Culture and Human Nature

Culture and Human Nature

THEORETICAL PAPERS OF

Melford E. Spiro * *Edited by*

Benjamin Kilborne *and* L. L. Langness

THE UNIVERSITY OF CHICAGO PRESS · CHICAGO AND LONDON

MELFORD E. SPIRO is the Presidential Professor of Anthropology at the University of California, San Diego. Among his many books are *Oedipus in the Trobriands,* also published by the University of Chicago Press, *Buddhism in Society, Gender and Culture,* and *Kibbutz: Venture in Utopia.*

BENJAMIN KILBORNE has taught anthropology at the Universities of California in Los Angeles and San Diego and is now a visiting lecturer in psychiatry at UCLA. He is also completing his psychoanalytic training and is in private practice. L. L. LANGNESS is professor of psychiatry and anthropology at UCLA. His books include *The Study of Culture.*

The University of Chicago Press, Chicago 60637
The University of Chicago Press, Ltd., London

© 1987 by The University of Chicago
All rights reserved. Published 1987
Printed in the United States of America

96 95 94 93 92 91 90 89 88 87   54321

Library of Congress Cataloging-in-Publication Data

Spiro, Melford E.
    Culture and human nature.

    Includes bibliographies and index.
    1. Culture. 2. Anthropology—Philosophy. 3. Ethnopsychology. I. Kilborne,
Benjamin. II. Langness, L. L. (Lewis L.), 1929–
GN357.S68 1987   306   87-5089
ISBN 0-226-76993-3
ISBN 0-226-76994-1 (pbk.)

Contents

Editors' Introduction

IN THIS volume are assembled for the first time twelve of the finest theoretical papers of Melford E. Spiro, one of the most distinguished figures in anthropology today. Professor Spiro founded the department of anthropology at the University of California, San Diego, where he is currently Presidential professor of anthropology. A member of the National Academy of Sciences, he combines long-standing interest in the philosophical problems of human existence with extensive anthropological fieldwork. In short, he is perhaps the most prominent figure in the country in psychological anthropology and culture and personality, and clearly one of the outstanding scholars in the areas of social and cultural theory.

This collection of papers, spanning the years between 1961 and 1984, appropriately demonstrates Spiro's contributions to the exploration of human nature and culture. It also addresses the fundamental issues of cultural relativism, the problem of explanation in the study of culture, and the anthropological study of religion and belief systems. Grouped according to theme rather than chronology, these papers have been selected and arranged so as to give a comprehensive view of Professor Spiro's theoretical works.

During the course of his career Spiro has developed a coherent and systematic body of theory modified by fieldwork, experience, and changes of mind. This body of theory has over the years provided him with a framework within which to develop his ideas and pursue various research projects in the field. Thus Spiro stands out as a scholar of unusual integrity, at once capable of changing his mind, of modifying his theories in the light of evidence, and of far-reaching efforts to understand the human condition. With an eye for well-constructed arguments, he incorporates ideas from a wide variety of sources.

One of the most fundamental emphases in Spiro's work has been on the need to consider both psychological and cultural forces and structures as part of any explanation of human behavior. In fact, a strong case can be made for the ineluctable necessity of doing this in the explanation of all behavior, although some anthropologists and sociologists would either deny or ignore it. Anthropologists inevitably employ psychological theories and premises whether or not they admit to doing so. As S. F. Nadel once put it, they "sneak them in through the back door." Psychological factors are, Spiro holds, an explicit and necessary part of any adequate theory of culture and human action. Indeed, it is difficult to see how a genuine and useful theory of culture could persist in the absence of an attempt to integrate within it a theory of the human mind. Spiro stands out as a foremost American anthropologist who has not wavered in his efforts to address the problems of human nature, and who has systematically linked theories of psychological motivation with social structure and belief systems.

The reader will note that Spiro consistently uses elements of psychoanalytic theory in his explanations and in his own theoretical constructions. While essentially a proponent of the ethnographic method, Spiro nonetheless holds that there are deep motivational structures underlying all human behavior, rational and irrational alike. His emphasis on psychoanalytic theory, which entails a theory of panhuman nature, constitutes one of the most fundamental thrusts of this book and, indeed, of Spiro's work in general. Thus, although psychoanalytic theory traditionally has been criticized and often dismissed by anthropologists, who assume that it is culturally relative and therefore of no use in ethnographic fieldwork and interpretation, Spiro makes it one of the keystones of his theorizing and methodology. He argues that psychoanalysis provides the best available coherent body of theory linking the (panhuman) structure of the family to concepts of individual motivation, on the one hand, and to concepts of culture and social organization, on the other. For example, in his *Oedipus in the Trobriands* Spiro demonstrates that the conclusions reached by Malinowski were far too hastily drawn. Spiro's reanalysis of Malinowski's material shows that there *is* an Oedipal constellation in the Trobriands, whereas Malinowski's work, *Sex and Repression in Savage Societies*, is commonly assumed to have proven there is not. Thus Spiro contends that the Oedipal complex can be used to explain Malinowski's Trobriand data with distinctly more parsimony and comprehensiveness than Malinowski employs in his theoretical revision of Freud.

In the first section, on human nature and culture, Spiro's debt to Freudian theory stands out clearly. While disagreeing with sociobiologists, he emphasizes the need for a theory of human nature implying panhuman psychological characteristics rooted in early childhood experience. Such psychological characteristics are, Spiro demonstrates, indispensable in understanding both anthropological questions and anthropological data.

In his interest in theories of human nature, Spiro resembles his friend and mentor, A. Irving Hallowell. The affinity between the two writers is palpable also in the second section of this book, where Spiro deals with motivations for the performance of roles defined as culturally important. Such sober doggedness in pursuing questions of rather fundamental significance characterizes both Hallowell and Spiro, and distinguishes these two writers from more fickle and sometimes also more popular contemporaries.

Notions of human nature and culture do not stay put in any bed of procrustean theory, whether of functionalism, structuralism, environmentalism, or of the superorganic. Because of this, these notions are better addressed directly and honestly than indirectly by way of whatever theories happen to be popular or appealing at the moment. Spiro has built his career largely on direct and forthright attempts to deal with the questions of human nature and culture, personality, and cultural values and beliefs, and he has sought to grasp these questions in all their complexity.

The first section of this book, *Culture and Human Nature,* includes papers representing Spiro's emphasis on a theory of human nature grounded in individual needs. The opening chapter, as well as those which follow, speak to the tendency in American anthropology toward both materialism and economic determinism. Spiro energetically criticizes the radical cultural relativism and determinism which he sees as characterizing much American anthropology. He has argued consistently over the past thirty years for the importance of a theory of human nature rooted in individual human needs, yet seen in terms of the perceptual configurations and meanings of symbols and symbol systems in specific societies at particular times.

In "Some Reflections on Cultural Determinism and Relativism . . ." (chapter 2), for instance, Spiro disputes the claims of cultural relativists by linking personality to culture as well as by refusing to concede that personality can ever be reducible to culture. Insisting on the psychological basis for the persistence of religious beliefs and cultural institutions, he also challenges the claims of the cultural materialists. Moreover, he strongly emphasizes both culture and human nature as manifested by the dynamics of the Oedipus complex and the nature of the human family. For Spiro, human nature (panhuman psychological characteristics) results from the interaction of phylogenetically determined biological (inherited) characteristics, and the functional requirements of any social system. As all human social systems depend upon the biparental family, it is in such families that the child's basic cognitive and motivational orientations are molded. Therefore, it is on these orientations that all social systems depend. In this sense, Spiro demonstrates that in fundamental respects the problem of the locus of culture is a specious one.

"Preculture and Gender" examines concepts of gender identity in kibbutz members. Whereas in works written earlier Spiro held that gender identity could be learned, in this chapter he explicitly holds that it cannot be understood merely in terms of learned roles. Spiro's change in emphasis is the direct result of fieldwork and his growing conviction that learning theory, while valuable, is not enough to account for what he saw in the kibbutz. A theory of human nature, of the human family, and of the ways in which families respond to human needs was required.

This theme (of the necessity of developing a theory of human nature and culture) is further elaborated in chapter 4, "Is the Oedipus Complex Universal?" In this paper Spiro argues that the Oedipus complex is structurally invariable (i.e., an expression of invariant features of the human family on the one hand, and of early stages of emotional cognitive development on the other). However, he points out, the Oedipus complex is variable when viewed functionally or culturally. The same material Malinowski relied upon has been reinterpreted convincingly by Spiro to demonstrate the presence of an Oedipus complex in the Trobriands as well as elsewhere.

The second section, *Functional Analysis,* presents an overview of Professor Spiro's theory of functionalism, and illustrates how he conceptualizes the functions of psychological drives and cultural systems and institutions.

The first paper of this section, "Social Systems, Personality, and Functional Analysis," attempts to explain the interrelationship between personality and culture. This chapter focuses, of course, on mutually dependent questions which have occupied social thought for centuries: How do human societies persuade their members to behave in conformity with cultural norms, and why do individuals feel motivated to conform to social values? Or, to put the questions differently: How are cultural values inculcated in individuals such that these individuals are motivated to conform to cultural norms? Where do social laws come from and why are they obeyed? In exploring these questions, Spiro analyzes the way in which human personality and motivational configurations affect the functioning of social systems. Indeed, he investigates how they make the functioning of social systems possible. When compared with scholars concerned only with putatively nonpsychological kinds of analysis (e.g., Leslie White, Marvin Harris), Spiro's position constitutes an important contribution to the entire field of social theory.

Spiro develops a "functional" view of personality and culture, which are interdependent. This position is illustrated in chapters 6 ("Religious Systems . . .") and 7, where he applies functional definitions of culture and personality to the analysis of religious systems. Once again he stresses the importance of early childhood experiences in linking family structure with religious taboo and guilt. Consequently, he can speak of "culturally constituted defense mechanisms," for religious systems (and other belief systems) serve defensive functions. These chapters, then, explore how the psychodynamic notions of "drive" and "defense" can be used in the functional analyses of cultural belief systems. Broadly speaking, chapters 5–7 illustrate the functional analysis of psychodynamic processes and cultural belief systems, as represented both in individual projective identification and projective mechanisms, and in culturally shared (and reinforced) means available to individuals for defensive reactions.

Chapter 7 ("Collective Representations and Mental Representations in Religious Symbol Systems") constitutes an attempt to show the relationship between cultural symbols and personal symbolism, between conscious and unconscious meanings both in the ways in which symbols are held and believed in, and in the ways in which they are explained. The chapter also discusses with particular cogency the distinctions between primary and secondary process thinking as defined and used in psychoanalysis. Primary process thinking reflects unconscious drives and fantasies; secondary process thinking is more rational, purposeful, acceptable, and explicable.

The final section of this book, *Religion and Myth,* illustrates in different ways Spiro's use of early family experience as an organizing principle. Religion, he shows, is necessarily rooted in the family. Furthermore, family dynamics are internalized in all human beings, who, as it were, "familiarize" themselves with the outside world on the basis of their own family experiences. Children internalize not only their perceived, experienced, and remembered relationships with their parents, but also their assessment of the judgments and evaluations which their parents have made of their own behavior, thoughts, and feelings. This process continues throughout life as adults read into adult relationships the wishes, fantasies, and fears of their own childhoods.

Thus Spiro's emphasis on the nature of the human family enables him to continue to pursue the questions—so alive in the nineteenth century but frequently believed to be superceded today—of taboo and the family. In this way he allows for the irrational, linking the human family to religious belief systems. Professor Spiro does not subordinate religion to a superordinate notion of social function, any more than he subordinates individual psychodynamics to such functions—and for similar reasons. However, the anthropological emphasis on context, together with the fieldworker's need to understand, for example, the Burmese beliefs from the inside, do not lead Spiro to the conclusion that human behavior is infinitely plastic (infinitely relative). What varies cross-culturally is surface structure, not deep motivational structure.

In "Religion: Problems of Definition and Explanation," Spiro reviews major definitions of religion, developing his own view. For him religion is "an institution consisting of culturally patterned interaction with culturally postulated superhuman beings." He then elaborates still further the arguments concerning the "truth" of religious beliefs, and analyzes their various manifest and latent functions, both psychological and sociological. Finally, he assesses "causal" as distinct from "functional" explanations for religious belief.

In "Virgin Birth: Parthenogenesis and Physiological Paternity," Spiro explores rationally and irrationally held beliefs. He points out that there are many kinds of connections between evaluations of how "true" or "false," how "rational" or "irrational" beliefs may be judged to be, thereby challenging structuralist assumptions that it is irrational to hold a false belief and rational to hold a true one. Once again Spiro stresses the pertinence of the functional/psychocultural view of explanation in anthropological studies of religion. Anthropologists are responsible for determining how beliefs are held (which entails psychodynamic analysis), as well as for understanding how they are labeled "true" and "false" by members of the society in question. When anthropologists proceed this way, Spiro shows, what beliefs "do" for their believers may be assessed with respect to empirical evidence.

"Whatever Happened to the Id?" succinctly lays out Spiro's propositions about human nature and culture. He shows that the often fanciful claims of structural analysis are frequently just that: fanciful. Reinterpreting the Bororo myth which Lévi-Strauss uses as evidence for the transition from the stage of nature to that of culture in *The Raw and the Cooked* (1969), he argues for a simpler, more obvious (less arcane) interpretation derived from psychoanalytic theory.

Chapter 11, "Some Reflections on Family and Religion in East Asia," applies Spiro's ideas about the importance of the family (and the Oedipus complex) toward understanding religion, emphasizing the panhuman character of the human family system and speculating on potential links between family tensions in East Asia and certain aspects of East Asian religions.

Finally, "Symbolism and Functionalism in the Anthropological Study of Religion" deals with the relationship of symbolic to functional analyses, and particularly with the relationship of cultural symbols to social experience. Spiro points to fundamental similarities between the symbolism of Judaism and Buddhism, linking certain religious beliefs to (culturally-defined) family roles. Religious symbols, he argues, are created not only, as Lévi-Strauss contends, to "think by," but also to "live by." Indeed, one of the strongest points of Spiro's theoretical orientation is his consistent attempt to ground theory in both behavioral and psychic reality.

This volume finally makes available a comprehensive collection of Professor Spiro's theoretical writings. Elaborations and variations on the major theoretical positions laid out in the papers here assembled may also be found in Spiro's numerous and important books. *Ifaluk: An Atoll Culture* (with E. G. Burrows) and *Kibbutz, Venture in Utopia* are early, primarily ethnographic works which lay the foundations for Spiro's subsequent interpretations of these cultures. *Children of the Kibbutz* explores the role of learning theories in making sense of observation and experience in the kibbutz. In this work Spiro analyzes the psychological dimensions of socialization and the acquisition of utopian values and aspirations.

In *Gender and Culture* (1979) Spiro returns to Israel, to the kibbutz materials and to his kibbutz experiences. He examines the relationship between human nature, sexual identity and social structure, social roles and family constellations in a radical attempt to engineer a utopian religious community. The entire venture of the kibbutz, together with its vicissitudes can, Spiro holds, be understood not only in terms of successful or unsuccessful social programs, but also in terms of the limits all social programs encounter in bending human nature to what might be construed by the actors as social purposes. What can be modified is surface structure; deep structure, rooted as it is in early childhood experience, is panhuman, and therefore beyond the reach of even the most high-minded and ambitious social reformers. The concluding chapter from *Gender and Culture* appears in this book (as chapter 3), demonstrating that human nature will show itself beneath the clothing of any social system.

Spiro's contributions to studies of religion and to articulations between personality systems, belief systems, and social systems are perhaps most apparent in his work on Burma and particularly on Burmese Buddhism. Spiro's *Burmese Supernaturalism* represents his first book-length treatment of a religious system; in this work he brings his concepts of cultural symbol systems and personality drive-defense theories to bear on the subject of Burmese folk religion.

Buddhism and Society (1970) develops the themes of religious needs (drive/defense) and social organization, of personality and culture. Specifically, he examines the meaning for the actors of discrepancies between their actual beliefs and the normative (canonical) doctrines of Buddhism.

Subsequently Spiro published yet another monograph, *Kinship and Marriage in Burma* (1977), pursuing his investigations of the cultural and psychodynamic dimensions of the Burmese world and applying functional, historical, and psychodynamic explanations to Burmese customs relating to kinship and marriage.

The papers that make up this volume, we hope, faithfully represent Spiro's most impressive corpus of scholarly anthropological inquiry and achievement. The portrait which emerges depicts his exceptional dedication to the problem of human suffering, to religious belief and scientific understanding. Such dedication and such contributions are, we believe, of particular value at a time when contemporary anthropology often appears to be rudderless, drifting aimlessly into literary criticism, idiosyncratic self-revelation, institutionalized routine and what Freud termed "the narcissism of small differences."

In sum, Spiro's theoretical contributions in this volume must be considered standard fare for all students of human nature, personality, and culture. This body of work cogently calls into question basic—and too often unquestioned—assumptions made by social scientists about the nature of belief and of scientific evidence, about the relation between society, personality, and culture. If anthropology fails to address problems of human nature, of human motivations and their relationship to cultural institutions, and of collective representations and individual action, the discipline of anthropology runs the risk of becoming trivial and, consequently, obsolete. Dealing with precisely these questions, the papers of Professor Spiro in this volume set exemplary standards for all students of culture and the human mind.

I CULTURE AND HUMAN NATURE

1   Culture and Human Nature

ALTHOUGH I have been asked to describe the development of my research findings and ideas, I cannot describe *what* I have done, or how I did it, without explaining *why* I did it.[1] Much of this paper, therefore, will be concerned with intellectual motivations and research strategies rather than with research operations or detailed research findings. Moreover, since I believe that any valid explanation is ultimately historical (genetic, evolutionary, developmental, etc.), a reliable account of *why* I did what I did cannot begin with my anthropological research, but must rather be rooted in my intellectual history. Hence, I shall first describe the intellectual (and other) interests that brought me to the study of culture and personality, and I shall then discuss one of the themes that, until relatively recently, has run through a great deal of my research. Since I am concerned with explaining the over-determined motivational structures that lie behind research choices and the complex decision structures on which research strategies are based, I do not have space to discuss other themes or to describe my more recent interests.

Beginnings

In an important sense, my intellectual interests have always been more philosophical than scientific, and just as in the Middle Ages philosophy was the handmaiden of theology, so for me anthropology has been the handmaiden of philosophy, a tool for the empirical investigation of some central issues concerning the nature of man. Although I have

Reprinted from *The Making of Psychological Anthropology*, edited by George D. Spindler (Berkeley: University of California Press, 1978), pp. 331–60.

1. I am grateful to Theodore Schwartz for his extremely helpful criticisms of an earlier draft of this paper.

3

worked in four different societies—the Ojibwa, Ifaluk, an Israeli kibbutz, and Burma—I have never been interested in ethnographic description, per se; and although I have published on a variety of institutions—family, kinship, politics, socialization, and religion—I have had little interest in institutional analysis, as such. Ultimately—so, at least, I have believed—these enterprises are useful to the degree that they can illuminate some aspect of the nature of man. Since, however, anthropology is primarily interested in society and culture, and since until recently it has been much more concerned with social and cultural differences than with universals, my choice of anthropology—rather than, for example, psychology—might seem rather strange. In the light, however, of the intellectual and political zeitgeist of the intellectually formative years of my life, this choice was not so strange after all.

For liberal intellectuals, like myself, coming to maturity in the late thirties and early forties, politics was an overriding concern. Existentialists without knowing it, we had to come to grips with the twin traumata of our time—the great depression at home, and the rise of Fascism abroad. Having escaped the seductions of Soviet Communism, while yet deploring the "poverty amidst plenty" which seemed to be characteristic of capitalism, we perceived in democratic socialism the only viable alternative to the horrors of both Fascist and Communist totalitarianism. As Marxists—and, in some sense, we were all Marxists in those days—we believed that men were the creatures of their social systems. If American society was characterized (as we thought) by competitiveness, exploitation, and injustice, these characteristics were not expressions of human nature, but of a particular social system. Hence, to abolish these evils it was only necessary to change the social system that produced them. In a social system, such as democratic socialism, whose institutions were based on equality and justice, they would disappear.

If Marxism was the ideological inspiration for these convictions, their intellectual underpinnings, at least for me, were derived from my philosophical studies. As a philosophy major, I had been persuaded— to be sure, I was prepared to be persuaded—by Locke, Hume, Rousseau, and the philosophers of the Enlightenment that man comes into the world as a tabula rasa; that anything that is eventually inscribed on the blank slate is put there by experience; and (though this was not shared by all these thinkers) that the most important types of experience are those derived from encounters with social institutions. Hence, the notion of a society in which men are motivated by cooperation, altruism, and mutual aid was not viewed as a utopian quest—nor was it viewed as a secular derivative of the religious visions of Amos or

Isaiah, those Hebrew prophets who had earlier influenced me—but as a logical deduction from the social theories of the eighteenth century philosophers of Reason. For if, indeed, man has no "nature," then his characteristics must be a product of history, as the latter is distilled by and concretized in the social institutions of his society.

But the capstone—and "proof"!—of the thesis of the malleability of man, and the omnipotence of social institutions, came from the writings of Durkheim, for Durkheim (as I viewed him) was not just another speculative philosopher; he was, rather, an empirical scientist. And if, as he had shown in *The Elementary Forms of the Religious Life*, the very forms of thought (space, time, causality, etc.) are ultimately derived from the structure of society, what else could be said on the subject? Durkheim, though a sociologist, had used anthropological data to sustain his arguments. This convinced me that it was from anthropology that I could best derive future intellectual nourishment, and when some years later I decided to pursue graduate studies in the social sciences, I turned to anthropology.

Although I earlier discovered Durkheim was not in good favor in anthropology—mostly because of Goldenweiser's critique of his theory of totemism—the regnant anthropological notions of that time were entirely consistent with (indeed, they might just as well have been derived from) Durkheim's view of society and culture. Still, these notions—cultural determinism and cultural relativism—provided a different conceptual, as well as rhetorical, basis for my views concerning the relationship between man and society. Since cultures vary across space and time, and since behavior is culturally variable, the inference that man's nature is similarly culturally variable seemed irrefutable. The concept of culture not only seemed to provide the definitive refutation of the notion of a universal human nature, but it appeared to be a refined tool for understanding group differences in behavior. Unlike the vague and rather metaphysical concept of social or historical "forces," the concept of culture could not only be broken down into observable units of empirical investigation, but it generated theories which seemed to account for group differences. (The culture theories of the time were inadequate to account for cultural invention, change, or deviance, but I did not perceive this as impugning their validity.)

Having discovered anthropology, I lost whatever interest I might otherwise have had in sociology or psychology. Focused on only one cultural variant—that of Western man—the findings of sociology, so it seemed to me, could shed little light on Man. Similarly, psychology, with its concern with subcultural psychological processes (learning, perception, cognition, and the like) as they could be studied in the laboratory, also seemed unlikely to shed important light on Man. Its findings were based either on the study of lower animals who, since they had no culture, seemed inappropriate models for the study of humans; or, they were based on the study of Western subjects, and since, as I believed, psychological processes are culturally shaped, these findings seemed culture-bound. Anthropology, on the other hand, seemed admirably suited to my interests. If man is the creature of culture, then the proper study of man, so l believed, is the study of culture; and since culture is variable, then the proper study of Man is the study of culture in all of its variability. If, moreover, each culture (as Ruth Benedict had argued in her seductive metaphor) has carved out a different arc from the total circle of cultural variability, and if (as she also contended) each primitive culture constitutes a natural experiment in cultural variability, then it further followed that the proper study of cultural variability entailed the study of primitive cultures. For me, then, anthropology was clearly the science of choice. This being so, it is important to sketch in greater detail the dominant anthropological notions concerning culture and human nature of that time, notions to which I and most of my contemporaries became, if we were not already, committed.

Since human behavior is culturally determined, and since cultures vary enormously, the only valid generalization that can be made about human nature is that it is enormously malleable ("plastic"). The existence of cultural universals does not require any qualification of this conclusion since culture, being "superorganic," does not reflect (and, hence, cannot be "reduced" to) noncultural, panhuman, biological or psychological attributes. Although, so far as biology is concerned, such anatomical attributes as hair form, eye color, and so on, are biologically determined (subject of course to cultural selection), biology has little, if any, determination on social behavior. Since the latter can be explained, without residue, by cultural determinants, the organism, like the psyche, is conceived as either an "empty" or a "black box." Since, according to one "empty box" model, culture affects behavior by a kind of Newtonian action-at-a-distance, the box remains perpetually empty. According to a second model, however, the empty box does not long remain empty for, as a consequence of "enculturation," the external culture is somehow incorporated by the social actors. Nevertheless, since the resultant "inside" (psychological) determinants of behavior are merely the "outside" (cultural) determinants that have become "internalized," and since, therefore, they vary as culture varies, these psychological determinants can hardly constitute the basis for a species-specific human nature. The "black box" differs from these two "empty box" models in that it does not deny the existence of "inside" variables; it merely denies their influence on social behavior. Since the latter, so the argument goes, is culturally variable, how can it be explained by biological or psychological determinants which are constant? Hence, even if these "inside" variables may be said to constitute or to determine a species-specific human nature, the latter is irrelevant to the understanding of man's social behavior.

Whatever the differences among these three models, it will be noted that all agree (if only by implication) there can be no conflict between the individual and culture. If there is nothing inside the individual (the first model), or if what is inside is either orthogonal to, or represents the internalization of, culture (the third and second models respectively), then the individual and culture are in a state of harmony. That is, what the individual wants to do is identical with what his culture requires him to do.

It should also be noted that although all three models explain behavior by reference to culture, culture itself is left unexplained. To explain culture by reference to some set of biological and psychological determinants (construed as the core, or nucleus, of human nature) is not only inconsistent with the empty and black box models, but it illustrates the fallacy of "reductionism." (For unexplained reasons, reductionism was taken to be a self-evident fallacy.) Hence, like Aristotle's First Cause, culture remains an Unmoved Mover. To be sure, since culture is in large part a symbolic system, man must everywhere have the capacity to invent, transmit, and acquire cultural symbols, and to that extent symbolization is to be included with plasticity as a second attribute of human nature. (Indeed, functionally or adaptively viewed, symbolization is to human plasticity what instinct is to animal specificity.) But since symbolization is culturally variable, the universality of symbolic processes does not imply the universality of symbolic meanings. Hence, so far as content is concerned, there is no universal human nature; there are only culturally specific—and therefore culturally variable—character structures.

Lest the above conceptions be used as a handle for racist arguments, the concept of cultural relativism—according to which all cultures, and therefore all culturally variable character structures, are equally valuable—was enlisted to do battle against racist notions in general, and the notion of primitive mentality, in particular. It should be noted, however, that cultural relativism was also used, at least by some anthropologists, to perpetuate a kind of inverted racism. That is, it was used as a powerful tool of cultural criticism, with the consequent derogation of Western culture and of the mentality which it produced. Espousing the philosophy of primitivism—akin to, but not identical with, Rousseau's notion of the Noble Savage—the image of primitive man was used by some few anthropologists as a vehicle for the pursuit of personal utopian quests, and/or as a fulcrum to express personal discontent with Western man and Western society. The strategies adopted took various forms, of which the following are fairly representative: (1) attempts to abolish private property, or inequality, or aggression in Western societies have a reasonably realistic chance of success since such states of affairs may be found in many primitive societies; (2) compared to at least some primitives, Western man is uniquely competitive, warlike, intolerant of deviance, sexist, and so on; (3) paranoia is not necessarily an illness, because paranoid thinking is institutionalized in certain primitive societies; homosexuality is not deviant because homosexuals are the cultural cynosures of some primitive societies; monogamy is not viable because polygamy is the most frequent form of marriage in primitive societies. Needless to say, the anthropologists of that period were neither the first, nor—as recent politically motivated resolutions advocated at meetings of the American Anthropological Association indicate—the last to use anthropological "findings" as "scientific" support for personal and political weltanschauungen.

Qualifications

Although many years were to pass before I finally discarded as untenable many of the ideas described in the previous section, the corrosive process began when I encountered the theories of A. I. Hallowell, my mentor at Northwestern University, and (through him) psychoanalytic and learning theory. From Hallowell's writings and teachings I came to realize that culture does not impinge directly on behavior, but is mediated through personality processes relating to individuals. The contours of these processes, I came to believe, were best delineated by Freud. It was the work of Kardiner, however, that persuaded me of the importance of the family and of socialization in the formation of these processes. From Kardiner, too, I became convinced of the importance of "projective systems" for the understanding of those aspects of culture that are not "reality" based. There remained, however, a missing ingredient. If social actors monitor their own behavior in accordance with cultural norms and rules, it was necessary to explain the acquisition of culture in each generation of social actors. Here, the social learning theorists—and especially Miller and Dollard—provided the key.

Hence, when I completed graduate work, my theoretical framework comprised an inchoate synthesis of cultural determinism, and cultural relativism, neo-Freudian personality theory, and social learning theory. In this loosely integrated synthesis, culture was viewed as a kind of master plan for group adaptation; it was transmitted primarily in the family, and in the early years of life, by traditional methods of socialization and enculturation; it was acquired as part of the personality by techniques of social reinforcement; its acquisition ("internalization"), however, often conflicted with and frustrated other personality "needs"; the conflict was resolved by the disguised satisfaction of these needs through culturally mediated symbolic systems ("projective systems").

It will be noticed that this synthesis, by including explicit attention to "personality," represented an important qualification of my earlier thinking. But this shift from a cultural to a culture-personality framework did not alter my earlier notions concerning human nature; on the contrary, it strengthened them. For, although influenced by psychoanalytic thought, the main thrust of the culture-personality school was precisely the reverse of psychoanalysis. While the latter postulated invariant stages and processes (and even invariant symbol formations and symbolic meanings) in the formation, structure, and functioning of personality, culture-personality (with some important exceptions) was primarily concerned to demonstrate their cultural variability. Since, according to this school, personality was determined by and constituted the internalization of culture, the range of personality variability across groups could hardly be smaller than the range of cultural variability. Indeed, since personality characteristics and personality configurations, respectively, were viewed as isomorphic with cultural characteristics and cultural patterns, the notion of a pancultural human nature was viewed as highly unlikely. On the contrary, it was assumed as almost self-evident that Zunis, Germans, Hawaiians, and Thais are much more different, not only in culture but also in personality, than they are similar.

These, then, were the views which I took with me on my first field trip—to the atoll of Ifaluk in the Central Carolines.

First Field Trip—Ifaluk

In those far off days—it was 1947–48—very few anthropologists thought of going into the field with a "problem," let alone with a hypothesis for "testing." Rather, the typical fieldworker immersed himself in the local society and culture and, with luck, he then came up with a problem that might provide the basis for a doctoral dissertation.

This, too, was my approach, and the problem I came up with was aggression. The choice of this problem was hardly accidental. In the first place, after some few months on the atoll, I was struck by the fact that I had not observed a single act of overt aggression. Reflecting on this remarkable fact, and reflecting on my own adjustments to atoll living, it was hard to escape the conclusion that the control of aggression was *the* central—or at least *a* central—problem confronting any group of 250 people attempting to live together on a land mass six-tenths of a mile square.

But, of course, the decision to study aggression was not that simple. What about the kinship system? The Ifaluk had a matrilineal descent system, based on matrilineages—a subject concerning which we knew very little at that time. What about the political structure? Ifaluk, though a small face-to-face society, had a complex system of hereditary chieftainship—a combination which would have evoked the attention of scores of anthropologists with backgrounds different from mine. What about the complicated redistribution system? The products of the fields and the oceans were periodically redistributed in Ifaluk by a mechanism which any Oceanist worth his salt would have investigated in minute detail. Although these, and other equally fascinating aspects of Ifaluk social structure commanded and deserved as much attention as aggression, there must have been other reasons for choosing the latter for study.

First, given my interest in human nature, it is understandable I would have been much more interested in social processes than in social structure. Second, among these processes, aggression had been a salient concern even prior to my trip to Micronesia, beginning with my political interest in the viability of socialism. This interest was supported by the culture-personality literature of that period, which had persistently held up the Pueblos as examples of nonaggressive, noncompetitive peoples, who constituted refutations of the Western notion that aggression and competition were universal social characteristics. Indeed, in this literature, the Hopi and Zuni were constantly contrasted with the Kwakiutl and Dobuans in support of the cultural relativist thesis concerning aggression and cooperation, and the Ifaluk seemed to offer yet additional support for this thesis. More immediately, as a student of Hallowell, my interest in aggression had been stimulated by three brilliant papers he had published on the psychocultural determinants of, and solutions to, the problem of aggression among the Berens River Saulteaux. These had left a deep impression on me. Finally, under Hallowell's guidance, and together with a group of graduate students, I had conducted field work on the Lac Du Flambeau

(Wisconsin) Ojibwa reservation the summer prior to leaving for Ifaluk, and I had been struck with (what I thought to be) a high incidence of aggression on that reservation. It was found at the social level (in interpersonal and intergroup behavior), at the cultural level (spontaneously told jokes and folk tales almost invariably displayed an aggressive theme) and at the personality level (as revealed in the Rorschach test). That the Ojibwa and Saulteaux are the same people, and that, though separated in space and living under different ecological and economic conditions, they yet exhibited similar aggressive tendencies—which, in turn, were similar (as Hallowell had shown in an ethnohistorical analysis) to those of their historical forbears—was an exciting finding, which reinforced my interest in aggression.

It is little wonder, then, that when observations in Ifaluk revealed almost no manifest aggression, I was struck by the contrast with what I had observed among the Ojibwa only six months earlier. The near absence of aggression in Ifaluk seemed clearly to support my views concerning the cultural relativism of human nature, and the cultural determinism of personality. Since the Ifaluk had a cooperative social system, since their ethos stressed the value of nonaggression, since there were few cultural pressures for competition for scarce resources, and since in this sociocultural context there was no observable aggression, it seemed to follow—as the Pueblo data had already suggested—that aggression is a function of historically specific cultural determinants, rather than an attribute of "human nature." This conclusion was also consistent with, and lent support to, the leading psychological theory of aggression—the frustration-aggression theory. For, when formulated in psychological terms, the Ifaluk observations seemed to indicate that in the absence of sociocultural frustration, there is no aggression.

After some additional work in Ifaluk, other observations, however, not only began to intrude on my attention, but they eventually compelled a change in my views about Ifaluk aggression. First, I had begun collecting personality data—Rorschach and TAT protocols and dreams—which clearly revealed the existence of hostile impulses at the personality level. In short, from the absence of aggression—a behavioral variable—in Ifaluk, l had wrongly inferred the absence of hostility—a psychological variable. (Here, and in what follows, "hostility" refers to such motivational and affective variables as anger, rage, hatred, and so on, while "aggression" refers to observable social action—verbal and behavioral—whose intent is harm, injury, damage, and so on.) Second, I had begun collecting data on cultural systems—folk tales, myths, and religious beliefs—which revealed important aggressive themes; and on the assumption that these systems constituted projective expressions of personality dispositions, these cultural data, too, revealed the existence of hostility in Ifaluk.

These findings not only challenged my conception of Ifaluk personality, but they posed two immediate problems. First, in the absence of a competitive culture, what explanation, other than recourse to the outmoded notion of "instinct," could be offered for Ifaluk hostility? Second, given the existence of hostility, why was it not expressed in aggressive social behavior?

Actually, I had been aware of what later appeared to be a partial solution to the first problem even prior to the empirical challenges to my original observations. Shortly after arriving in Ifaluk I was (rather annoyingly) awakened every morning by the cries of babies who, at dawn, are brought by their mothers to be bathed in the chilly waters of the lagoon. Invariably, the infants would react to this experience with cries of rage, and although I could not say the experience was traumatic, there was no doubt that it was painful for the infant. When queried, mothers said they knew that it was a painful experience, but custom nevertheless required that infants be bathed in that way and at that time. When, some months later, I was perplexed by the presence of hostility in people living in a cooperative and nonfrustrating culture, it occurred to me that it might be related, at least in part, to this bathing experience. Since Ifaluk *adults* did not suffer important frustrations, perhaps, so I reasoned, their hostility was not situational, but characterological, their hostile impulses representing motivational dispositions produced by those conditions that are formative of personality dispositions in general, viz., infant and childhood experiences. Although it seemed to me doubtful that one type of frustrating and painful experience—even one that was repeated daily for a long period—could produce a permanent character trait, it seemed reasonable that perhaps other types of early frustrating experiences might also be discovered. Hence, changing the focus of my study from adults to children, I began a three-pronged program of investigation, including observations of parent-child interaction, interviews of parents and of children concerning processes of socialization, and interviews of children concerning their reactions to these socialization processes and their consequent feelings toward parents and siblings.

From these investigations it was discovered that in addition to their early bathing experience, Ifaluk children do indeed have other frustrating (perhaps traumatic) experiences, and I became increasingly convinced that adult hostility in Ifaluk was traceable to this configuration of early childhood frustrations. Although, as is the case with all naturalistic studies, the absence of controls did not permit this conviction to be converted into a conclusion, its status as a highly likely hypothesis seemed warranted on theoretical-deductive grounds. That is, on the assumption that hostility is not "instinctive," and on the further assumption that it is produced by frustration, then, since there appeared to be few situational determinants of hostility in Ifaluk adulthood, it seemed to follow that it was produced by the frustrations of childhood.

Having discovered a tentatively satisfactory answer to the first question raised by Ifaluk hostility, I still had to find an answer to the second: given that the Ifaluk do indeed have hostile impulses, what accounts for their nonaggressive behavior? Why isn't hostility expressed in observable social aggression? Two answers suggested themselves—one based on the Freud-Kardiner theory of religion, the other on my observations of chieftainship. Since Ifaluk religion postulates the existence of a class of spirits who are purely evil—their sole aim is to cause human suffering—I reasoned that much of the hostility of the Ifaluk is expressed (both displaced and projected) in their hostile feelings to the *alus,* as these spirits are called. Moreover, since rituals are periodically performed to drive away these evil spirits, I inferred that much of their hostility is discharged in the performance of these "aggressive" rituals. Since the characteristics of these spirits are, on a number of dimensions, isomorphic with those of the parents of their childhood, the expression of hostility in this form could be seen as a symbolic expression of the hostility which, though repressed, was originally aroused by the frustrating parents. In short, viewed as a projective system, Ifaluk religion seemed to afford one avenue for the expression of hostility.[2]

Although, ex hypothesi, religious beliefs and rituals channeled the expression of hostility, permitting the discharge of hostile impulses through projection and displacement, this hypothesis did not explain why the Ifaluk complied with this culturally approved form of aggression, rather than expressing their hostility in aggression against their fellows. Why, in short, did they follow their cultural ethos, which prohibits any social aggression? The ethos itself, so I assumed, is a highly adaptive cultural trait for a group living in a tiny land mass (in which physical avoidance of others is impossible), but, like any other func-

2. Since that time, I have become convinced that there are sources of frustration—especially related to esteem—in the adult social system, and that there are other expressions of hostility in addition to projective expressions. Moreover, Theodore Schwartz (personal communication) has called my attention to the aggression in the Ifaluk treatment of infants and children.

tional explanation of culture derived from a biological evolutionary model, it does not explain the conditions for the persistence of the ethos, or for compliance with its dictates. The latter condition must be explained not by some functional requirement—a "final" cause—but by some condition in the immediate social field of the actors—an "efficient" cause. This condition, it seemed to me, consisted in the institution of hereditary chieftainship, especially the prescribed behavior and persona of the chiefs, qua chiefs.

In Ifaluk, the chiefs are moral mentors. At periodic assemblies they exhort the people to do "good," and much of this exhortation is concerned with admonitions to behave in accordance with the ethos of nonaggression. In addition, they periodically monitor the behavior of their subjects by regular inspections of their districts—there is one chief for each district—to assure that this ethos is complied with. The chiefs, to use their own expression, are the "fathers" of their people. Moreover, from observations of the Ifaluk in interaction with the chiefs, and from interview and test protocols, it seemed as if, reciprocally, the chiefs were, in the people's eyes, benevolent parental figures, whose approval was of vital importance for their self-esteem and positive self-image. Desire for the approval of chiefs, and fear of their disapproval, seemed to be the most important social determinant of the Ifaluk adherence to the ethos of nonaggression.

With this, I felt that I had tentatively, and in large part, solved the problem of aggression in Ifaluk, and in a manner entirely consistent with my views of culture and human nature. However disappointing, especially after my original impressions, to discover hostility in the Ifaluk, this discovery neither supported the notion of a pancultural human nature, nor did it challenge my own notion of historically specific cultural determinism. Although the social system did not engender hostility, the socialization system did, and this clearly supported my view that hostility is culturally relative. For, if the Ifaluk socialization system engenders hostility, then, so it seemed to me, other socialization systems could surely be found which do not. Moreover, despite the presence of hostility at the personality level, the Ifaluk case demonstrated that its expression, like its instigation, is culturally relative. Instead of permitting hostility to be expressed in social relations, Ifaluk culture directed its expression into other, less disruptive, channels.

Although for me, at least, the foregoing interpretation of the instigations to, and vicissitudes of, aggression in Ifaluk seemed convincing, it was obvious, as I have already indicated, that its various hypotheses remained unproven. Without controls there can be no proof, and in naturalistic studies of society and culture, there are really only two types of controls. One can study different groups under the same conditions (this, in effect, characterizes the comparative method in all of its variants), or the same group under different conditions. The latter method (which, for reasons I cannot develop here is the much more satisfactory) exploits historical change to test interpretations previously offered for the status quo ante. Thus, if my interpretations of Ifaluk aggression are valid, it follows that were its religious beliefs and rituals to change, and were chieftanship to be abolished (or otherwise lose its meaning), then—if there were no functionally equivalent structural alternatives for these institutions—hostility should be expressed in overt social aggression, or (if it is inhibited by external sanctions) in predictable clinical symptoms. This prediction not only provides a clear empirical test of the hypotheses discussed above, but it is now possible to perform this test. In the quarter century that has elapsed since my study of Ifaluk, there have been important changes both in its religious and its political system. Christianity, introduced by the missionaries, has replaced the traditional religion, and elective government, introduced by the United States, has replaced traditional chieftainship. I hope to return to Ifaluk to assess the psychological consequences of these changes and, thereby, to test the hypothesis described here.

Second Field Trip—Israel

Although the Ifaluk findings were consistent with traditional culture-personality views, they nevertheless left unanswered the basic question with which I had been concerned—can culture (in the holistic sense) form the psychological structure of human beings into any mold it chooses? Still, I was sufficiently wedded to the traditional anthropological paradigm to remain committed to the conventional culturalist answer to this question. In 1950, having recently completed my Ph.D. thesis on Ifaluk aggression, I decided to explore this question in an Israeli kibbutz.

Although I still believed, on the grounds adduced by Benedict, that anthropology ought to be concerned with primitive societies, the rationale for studying this, a modern group, was precisely that which Benedict had offered for the study of primitives—it represented yet another, and an unexplored, arc of the total circle of cultural variation. Within this particular arc, I was concerned with two problems especially. First, since children are reared outside of the domestic family, to what extent do they exhibit the same stages of psychosexual development which psychoanalysis had postulated as universal, and more especially, to what extent do they develop an Oedipus complex? Second, referring back to the Ifaluk study, to what extent had the kibbutz succeeded in producing children without hostility? It seemed particularly desirable to explore the second question in a kibbutz since the latter is not only one of the few *modern* examples of a cooperative group, but it is one that practiced a form of democratic socialism which had been of such great interest to me in my early life. Here, I shall treat the latter question only.

On the basis of the meager available literature, it was evident that the kibbutz movement had ushered in a new type of human society. Rejecting the traditional social structures of the West, this movement had initiated a radical experiment in voluntary, comprehensive, cooperative living. Not only were the means of production collectively owned, and not only was the system of distribution based on the socialist principle of "from each according to his abilities, to each according to his needs," but even the children were raised by (and for) the community, rather than in individual families. Living in communal children's houses, rather than with their parents, they were reared by professional nurses and teachers, whose primary goal was the transmission of the cooperative values of kibbutz culture. If, then, there is no universal human nature, if the psychological characteristics of social actors represent the internalization of the historically specific cultural values of their group—if, in a word, personality is the culture writ small—then, if the kibbutz values of sharing and cooperation were in fact internalized by the children, it would be expected that they would exhibit little if any competitive or hostile characteristics. This at least was the premise which guided my kibbutz field work.

The findings of the kibbutz study had a strong—and thus far a lasting—impact on my image of man and on my conception of anthropology. Although the kibbutz children were raised in a totally communal and cooperative system; although their socialization had as its primary aim the inculcation of a cooperative, noncompetitive ethic; although the techniques of socialization were mild, loving, and permissive; although the target responses were properly reinforced; although, in a word, almost all of the culture conditions were designed to exclusively promote cooperation and sharing, the data clearly indicated that kibbutz children, like other children, do not wish to share scarce and valued goods—they want them for themselves and they resist the attempts of adults to get them to share them. They view as rivals those with whom they are obliged to share, and they aggress against those who frustrate their desires to monopolize (or at least to maximize) these scarce goods. Although they learn to cooperate, their cooperative motives do not lead to the extinction of their learned competitive and rivalrous motives. In short, although they learn to view aggression as wrong, when they are frustrated they become angry, and their anger—when not controlled—leads to overt aggressive behavior.

This does not mean, I hasten to point out, that the kibbutz has been unsuccessful in transmitting its ethic of sharing, equality, mutual aid, and cooperation to its children. It has, on the contrary, been surprisingly successful, if "success" is defined as the perpetuation, by successive generations of adults, of the social and cultural systems for which they were socialized. But if "succcss" means not only the internalization of the above values, but the absence of any competing and conflicting tendencies—i.e., if "success" means the development of a "new man," (as the kibbutz puts it)—one without competitive, hostile, or acquisitive motives—then, of course, the kibbutz has not been successful. But only a utopian or—what is the same thing—a radical cultural relativist would have ever thought that the creation of such a "new man" was possible. Indeed, from a nonutopian point of view the real mark of kibbutz success is that although its children have developed competitive and acquisitive, as well as cooperative and sharing dispositions, when, as adults, they experience conflict between them, they usually resolve the conflict in favor of the latter dispositions. In short, the kibbutz values have penetrated to that part of the personality which is the true measure of the internalization of cultural values—the superego.

On the basis of the kibbutz study (and on the basis of everything I have studied, read, and reflected upon since) I slowly and painfully came to the conclusion that the belief that competition, rivalry, hostility, and so on, are culturally relative rather than generically human is a misguided and false notion which, invented by Rousseau, continues to be perpetrated by the latter day believers—true believers—in the noble savage. This is so, I came to believe, because although the intensity of competitive and hostile motives is culturally (and individually) variable, and although culture can tame and domesticate these motives, it is culture itself (interacting with characteristics of man's mammalian biology) which also, and universally, creates them. This conclusion is based on a number of assumptions that will be examined in the last section of the paper.

Third Field Trip—Burma

From my earlier exposure to Durkheim, I had acquired a persistent interest in the study of religion, but it was the influence of Max Weber, whose religious sociology I became acquainted with only after returning from Israel, that led me to turn my research attention to religion. *The Protestant Ethic* opened my mind to a point of view and method of analysis which were revolutionary and enormously exciting. Moreover, Weber's essays on the sociology of religion, and especially his work on the religions of India, stimulated an interest in Asia and Asian religions which has not yet run its course. Again, however, this interest was very much related to my concern with human nature. Although man's basic motives, I had already decided, are culturally universal, Weber's work strongly suggested that world views are culturally relative, and the religions of India, Hinduism and Buddhism—but especially the latter—seemed to constitute convincing proof for this thesis. If the adherents of one of the world's great religions believe that the self is an illusion, that there are no gods, that life is suffering, that suffering can only be avoided by rejecting the world and all worldly desires, that (therefore) the quest for immortality is a quest for eternal suffering, that salvation consists in the cessation of life (i.e., of rebirth)—if, that is, Buddhists believe in these, and in many other, principles that are directly opposed to accepted Western principles, it seemed to follow that world views—those fundamental cognitive orientations by which men order their lives—are historically conditioned and therefore culturally relative.

In order to study both the determinants and the consequences of the Buddhist world view "on the ground," I determined that my next field trip would take place in Asia, and from 1961 to 1962 I was fortunate to have the opportunity to conduct such a study in Upper Burma. Subsequently, in the summers of 1969 to 1972 I continued these studies among the Burmese expatriates in Thailand. As an anthropologist, especially one committed to functionalism, I did not, of course, restrict my studies to Buddhism. But I shall avoid any discussion here of the findings concerning kinship and politics, of folk religion and folk medicine, not to mention aggression, though the latter is directly related to the previous sections of this paper. Instead, this discussion will be confined to elements of the Burmese Buddhist world view in their relationship to human nature.

As was the case in the earlier field trips, the expectations I took to Burma proved to be chimerical, for I discovered that the religious beliefs of Burmese Buddhists—and subsequent studies of other scholars revealed this was also the case in Ceylon and Thailand—were in many respects rather discrepant from those described in Western works on Buddhism, not excluding that of Weber. The discrepancies were based on two errors. One error was mine, in expecting congruence between canonical texts and beliefs held by religious actors, for, of course, it is never the case that the belief systems of religious actors accurately mirror their canonical texts. The other error was that of Western interpreters of Buddhism, who, by their often inaccurate renditions of canonical beliefs, had presented a distorted conception of Buddhism. One example of such a distortion is the alleged atheism of this religion. Although in the metaphysical or theological sense of denying the existence of a Creator or Redeemer, canonical Buddhism is indeed atheistic, it is nevertheless far from being the kind of Ethical Culture movement that it is often portrayed to be. On the contrary, Buddhism explicitly affirms the existence of a host of superhuman beings—gods, godlings, and spirits—and it prescribes various types of ritual for enlisting the help of the benevolent, and appeasing the wrath of the malevolent, ones. It is metaphysically important that these superhuman beings are not eternal, that they, like humans, are subject to the law of karma and, hence, to the wheel of rebirth, but it is irrelevant to the religious concerns of the Buddhist actor who, like religious actors everywhere, turns to these beings for help in time of need, and invokes their activity to explain his suffering. For him, life is inconceivable without the help of the benevolent superhuman beings, and most of life's vicissitudes are inexplicable without his belief in the malevolent.

To be sure, the superhuman helpers of Buddhism are of no assistance—as they are in some other religions—in the Buddhist's quest for salvation, for their help is confined to this world. Even the Buddha, Himself, though He has shown the Path to salvation, is not—as is Christ, for example—a Savior. To be saved every man must walk alone on that Path, without external guidance or intercession. Man, as it were, must save himself. To this extent, Western interpretations of Buddhism are correct. What they usually fail to observe, however, is that this Path is not one on which many Buddhists desire to walk because its soteriological goal, nirvana, is not one which they usually aspire to attain. The reason is simple. Nirvana, a knotty concept at best, is not a state of being—not, at least, in the ordinary sense of "being." Indeed, in the latter sense, nirvana is best characterized as a state of nonbeing, signalling the end of the wheel of rebirth in all of the planes of existence postulated by Buddhist cosmology. But Buddhists, for the most part, are no more interested in the extinction of their future rebirths than are Westerners in the extinction of their *present* birth. Although paying lip service to the notion of nirvana, most Buddhists, in fact, conceive of salvation in highly concrete and material terms, much as it is conceived in most other religious systems. That is, salvation for them is a state of being in which wants and desires are fulfilled, and in which suffering is extinguished. Such a state of affairs they project into future rebirths, in which they are reborn either as wealthy human beings, or—if they dare to aspire to it—as gods in one of the Buddhist material heavens. (They explain that they do not aspire to the normative goal of nirvana by the fact that their present spiritual attainments are still underdeveloped. They hope, however, that after many future rebirths they will eventually develop higher spiritual qualities by means of which they will be able to aspire to this superior vision of salvation. In this regard they are like the young St. Augustine, who prayed he might achieve celibacy, "but not yet.")

But in addition to these findings, there were still others that also disabused me of my earlier view that basic human cognitive orientations are entirely culturally relative and wholly historically conditioned. Thus, for example, the all too human hope which the Burmese evince for a continuous existence is expressed not only in their desire for continuous rebirths, but also in the prevalence of alchemic beliefs and practices whose aim—like the alchemic aims of China—is not the transmutation of base into precious metals, but the attainment of "immortality." To be sure, this goal is not defined as immortality because, as Buddhists, the Burmese profess belief in the normative doctrine of the impermanence of sentient existence. Hence, this goal is defined as—and the alchemic beliefs hold up the possibility of—a continuous existence of only sixty thousand years duration. One could, of course, debate the issue (though probably without much profit) of whether, for the average human mind, sixty thousand years is or is not tantamount to immortality.

Now in pointing, by implication, to the similarities between certain dimensions of the Burmese world view and those of traditional Western culture, I am not suggesting the two are similar on all dimensions. Since, even within the same social group, there are individual differences in cognitive orientations, it is a fortiori the case that there are group differences in cognitive orientations, as well, and the latter are obviously a function of cultural differences. I am suggesting, however, there are some basic cognitive orientations that are not culturally variable (though they may be culturally determined), and among these must be counted those mentioned here in this brief description of some of the cognitive orientations found in Buddhist societies, viz.: the desirability of life, and hence the desire for its prolonged duration; the desirability of material and physical pleasures, and hence the desire to maximize these pleasures; belief in superhuman beings, both of good and evil, and the corollary belief that human action (religious ritual, etc.) can influence their activity by invoking the assistance of the former and repelling the harm of the latter. It is especially instructive that Buddhist actors share these panhuman orientations because in their case these orientations (except for the third) are in direct opposition to the normative teachings of the religion which they genuinely—indeed passionately—revere.

In sum, although the differences in the normative values and official codes of different cultures may, in some instances, lead to the conclusion that culturally constituted cognitions are so different as to constitute (as many contemporary ethnoscientists believe) incommensurable world views, on the basis of the Burmese study I have come to believe this conclusion is entirely unwarranted. I now believe, on the contrary, that when the values and codes of social actors are studied directly, rather than inferred from normative cultural concepts, many cultural differences in basic cognitive orientations are seen to be more apparent than real; to a large extent these differences are merely the manifest expressions of the same underlying cognitive orientations which, being historically conditioned, take different cultural forms.

In short, just as the kibbutz and Ifaluk studies convinced me that many motivational dispositions are culturally invariant, the Burmese study convinced me that many cognitive orientations are also invariant. These invariant dispositions and orientations stem, I believe, from panhuman biological and cultural constants, and they comprise that universal human nature which, together with received anthropological opinion, I had formerly rejected as yet another ethnocentric bias.

Conclusions

Having described how I gradually and painfully came to discard much of the received anthropological wisdom, I now wish to explore (what I consider to have been) the fallacies in traditional anthropological thinking that led to the adoption of cultural determinism and, hence, to the cultural relativistic view of human nature.

I have already noted that in the traditional conception, "culture" referred to all aspects of a group's environment, except the physical, and to all aspects of man, except the biological. Given, then, that man constitutes a single biological species and that, nevertheless, social behavior reveals a wide range of cross-cultural variability, it seemed to follow that the organism is an empty or a black box, and that social behavior, therefore, is determined by culture. Given, too, that personality characteristics were believed to exist in a one-to-one relationship with behavioral characteristics, the former being thought to be *directly* deducible from the latter, it seemed to follow that personality is also culturally determined. This meant that no psychological characteristic—no affect, no need, no wish, no belief—could be part of human personality unless culture put it there. Given, moreover, that culture is variable, personality (it was further argued) must similarly be variable; historically specific cultures produce culturally variable personality characteristics. Given, finally, that depending on their culture, human beings may acquire *any* empirical subset of the total conceivable set of human psychological characteristics, any member of the latter set (it was concluded) is culturally relative; none is an invariant characteristic of a universal human nature. Any psychological characteristic—the feeling of love or hate, the wish for mortality or immortality, the belief in the talion principle or its reverse—might or might not be found in any social group as a function of its cultural program.

Skipping over some logical and empirical problems in its global[3] and holistic[4] conception of culture, this conceptual structure falters, I be-

3. The logical problem raised by the global conception of culture is easily stated. If culture includes (among other things) behavioral patterns and personality traits, to say that culture determines behavior and personality is obviously circular. Although this difficulty is easily resolved—by excluding behavior and personality from the definition of "culture" and thereby rendering the culture concept less global—yet another problem with respect to personality remains. For if personality is not part of culture, and, moreover, if personality (as we shall see below) is not isomorphic with behavior—if, on the contrary, personality is viewed as a system of cognitive, perceptual, motivational, and affective dispositions "underlying" behavior—it cannot be so blithely assumed that cultural (and, therefore, behavioral) variability is associated with personality variability. This latter thesis now becomes an empirical hypothesis, to be tested by direct examination of personality, rather than an a priori assumption whose proof consists in pointing to the cross-cultural variability in behavior. In short, if personality is not, merely by definition, a part of culture, and if the isomorphism of personality and behavior is not accepted as an unchallenged assumption, then the question of pancultural psychological characteristics remains open.

4. The empirical problem raised by the holistic conception of culture is also easily stated for, given this conception, it is difficult to know which of the various elements comprising a culture are the determinants of personality: Art styles? Religious beliefs? Descent systems? Modes of production? Child rearing? Some of these? All of these? In short, so long as culture is taken as an undifferentiated whole, a seamless web, the thesis of cultural determination of personality is not very illuminating, since (even in the now restricted conception of culture) the only things that are excluded as possible determinants are characteristics of the organism and of the physical environment. Even Margaret Mead, much of whose work has concentrated on (and has illuminated so much of) the relationship between child training and personality, has disclaimed any notion that the former is an especially important cultural determinant; rather, she claims, it is merely a convenient way of entering into the total configuration of cultural determinants.

lieve, on two related, but separable, theses, both of which are (I believe) untenable. These are: (1) culture is the exclusive determinant of personality; and (2) personality consists exclusively of the internalization of culture. Let us begin with the first.

1. *Culture is the exclusive determinant of personality.* Culture determinist theories of behavior and of personality were developed in the first instance as alternatives to and refutations of biological determinism. Given the demonstrable cross-cultural variability in behavior and personality, anthropology (validly) argued that social behavior cannot represent an expression of instincts, and personality formation cannot represent an unfolding of genetically programmed psychological traits. Rather, both must be (in a large part, at least) a result of learning, which is to say (since anthropology is concerned with group, rather than individual, variability) that they are the products (in large part, at least) of social and cultural determinants. So far, so good. To have concluded, however, that cultural determinism implies the absence of any invariant pancultural psychological characteristics—in short, that all such characteristics are culturally relative—is an invalid conclusion which is based, I believe, on three interrelated fallacies.

The fallacy of assuming that the cross-cultural variability in social behavior and personality implies that the organism is an empty or black box. Despite the variability in culture, it does not follow that man has no invariant psychological characteristics, because some, at least, are biologically determined. Far from being an empty or black box, some of the properties of the organism are important determinants of social behavior as well as personality. Although space does not permit a detailed, let alone an exhaustive catalogue of these properties, I might mention a small subset, viz., those relevant to the problem of hostility and aggression discussed in earlier sections of this paper.

Because of prolonged helplessness, requiring dependency on others for the satisfaction of their survival needs, children are everywhere raised in family or family-like groups whose members, to a greater or lesser extent, provide them with nurturance, gratification, and protection. As a result, children everywhere have the following characteristics: the need to receive love from, and the motivation to express love for, the loving and loved objects; feelings of rivalry toward those who seek love from the same (scarce) love objects; hostility toward those who would deprive them of these objects; and so on. In short, everywhere (due to Oedipal struggles and conflicts with siblings) children's need for love is necessarily thwarted, as well as gratified, to some extent. Moreover, because everywhere man lives in social groups—yet another biological requirement of the human organism—and since the requirements of a human social order demand that children learn to behave in compliance with cultural norms, everywhere their needs, desires, and wishes are necessarily frustrated, as well as gratified, to some extent. Everywhere, therefore, if for only these reasons, hostile, rivalrous, and competitive feelings, as well as those of love and mutual aid, will be found to some extent.

The expression "to some extent" underscores the fact that the intensity of these various types of frustrations, and hence the intensity of these feelings, are highly culturally variable. Similarly, and for the same reason, the targets of these feelings, the degree to which they are permitted expression in aggressive behavior, the social domains in which they are permitted expression (whether in kinship, religion, politics, and so on), the manner in which they are expressed (whether directly, through displacement, projection, and so on)—all these are culturally determined and culturally variable. Nevertheless, although different cultures channel these feelings in a bewildering variety of social and cultural forms—some more, some less adaptive—all cultures produce them to some extent. They are, in short, among man's invariant psychological characteristics.

The fallacy of confusing "a culture" with "culture" in the expression "cultural determinism." The theory of cultural determinism was based on the following (valid) argument. Given that human beings are born without instincts, the gratification of human "needs" depends on learning. Given, moreover, that they are born entirely helpless, they are wholly dependent on adults for the acquisition of the means for their gratification. Given, finally, that they live in social groups, these means must be shared and, therefore, prescribed, i.e., they must be cultural. Thus, the properties of the organism, interacting with those of the social environment, *require* that a human existence be a culturally constituted existence. In short, if other animals adapt by means of species-specific biological specializations, human adaptation is achieved by means of a species-specific nonbiological specialization, viz., culture. If this is the case, then, for a human primate to be classified as man— i.e., to be characterized as more than a bipedal, big-brained, primate—it is not enough that he have those biological characteristics a zoologist would designate as the distinguishing features of Homo sapiens. It is also necessary that he have those characteristics—socially shared and transmitted symbols, values, rules, and so on—that an anthropologist would designate as the distinguishing features of a cultural mode of adaptation. But if culture is as important an adaptive human requirement as food or water, then culture and the psychological products of culture—the drives, needs, cognitions, and the like, that are produced by culture—are as much a part of man's nature as his biological characteristics and *their* psychological products. Indeed, since many of man's biological and biologically derived psychological characteristics are found in the entire class of mammals, it may be said that since his cultural and culturally derived psychological characteristics are man's species-specific characteristics, they are the uniquely *human* part of his nature.

These, then, were the insights that were originally captured by the notion of cultural determinism. They were valid then and, in my opinion, they are valid now. When, however, anthropology became increasingly impressed with cultural differences, this original notion of cultural determinism underwent (as we have seen) two changes. First, instead of being taken as *a* determinant, culture was taken as *the* determinant, of human nature, for when anthropologists began to view culture as internalized by social actors, they also began to argue that culture was the exclusive (or the exclusively relevant) content of the black or empty organism. Second, since culture is found in a bewildering variety of local manifestations, anthropologists came to view each culture as a more or less historically unique creation, each producing a culturally unique human nature. Consequently, it came to be believed that there is little basis for postulating any set of invariant psychological characteristics that might comprise a universal human nature.

Almost without recognition, therefore, the meaning of "cultural determinism" has undergone a gradual shift. Beginning as a statement about man's nature, it has come to be a statement about his history. From a theory of the generic cultural determination of single pancultural human nature, it has become a theory of the historically specific cultural determination of many culturally relative human natures.[5] The fallacy in this shift is obvious. Since cultural variability does not mean that culture is distributed across space and over time in a series of discrete configurations, each incommensurable with every other; since, on the contrary, culture is known to be distributed in a series of overlapping configurations; since, in short, despite the variability of culture, there is clearly discernible (what Wissler termed long ago) a "universal culture pattern," then, if personality is determined by culture, there must also be a universal personality pattern—a set of

5. Certain trends in current anthropology are even more relativistic. Thus, for example, the movement alternatively referred to as the "new ethnography," ethnosemantics, or ethnoscience, rejects the very notion of objective categories of ethnographic description. Arguing that cultures are incommensurable, the members of this movement insist that "etic" (i.e., cross-cultural) categories distort, when they do not falsify, the meanings of intracultural concepts, and that "emic" categories alone can convey their meanings. In my view this is not only the reductio ad absurdum of cultural relativism, but it leads to the demise of anthropology as a science.

invariant psychological characteristics produced by all cultures. In sum, even an exclusively cultural determinist theory of personality does not entail a cultural relativistic theory of human nature. For if certain cultural characteristics are pancultural, then, ex hypothesi, certain personality characteristics are also pancultural, and they, at least, comprise man's pancultural human nature.

The fallacy of not distinguishing the phenotypic from the genotypic, or (using a more fashionable metaphor) surface structure from deep structure, in culture. Culture, as man's most important adaptive specialization, mediates the interaction between the properties of his psychobiological organism and those of his social and physical environments. But in its role as mediator, culture is necessarily variable across space and over time because, as a product of man's symbolic capacities, culture can (and must) vary with a host of variable historical conditions—ecological settings, diffusionary opportunities, politically powerful or charismatic leadership, unpredictable physical and social events (war, drought, invasions), and so on. If, then, culture is the means by which men and groups adapt to the functional requirements of individual and group existence, it is not surprising to find a wide range of differences in the form and content of culture as a function of an equally wide range of differences in man's historical experience.

Variability in the form and content of culture does not, however, imply variability in the substance of culture, nor, a fortiori, does it entail variability in personality. Indeed, identical psychological structures can be associated with (and eventuate in) manifestly dissimilar cultural structures, for though phenotypically different, the latter may be genotypically identical, i.e., they may be functionally equivalent structural alternatives for coping with the identical functional requirements of individual and group existence. Different religions, for example, exhibit wide variability in their belief and ritual systems, and yet these different systems may all satisfy (among other things) a common human wish for dependency on powers greater than man. Thus, the gods of different cultures may differ in form and content (cultural phenotype), but, as powers greater than man (cultural genotype), they all reflect a pancultural human psychological characteristic (dependency need).

If, then, differences in cultural phenotypes do not imply differences in genotype, culture is less variable than it seems. Hence, phenotypic cultural differences do not in themselves justify the inference of personality differences, and phenotypic cultural variability does not in itself imply the cultural relativity of human nature. Unless these phenotypic differences can be assumed to be more than historically conditioned variable expressions of the same cultural genotype, such differences are entirely compatible with a pancultural human nature.

The foregoing critique of cultural determinism, and its corollary, cultural relativism, may be summarized as follows: the nature/history dichotomy is a false dichotomy; although personality, to some extent, is culturally relative, man has a nature as well as a history; this is so because even a radical cultural determinism does not imply a radical cultural relativism; however much societies may differ, they all must cope with man's common biological features, especially his prolonged infantile dependency; the adaptively viable means for coping with the latter condition exhibit common social and cultural features across a narrow range of social and cultural variability; these common biological, social, and cultural features are a set of constants which, in their interaction, produce a universal human nature.

2. *Personality consists exclusively of the internalization of culture.* Although the thesis that culture is the exclusive determinant of personality accounts, in part, for the traditional denial of a pancultural human nature, the thesis that personality is the internalization of culture has been even more decisive in this regard. For since culture is variable, and since, ex hypothesi, personality is merely culture as it is internalized in social actors, it follows necessarily that there can be no pancultural human nature; there can only be culturally relative human nature. But this undifferentiated model of personality (personality as constituted exclusively of culture) is even less tenable than the global model of culture held by its champions. If, instead, we were to adopt a more sophisticated model of personality—one in which personality, conceived as a system, consists of differentiated structures, each with distinctive functions—cultural variability need not imply personality variability (and, for that matter, cultural similarities need not imply similarities in personality).

Consider, for example, the Freudian model according to which personality, as a system, consists of three differentiated, but interrelated structures. Over-simply put, these structures consist of an impulse system, or id; a cognitive-perceptual system, or ego; and a normative-prescriptive system, or superego. This model is not only much more complex than the internalization-of-culture model, but one of its postulated structures—the id—comprises wishes and desires, many of which are in frequent, if not persistent, conflict with culture. Moreover, since the id is only one structure of the personality, and since another of its structures—the superego—comprises (among other things) internalized cultural values, many wishes of social actors are not only in conflict with the cultural requirements of their group (external conflict), but one part of their personality is frequently in conflict with another (internal conflict). In the latter case, the ego experiences conflict between impulses which seek gratification and internalized cultural values which proscribe their gratification. To complicate the picture even more, this conflict may be unconscious, as well as conscious.

According to this model of personality, social behavior is often neither a direct expression of an undifferentiated personality, nor a simple result of the influence of external cultural norms. It is more likely to be the end product of a chain of interacting psychological events, including impulse (id), cultural and personal values (superego), conflict between them, and defense against conflict (ego), which only then eventuates in behavior. In most cases, to be sure, behavior—the end product of this chain—conforms to cultural norms, for the actor usually complies with his superego, and resolves the conflict by controlling the forbidden impulses—either by the conscious mechanism of suppression, or by a variety of unconscious mechanisms of defense (including the defense of repression). In short, according to this model of personality, social actors are not merely the creatures of their culture, formed in its mold, and reflecting its values. Although typically conforming with them, a comprehensive description of their values is only a partial description of their personality. Indeed, their values, which comprise one part of their motivational system, are often in conflict with equally strong motives which oppose them. The latter may be kept under control, but since control does not mean extinction, culture, as Freud argued, necessarily produces "discontents"—a condition in which the social actor is frequently at odds with himself and with his culture.

Since both models of personality, the Freudian structural model and the internalization-of-culture model, make the same behavioral predictions—both predict behavior will conform with cultural norms—what difference does it make regarding which of the two one chooses? (Indeed, the principle of parsimony would suggest the adoption of the latter, or cultural determinist model.) Although this choice makes little difference for the prediction of social behavior, it makes a great difference for the understanding of personality (not to mention the understanding of the psychic costs of culture, mental illness, social deviance, and so on). According to the internalization-of-culture model, behavior is the direct (unconflicted) expression of cultural norms as they are internalized in the personality. Hence, for example, if one observes little aggressive behavior in some social group, it could be inferred that, having internalized a set of cultural values opposing aggression, the social actors are nonhostile—for hostility, according to this model, is determined by cultural values which favor aggression. According to the

Freudian model, however, this inference may be entirely unwarranted, for these nonaggressive actors may (as a result of any number of punitive and frustrating conditions) have strong hostile impulses which, however, because of strong superego disapproval of aggression, are kept under rigid control.

Just as the internalization-of-culture model may invalidly deduce personality from behavior, it may similarly invalidly deduce culture from behavior. Thus, if one were to observe a great deal of aggression in a social group, then, in accordance with this model, it could be inferred that the actors have internalized a set of cultural values which favor aggression. According to the Freudian model, however, this may not be the case at all. Rather than expressing cultural values, aggressive behavior may in fact be in direct violation of them. The aggression (stemming from socially induced hostility) may instead be the result of an immature ego (with little impulse control), or a weak superego (which has insufficiently internalized the cultural values opposing aggression), or of a powerful id (with strong hostile impulses).

In sum, when personality is viewed as a system with differentiated structures and functions, the simple isomorphism between culture, behavior, and personality postulated by the internalization-of-culture model is frequently found wanting. As we have seen, a group which exhibits very little aggressive behavior may, nevertheless, be characterized by strong (probably unconscious) hostility; and a group which exhibits a great deal of aggressive behavior may nevertheless be characterized by cultural values which oppose aggression. (In the latter case, of course, the aggression will probably be expressed—displaced, projected, and the like—in socially acceptable forms). To take a classic case, the Hopi may be no less hostile than the Sioux, despite the fact that the latter exhibit much more social aggression, and that their cultural values concerning aggression are much different. Rather than reflecting differences in hostility, resulting from differences in culture, the differences in their aggressive behavior may instead reflect differences either in the social canalization of aggression, or in the relationships among the id, ego, and superego components of their respective personalities. Indeed, their strict avoidance of interpersonal aggression might suggest the hypothesis that Hopi hostility may be even stronger than that of the Sioux, but that, because of a stricter superego, they inhibit their dangerous hostile impulses.

This example suggests that although group differences in behavior say a great deal about differences in culture, in themselves they may say little about differences in personality, and even less about the cultural relativity of human nature. It also suggests that different models of personality do indeed make a difference for our understanding of human nature. The internalization-of-culture model, which assumes that personality differences are isomorphic with behavioral and cultural differences, leads to the cultural relativistic view of human nature. The model of a structurally and functionally differentiated personality, which makes no assumptions about social-culture-personality isomorphisms—and which therefore requires that personality be investigated independently of both behavior and culture—supports the view of a pancultural human nature.

References

The following entries pertain exclusively to the author's three research projects discussed in this chapter.

Ifaluk
> 1950. *A psychotic personality in the South Seas. Psychiatry* 13:189–204.
> 1951. Some Ifaluk myths and folk tales. *Journal of American Folklore* 64:280–303.
> 1952. Ghosts, Ifaluk and teleological functionalism. *American Anthropologist* 54: 497–503.
> 1953. *An atoll culture,* with E. G. Burrows. New Haven: Human Relations Area Files.
> 1953. Ghosts: An anthropological inquiry into learning and perception. *Journal of Abnormal and Social Psychology* 48:376–82.
> 1959. Cultural heritage, personal tensions, and mental illness in a South Sea culture. In *Culture and mental health,* ed. M. K. Opler. New York: Macmillan.
> 1961. Sorcery, evil spirits, and functional analysis. *American Anthropologist* 63:820–24.

Kibbutz
> 1954. Is the family universal? *American Anthropologist* 56:839–46.
> 1955. Education in a communal village in Israel. *American Journal of Orthopsychiatry* 25:283–92.
> 1956. *Kibbutz: Venture in Utopia.* Cambridge: Harvard University Press. (New augmented edition, 1971, with a new chapter.)
> 1957. The Sabras and Zionism: A study in personality and ideology. *Social Problems* 5:100–110.
> 1958. *Children of the kibbutz.* Cambridge: Harvard University Press. (New augmented edition, 1975, with a new chapter.)

Burma
> 1965. Religious systems as culturally constituted defense mechanisms. In

Context and meaning in cultural anthropology, ed. Melford Spiro. Glencoe: Free Press.

1966. Buddhism and economic saving in Burma. *American Anthropologist* 68: 1163–73.

1967. *Burmese supernaturalism: A study in the explanation and resolution of suffering.* Englewood Cliffs, N.J.: Prentice-Hall.

1968. Religion, personality, and behavior in Burma. *American Anthropologist* 70:359–63.

1968. Politics and factionalism in Upper Burma. In *Local level politics,* ed. Marc Swartz. Chicago: Aldine.

1969. Religious symbols and social behavior. *Proceedings of the American Philosophical Society* 113:341–50.

1969. The psychological functions of witchcraft: The Burmese case. In *Mental health in Asia and the Pacific,* ed. Caudill and Lin. Honolulu: East-West Center Press.

1971. *Buddhism and society: A great tradition and its Burmese vicissitudes.* New York: Harper and Row.

1972. Violence in Burmese history: A psychocultural interpretation. In *Collective violence,* ed. Short and Wolfgang. Chicago: Aldine.

1973. Social change and functional analysis: A study in Burmese psychocultural history. *Ethos* 1:263–97.

1974. The Oedipus complex in Burma. *Journal of Nervous and Mental Disease* 157:389–95.

1975. Some psychodynamic determinants of household composition in village Burma. *Contributions to Asian Studies* 8:126–38.

1977. *Kinship and marriage in Burma: A cultural and psychodynamic analysis.* Berkeley: University of California Press.

1979. Symbolism and functionalism in the anthropological study of religion. *Proceedings of the Study Conference of the International Association for the History of Religion.* In *Science of religious studies in methodology,* ed. Lauri Honko. The Hague: Mouton.

2   Some Reflections on Cultural Determinism and Relativism with Special Reference to Emotion and Reason

A Conception of Culture

As I SEE IT, "culture" designates a cognitive system, that is, a set of "propositions," both descriptive (e.g., "the planet earth sits on the back of a turtle") and normative (e.g., "it is wrong to kill"), about nature, man, and society that are embedded in interlocking higher-order networks and configurations. Cultural and noncultural propositions differ in two important dimensions. First, cultural propositions are *traditional*, that is, they are developed in the historical experience of social groups, and as a social heritage, they are acquired by social actors through various processes of social transmission (enculturation) rather than constructed by them from their private experience. Second, cultural propositions are encoded in *collective*, rather than private, signs (indices and icons, to employ Peirce's distinctions, as well as symbols). Hence, they exist and (in the first instance) are discoverable by anthropologists in the collective representations of social groups without their having to probe for them in the private representations of social actors (though, as I shall soon argue, many of them are also found there, albeit in a different form). This is not to say that cultural statements, rules, values, norms, and the like are always stated in propositional form, for clearly they are not, but that they are susceptible of statement in that form.

This restricted conception of culture has important implications for what "culture" does not designate. First, although by this conception,

Reprinted from *Culture Theory: Essays on Mind, Self, and Emotion*, edited by Richard A. Shweder and Robert A. LeVine (Cambridge: Cambridge University Press, 1984), pp. 323–46. © 1984 by Cambridge University Press. Reprinted by permission of the publisher.

Although we continue to disagree on some key issues, this chapter has importantly benefited from the suggestions and comments of Roy D'Andrade, Richard Shweder, Marc Swartz, and Donald Tuzin.

culture is obviously an important—though only one—determinant of behavior, culture as such does not consist of behavior. Moreover, although culture—to broaden this implication—includes propositions referring to social structure, social organization, social behavior, and the like, culture as such does not consist of them. It might be added that because the latter have noncultural (situational, ecological, economic, political, biological, emotional, etc.) as well as cultural (ideational) determinants, the cultural propositions comprising the emic models of social structure, social organization, and the like cannot in themselves provide a reliable basis for predicting their content or their shape. For the same reason, cultural models cannot be reliably deduced from the observation of social behavior alone.

Second, although by this conception "culture" designates a cognitive system, it is not the only—though it is clearly the most important—source of the cognitions and schemata held by social actors. The other source, of course, consists of their own experience. Thus, on the basis of their social experience, a group of actors may come to construct a conception of their social universe as hostile and threatening even though such a conception is not transmitted to them by intentional enculturative processes and may even be inconsistent with cultural propositions that convey the very opposite message. Although conceptions of this type—beliefs or cognitive orientations constructed by social actors as an unintended consequence of social experience—have important effects on the social behavior, social structure, and world view of social groups, they are not, by our definition, "cultural." Usually, but not always, unconscious, they are not encoded in collective signs, and they are (therefore) not transmitted by means of intentional enculturative processes. (They are discovered by the anthropologist as an inference from clinically oriented interviews, dreams, projective tests, and culturally constituted projective systems such as myths, folklore, and the like.)

Third, although many cultural propositions have emotional antecedents, and although others have emotional consequences—they arouse emotional responses in social actors—and although some even prescribe the proper conditions for the expression of emotions, culture as such—a cognitive system encoded in collective representations—does not consist of emotions.

The exclusion of emotion from this conception of culture is not based on the view—which, it might be thought, I hold either from ignorance or foolishness—that emotions occur without thought or thought without emotions. Even if I held such a misguided view (which I do not), it would hardly be germane to the present issue because—although I have defined "culture" as a cognitive system—culture does not consist of thought (thinking) any more than it consists of emotion (feeling). As thinking and feeling are properties of persons, and as culture—neither by this definition nor by any other that I am aware of—does not consist of persons—though society does—it is hard to see how either could be part of culture.

Although not a part of culture, thinking and feeling are often determined by culture. That is, we most often think by means of the concepts comprising cultural propositions, and our emotions are often aroused by them; in short, many of our thoughts and emotions are (what might be termed) "culturally constituted." But just because thoughts and emotions are culturally constituted, it is logically impermissible to conclude that culture, as such, consists of emotion or thought any more than it can be concluded that culture consists of behavior or social structure, although they too are culturally constituted (cultural propositions serve to motivate behavior and to provide a model for special structure). The conflation of culture and culturally constituted phenomena is based on a confusion of logical types, of cause with effect, structure with function, producer with product. (It is that very confusion that invalidates my earlier attempt ([Spiro 1950] to understand the relationship between mind and culture by arguing—as I now see it—fallaciously that "culture" and "personality" are synonymous.)

If, then, the exclusion of emotion from this conception of culture is not based on the misguided view that feeling is isolated from thinking, neither is it based on the view that while emotions (because they are "located" in the mind) are private events, thoughts (because culture is "located" in collective representations) are public. In fact, I reject that view, not because I believe that emotions are public—although their expression is—but because I believe that thoughts are also private. Hence, as culture is a public system, thoughts no less than emotions are, by definition, excluded from "culture."

Culture is public because it consists of propositions that are encoded in collective representations, or public signs, usually, but not always, symbols. It is precisely for that reason that anyone—and not only a native—can learn the culture of any social group. Since, then, the "meanings" of those signs consist of the concepts they designate and represent, cultural propositions are public because—as Saussure (1966) has shown—their meanings are "located," as it were, in the signs themselves: the signs, to employ his terms, function simultaneously as both signified (concept) and signifier (sign vehicle). When, however, cultural propositions are learned by social actors, they become personal thoughts that, like emotions, are private; they are now "located" in the mind.

However, because these private thoughts are derived from, though they may be less than isomorphic with, cultural propositions, they are (to employ a term introduced earlier) culturally constituted. Nevertheless, inasmuch as they are "located" in the (private) mental representations of social actors, rather than in the (public) collective representations of their group, to conclude that culture consists of these culturally constituted thoughts is to commit the logical fallacies mentioned earlier.

Finally, this conception of culture does not imply that the meanings of the symbols and other signs—both "discursive" and "presentational"—in which cultural propositions are represented are only conscious, nor (in the latter case) only denotative. This conception of culture recognizes that cultural symbols have unconscious and connotative meanings, as well—the meanings that are expressed in metaphor, metonymy, and other tropes. Moreover, as it is in these meanings that most of the emotional action of symbols is found, it is in respect to them that the interaction between culture and emotion is most pronounced. As these meanings, however, do not constitute the (conventional) meanings *of* symbols but are rather the meanings that social actors, consciously or unconsciously, *intend* for them to have, they are "located" not in the symbols themselves but in the minds of social actors. Hence, if we distinguish between the meanings *of* cultural symbols and the meanings that they have *for* social actors, the range of meanings that a culture has *for* social actors is much broader than the range of meanings *of* (conventional) cultural symbols.

Because of this difference in range, although anyone, not only the natives, can learn a culture, the meanings that it has for the natives may be very different from those that it has for non-natives. In learning a foreign culture a non-native may acquire as firm a grasp of the meanings *of* the culture as a native, but not having been socialized in the group, he or she has not had those social experiences that, alone, serve to invest the culture with those surplus meanings, that it has *for* the native.

That is why, too, we must distinguish between learning a culture and becoming enculturated. To learn a culture is to acquire its propositions; to become enculturated is, in addition, to "internalize" them as personal beliefs, that is, as propositions that are thought to be true, proper, or right. This is especially the case for those propositions that Shweder (1984) calls "cultural frames," propositions that can be neither proved nor disproved. Thus, for example, a non-Buddhist scholar of Buddhism may have studied its textual doctrines and may know their meanings in much greater detail than a Buddhist. Nevertheless, the scholar is rarely converted to Buddhism—its textual doctrines do not become personal beliefs—because, not having been socialized in a Buddhist society, its textual doctrines do not have for him the connotative meanings, nor do they arouse in him the emotional responses, that alone serve to transform cultural frames into culturally constituted beliefs. I shall return to this thesis later.

That is also why, even for the natives themselves, many cultural frames are, or become, what might be called "cultural clichés"—propositions to which actors may give nominal assent but which are not "internalized" by them as personal beliefs. Although this may occur for many reasons, the most important, in my view, is that these particular propositions do not have, or have lost, emotional importance for them.

Finally, that is why the anthropologist who is interested in the meanings that a culture has *for* the social actors must investigate the personality of the actors with the same diligence that he investigates their cultural symbol systems. For, in addition to the fact that, as D'Andrade has observed (1984), there is considerable slippage in the transformation of cultural propositions into (culturally constituted) beliefs, the surplus meanings of cultural symbols are "located" in the minds of the actors.

The Aims of This Chapter

Given the cognitive and public conception of culture sketched in the preceding section, the primary questions I wish to address in this chapter are the questions of cultural determinism and relativism. The reason for addressing these traditional questions in particular is that they form the core issues of the essays I was asked to discuss at the SSRC conference—the essays by Shweder and Rosaldo—and the excellence of those essays, together with the ensuing discussion of them, served to focus in sharp relief those dimensions of cultural determinism and relativism from which I dissent. In my view the essays and discussion alike attribute much more social and psychological power to particular cultures than I believe is justified; and from the variability among cultures, they draw relativistic conclusions that are more radical than I believe is warranted.

Almost all anthropologists, I take it, would agree that descriptive cultural propositions related to scientific (or ethnoscientific) domains can be judged to be true or false by normal canons of scientific evidence. Hence, what is at issue here is that subset of cultural propositions, both descriptive and normative, that Shweder calls "cultural frames." Cultural frames, of course, constitute a large—perhaps the largest—proportion of all the propositions comprising any culture.

That cultural systems display a wide range of variability in their cultural frames is of course an empirical generalization that anthropology has documented both richly and abundantly. However, that no comparative judgments can be made, as some relativists claim, concerning these frames is, in my view, a non sequitur. For if, as I believe, the processes that characterize the working of the human mind are the same everywhere—even though human cultures are different—then there are certain psychological criteria by which such judgments can be made. For example, judgments concerning the rationality of cultural frames can be made according to the criterion of "reality testing": that is by the degree to which they rest on a failure to distinguish fantasy from reality. Again, judgments concerning their utility can be made according to the criterion of functional consequences, that is by the degree to which they lead to an emotional disturbance and to disruptive social relationships rather than the reverse, and so on. These and other criteria will be examined in detail.

The validity of these criteria, of course, rests on the assumption that, as mentioned earlier, the human mind works (or has the capacity to work) the same everywhere so that, in respect to my examples, their validity presumes that all humans have the capacity to distinguish fantasy from reality, to prefer pleasurable to painful feelings, to welcome nonconflictual over conflictual relationships, and so forth.

Having mentioned two psychological criteria for comparing the relative merits of different cultures, I am not suggesting that culture can be "reduced" to psychology. Far from it. For to say (as I have) that the propositions comprising culture are "traditional" propositions is to say that culture is quintessentially a historical product. Hence, any adequate account of culture is necessarily a historical account. Nevertheless, once a cultural proposition is acquired as a personal belief by social actors, its acquisition is a psychological event, and that event requires a "psychological" explanation. This can perhaps be best understood by reference to the concept of the cognitive salience of cultural propositions.

Somewhat schematically, and in ascending order of importance, those propositions that, following Shweder, we are calling "cultural frames" may be said to comprise a hierarchy of cognitive salience consisting of the following five levels.

1. As a result of normal enculturative processes, social actors *learn about* the propositions; they acquire an "acquaintance" with them, as Bertrand Russell would say.

2. In addition to learning about the propositions, the actors also *understand* their traditional meanings as they are interpreted, for example, in authoritative texts or by recognized specialists.

3. Understanding their traditional meanings, the actors "internalize" the propositions—they hold them to be true, correct, or right. It is only then that they are acquired as personal beliefs. The transformation of a cultural proposition into a culturally constituted belief does not in itself, however, indicate that it importantly affects the manner in which the actors conduct their lives, which leads to the fourth level.

4. As culturally constituted beliefs, cultural propositions inform the behavioral environment of social actors, serving to structure their perceptual worlds and hence, to *guide* their actions.

5. At this level, culturally constituted beliefs serve not only to guide but to *instigate* action, that is, they possess emotional and motivational, as well as cognitive, salience. Thus, for example, one who acquires the religious doctrine of infant damnation as a personal belief at this level of cognitive salience not only incorporates it as part of his (theological) belief system but also internalizes it as part of his motivational system: It arouses strong affect (anxiety), which, in turn, motivates him to action (the baptism of his children) whose purpose is to save them from damnation. (For a detailed explication of the consequences of this hierarchy, see Spiro 1982.)

A cultural frame that is acquired as a personal belief at the highest three levels of cognitive salience has a legitimacy and a moral and emotional urgency that are absent from other cultural frames. Thus, as was noted earlier, although the existence of such a frame as part of the cultural heritage of the group requires a historical explanation, its internalization as a personal belief requires a "psychological" explanation. This can perhaps be clarified by the example of the Augustinian doctrine of infant damnation.

The doctrine of infant damnation, a cultural proposition that is part of the theological system of certain Christian denominations, must be explained, in the first instance, by the history of Christian theology. The moment, however, that some Christian actor says, "By God, it's true!" it is internalized as a personal belief, and its internalization requires a psychological explanation. For why this actor (or any other) should believe that a just God would condemn little children to damnation must now be explained by reference not to the history of Christian doctrine (which the believer is probably ignorant of anyway) but to the cognitive orientations, perceptual sets, and motivational dispositions that led him to assent to its truth.

Again, in saying that the transformation of a cultural frame into a personal belief entails an explanatory shift from a historical to a psychological perspective, I am not saying that this represents a shift from a group to an individual level of explanation. For the psychological characteristics of social actors must also be explained by reference to a group phenomenon—not, however, by reference to culture but, rather, at least in my view, to society, a distinction that (for me at any rate) is crucial. If "culture" refers to traditional propositions about nature, man, and society, then "society," as I am using that term, refers to traditional forms of social relations, in which "social" refers to a range extending from a dyad to a nation-state.

Cultural acquisition begins in childhood, and children acquire culture from persons who are their "significant others," that is, persons—usually parents or parent surrogates—with whom they have a powerful emotional involvement, both positive and negative. Hence, their mental representations of these parenting figures not only persist; they often constitute as well a template for their perception of other superordinate beings, both human and divine. It is the mental representation that a child forms of a particular type of parenting figure that explains (in part) how an otherwise benevolent Christian might come to believe that a just God can send unbaptized infants to hell. For in their modes of socialization and enculturation, not only do parents intentionally transmit the meanings or messages *of* cultural propositions to their children, but they also unintentionally transmit another set of messages to them: messages about the kinds of persons they (the parents) are, the conditions under which they offer and withhold love, and punishment, and the like. It is from these latter messages, acquired by (as Bateson calls it) deutero-learning, that children form their parental representations. If the particular concept of God that is implicit in the doctrine of infant damnation is consistent with the child's parental representation, then, when he later learns that doctrine, it makes "psychological" sense to him and that is one reason he might internalize it as a personal belief.

That cultural frames make emic, or intracultural, sense does not imply, however, that they are immune from valid transcultural, or etic, judgment (as Shweder argues), let alone that they are the primary, if not the exclusive, determinants of what social actors think and feel or how they behave (as Rosaldo argues). Before examining these arguments, however, I wish to emphasize that where I disagree with them, my disagreement is with the two dominant themes of contemporary culture theory that they represent and not with Rosaldo's and Shweder's able formulations of these themes. Indeed, because their formulations are clearer and more cogent than any I previously encountered, I was able to more clearly discern my own disagreement with these two themes—the themes (as I shall call them) of *particularistic* cultural determinism and *normative* cultural relativism.

Particularistic Cultural Determinism

"Culture patterns," Rosaldo wrote in an earlier draft of her essay, "provide a template for *all* human action, growth, and understanding" (my italics), and again, "culture does not dictate simply *what* we think but how we feel about and live our lives" (italics in original).[1] Such comprehensive claims, no doubt, gratify our anthropological egos, for as the main keepers of the flame of culture, we thereby assure ourselves that we travel the royal road to human understanding. Gratifying as it is, we must nevertheless ask to what extent such claims are true. Is there nothing in biology or in social relations, for example, that might also affect our action, growth, and understanding? And is there nothing in imagination and fantasy that might also affect the way we feel about and live our lives? In short, to advert to the first question, are our "action, growth, and understanding" never influenced by our transcultural biologically acquired drives and socially acquired selves or are they only influenced by culture patterns? Moreover, to advert to the second question, do our egos never transcend the constraints of all three determinants—the biological, the social, and the cultural alike—and thereby achieve some degree of autonomy, if only in fantasy and imagination?

Now because, as Rosaldo claims, culture dictates what we think and feel, *we* (following the dictates of *our* culture) "think of hidden or forgotten affects as disturbing energies repressed [and] see in violent actions the expression of a history of frustrations buried in a fertile but unconscious mind," but the Ilongots (following the dictates of *their* culture) think and see nothing of the kind.

Although I am not convinced that, except for some few Freudian theorists, most of *us* do not think and see things as the Ilongot do, the

1. In its published version, this quotation has been modified to read, "Culture makes a difference that concerns not simply *what* we think but how we feel about and live our lives." Since this modified version is one that every anthropologist, not only a cultural determinist, would unqualifiedly assent to, I have used the earlier version as representing the view of particularistic cultural determinism, even though Rosaldo herself apparently no longer subscribed to it.

relevant issue is not whether we, but not they, entertain the former theory about the relationship between affects, frustration, and violence, but whether that theory—let us call it the "Western" theory—can account both for their behavior and ours. For if it can, then much of *their* behavior and *ours*, alike, must be explained not by the "dictates" of our respective (and different) culture patterns but rather, as the "Western" theory claims, by the transcultural characteristics of the human mind. Let us briefly examine that claim by examining the paradigmatic case that Rosaldo cites from her fieldwork among the Ilongot.

In that case, a man who was ostensibly offended by the carelessness of his "brother" in making some plans got drunk and fought with him. That his aggression was not caused (as the Western theory would claim) by some "repressed" resentment, which finally surfaced when he was drunk, is proved, Rosaldo says, by the absence of "symptoms" of resentment in his subsequent sober behavior. Hence, she argues, these "brothers" (and the Ilongots in general) were and are successful in "keeping 'anger' from disrupting bonds of kin suggests that in important ways their feelings and the ways their feelings work must differ from our own" (1984).

Although that is one possible conclusion, it is not the only one. In the first place, so far as the working of "our own" feelings is concerned, the Ilongot case can surely be duplicated in spades in our own society. The documentary evidence—from history, biography, sociology, psychoanalysis, and, of course, fiction, let alone the evidence from our personal observations of kin relations (if not of others, then of our own)—is too abundant to require comment. Indeed, it is the very abundance of that evidence that led, in the first instance, to the development of the theory of repression and to the study of the various defense mechanisms by which, according to the "Western" theory, repressed emotions and motives find disguised expression.

In the second place, to return to the Ilongot case, it is not at all clear from the available data that the brothers in fact did not "repress" their anger for each other or that the frustration-induced anger in their relationship is in fact not expressed in violent action—not, to be sure, against each other, but in culturally approved violence against enemies. In the absence of the relevant psychological data for testing this hypothesis, I am not claiming that this in fact is what *does* occur, but in the absence of the relevant data it cannot be concluded that it does *not* occur. At the same time there are hints in Rosaldo's description that suggest that it *might* occur.

The Ilongots, Rosaldo informs us, "think of 'anger' as a thing that, if expressed, will necessarily destroy social relations . . . . [they] respond to conflict with immediate fear of violent death; they say they must forget things lest expression make men kill; [therefore] disputing persons either separate or fight—and the expression of violent feelings is seen as always dangerous" (ibid.).

Now I would submit that a psychocultural context in which it is believed that the expression of anger destroys social relations and that any conflict arouses fear of homicide is a context, par excellence, in which the "repression" of anger and the "denial" of conflict, most especially in kin relations, are most expected, as the Ilongots themselves explicitly recognize. For what else can the injunction to "forget things lest expression make men kill" possibly *mean* if it does not mean, "Since anger (my own and alter's) is so powerful that once aroused it leads to murder, in order to avoid such a consequence (either for me or for alter), it is crucial that I (and he) 'deny' those frustrating events that arouse our anger."

Now what there is about Ilongot social relations that arouses anger of such intensity or what there is about the lack of controls in Ilongot personality that transforms anger into homicidal impulses, we do not know. However, that the one or the other (or both) should lead to "'forgetting anger' in those contexts [kinship] where a show of violence has no place" (ibid.) is now not only understandable but also predictable by the "Western" theory. Is there any other way that a kin-based, face-to-face society, whose members have those personality characteristics, might possibly survive? In short, rather than confuting the view of the "Western" theory that the human mind, including its affective dimension, works the same everywhere, the Ilongot case in fact supports it. More particularly, it supports its claim that profoundly disturbing affects and events are dealt with, *inter alia,* by repression and denial regardless of cultural differences and the "dictates" of culture patterns.

But what about the other claim of the "Western" theory, the claim that "violent actions [are] the expression of a history of frustrations buried in a fertile but unconscious mind." That claim is especially confuted, Rosaldo argues, by the fact that, in the case of the two brawling Ilongot "brothers," no "symptoms" of any antagonism were evident in the antagonist once he became sober. But given the psychocultural context that has just been described, the "Western" theory would not expect such "symptoms" to be evident in the relationship between the "brothers." Rather, it would predict precisely what Rosaldo describes, *namely,* that the Ilongot would be "quite capable of 'forgetting anger' in those contexts where a show of violence has no place," the fraternal relationship being, par excellence, one of those contexts.

That theory would also predict, however, that their "forgetting anger" in their relationship with each other does not mean that the anger of the "brothers" had disappeared. Rather, it would predict that having "repressed" the anger that is aroused in the "history of frustrations" with each other, they would express it in symbolic disguise in other "contexts where a show of violence has [its] place."

Given that prediction, however, I do not know enough about the Ilongots to describe or even to guess at the various symbolic forms by which, or the various contexts in which, repressed anger between siblings (or anyone else) might be expressed. However, because the Ilongots have a long tradition of headhunting and because few actions are as violent as hacking off a man's head (which is what Ilongot headhunters do), I would suggest that the headhunting expedition is perhaps the most important symbolic form by which—just as "enemy" territory is a most important context in which—repressed anger toward their fellows (including siblings) is both displaced and gratified. This suggestion, of course, can only be verified by a symbolic investigation of Ilongot headhunting to determine whether the headhunter's victim is an unconscious symbolic representation of his frustrating fellows. Although the data for that kind of analysis are not available, this suggestion is consistent with the following characteristics of Ilongot headhunting, described in R. Rosaldo's *Ilongot Headhunting*.

Item 1. Although headhunting expeditions are usually instigated by insults or wrongs, some of them (at least from our point of view) are trivial in the extreme. Moreover, they are sometimes undertaken without any recognizable motive at all as, for example, when the prospective victim is in a "vulnerable" state and happens to fall victim to "youths with characteristic relentless zeal to take heads as they grow into manhood" (Rosaldo 1980:63).

Item 2. Even when ostensibly instigated by some insult, retaliation is seldom directed to the offender or even his family; rather, it will "encompass a wider target of population, including men and women and adults and children, all equal in their shared liability as victims" (ibid.).

Item 3. One of the characteristics of the relentlessly zealous headhunting youths is their emotional volatility, "their moods and passions [being] subject to dramatic ups and downs; and many youths describe themselves in song and story alike as weeping in their fierce, as yet frustrated, desire to 'arrive' and take a head" (ibid., 139).

Item 4. The source of their fierce desire "is above all envy of their peers and elders, those men who . . . have taken a head and thus won the coveted right to wear [the insignia of a headhunter]" (ibid., 140).

Item 5. "The point in Ilongot headhunting . . . [is] not to capture a trophy, but to 'throw away' a body part, which by a principle of sympathetic magic represents the cathartic throwing away of certain burdens of life—the grudge an insult has created, or the grief over the death in the family, or the increasing 'weight' of remaining a novice when one's peers have left that status" (ibid.).

Item 6. "Taking a head is a symbolic process designed less to acquire anything . . . than to remove something. What is ritually removed, Ilongots say, is the weight that grows on one's life like vines on a tree. Once cleansed [by taking a head] the men are said to become 'light' in weight, 'quick' of step, and 'red' in complexion. . . . In other words, the raiders regress through this ritual process to a culturally idealized phase of life" (ibid.).

Item 7. After hacking off the victim's head, the men (in one reported case, presumably not atypical, that was taped by Rosaldo) "vented their pent-up anger on the cadaver and chopped it up until 'it had no body and you couldn't see its bones,' until 'it was like ashes'" (ibid., 162).

Item 8. Following the decapitation, the men fled, pausing "now and again to shout and to sing the song of celebration" (ibid., 162).

Item 9. Before stopping for the night, they collected some fern leaves and tucked them into their armbands, "in order to modify and preserve the smell of their victim" (ibid., 163).

Item 10. Upon their return to the village, both men and women joined in the song of celebration and dancing and singing throughout the night while their "hearts lengthened with joy" (ibid., 163).

Although these characteristics of Ilongot headhunting speak for themselves as implicit support of the prediction of the "Western" theory, still it might be well perhaps to indicate explicitly why I believe they support my suggestion that the Ilongot handling of anger is entirely consistent with the "Western" theory of emotions. Because the victims of headhunting are clearly not the instigators of the hunters' anger (Items 1 and 2), the violence that the Ilongot display in hacking off the head of an 'enemy' and in their treatment of the cadaver (Item 7) expresses anger that is clearly displaced from somewhere else. That that anger, whatever its instigation, is repressed and consequently (in an almost classical hydraulic model of the emotions) presses for discharge is equally clear (Items 1 and 3). That their anger is instigated in the first instance by frustrations within the group, frustrations related (among other things) to envy and status rivalry, is also clear (Item 4), and I would guess that their envy and, therefore, their repressed anger have a long history, beginning with sibling rivalry in early childhood.

That this might be so is suggested by the Ilongot metaphor according to which men carry a "weight" in them, the removal of which is the motive for, and is achieved after, a successful headhunting raid (Item 6). The latter has the cathartic effect of removing that burden (Item 5), so that the headhunter "regresses" to that "idealized phase of life" (pre-sibling rivalry?) prior to the imposition of that weight (Item 6). That that "weight" represents their "pent-up" (repressed?) anger is shown both by the savoring of their victim's memory even after their hacking him to bits (Item 9) and especially by the exaltation (a manic state?) that they both feel and express following the violence displayed in the raid (Items 8 and 10).

To sum up this discussion, I would suggest that it is not the case, insofar as anger is concerned at least, that "in important ways [Ilongot] feelings and the ways their feelings work must differ from our own" (Rosaldo 1984). To be sure, their anger seems to be much more intense than ours, and its expression is much more violent, but, these quantitative dimensions aside, their anger and ours seem to work in similar ways. They, like we, get angry when frustrated, and they, like we, usually repress their anger in culturally inappropriate contexts only to express it symbolically in culturally appropriate ones. This indicates, I would suggest, that human feelings and the ways in which they work are determined not so much by the characteristics of particularistic culture patterns but by the transcultural characteristics of a generic human mind.

That those characteristics are in turn determined in large measure, however, by the transcultural characteristics of a set of universal culture patterns is of course—for me at least—axiomatic. But that kind of *generic* cultural determinism—one that rests on certain assumptions about the universality of human biological and social characteristics (which we cannot go into here) and their symbolic expressions and cultural transformations—is very different from the *particularistic* cultural determinism proposed by cultural determinists of the relativistic school.

Briefly put, particularistic cultural determinism views the process of enculturation as a process by which a neonate learns to become a completely enculturated Iatmul, Ifaluk, Ifugao, and the like—a process according to that view, by which each of the three learns to become radically different from the others. Although in one sense that thesis is also held by generic cultural determinism, the latter views enculturation as first and foremost a process of *humanization*, a process, that is, in which the neonate, by becoming an Iatmul, Ifaluk, or Ifugao, is also transformed from a mammal into a human being.

This is not to deny, on the one hand, that having become enculturated the human being is no longer a mammal—much of this chapter
argues that the contrary is the case. Nor is it to deny, on the other
hand, that an Iatmul human being is different in important respects
from an Ifaluk human being—human beings do come in different cultural shapes and forms. Rather, it is to affirm (to advert to the second
point) that insofar as it is culture that makes us human and insofar as an
enculturated Iatmul, Ifaluk, and Ifugao are equally human, the deep
structural similarities in their cultures (and in all other cultures) comprise a set of universal culture patterns, which, in interaction with a
common biological heritage and common features of social interaction,
create a generic human mind. It is to affirm, in short, that despite the
surface structure differences in their cultures—and perhaps in their
deep structures too—the minds of the Iatmul, the Ifaluk, and the
Ifugao (and everyone else) work in accordance with the same principles
("the psychic unity of mankind"). Starting from different premises and
concerned with different intellectual problems, Chomsky and Lévi-
Strauss, of course, among others, have most notably propounded the
psychic unity thesis in our time.

So far as the emotions are concerned, the perspective and strategy
of generic cultural determinism is very different from that of particularistic determinism. Whereas the former type leads to a search for a
set of universal principles that, insofar as they are derived from the
transcultural characteristics of the human mind, underlie the manifest
cultural differences in the display of emotions, the latter type views
such a search as futile. Perhaps so. But if the preceding analysis of
Ilongot anger is valid, it may not be so futile after all.

Normative Cultural Relativism

Because, according to the theory of particularistic cultural determinism, emotions and the self (and almost everything else) are determined
by culture, and because particular cultures are markedly different, it
follows, according to what might be termed "descriptive cultural relativism," that emotions and the self (and almost everything else) vary as
a function of the variability in cultures. To what extent those cultural
variations are themselves susceptible of judgments concerning their
relative worth is a question that descriptive cultural relativism does not
address, and Rosaldo does not address it.

Shweder, on the other hand, addresses that very question, for his
essay (1984) is a defense of what might be termed "normative cultural
relativism," the second strand in the classical theory of cultural relativism. Because, according to this strand, there are no transcultural

standards by which the variable propositions of particular cultures can be validly evaluated, there is no way by which their relative worth can be judged. (A similar distinction between these two kinds of relativism is made by Swartz and Jordan 1976:701–2.)

Shweder, however, both broadens and narrows this claim. He narrows it by restricting it to a subset of cultural propositions, which he calls "cultural frames." He broadens it to include explanation as well as evaluation. That is, he also claims (for reasons to be elucidated later) that there are no transcultural theories by which cultural frames can be validly explained.

"Cultural frames," as I have already indicated, consist of that subset of cultural propositions that are susceptible of neither confirmation nor disconfirmation. They can be neither confirmed nor disconfirmed according to Shweder, because they are (1) *arbitrary*, being grounded in neither logic nor experience, and (2) being arbitrary, they are neither rational nor irrational but *nonrational*. These characteristics of cultural frames have two implications so far as their explanation and evaluation are concerned. As for the former, cultural frames "fall beyond the sweep of logical and scientific evaluation," so that the most the anthropologist can hope to do is "document" the differences among the cultural frames of different cultures and explicate the "internal rules of coherence" of those comprising the same culture. As for evaluation, "there are no standards worthy of universal respect dictating what to think or how to act," so that alternative frames are neither "better" nor "worse" but only "different." In short, the "whole thrust [of this position] is to defend the co-equality of fundamentally different 'frames' of understanding" (ibid.).

Finally, the cultural frames of different cultures are not only "fundamentally different," but they are "irreconcilable" (ibid.); and because there are no "deep structures" underlying their surface content, "the more we attend to surface content, the less common is the culture of man" (ibid.). Since, therefore, cultural frames do not reflect but rather construct reality, there is no single reality—none at least that can ever be known; there are only "diverse realities."

Although there is much in this argument with which I agree, I believe that it is both over- and understated. Specifically, I believe, on the one hand, that cultural propositions are less arbitrary and, on the other, that they are more irrational than normative cultural relativism claims. That being the case, I believe that cultures are susceptible of a greater degree of explanation and comparative evaluation than a relativistic view allows. I shall begin with the degree of arbitrariness of cultural propositions.

In my view cultural relativism overstates the arbitrariness of cultural propositions because, despite their undoubted variability, their range is not all *that* variable. For any cultural domain, and for any sample of cultures, the diversity of cultural propositions is much smaller than the number of cultures comprising the sample; and the diversity becomes smaller yet when we observe that even at the level of surface content—let alone at the level of deep structure, which Shweder rejects—the diversity can be radically reduced to, and yet adequately described by, a small number of types.

Although cultural propositions (including cultural systems of classification) may be arbitrary, they are not all *that* arbitrary. Shweder is correct, of course, when he says that "logically, any classification is possible." But he himself adduces an important constraint when he observes that any actual classification is a function of "some special purpose of man." Given this relationship between "purpose" and classification (and even omitting unconscious purposes), the fact that in our kinship system parents' brothers and parents' sisters' husbands are classified as "uncle" does not, as Shweder claims, make such a classification of these kin types "arbitrary." Indeed, in discovering their classificatory principles, Kroeber (1909) and others have been able to elucidate the logic not only of the putatively nonrational and arbitrary classification of these kin types but also of the entire classificatory systems in which they are embedded. Moreover, by demonstrating systematic relationships between kinship systems and a small set of ecological, political, economic, and other determinants, Murdock (1949) and others have been able to causally *explain* the distribution of these types.

To be sure, were we to discover a system in which not only parents' sisters' husbands, but parents' brothers' wives, or brothers' sons' wives, as well, were also classified with parents' brothers, that would certainly count as "arbitrary." But there is no need to reach for such extreme counterfactual examples to make my simpleminded point that, inasmuch as the range of cultural variability is not unconstrained, many cultural classifications are only apparently nonrational.

That still leaves, of course, a large number of cultural propositions that are unquestionably nonrational: They are grounded in neither logic nor evidence. That they are, therefore, arbitrary (thereby eluding the net of causal explanation) is perhaps true of some of them. To claim, however, that it is true of all of them is to overlook another possible determinant of cultural propositions.

Although, beginning with its title and persisting as a pervasive theme of the chapter, Shweder argues that "there's a lot more in the mind than reason and evidence," including "culture, the arbitrary, the symbolic, the expressive, the semiotic," he does not mention the emotional part of that "more," nor does he explicitly attend to emotions in his discussion. If, however, we attend to that emotional part, then, although many cultural propositions may not be determined by logic or evidence, it may nevertheless not be the case that they are arbitrary, for they may be determined by emotion. In that case, they do not—in principle at least—elude the net of scientific explanation, if by "explanation" is meant the discovery of systematic relationships or regularities between cultural propositions and noncultural conditions that might account for cross-cultural variation.

Even if relativists were to concede that some cultural propositions might be grounded in emotional needs, they might counter that they are nevertheless arbitrary precisely because there seems to be no systematic or predictable relationship between such propositions and their putative emotional determinants. Food taboos and witchcraft propositions, to take but two examples, are often claimed to have emotional determinants, and yet there is no obvious reason why this should be the case, nor are there any predictable emotions to which they are attached.

This riposte is well founded if we attend exclusively to the public and conscious meanings *of* cultural propositions. If, however, we also attend to the cognitive meanings that they have *for* social actors—especially their unconscious meanings—it is often the case that their emotional determinants can be discovered, for (like the emotional determinants of dreams) they are most frequently related to the unconscious meanings that they have for social actors.

That conclusion rests on two assumptions. First, in some cases, at least, the conscious meanings of cultural propositions (like the manifest content of dreams) are "surface structure" meanings, and their unconscious meanings (like the latent content of dreams) are "deep structure" meanings. Second, the latter meanings are unconscious because conscious awareness of them (like the conscious awareness of the latent content of dreams) arouses anxiety, shame, guilt, and the like. On these assumptions the emotional determinants of cultural propositions can only be discovered by investigating their possible deep structure meanings. Until such investigations are undertaken in regard, say, to food taboos, witchcraft propositions, and others, we cannot assume a priori that they are arbitrary even when they appear to be in respect to their conscious meanings.

This thesis also applies to seemingly arbitrary and inexplicable classifications. Classes whose members appear to share no distinctive features may nevertheless be shown to be logically classified when their unconsciously perceived similarities are discovered. In that case it is usually found that class membership is based on the same logical principles by which tropes are constituted, particularly the type of trope referred to as synechdoche. For example, one of the reasons that, in his "maternal transference," a psychoanalytic patient classified his therapist with his mother is that (as he saw it) the vital "nourishment" that the therapist gave him in the form of words was an unconscious symbolic representation of the nourishment that, as a child, he had received from his mother in the form of milk. The use of unconscious distinctive features as the basis for seemingly bizarre classifications applies not only to private but to cultural classification as well.

By attending to the relationship between emotion and culture, we may discover not only that many cultural propositions (because they are not arbitrary) are susceptible of scientific explanation but also that alternative cultural frames are susceptible of being judged as "better" or "worse." That is because cultural propositions may have not only emotional antecedents, as in the case of the previous example, but emotional consequences as well. If those consequences are ignored, then, viewed "in terms of comparative adequacy," it might indeed be the case, to take Shweder's example, that the only judgment that can be made as between those who empathize with starving Armenians and those who take the heads of their neighbors is that they are "obviously different." Many of the headhunters that I have read about— and the one that I knew—do not, however, share that view, not because they necessarily share the Western cultural frame that to give life is better than to take it but because in headhunting societies the hunter is also the hunted, a prospect which leaves him in a state—actual or potential—of terror.

Now some relativists might retort that the emotional consequences of nonrational ideas and actions cannot constitute a measure of "comparative adequacy," because inasmuch as the assessment of emotions, like the assessment of reality, is culturally relative, headhunters, unlike Americans, may prefer to live in terror. Such a retort, however, would constitute an empirical disagreement, which, presumably, could be resolved by collection of the relevant data.

By not attending more explicit to the relationship between emotion and culture, Shweder, in my view, not only *overstates* the arbitrariness of culture but he also *understates* its irrationality. For Shweder, the "irrational" is confined to errors in thinking or thought (the verb). But inasmuch as cultural propositions are *traditional* ideas or thoughts (the noun), they are acquired by social actors from the cultural heritage of their group, not as a product of their own thought (the verb). Since they therefore elude Shweder's criterion for assessing "irrationality," by an unintended sleight of hand many cultural propositions become "nonrational"—neither rational nor irrational. To the degree, however, that the internalization of cultural propositions is motivated by the wish to satisfy emotional needs, many of those that are internalized at the highest three levels of cognitive salience mentioned previously are arguably "irrational" rather than "nonrational." I am referring to the subset of emotionally motivated propositions that are *emotionally driven* and are therefore obsessional and "magical." To better understand this contention, let us briefly describe the characteristics of "obsessional" and "magical" thoughts, beginning with the former.

An obsessional idea or thought is an all-consuming thought, that, typically, is driven by a powerful emotional need to prevent an unconscious thought, which it has replaced, from entering consciousness because the latter arouses an uncontrollable, forbidden, or painful emotion, such as lust, hatred, or guilt, respectively. In short, an obsessional thought is a defense against powerful and potentially overwhelming anxiety. The reason for calling thoughts of this type, whether privately or culturally constituted, "irrational" is that they are impervious to reason or evidence. Even when confronted with logical inconsistencies in holding them, or with disconfirmatory evidence in respect to them, those who hold such thoughts resist any change—lest the anxiety they are defending against erupt into consciousness. Held in thrall by these thoughts, they cannot let them go. Although clinical psychiatry is a storehouse of thoughts (including cultural propositions) of this type, let us illustrate them by an example taken from the storehouse of ethnography.

Consider, for example, the widely prevalent cultural proposition that various forms of misfortune are caused by witchcraft. As a proposition—but not necessarily as an internalized belief—this appears to be a good example of a cultural frame. Indeed, when found in prescientific societies, one might go so far as to call it a "rational" proposition even though, from a modern scientific perspective, it is false. In the former societies, such a proposition is validly deduced from a culturally constituted world view; it is inductively supported by a great deal of empirical evidence; it is compatible with whatever reliable scientific knowledge is available in those societies; and it is consistent with all the other cultural propositions of those societies. In short, it is a proposition that in prescientific societies does not rest on fallacious inductive or deductive reasoning, does not violate the law of contradiction, and—given their scientific knowledge—is not empirically absurd.

Whether rational or nonrational, however, if the social actors, driven by imperious emotional needs, develop an obsessional concern with witchcraft—as happened, for example, in sixteenth- and seventeenth-century Europe and seventeenth-century New England—their witchcraft propositions can be said to be neither rational nor nonrational, but irrational. Having become obsessive, they are no longer just another of those many cultural propositions that social actors are taught and to which they give assent. Rather, being emotionally driven, the actors are not free—regardless of evidence, logic, or reason—to let them go.

The same may be true not only of relatively dramatic cultural propositions like those concerning witchcraft but also of seemingly trivial ones like those concerning food preferences. One need only observe, for example, the obsessional concern of some few orthodox Muslims, Jews, or Hindus with their respective food taboos to realize that some food preferences, at least, can hardly be characterized as merely nonrational. That they are rather irrational is evidenced by the acute anxiety the actors suffer even by the prospect, let alone the act, of violating them.

That in neither of these cases, clearly, is there anything in the (conscious) meanings *of* these propositions that would explain—or permit us to predict—why they should be emotionally driven, and hence obsessive, suggests that the explanation lies in the (unconscious) meanings that they have *for* the social actors. To uncover those meanings, of course, requires a separate investigation of each of these frames, case by case, in their ethnographic context.

Emotionally driven cultural frames are sometimes not only obsessional but also magical, and all the more irrational. A "magical" thought, as I am using it here, is based on an impairment in "reality testing," that is, the ability to distinguish mental events that occur in the inner world (the mind) from physical events that occur in the external world. By this definition, if a cultural proposition asserts that heaven is populated by seven gods, each possessing seven heads, it is not based on any impairment in reality testing. Nor could it properly be said to rest on such an impairment even if, driven by powerful emotional needs, the social actors have a fantasy of such a heaven. If, however, they were to construe such a fantasy—an image in their minds—as a perception of such a heaven, then inasmuch as the fantasy had become a hallucination, the proposition is now based on impaired reality testing, and is "irrational."

In short, to say that a "magical" thought is based on an impairment of reality testing is to say that it is a thought in which inner reality is mistaken for outer reality, impulses stemming from the internal world are mistaken for stimuli coming from the external world, a mental representation of an object or event is mistaken for the object or event that it represents, and so on. If, then, because they are emotionally driven, cultural propositions are based on an impairment in reality testing, they are clearly irrational as they are based on the most primitive form of empirical error. (For a smiliar view of the relationship between culture and the irrational, see Devereux 1980:chap. 1.)

For an actual, rather than a hypothetical, example of the relationship between cultural frames and magical thinking, let us turn once again to witchcraft. From the cultural frame that misfortune is caused by witches, not only do social actors acquire a belief in the existence of such a class of malevolent human beings, but they also form composite mental representations of them, which (more or less) correspond to the collective representation of witches. Their mental representations of witches can be called a fantasy—a culturally constituted fantasy—and so long as they are just that, they reflect no impairment of reality testing. If, however, driven by emotional conflicts, an actor comes to believe that some specific person, X, is a witch and that X is bewitching him, his belief *is* characterized by magical thinking because the fantasy is now mistaken for reality.

Take, for example, the ailing Burmese villager, Mr. G, who told me that he was being attacked by a witch, whose spirit or soul has possessed him, and that the witch was in fact his wife. This belief, in my view, was based on a complex set of obsessional and magical thoughts. Enraged by his wife's repeated and flagrant adulteries, but unable to cope with his rage, Mr. G projected it onto his wife, thereby constructing a mental representation of her as malevolent and punitive. Identifying this mental representation of his wife with his composite mental representation of witches, he thereby perceived his wife to be a witch. That is, he modified his mental representation of his wife to correspond to that of a witch, although she is not one.

But if that is not irrational enough, consider then that his belief that his wife, now a witch, possessed him was based on an even more serious impairment in reality testing. For his sensation of his body having been invaded by her could only be based on first, the reification of his mental representation of the witch, and second, mistaking it for the witch herself. As a reification, her mental representation was no longer experienced by him as an image that he "located" in his mind; rather, he experienced it as his wife herself (more accurately, as her spirit or soul), which he now "located" in his body.

Although witchcraft beliefs, as such, may be nonrational, if—because emotionally driven—they are based on, or eventuate in, an impairment of reality testing, they are clearly irrational. Relativism rejects this view on the grounds, it will be recalled, that inasmuch as culture constructs reality, there is no other reality that can be used to judge them. Hence, there is no criterion "worthy of universal respect" by which such beliefs and other beliefs that are logically consistent with them can be judged on a scale of rationality. And that is where the issue is joined. Although Mr. G's belief that he was possessed by a witch is entirely consistent with the cultural frame of Burmese witch-craft, and although his fellow villagers, therefore, fully shared his belief that he was possessed, in my view his belief was no less irrational than if it had been inconsistent with it. For in both cases such a belief is based on an hallucination—on a confusion of fantasy with reality—as those terms have been defined here.

In sum, in ignoring—either from principle or from neglect—the emotional motivation for the internalization of cultural propositions, normative cultural relativism underestimates the degree of irra-tionality in cultural propositions by construing many of them as nonra-tional—as cultural frames—when (as I have attempted to demonstrate) they are more properly construed as irrational. Hence, by the two criteria that I suggested for the assessment of irrationality—there may be others—we may conclude this section by drawing the following—antirelativistic—conclusions. (1) The alternative cultural propositions comprising different cultural systems can be compared on a scale of rationality. (2) On such a scale, many cultural propositions are cultural frames—nonrational—and are therefore merely "different" from each other. (3) Many cultural propositions that are seemingly nonrational, and are so viewed by cultural relativists, can be assessed by this scale as irrational, and they may therefore be judged as either "better" or "worse" than their cross-cultural alternatives. (4) If total cultural sys-tems differ in the extent to which they comprise irrational proposi-tions, by such a scale cultural systems can be similarly judged to be "better" or "worse."

Concluding Remarks

I should like to conclude with some personal observations. Thus far I have examined particularistic cultural determinism and normative cultural relativism in theoretical terms alone. But theories also have consequences, and these theories have some (largely unintended) con-sequences, which—given my values—I consider unfortunate. Because values, whether personally constructed or culturally constituted, may be frames, it would be a conceit to claim that the values on which this judgment is based are grounded in logic or evidence or that they are free of emotional determinants. Because the contrary is very likely the case, I refer to these remarks as "personal observations."

Shweder, entirely correctly in my view, places (normative) cultural relativism in the "romantic" movement, a movement that tends to place a high value on the nonrational. Hence, (normative) cultural relativism not only defends the "coequality of fundamentally different 'frames' of understanding" but, consistent with its intellectual heritage, also celebrates them precisely because they are nonrational. Shweder puts this view forthrightly: "Don't knock the mystical, the transcendental, or the arbitrary," he exhorts us even though the "arbitrary" in his discussion ranges, on the one hand, from differences between one kin type classification and another to the difference between taking heads and feeding starving Armenians, on the other.

Now, by this time it should be abundantly clear that I fully agree with Shweder's twin contentions that "there's something more to thinking than reason and evidence" and that reason is in short supply. But it is precisely because reason is in short supply, and because (in my view) its alternatives are not only the nonrational and the logically fallacious irrational but also the emotionally driven irrational, that I believe that it is reason and those aspects of culture that are based on it that should be celebrated. To be concrete, it is not only because the emotionally driven irrational leads to witchcraft accusations, food taboos, and head hunting, but because it also leads to the destruction of scholarly papers and scientific laboratories—and I am referring not only to the Arabian armies that sacked Alexandria in 640 but also to the university students who sacked Columbia, Cornell, and Wisconsin in the 1960s—that I am dubious about celebrating the mystical, the transcendental, and the arbitrary. In short, it is because reason is in short supply that I prefer—as Freud once put it in expressing the goal of psychoanalytic therapy—"where id was, there ego shall be."

By the same token, it is because the emotionally driven irrational has no limits or—to be more cautious—because its limiting case is Auschwitz, that I believe that there *are* standards "worthy of universal respect" by which cultural frames can be evaluated. That is the case, of course, only if it can be agreed that those standards—to advert to Freud's metaphors for the different parts of the mind—are the standards not of the "id" but of the self-reflective "ego." Assuming agreement on that, then, inasmuch as the preference for headhunting over the feeding of starving Armenians is based on the standards of the former, while the contrary preference is based on those of the latter, the latter preference can then be judged to be superior to the former.

To be sure, not all social actors have self-reflective egos. But on the assumption that self-reflection is a characteristic at least of philosophers and saints, and that all societies, including—as Radin has observed—primitive societies, have their philosophers (and probable saints too), the preference for feeding starving Armenians over the taking of heads is based on a standard that, I would argue, is universal in that it is found in at least the reflective members of all societies.

If, however, it turned out that in some headhunting societies—the Ilongot, for example—even the philosophers judged headhunting to be preferable to feeding, say, the starving Ifugao, I would then argue that the contrary judgment of the Buddha and Christ, of Isaiah and Laotzu, of Socrates and Gandhi is worthy of greater respect. For, I would contend, the Ilongot philosophers are unable because of emotional constraints to apply the standards of their self-reflective ego to this question.

Given my values, particularistic cultural determinism and normative cultural relativism have a second consequence that I consider to be unfortunate. As these theories have come increasingly to dominate anthropological thought, the vision of anthropology as the "study of man" has been gradually eroded and replaced by the vision of anthropology as the "study of men."

The latter vision, which represents a departure from an attempt to discover cross-cultural regularities and to formulate theories that might explain them, challenges the status of anthropology as a "science" (as I characterized that term earlier) because it views each culture (so far at least as its cultural frames are concerned) as a kind of Leibnitzian cultural monad. The diversity of cultures, from the perspective of this new vision, represents a very Babel of voices, each expressing a set of arbitrary ideas encoded in a set of arbitrary symbols. The noncommensurability of cultural frames renders them incomprehensible to each other and recalcitrant to scientific explanation, and their power—like that of God's voice at Creation—is sufficient to construct reality itself.

The result of this vision is well known. Although anthropology has made much progress in the meticulous recording and reporting of the ideas and institutions of particular cultures, it has made little progress in relating its findings to the development of a theory of culture. The latter enterprise, we are now increasingly told, is precluded in principle by the proclaimed incommensurability of cultures. Thus, we can't have a cross-cultural theory of incest taboos, for example, because "incest" has different meanings in different cultures; we can't have a cross-cultural theory of religion, because "religion" means very different things in different cultures and so on.

That view, in my opinion, is unfortunate, and has the potentiality for becoming even more unfortunate. For as the premises of this new vision gain currency, it might then be contended—as indeed some have already contended—that one or more of the following conclusions may be derived from those premises. (1) Anthropologists cannot adequately describe, let alone explain, any culture different from their own. (2) For any culture to be adequately described and understood, it must be investigated by an anthropologist who himself has been enculturated in it. (3) For the latter to adequately convey the ideas and institutions of that culture, they must be reported in the native language, for there is no adequate way of rendering the conceptual system of one culture by the concepts of another—not even those of (anthropological) science, which is just another culture-bound (Western) conceptual system. All science is ethnoscience.

Such a scenario may be the *reductio ad absurdum* of the new vision of culture rather than its logical entailment. Nevertheless, we have seen it enacted (sometimes with the encouragement of anthropologists) in another form in some American universities. Thus, there are some few programs in ethnic and women's studies that claim that only ethnics are qualified to teach the former and women the latter. Given the new vision of culture, why should the same logic not apply to the teaching of Confucian philosophy, the Old Testament, or the French Revolution?

However, even if the former scenario is only the *reductio* of the new vision of culture, insofar as it is a potential consequence of that vision, I would hope that the present ascendancy of particularistic cultural determinism and normative cultural relativism might be subjected to continuous and searching scrutiny.

References

D'Andrade, Roy G. 1984. Cultural meaning systems. In *Culture theory: Essays on mind, self, and emotion*, ed. Richard A. Shweder and Robert LeVine, 88–119. Cambridge: Cambridge University Press.

Devereux, George. 1980. *Basic problems of ethnopsychiatry*. Chicago: University of Chicago Press.

Kroeber, A. L. 1909. Classificatory systems of relationship. *Journal of the Royal Anthropological Institute* 39:77–85.

Murdock, George Peter. 1949. *Social structure*. New York: Macmillan.

Rosaldo, Michelle Z. 1984. Toward an anthropology of self and feeling. In *Culture theory: Essays on mind, self, and emotion*, ed. Richard A. Shweder and Robert LeVine, 137–57. Cambridge: Cambridge University Press.

Rosaldo, Renato. 1980. *Ilongot headhunting*. Stanford, Calif.: Stanford University Press.

Saussure, Ferdinand de. 1966. *Course in general linguistics*. New York: McGraw-Hill.

Shweder, Richard A. 1984. Anthropology's romantic rebellion against the enlightenment, or there's more to thinking than reason and evidence. In *Culture theory: Essays on mind, self, and emotion*, ed. Richard A. Shweder and Robert LeVine, 27–66. Cambridge: Cambridge University Press.

Spiro, Melford E. 1950. Culture and personality: The natural history of a false dichotomy. *Psychiatry* 13:9–204.

————. 1970. *Buddhism and society: A great tradition and its Burmese vicissitudes*. New York: Harper & Row.

————. 1982. Collective representations and mental representations in religious symbol systems. In *On symbols in cultural anthropology: Essays in honor of Harry Hoijer*, ed. Jacques Maquet. Malibu, Calif.: Udena.

Swartz, Marc J., and David K. Jordan. 1976. *Anthropology: Perspective on humanity*. New York: Wiley.

3   Preculture and Gender

A Precultural Interpretation

ANY ATTEMPT to assess the possible determinants of the counter-revolutionary changes that have occurred in the kibbutz movement in such institutions as marriage, the family, and sex-role differentiation is beset with formidable difficulties. The problem is too complex, the data are too limited, and our methods of investigation were too primitive to permit an unequivocal interpretation. The weight of the evidence nevertheless suggests that although several possible cultural determinants may have contributed to these changes, on balance they do not appear to have been decisive. Evidence from sabra childhood behavior suggests, instead, that these counterrevolutionary changes were more probably brought about not primarily as a response to external cultural conditions nor by culturally acquired motives, but by precultural motivational dispositions.

Since, however, it is a basic axiom of the social sciences that human behavior and motives are primarily, if not exclusively, culturally programmed, I wish to observe, lest this conclusion be rejected on axiomatic grounds, that the counterrevolutionary changes in the above domains were not the only (nor even the most dramatic) changes brought about by the sabras. A perhaps even more dramatic change occurred in the sexual domain. Hence I would like to examine briefly this latter change which constitutes a rather unequivocal exception to our social science axiom.

According to the ideology of the kibbutz pioneers, attitudes and orientations to sexual behavior and sexual anatomy are cultural artifacts. Hence, so they believed, if children were raised in a sexually

Reprinted from Melford E. Spiro, *Gender and Culture* (Durham, N.C.: Duke University Press, 1979), pp. 97–110. © 1979 by Melford E. Spiro.

permissive and enlightened environment, in which boys and girls, living together, were acquainted with each other's bodies and were taught to view nudity as natural, so that notions of shame were not attached to the exposure of sex organs—in such an environment, differences in sexual anatomy would assume little more importance than any other kind of anatomical differences. This belief was important for the pioneers not only because of their commitment to healthy sexual attitudes, but also because of their conviction that sexual equality (in its "identity" meaning) required an attitude of indifference to sexual dimorphism. If, as they believed, the only "natural" difference between the sexes consists in differences in sexual anatomy, if children were raised to view this difference as inconsequential, the road to sexual equality (as they conceived it) would then have been paved.

Acting upon their beliefs, the pioneers established an entirely "enlightened" sexual regime in the children's houses. Boys and girls used the same toilets, dressed and undressed in each other's presence, walked about their dormitory rooms (if they chose) in the nude, showered together in one shower room, and so on. This system worked (and works) as the pioneers expected until the first intimations of puberty in the girls—in general, girls enter puberty a year or two before the boys—at which time the very girls who had been raised in a sex-blind environment developed intense feelings of shame at being seen in the nude by the boys. Sometime before our 1951 study, the girls in Kiryat Yedidim, for example, initiated an active rebellion against the mixed showers: they began to shower separately from the boys, refusing to admit them into the shower room at the same time. Consistent with this attitude, some of the girls would return early to their children's house at night to undress and be in their pajamas before the boys arrived.

Despite the girls' active opposition, the educational authorities refused to change the system of mixed showers. Moreover, when high schools were built in the kibbutzim, mixed showers and bedrooms were instituted in the high school dormitories as well. By 1951, however, the mixed showers in most kibbutz high schools had been unofficially abandoned. As one teacher in Kiryat Yedidim put it, the mixed showers had become "a form of torture" for the girls, their shame at exposing their nude bodies in front of the boys being intensified by the latter's teasing. Hence, though the high school authorities did not officially sanction it, arrangements were made for boys and girls to shower at different times. In a survey I conducted in Kiryat Yedidim in 1951, only three students in the entire student body favored a return to the mixed showers. Today, the sexes not only shower separately, but in almost all kibbutz high schools there are now separate shower rooms for boys and girls.

The same process has taken place with respect to the dormitory rooms. I have already noted that even in the grade school the older girls felt considerable discomfort about undressing in the presence of the boys. Their discomfort was exacerbated in the high school. In 1951, for example, although boys and girls in the high school in Kiryat Yedidim shared the same rooms (usually three boys and three girls to a room), they were careful to undress in the dark with their backs to each other. Moreover, so that their bodies would not be exposed, the girls wore pajamas (regardless of the heat) even though they slept under sheets. Despite these precautions, succeeding generations of students have been persistently unhappy with these living arrangements until, seven years ago (and after many generations of female protest), the high school authorities capitulated to the girls' demands, and instituted unisexual bedrooms. Similar changes have been introduced in most other kibbutzim as well.

In sum, the original kibbutz belief, that in the proper learning environment children would be sex-blind, was proven to be false even in the sexually enlightened conditions in which these children were raised. Even if it were the case that the only natural difference between males and females is one of sexual anatomy, this one difference apparently is not as trivial as had been assumed. In this instance, at least, it had important social and psychological consequences which could hardly have been culturally determined, for these children (as we have seen) developed a sense of sexual shame not as a result of, but in opposition to, the cultural values of their learning environment.[1] Apparently, nudity on an impersonal and anonymous bathing beach is one thing; but in an intimate and potentially sexually charged small group, it is quite another. When, then, the social institutions that em-

---

1. In 1951, under the influence of kibbutz ideology, the high school personnel attributed the sabras' reactions to the influence of students from the city who had imbued them with feelings of sexual shame. Being a cultural determinist at that time, I too found this to be a persuasive explanation although, in retrospect, its flaws are obvious. First, these shameful feelings were almost always aroused during (or shortly before) pubescence when most girls, still in the grammar school, were not yet exposed to city students. Second, even for those whose puberty was delayed till high school, the assumption that the cultural values of a tiny minority of outside students could prevail over those of the majority, especially when the latter were natives (supported by the entire weight of their native and much more prestigeful environment) makes little sense. Moreover, if the absence of sexual shame is natural and its acquisition cultural, this explanation makes even less sense, for one would then have expected the cultural to give way to the natural. If the kibbutz students were indeed influenced by the city students, it is more reasonable to believe that they were ready to be influenced because this influence was syntonic with their natural dispositions.

bodied these cultural values became too painful for the children, they pressed for their abolition in violation of the attitudes in which they had been imbued and over the opposition of the adults.[2]

Is this not the same process that describes the counterrevolutionary changes in the family and sex-role differentiation which were instituted by the sabras upon becoming adults? In the case of these children, reared in a learning environment that was predicated on the assumption that sex differences in behavior and psychology are cultural artifacts, that boys and girls differ only by virtue of their sexual anatomy, and that this difference becomes socially important only so far as culture makes it so—in the case of these children the sex differences in behavior that they exhibited very early in their lives were exhibited in spite of and in opposition to their learning environment. This being so, it seems most likely that these sex differences (like their sense of sexual shame) were brought about not by culture, but by the triumph of human nature over culture, that is, by motivational dispositions based on sex differences in precultural, rather than culturally constituted, needs. If, then, the counterrevolution of the female sabras was motivated by precultural needs, these needs cannot be unique to them; rather, all things being equal, it is probable that they are shared by females in any society. Hence, having thus far avoided any discussion of the types of precultural needs that might explain these sex differences in motivation, we must finally address this issue directly.

Precultural Needs and the Sabra Counterrevolution

In a typology of possible determinants of the sabra counterrevolution three types of precultural needs can be distinguished. One type ("biological needs") consists of genetically inherited drives. The other two ("psychosocial" and "psychobiological" needs) consist of experientially acquired wishes and desires. Here, then, we have three types of determinants of sex differences in motivational dispositions which are present prior to (or, as in some cases, independent of) the acquisition of culturally constituted motives. Although the latter two types are experientially acquired, they are no less panhuman than those genetically

2. It is pertinent to observe here that these children, whose behavior refuted the assumption that the shame aroused by sexual dimorphism is cultural, are the same children who, upon becoming adults, reversed the attempts of the pioneers to minimize the importance of dimorphism by eschewing feminine clothing, jewelry, and cosmetics. Today, as we have seen, female sabras attempt to enhance their feminine appearance by these cultural means, and male sabras obviously approve of these attempts.

inherited because the experiences by which they are acquired are dependent either on certain invariant characteristics of the human organism or on those characteristics of human society that are invariant. Since the invariant characteristics of human society (biparental families, group living, socialization systems, and the like) are institutional solutions to adaptive requirements of human beings (the satisfaction of early dependency needs, for example) which they share by virtue of their constituting a common biological species, these needs too are indirectly "psychobiological." From this perspective, then, those precultural needs that are experientially acquired are no less a part of "human nature" than those that are genetically inherited. In the present stage, at least, of human biological and social evolution, both are invariant characteristics of human personality and both constitute panhuman bases for human behavior. (For the most important anthropological statement of this thesis, see La Barre 1954.)

Although precultural needs, then, may be either genetically or experientially acquired, the research strategy employed in this study does not permit us to decide whether the motivational determinants of the sabra counterrevolution—and, therefore, of precultural sex differences in motivation anywhere—are the one or the other. That the counterrevolution was motivated by precultural needs is an interpretation, it will be remembered, that was adopted only after the cultural hypotheses comprising our explanatory paradigm were finally rejected as incompatible with the data. The precultural interpretation was then adopted not only because it was the one remaining hypothesis in the explanatory paradigm but because it was the one interpretation that was compatible with the entire array of data. On the basis of these data, however, there is no way of deciding whether the sex differences in precultural needs that are reflected in the counterrevolution are genetically or experientially acquired. Hence, the only thing we can do is delineate the shape of these competing types of precultural interpretations by offering examples of the more prominent theories which exemplify each type.

To simplify our task, I shall concentrate on only one need for which, according to our analysis of the behavior of sabra children, there are precultural sex differences. For this purpose I have chosen the parenting need because, in one sense, it is the cornerstone of all the changes that comprise the counterrevolution. The aim of the feminist revolution of the pioneers, it will be recalled, was to minimize the woman's involvement in family, and especially in mothering roles because (it was believed) this would maximize her involvement in extrafamilial roles. This, in turn, was expected to lead to the dissolution of sex-role differentiation, and thereby to sexual equality (in its "identity" meaning). Hence, the feminine counterrevolution, as I have often emphasized, is essentially a phenomenon of sabra females, for while the males have persisted in economically traditional male roles, the females have rejected the more "masculine" of the traditional male roles in favor of other kinds. Moreover, to a much larger extent than the males, the females have also reemphasized the very family—and especially parenting—roles which the pioneers had attempted to deemphasize. Since, then, the parenting need (like most other precultural needs) is shared by both sexes, it is with respect to its greater strength in females that examples of alternative types of precultural interpretations will be examined. In the following discussion, then, "the female parenting need" is used as an ellipsis for "the greater strength of the parenting need in females."

According to one prominent example of a biological interpretation, the female parenting need is an instance of those precultural needs which are genetically determined. Phylogenetically inherited, this need is interpreted in the same manner as any other biological characteristic that is the product of biological evolution, namely, by natural selection. Such an interpretation would hold that in the conditions obtaining in the early history of our species, a strong mother-child bond was an adaptive requirement, so that a strong parenting need in women had a selective advantage. Tracing this advantage to the adaptive requirements of the hunting stage of human evolution, this is precisely the interpretation offered by Tiger and Shepher (1975:274–77) for the female parenting need and, therefore, for the counterrevolution in the orientation of the female sabras to the family.[3] According to this interpretation, then, the female parenting need is conceptualized as a "biological" need which, phylogenetically inherited, serves as an internal stimulus to behavior.

We now can turn to examples of those theories of the female parenting need according to which this need, though precultural, is experientially acquired. According to one example, the female parenting need is a "psychobiological" need which is acquired as a result of psychological experiences derived from a biological characteristic of the female organism. Specifically, this need is explained as the motivational con-

3. There are, of course, alternative biological interpretations of the female parenting need which, departing from classical Darwinian theory, one might mention—parental investment theory, for example (Trivers 1972). I do not discuss this theory here because although our research design does not permit us to decide whether, as a precultural need, the female parenting need is biologically or experientially acquired, this does not hold for this particular biological theory which (for reasons which would require an extensive discussion) does not seem to adequately explain the kibbutz data.

sequence of the girl's cognitive and emotional reactions attendant upon her psychic awareness of the structure of her reproductive organs. This theory, as most prominently formulated by Erikson (1963:91), anchors many sex-linked needs in what he calls the "ground plan" of the body. Given that boys and girls have a different "ground plan," each is characterized by "a unique quality of [inner] experience." The experience of girls is different from that of boys as a function of (among other things) the "inner space" that characterizes the female reproductive organs. This experience, which is "founded on the preformed functions" of the "future childbearer," provides girls with a motivational disposition for childbearing and hence for parenting. This thesis has been more extensively developed by Bardwick (1971:15). It is because of the girls' creative inner space, so her thesis goes, that "an anticipatory pleasure and rehearsal of future maternity . . . looms large in the girl."

Perhaps the most influential (and controversial) examples of a "psychosocial" interpretation of the female parenting need are those formulated by Freud (1964, ch. 33). For Freud, like Erikson, this need is acquired as a result of experiences related to female sexual anatomy, but since for Freud these experiences are social (consisting in the girl's interaction with significant others), it seems more accurate to say that for him the female parenting need, though precultural, is more a "psychosocial" than a "psychobiological" need.

According to the first of Freud's hypotheses, if the young girl feels loved by her mother, then, given the dependency need of children, she develops a libidinal attachment to and identifies with her. Since, for the growing girl, the mother's parenting role is her most important characteristic, the girl's identification with her mother is the basis for her desire to emulate that role particularly. To be sure, the earliest identification of the boy is also, and for the same reason, with the mother; and by this explanation of the girls' acquisition of the parenting need, one would expect that boys would acquire a parenting need no less strong. This is exactly what psychoanalytic theorists like Bettelheim (1954) and others have suggested, a suggestion which receives support from the fantasy play of the sabra children in which, it will be recalled, the second most frequent identification of the boys was with parenting women. Nevertheless, the boy's identification with the mother does not persist because, according to these latter theorists, with his discovery of the anatomical differences between the sexes, he realizes that he cannot become like her. For Freud, however, it is not because he cannot become like her, but because his fear of castration leads him to give up his desire to become like her, that is the crucial factor in the boy's disidentification with his mother. On either interpretation, although boys may subsequently come to envy women for their childbearing function, they give up their identification with the mother.

For the girl, on the other hand, the discovery of the anatomical differences between the sexes has a rather different consequence, which leads to Freud's second hypothesis. When the girl makes this discovery, disappointment supersedes her attachment to the mother as the basis for her parenting need. Viewing herself as having been deprived of a penis, the girl develops a strong wish to acquire one. Eventually, however, she must accept the fact that she cannot gratify this wish (just as the boy must accept the fact that he cannot gratify his wish to bear a child). When, then, the girl gives up her wish for a penis, she puts in its place a wish for a child, and the latter wish acquires all the intensity of the former.

The above four theories are among the most prominent examples of precultural interpretations of the female parenting need. Since, in our present state of knowledge, there is no way of assessing their relative merit, we can only say that all of them can account (in principle) for the precultural existence of this need. But even if all four examples were to be disconfirmed, this would not invalidate the conclusion of this study that the female parenting need is precultural. For if the findings reported here are reliable, the disconfirmation of the above examples of precultural interpretations of this need would merely oblige us to search for alternative interpretations.

On the assumption that the female parenting need is a precultural need, we can not only explain the counterrevolutionary attitudes of the female sabras to the family, but we can also explain the vicissitudes of the revolutionary attitudes of their mothers and grandmothers. For on this assumption, when the kibbutz pioneers rejected (and physically abandoned) their biological family of origin, it is entirely understandable (and in hindsight, at least predictable) that they would have created a sociological family to take its place. Thus it is that the kibbutz, as we have seen, became for them a surrogate family, one, however, in which culture took the place of biological kinship as its basis. Moreover, their repressed parenting need—the women's exaggerated expressions of affection for their grandchildren is evidence for its repression and for the subsequent "return of the repressed"—was initially satisfied by the maternal attitudes they displayed to all kibbutz children. In short, although in the early years of the kibbutz few women performed the role of genitrix, any could (and many did) perform the role of mater.

But a surrogate family can take the emotional place of the biological family only until one's own family of procreation becomes psychologically important; and on the assumption that the female parenting need is precultural, this must inevitably happen unless the initial motive for the repression of this need is transmitted from one generation to the next. In the kibbutz case, the motive for its repression (whatever it may have been) was obviously not transmitted to the second generation, for the sabras have not only established larger biological families than their mothers, but they have also transferred a significant measure of their familial emotions from the sociological family (the kibbutz), which had been the focus of the familial emotions of the kibbutz founders, to the biological family which each has created herself. This is the process, or so at least it seems to me, by which the kibbutz has been transformed from one, undifferentiated child-oriented community to a structurally differentiated community consisting of separate (though integrated) child-oriented families.

But this is not all. Insofar as the female sabras value parenting as a phase-specific role in the life cycle, the gratifications they derive from this "feminine" role obviate the need to strive for status in "masculine" roles. Confident in and valuing their status in the family domain, their desire, however, for sexual equality in extrafamilial domains has in no way diminished, although it has taken a different form from that desired by women who disvalue the maternal role. Instead of seeking "status identity" with men in a system of sex-role uniformity, the sabras seek "status equivalence" in a system of sex-role differentiation. It is all the more significant, therefore, that although many of them have been frustrated in this attempt by the narrow range of occupational opportunities available to women, they have neither abandoned their familistic orientation, nor have they attempted to reinstate the pioneers' "identity" meaning of sexual equality.

These kibbutz findings, if I may be permitted a personal note, forced upon me a kind of Copernican revolution in my own thinking. When I returned to Kiryat Yedidim in 1975, I realized that my understanding of what I thought I had been doing in the kibbutz in 1951 was very different from what I found myself doing in 1975. As a cultural determinist, my aim in studying personality development in Kiryat Yedidim in 1951 was to observe the influence of culture on human nature or, more accurately, to discover how a new culture produces a new human nature. In 1975 I found (against my own intentions) that I was observing the influence of human nature on culture; alternatively, I was observing the resurgence of the old culture (in modern garb) as a function of those elements in human nature that the new culture was unable to change. If this is so, then what is really problematic about the data I have presented is not the feminine counterrevolution of the sabras, but the feminist revolution of their parents and grandparents. For if, as these data suggest, many of the motivational differences between the sexes are precultural, and if, moreover, these differences are more or less accurately reflected in the system of sex-role differentiation presently found in the kibbutz (and in almost every other human society), then the challenge for scientific inquiry presented by the kibbutz experience is not why the sabras, in their system of sex-role differentiation, conform to "human nature," but why the kibbutz pioneers had attempted to undo it. Since, however, a nonspeculative answer to this question requires historical data which I do not command, and since in any event the question is best answered by a study of contemporary movements in the West that are making the same attempt today, there would be little gain in offering a speculative answer. Instead, I wish to turn to some of the broader issues implicit in the kibbutz experience.

Unlike cultural theories, which attribute sex differences to sexually appropriate role modeling, our analysis of the kibbutz data has suggested that the obverse is closer to the truth; that is, sexually appropriate role modeling is a function of precultural differences between the sexes. Implicit in this difference between cultural and precultural interpretations of the motivational bases for role modeling is an even more important difference with respect to the origin and persistence of systems of sex-role differentiation. Since, according to cultural interpretations, there are no precultural differences between the sexes, it follows that sex-role differentiation is itself culturally determined. Hence, it is just as feasible for social systems to be constructed on (or to evolve into) a "plan" of sex-role uniformity as of sex-role differentiation. According to precultural interpretations, however, the former alternative is not feasible, for the precultural motivational differences between the sexes render it highly probable that these differences will inevitably be institutionalized in some type of sex-role differentiation.

Of course, the content of any system of sex-role differentiation is culturally constituted, so that such systems can—and many do—become ossified and exploitative. If, then, as a reaction to such a situation, a particular system were to be abolished, it is highly likely, as the kibbutz experience suggests, that another, albeit nonexploitative system, would take its place. For if many sex differences in motivation are precultural, then systems of sex-role differentiation not only create sex differences in motivational dispositions, but they also constitute important institutionalized means for the expression and gratification of these precultural dispositions. Lest I be misunderstood, I should like to make explicit some of the implications of this conclusion.

1. To say that sex-role differentiation is a consequence of sex differences in precultural needs does not imply that all differences in sex roles are a result of these differences; this inference is both theoretically untenable and empirically false. Moreover, to say that the sexes differ in precultural needs is not to say that they differ in all precultural needs, nor is it to say that they differ only in precultural needs, for both statements, again, are theoretically untenable and empirically false.

2. To say that sex-role differentiation, as such, has its origin in sex differences in precultural needs is not to say that sex roles are themselves precultural in origin. Any system of sex-role differentiation is a culturally constituted system; that is, it consists of a set of rules and norms which, viewed as cognitive messages, inform social actors of the appropriate behavioral means by which their needs may be gratified. This being so, although the motivation for performing certain sex roles may stem from a desire to gratify needs, their performance is governed by cultural rules and norms.

3. To say that the performance of some sex-roles gratifies precultural needs (among others) does not imply that sex differences in these needs are differences in kind; rather (as the evidence from sabra children demonstrates) they are typically differences in degree. This is especially true of those needs whose expression and gratification are institutionalized in sex-role systems. Hence, the fact that such systems tend to classify social roles categorically as either male or female does not mean that sex differences in precultural needs are categorically different. On the contrary, so far as these needs are concerned, human beings are most probably bisexual. The behavior of sabra children indicates that both sexes share the same needs, the differences between them consisting of differences in the strength of these needs. Nevertheless, although the differences are in degree, rather than in kind, if the sex-role system does not recognize these differences, then, as the kibbutz data suggest, the social actors will eventually change it.

There is, however, another side to this coin. Whether they are genetically or experientially acquired, it often happens that a reversal occurs in the relative strength of precultural needs. Some males, for example, may exhibit an especially strong parenting need, while some females may exhibit a relatively weak one. This being the case, we may expect that in any society there will be a certain percentage of social actors for whom the culturally appropriate sex roles are psychologically inappropriate. If, then, inflexible boundary rules deny these actors access to the complementary set of sex roles found in their society, or if they are not provided with alternative roles, we may also expect that such actors will exhibit psychological dislocations which, in the absence of relevant structural changes, will lead to sociological dislocations.

4. From the last point it follows that, as a principle of social policy, no social role should be barred to any person on the grounds that his or her recruitment is inconsistent with the current system of sex-role differentiation. In short, no individual or group of individuals should be prohibited from achieving sexual equality in the "identity" meaning of equality. If, however, our findings are reliable, attempts to correct the inequities in any particular system of sex-role differentiation should most effectively be addressed to the achievement of sexual equality in its "equivalence" meaning, for it is the latter meaning of equality that is important for most people to achieve. Hence, for any group of individuals to attempt to impose their particular reversal of a panhuman distribution in sex differences upon others, is an insult to their basic human dignity. If, moreover, the political or media influence of such a group assures their attempts a measure of success, the ensuing social and psychological dislocations for the larger society can be expected to be as serious as those attendant upon the reverse kind of straightjacketing (except that in the latter case the consequences are felt only by a minority). For if systems of sex-role differentiation, as such, are in large part a function of sex differences in motivational disposition, attempts to convince women that sexual equality, for example, is worthwhile only in the "identity" meaning of equality, and that "feminine" careers—even if they achieve equality in its "equivalence" meaning—are unseemly pursuits imposed on them by a sexist society, may (if successful) deprive them of important sources of human gratification. Moreover, to the extent that some women are persuaded by this ideology, but continue to be motivated by powerful countervailing needs, the resulting inner conflict may lead, as one psychiatric study has shown (Moulton 1977), to painful feelings of guilt and depression.

Single cases prove little; they are primarily useful insofar as they challenge received opinion. The kibbutz case does not prove the existence of precultural sex differences. Rather, it challenges the current intellectual and political pieties which deny the existence of such differences (just as they deny the existence of other group differences) on the grounds that to be different is ipso facto to be unequal. That individuals and groups must be identical in order to be equal is surely one of the more pernicious dogmas of our time, and the fact that, ironically enough, it has become a liberal dogma does not make it any the less so. Until or unless the kibbutz data are interpreted differently, the kibbutz case constitutes a challenge to this dogma so far as sex differences are concerned. Of course, the strength of this challenge cannot be determined without much more extensive research—especially longitudinal research—in a variety of cultural settings. Until then, prudence suggests that scientific formulations and public policies related to sex differences proceed with caution.

References

Bardwick, Judith M. 1971. *Psychology of women*. New York: Harper and Row.

Bettelheim, Bruno. 1954. *Symbolic wounds*. Glencoe, Ill.: The Free Press.

Erikson, Erik H. 1963. *Childhood and society*. 2d. ed. New York: W. W. Norton.

Freud, Sigmund. 1964. *New introductory lectures on psychoanalysis* [1933]. In *The standard edition of the complete psychological works of Sigmund Freud*, vol. 22. London: Hogarth Press.

La Barre, Weston. 1954. *The human animal*. Chicago: University of Chicago Press.

Moulton, Ruth. 1977. Some effects of the new feminism. *American Journal of Psychiatry* 134:1–6.

Tiger, Lionel, and Joseph Shepher. 1975. *Women in the kibbutz*. New York: Harcourt Brace Jovanovich.

Trivers, Robert L. 1972. Parental investment and sexual selection. In *Sexual selection and the descent of man 1871–1971*, ed. Bernard Campbell. Chicago: Aldine.

4   Is the Oedipus Complex Universal?

IN PREVIOUS work I attempted to achieve two separate, but related, goals. First, I attempted to demonstrate that its empirical foundation is too weak to support Malinowski's argument that a matrilineal complex exists in the Trobriands. Second, I attempted to show that the evidence indicates to the contrary that an unusually strong Oedipus complex exists in the Trobriands. Here I wish to examine the implications of these Trobriand findings for human societies in general.

Malinowski and those who follow his lead have argued that the male Oedipus complex is culturally relative because it is produced not by the boy's experience in the family in general, but by his experience in the "patriarchal" family uniquely. Since, so they argue, it is the authoritarian father—the nineteenth-century European father being paradigmatic of the class—who arouses filial hostility, matrilineal societies whose family structure does not conform to the "patriarchal" type— the Trobriands being paradigmatic of the class—would not be expected to produce an Oedipus complex.

In a sophisticated and perceptive explication of that argument, Campbell and Naroll (1972:437) quite properly observe that in principle the boy's hostility to the father may be motivated either by his rivalry with him for the love of the mother (as Freud claimed) or by the father's punitive authority (as Malinowski claimed). Freud, they argue, confounded these two motives in his construction of the Oedipus complex because, in his European patient population, the father was both the authority figure and the mother's lover. Since in the Trobriands, however, these roles are performed by different persons rather than by one and the same person, and since the boy's hostility, according to Malinowski, is directed to the authority figure (mother's brother)

Reprinted from Melford E. Spiro, *Oedipus in the Trobriands* (Chicago: University of Chicago Press, 1982), pp. 144–80.

rather than the mother's lover (father), the hostility dimension of the Western Oedipus complex is brought about not by the son's sexual rivalry with the father, they argue, but by his resentment of the latter's authority.

That argument can now be faulted on three grounds. First, there are no a priori grounds for assuming that hostility to the father cannot be motivated by both sexual rivalry and resentment against his authority. Indeed, that is the view I have adopted in distinguishing between Oedipal and non-Oedipal grounds for filial hostility. Second, there are no evidential grounds for claiming that in the Trobriands the jural authority of the mother's brother is exercised either frequently or punitively. Hence, even if the boy's *conscious* hostility is directed toward the mother's brother, it cannot be a function of the latter's punitive authority. Third, the findings I have presented demonstrate rather conclusively that in fact it is the father who is the prime target of the boy's hostility in the Trobriands, and moreover his hostility is Oedipal in motivation, i.e., it is motivated by his rivalry with him for the love of the wife-mother.

Even, however, without that empirical demonstration, the claim that the male Oedipus complex would not be expected in matrilineal societies because the father is not an authority figure can be faulted on theoretical grounds alone. In order to sustain that claim, it would have to be demonstrated that in matrilineal societies it is the case not only that the father is not an authority figure for the son (however important that might be for the non-Oedipal dimensions of the father-son relationship), but that the mother is not a love-object for him. For if it is the case that the son has a libidinal attachment to the mother in matrilineal as well as in "patriarchal" societies, the contention that he would nevertheless not be hostile to the father—or anyone else that he perceived to be the rival for her love—would be warranted only on the assumption that hostility to a rival is a phenomenon which is restricted to patriarchal societies. That assumption, however, is easily refuted, if only by the abundant evidence to the contrary reported by Malinowski for the Trobriands. That being the case, unless it were demonstrated that a libidinal attachment to the mother is restricted to boys in patriarchal societies, then, all things being equal, it would be no less likely for the Oedipus complex to be found in matrilineal societies than in patriarchal ones.

Malinowski, who waffled on this issue of the boy's relationship to the mother—on the one hand he claimed that in the Trobriands the young boy has a "passionate" attachment to his mother, on the other that this attachment disappears spontaneously prior to the normally expected onset of the Oedipus complex, a point to which we shall return—nowhere adduced any structural feature(s) peculiar to matriliny that might account for the absence of a libidinal attachment to the mother in matrilineal societies. Unless such a feature can be identified, it seems judicious to go along with the large body of evidence which suggests that a motivational disposition to nuclear family incest in general, and to mother-son incest in particular, is a panhuman characteristic. Since Lindzey (1967) has brought together much of the evidence pertaining to incest in general, our discussion of that topic will take its departure from his excellent paper, following which we shall turn to mother-son incest, which is our primary concern here.

The evidence marshaled by Lindzey can be classified into two categories, indirect and direct. Beginning with the former, we might mention in the first place the abundant social-psychological findings which suggest that "personal attractiveness and interpersonal choice are mediated, or determined, by similarity in attitudes, values, needs, and background factors," and that "positive social choice is strongly facilitated by physical or geographic proximity" (Lindzey 1967:1056). When these social-psychological findings are combined with the sociological findings concerning homogeneity of mate selection and the demographic findings concerning assortative mating (which indicate that the grounds for preferential choice in nonsexual domains apply to the sexual domain as well), their cumulative force suggests that in the absence of countervailing factors (most notably, incest taboos) sexual choice within—but not restricted to—the nuclear family would be a likely outcome.

That suggestion is supported by the direct evidence regarding the motivational disposition to nuclear family incest. Consider, first, the psychiatric findings concerning the existence of incestuous wishes at least in clinical populations. Consider, again, the psychological findings concerning the frequency of incestuous wishes, both overt and covert, in the dreams of normal populations. Consider, moreover, the anthropological findings concerning the near-universal incidence of the incest motif in myths, legends, and folktales, as well as the universality of nuclear family incest taboos. Consider, in addition, the sociological findings concerning the prevalence of incestuous behavior in the United States. For example, one out of every twenty persons questioned in 1970, according to an authoritative estimate, had had an incestuous experience (Justice and Justice 1979:17). Consider, finally, the ethological findings (Bischof 1975) which indicate a near-universal motivation to incest in infrahuman mammalian societies.[1] If, then, we consider the cumulative force of these various kinds of evidence, it is hard to avoid the conclusion that the existence of a panhuman motivational disposition to incest is a highly probable hypothesis. This hypothesis, I hasten to add, does not entail the conclusion that nuclear family members are the strongest objects of sexual desire—though that too may sometimes occur—but only that they, among others, are members of that class.

Although almost all anthropologists, representing the entire range of anthropological thought, accept this conclusion, it has always had its opponents. If, so their counterargument goes, incestuous behavior is rare in human societies, it is not because of social or cultural pressures, most notably the implementation of incest taboos, which lead to its inhibition (as the proponents of the incest hypothesis argue), but because (to quote a recent statement of a distinguished critic) "human beings are 'naturally' non-incestuous" (Fox 1980:14). (Fox's view is much more complex than this quotation suggests, as will become apparent when we return to it below.) Hence, before turning to the motivational disposition to incest in the mother-son dyad (our concern here) it is necessary to examine this counterargument, especially since prominent findings from China and Israel have recently been adduced on its behalf.

Various of its proponents base the counterargument to the incest hypothesis on different theoretical grounds, but they all agree with Westermarck (who first proposed it) that sexual indifference or aversion, rather than attraction, develops between any persons (including family members) who live together from an early age. It is this naturally developing aversion that then accounts for the relative infrequency of incestuous behavior (Westermarck 1906–8:vol. 2, p. 368). In order to fully grasp this counterargument it must be emphasized that none of the proponents of the incest hypothesis argue that—except for young children—members of the nuclear family have a conscious wish

---

1. Despite their motivational disposition, incestuous behavior is infrequent in mammals because of a variety of structural constraints—most notably the formation of all-male adolescent groupings, adolescent extrusion, and dominance structures—which are summarized by Bischof (1975) in his admirable survey of the mammalian evidence. Although Bischof, a zoologist, shows that in the absence of these structural arrangements incest would be prevalent in mammalian societies, and although he argues that these arrangements are the evolutionary result of a selection process to constrain its occurrence, he then, strangely, concludes that the infrequency of mammalian incest indicates the absence of motivation to incest. It is hard to account for this non sequitur in an otherwise exemplary study.

to take one another as sexual partners. They, no less than Westermarck, are fully aware that, consciously, most individuals are either indifferent or aversive to having sexual relations with family members. For them, however, sexual indifference or aversion is a consequence not of childhood propinquity but, rather, of the internalization of incest taboos and the consequent repression or extinction of the incestuous wishes.

Although Westermarck's theory has been persistently rejected by social scientists, most particularly on the grounds—first adduced by Frazer ([1887] 1910:vol. 4, p. 97 ff.)—that the universality of nuclear family incest taboos implies that the motivational disposition to incest is also universal, it has recently been defended on the basis of two sets of findings, one from China, the other from Israel. Since these findings, both confined to the question of sibling incest, have been widely heralded as constituting conclusive support (cf. Bischof 1975; Demarest 1977; Fox 1980:chapter 2; Money 1980; Wilson 1978) for Westermarck's theory, it is important to examine them rather carefully.

The Chinese case, which has been extensively studied by Wolf (1966, 1968, 1970) and by Wolf and Huang (1980), concerns a type of marriage known as *simpua* marriage. In this marriage type, a boy's parents choose as his future bride a young girl, often orphaned or from a poor and socially inferior family, who is adopted as a daughter, who lives in the family household throughout childhood, and whom he subsequently marries at the appropriate age. In short, prior to their marriage the structural relationship between the boy and his chosen bride is little different from that of biological siblings raised in the same family. According to Wolf's findings, the adultery and divorce rates found in *simpua* marriages are higher and the fertility rate is lower than those found in regular Chinese marriages. Taking these rates as a measure of sexual dissatisfaction, Wolf argues that the greater sexual dissatisfaction in *simpua* marriages is a consequence of the sexual aversion that develops between the boy and girl in childhood, which supports Westermarck's theory that propinquity leads to sexual aversion.

Convincing as it might seem, Wolf's argument, I believe, is invalid on both empirical and theoretical grounds. Empirically, Wolf's findings regarding *simpua* marriage do not sustain the conclusion that children who live together typically develop a sexual aversion for each other, for although these marriages are characterized by higher rates of divorce and adultery and a lower rate of fertility than regular marriages, it is nevertheless the case that the great majority of them do not display these characteristics. If it is then claimed that these findings indicate that there is a greater likelihood for childhood propinquity to lead to sexual aversion, even this lesser claim can be sustained only on the dubious assumption that adultery, divorce, and low fertility are necessarily (as Wolf takes them to be) measures of sexual dissatisfaction. Surely, other factors also contribute to these forms of behavior in China—in regular and *simpua* marriages alike—as we know to be the case elsewhere.

But even accepting the assumption that sexual dissatisfaction is the sole determinant of divorce, adultery, and low fertility, Wolf's ethnographic data cast considerable doubt on his contention that the postulated sexual dissatisfaction found in *simpua* marriages is primarily determined by the sexual aversion that, putatively, the couple develop as a result of their living together in childhood.

Consider in the first place that the boy, according to Wolf, feels cheated and frustrated by a *simpua* marriage because it deprives him not only of honor and prestige—these marriages are viewed as "vulgar and inferior" and are therefore "socially despised"—but of a dowry, affinal alliances, and other advantages of a regular marriage, as well. Considering all of these disadvantages, it is hard to credit Wolf's contention that although the boys "resent their having their best interests sacrificed by their parents," their resentment is nevertheless "not likely to disrupt permanently their relationship as husband and wife" (Wolf 1970:506). I would assume, on the contrary, that their resentment would have that effect precisely.

Consider, again, that a girl adopted for a *simpua* marriage is an object of "abuse" by her adoptive family; indeed, such girls are treated so badly that they are the very "symbol of the life of misery." Consider, too, that (presumably as a result of this treatment) the girl is hostile to the members of her adoptive family, including her "brother" (and future husband), of whom she is jealous and toward whom she displays "sibling" rivalry. It is again hard to credit Wolf's contention that these factors do not importantly affect the girl's subsequent relationship with the boy when she becomes his wife. It is also difficult to believe that the girl's abusive treatment by his parents does not affect the boy's perception of her as an inferior person, one who is unworthy of esteem and affection. Indeed, since the main reason for a *simpua* marriage is the wish of the boy's mother to have a subordinate daughter-in-law, one who will not be a rival for her son's affection (as is the case in regular marriages), it would seem not unlikely that she goes out of her way to prevent her son from establishing an affectionate relationship with his "sister."

In short, given all of these considerations, it is hard to credit Wolf's claim that the boy's "resentment" and the girl's "misery" have no influence on their feelings for each other, and that these feelings, in turn, have no effect on their subsequent relationship as husband and wife, most especially their sexual relationship. Indeed, everything that we know about the influence of emotional attitudes on sexual desire and performance supports the contrary assumption. Hence, even if it were the case that the differences in the rates of fertility, divorce, and adultery in regular and *simpua* marriages are exclusively determined by a higher incidence of sexual dissatisfaction in the latter marriages, it is hard to believe that all of these social and cultural factors have no influence on that dissatisfaction. Indeed, given those factors it is a wonder that these marriages do not display a much greater degree of dissatisfaction.

When, then, to these social and cultural impediments to a satisfactory sexual relationship that are contained in Wolf's data we add the observation that in *simpua* marriage the boy and girl must marry each other even if, being sexually unattracted, they would not have married had they been raised separately; and when to that we add the additional observation that almost everywhere divorce in early marriages is higher than in later ones, so that the higher divorce rate of *simpua* marriages (in which twice as many couples marry before seventeen than in regular marriages [44 as against 22 percent]) would be expected as a function of the couple's age at marriage—when these observations are also taken into account, I would then submit that Wolf's contention that the case of *simpua* marriage proves Westermarck's theory that childhood propinquity leads to sexual aversion rests on a very shaky foundation.

Let us then turn to the second ethnographic case that allegedly proves Westermarck's theory, the Israeli kibbutz movement. In 1958 I reported that in the kibbutz I had studied none of the children who had been reared together from birth had married each other, and that to the best of my knowledge none had had sexual intercourse with each other (Spiro 1958:347–48). These findings were replicated in a later study by Talmon (1964) in three kibbutzim. Still later, based on a study of the marriage records of kibbutz children in all kibbutzim—2,769 marriages in all—Shepher (1971) reported that in not one case had there been a marriage between children reared together from birth through the age of six years. Shepher also reported that so far as he was able to ascertain, this finding also applied to love affairs, those at least that were publicly known.

Now what makes these three reports of considerable interest is that no marriages (and probably no love affairs) have taken place among members of the same peer groups *despite the fact that such marriages are not prohibited.* It is understandable, therefore, that these findings have aroused a great deal of attention.

I interpreted my own findings as indicating that members of the kibbutz peer group repress their sexual feelings for each other. This interpretation was based on two sets of data. First, with one exception they themselves attributed the absence of marriage within the peer group to the sexual indifference which, they explained, arose from their perception of each other as "siblings." Second, the data regarding sexual behavior and socialization in these peer groups, to which I shall advert below, suggested rather strongly that their sexual indifference did not develop spontaneously.

Some (but hardly all) incest theorists, especially those acquainted with Shepher's subsequent large-scale report, interpreted the kibbutz findings, as did Shepher himself, as supporting Westermarck's theory that children reared together in childhood (whether or not they are siblings) develop a sexual aversion for each other. Since the latter interpretation, however, was offered without giving any consideration to (what I believe to be) the crucial data on sexual socialization, in order to evaluate these competing interpretations it is necessary to summarize those data for the particular historical period—because much has changed since then—for which the marriage findings were reported (for details see Spiro 1958:chapters 9, 11, 13, 14).

In that period, consistent with the kibbutz ideology of sexual freedom, young children were almost entirely free to engage in sexual play without interference or punishment by their caretakers. Since, therefore, boys and girls of the same age not only lived together in one dormitory, but also slept and showered together and had frequent other opportunities to see each other in the nude, it is not surprising that they also engaged in (childlike) sexual behavior and that they displayed little sexual shame (Spiro 1958:219–28). An important change in their behavior occurred, however, around eleven or twelve, when girls, who were beginning to show the first signs of puberty, refused to shower together with the boys, and in general began to display overt signs of sexual shame. At the same time, sexual behavior no longer occurred, and was replaced by a great deal of bickering and hostility between the sexes. Although the bickering and hostility gradually disappeared, sexual shame, including the avoidance of mixed showers, persisted throughout high school, and there was no return to the sexual play that characterized early childhood, nor was there an assumption of sexual behavior of a more mature form.

With this brief behavioral description, we may now examine the cultural and structural factors associated with these behavioral changes.

First, despite their differential physical maturation at puberty, boys and girls of the same peer groups continued to live and sleep together. This meant that physically immature boys continued to be the roommates of girls who may have begun to menstruate, and whose secondary sexual characteristics—the development of breasts, the growth of pubic hair, and the like—were becoming prominent. Hence, although the girls were beginning to experience the sexual tensions of puberty and a concern with the physical changes in their bodies, the boys remained physically immature. It is not surprising, then, that the girls displayed no interest in the boys, and that in some cases the latter were put off—even frightened—by the girls, while others (outsiders) were sexually aroused by them.

Even at a later age, however, when the boys' maturation caught up with the girls', two other factors intervened. First, in the case of the older children—beginning around prepuberty and continuing until the end of high school—the permissive ideology of the kibbutz regarding the sexual play of young children was replaced by a strong prohibition on sexual behavior. The introduction of such prohibitions at this age was not based—not, at least, officially—on sexual puritanism, but on the assumptions that sexual behavior disrupts the learning process, that intellectual development is enhanced when the sex drive is sublimated in intellectual pursuits, and that pair bonding, which often results from sexual behavior, interferes with the intensive group interaction and group identification that the kibbutz viewed as paramount values. Hence, at this age strong pressure was exerted on the children to defer all sexual encounters until graduation from high school, and especially to avoid the formation of permanent liaisons. The latter in particular were the object of strong social sanctions.

Second, despite these sexual prohibitions and their attendant sanctions, kibbutz educators believed that to encourage children to develop a wholesome attitude toward sex and a "natural" attitude toward the body and its functions, it was important that boys and girls live together not only in early childhood but throughout their educational careers until graduation from high school. Beginning, however, in the seventh grade the group of approximately sixteen age peers, who had previously shared one barrack-like dormitory room, was divided into groups of four—two males and two females—each group sharing one bedroom.

Here, then, I would submit, is a classic example of incompatible demands. On the one hand, we have a group of teenagers, at a physiological developmental stage of maximum sexual tension, who are exposed to persistent sexual stimulation induced by living in close quarters with members of the opposite sex, who dress and undress in one another's presence—though it was expected that they avert their eyes during this process—and who sleep in adjacent beds. At the same time, these same teenagers are expected to comply with a cultural norm which prohibits sexual behavior between them on pain of serious social sanctions. Such a contradiction, I would submit, can only result in intolerable conflict and unbearable sexual frustration. Edith Buxbaum, a child therapist, highlights this contradiction in her discussion of a fifteen-year-old kibbutz boy who could not sleep because of his urge to touch a girl, and who was advised to seek psychiatric help for his "problem." It seems paradoxical. Buxbaum (1970:286) writes

that people should consider it abnormal for a fifteen-year-old boy to want to touch a girl with whom he sleeps in the same room. Indeed, it would be extraordinary if he did not want to. Yet, this is what kibbutz educators expect and the children expect of themselves. They are not supposed to have these feelings, or if they have them, they are not supposed to act on them.

That, however, only a small percentage of these teenagers required professional help to cope with the tensions induced by this contradiction suggests that the majority managed to erect strong psychological barriers against them. These barriers, as I suggested above—and as Buxbaum (1970:285–90) and Bettelheim (1969:235–40) have suggested elsewhere—could only have consisted in the repression of their sexual wishes (which would explain how they might have consciously become sexually indifferent to each other) and, if that were not sufficient, in the formation of a reaction against them (which would explain how they might have consciously developed a sexual aversion for each other).[2]

There are three reasons, I would submit, for preferring this interpretation of these kibbutz findings to that of Westermarck's fol-

---

2. If correct, this analysis confutes Fox's attempt to salvage Westermarck's theory. The latter theory, according to Fox (1980:chapter 2), only applies to children who not only live together but also engage in intense physical interaction. Since, he argues, their physical contacts lead to sexual arousal, and since immature children have no means of physiological discharge, their painful frustration leads to a consequent sexual aversion for the children (later adults) who are responsible for their pain. If, however, children who live together have no physical interaction and, therefore, no history of painful sexual frustration, Westermarck's theory does not apply. The kibbutz case, according to Fox, supports this argument because it involves physical interaction in childhood followed by aversion at adolescence.

According to my analysis, however, it is not the physical interaction in childhood, but the sexual prohibition at adolescence in the face of powerful sexual stimulation that leads to sexual aversion in the kibbutz. By my argument, the sexual stimulation leads to sexual arousal, which is frustrated by sexual prohibitions, and the resulting painful tensions are defended against by repression and reaction formation which, if effective, lead to sexual aversion.

lowers. First, the early sexual play of kibbutz children for the period under discussion was replaced by sexual abstinence only after the sexual permissiveness of childhood was replaced by the sexual prohibitions of adolescence. This suggests, pace Westermarck, that their sexual aversion for each other—if that is what it was—did not develop endogenously. Second, the sexual abstinence of the adolescents applied not only in regard to the members of their peer group—the group with whom they lived as children—but to other groups as well—those with whom they did not live as children. Third, and most important, this interpretation is supported by the recent findings of Kaffman (1977), a psychiatrist employed by the kibbutz movement, regarding sexual behavior in the kibbutz.

Although Kaffman's findings regarding peer-group marriage do not disagree with the early findings reported above, those regarding love affairs are at variance with them. "There is hardly a kibbutz," Kaffman writes, "without its report of heterosexual relationships between adolescents brought up together from infancy" (Kaffman 1977:216). Such relationships, he claims, "may not be typical, but [they are] not all that rare either" (ibid.). Kaffman also reports that whereas in an earlier study of seventeen-year-old kibbutz children, 66 percent of the sample were opposed to sexual relations, in 1973 only 7 percent of the males and 11 percent of the females voiced opposition.

How, then, are the discrepancies between Kaffman's report and the earlier reports to be explained? And what light do these discrepancies shed on the conflicting interpretations of the earlier reports? Kaffman's findings are based on studies conducted some few years after two major changes had begun to take place in the kibbutz movement. In the first place, many kibbutzim changed the living arrangements in the high school dormitories from mixed to unisexual bedrooms. In many of them, too, the prohibition on teenage sexual behavior has been informally if not formally abolished. According, then, to my interpretation of the earlier findings, Kaffman's findings are exactly what one would expect from such changes: no longer suffering the severe sexual tensions aroused by a contradiction between their living arrangements and sexual norms, adolescents in those kibbutzim which had undergone these changes had no need to create psychological barriers (repression and/or reaction formation) to their sexual feelings. As more and more kibbutzim make these structural and cultural changes, we would then expect the sexual changes reported by Kaffman to become more widespread. It is difficult, however, to accommodate Kaffman's findings to Westermarck's theory. Since, according to that theory, sexual aversion results from joint living in childhood, and since no changes in the children's living arrangements were associated with the sexual changes reported by Kaffman, his data are clearly inexplicable by that theory.

If, then, my interpretation of the earlier reports is correct, why is it that the structural and cultural changes pointed to above have not had an even greater effect on the incidence of intragroup love affairs and marriage? There are at least two answers to that question. In the first place, the fact that individuals who live together in childhood (whether they are siblings or nonsiblings) acquire sexual wishes for each other does not mean, as I observed above, that these are their strongest sexual wishes. When we consider, then, that kibbutz peer groups, as Kaffman observes, are small and the range of sexual choice limited, and when we consider too the different maturation rates of boys and girls, we would not expect a surge of sexual behavior within the per group despite those changes. In the second place, since sexual attractiveness is hardly the only basis for marriage, we would not expect all couples who are sexually attracted to each other to wish to enter into a marriage.[3]

I would conclude, then, that the kibbutz case no more than the Chinese constitutes proof for the Westermarck theory. Indeed, if my analysis is correct, the kibbutz case provides strong support for the contention of the vast majority of incest theorists that individuals who live together (whether they are family or nonfamily members) do indeed develop and retain sexual feelings for each other unless they are inhibited by countervailing social and cultural pressures.

This analysis of the Israeli case is supported by yet another case, one which was reported only some few years following the claim that the kibbutz and Chinese cases support the Westermarck theory. This case, which has already been mentioned in a previous chapter, consists of brother-sister marriage in Roman Egypt. For two centuries, brother-sister marriage, according to Hopkins (1980:310), was a "frequent practice" in Roman Egypt. According to second century census returns, for example, 23 of 113 recorded marriages were between brother and sister. More important for the terms of this discussion is that these marriages, which were considered to be entirely "normal"—hence, not

---

3. Those incest theorists—the so-called alliance theorists—who see the unchecked motivational disposition to incest as a barrier to the formation of interfamily alliances have primitive and prehistoric families as their model. Since the latter (hunting and gathering) families are frequently isolated from other families in their bands, mating with a family member is much more likely—unless it is checked by incest taboos—than in families in which a wide range of sexual partners, in addition to family members, are available. Physical isolation of the family, as we have previously observed, is an important condition for incest in modern families as well.

prohibited by an incest taboo—were based not on economic or other practical considerations, but on "love and sexual passion." Hence, when such marriages came to an end in the third century, it was not because love and passion between brothers and sisters came to an end, but because Egypt came under Roman law, which prohibited incest.

If, then, the Chinese case does not refute the generalization that siblings who are reared together develop incestuous feelings for each other, and if the kibbutz and Egyptian cases offer strong support for that generalization, we may now turn to the question of incestuous feelings in the dyad that is relevant to the Oedipal problem, the mother-son dyad.

There is nothing in the evidence summarized above regarding the existence of a motivational disposition to nuclear family incest which suggests that the boy's incestuous feelings for his mother are less strong than those for his sister. Indeed, given the nature of the mother-son bond in humans, it is reasonable to assume that, typically, his incestuous feelings for the mother are stronger by far than those for his sister, and that this generalization holds even when the mother is not seductive, as she is (according to my argument) in the Trobriands. Moreover, given the nature of the mother-child bond in humans, the incestuous feelings for the mother in our species, so I shall argue below, are much stronger than those found in any other species. In short, contrary to most incest theorists, I shall argue that if the (mother-son) incest taboo represents the transition from the state of nature to that of culture, it is because the intensity of the incestuous attachment to the mother is much stronger in human (culture) than in animal (nature) societies. A comparison of human with infrahuman primate societies— for convenience's sake this discussion will be restricted to primates, our closest animal relatives—can reveal why this is the case.

For obvious biological reasons it is the mother with whom any primate infant, human or infrahuman, sustains its most intimate emotional and physical relationship. It is she primarily who suckles, trains, and plays with him. It is her voice, her body, and her face that the infant knows best, and it is she whom above all others he seeks out for pleasure, protection, and comfort. As a consequence, it is the mother who is the primary object of the infant's emotional attachment. If, then, even the infant is a sexual creature and capable of sexual arousal, it is not unreasonable to assume that the early attachment to the mother has important libidinal overtones, and that the mother, therefore, is the object of the earliest libidinal attachment. Despite these similarities between humans and other primates, the incestuous attachment to the mother is much stronger and especially problematic in humans because of two important biological characteristics that are unique to humans: the suppression of estrus and prolonged infantile dependency.

Among infrahuman primates there is an incompatibility between sexuality and mothering because at the height of estrus, when the females are in a state of sexual "mania" or "frenzy," as the primatologists call it, they have little interest in mothering or, for that matter, in any other activity except sex. Hence, mothering can only occur during anestrus—the period in which the female is not sexually receptive—which, apart from the normal sexual cycle, begins immediately following pregnancy and continues until the end of lactation. When, at the end of lactation, estrus returns, the juvenile is already weaned, and since typically infantile helplessness does not extend beyond weaning, the mother's indifference to her offspring during estrus does not endanger their welfare since they are no longer dependent upon her for care and nurturance. Indeed, at the conclusion of weaning the juvenile's relationship with the mother is typically and abruptly severed. Thus, in those primate societies consisting of mother-child families, the juvenile is usually driven off by the mother when, at the conclusion of weaning, she enters estrus, while in those with biparental families, he is usually driven off by her consort. In either case, he usually joins a group of juveniles who, with some few exceptions, are permanently "peripheralized" (as the primatologists say).

Since, then, mother and son are separated following weaning, and since their separation is socially enforced at least until the son achieves maturity—when, in a few cases, he may force himself upon the dominant adult male(s)—there is no opportunity for his early attachment to the mother to become intensified by a continuing relationship with her. (For a more extensive treatment, see Bischof 1975; Chance and Jolly 1970; Fox 1980; Lancaster 1979; Rowell 1972.)

Among humans, the mother-child relationship is very different. Since infantile helplessness is prolonged, and cultural acquisition complex, it is necessary that the child remain dependent upon the mother (or mother surrogate) long after the completion of weaning. And since, with the suppression of estrus, the human female is not characterized by sexual mania, her interest in sex, though continuous, does not interfere with her motivation or ability to care for her young children. Since, then, there is no incompatibility between mating and mothering among humans, human offspring live with and remain dependent upon their mothers for many years, not excluding the "phallic" period (when the early libidinal attachment to the mother receives strong reinforcement) and puberty (when sexuality may erupt explosively).

In short, since the son's relationship with the mother may persist throughout childhood and even into puberty, thereby intensifying his early emotional attachment to her, and since that attachment is based on *both* libidinal and dependency feelings, it is reasonable to expect the incestuous attachment of the son to the mother to be much stronger in humans than in primates. For the same reason, one would expect the attachment to the mother to be much stronger than the incestuous attachment to the sister. Although brother and sister live together, they never have—indeed, they are prohibited from having—the intimate physical relationship that the son has with his mother.

Strangely enough, Malinowski (unlike most of his followers) fully recognized the strength of the boy's incestuous attachment to the mother, as well as the critical challenge that it posed for his contention that the Oedipus complex is confined to "patriarchal" families of the Western type. Indeed, in a long rhapsodic passage he expatiates in concrete detail on the erotic feelings of the young boy for his mother (SR:212–14). At the same time he also observes that since lovers employ the same organ zones and behavioral modes in their physical interaction with each other that mother and child employ in their interaction, the male's later induction into the "erotic life" may arouse in him "disturbing memories" of the relationship with his mother, because she "remains in the foreground of [his] emotional interests throughout his life." That being the case, Malinowski continues, before the boy reaches sexual maturity it is necessary that "all sensuality felt toward the mother become repressed." That is achieved by inculcating in the boy emotions of "reverence, dependence [and] respect" toward the mother so that if a "subconscious temptation of incest" is aroused when he is mature, it is muted by its "blending" with these nonsexual emotions.

The above analysis represents Malinowski's conception of what happens to the early incestuous attachment to the mother in the West (and some other societies), but it is not what happens (according to him) in matrilineal societies, in which the "passionate" attachment of the infant to the mother spontaneously disappears by the time the boy reaches the "phallic" stage of development, the very stage when genital love for her is normally expected to appear. Unfortunately, however, his argument on behalf of this claim is less than convincing. In a nutshell, Malinowski nowhere indicates how or why the spontaneous disappearance of the boy's passionate attachment to the mother occurs. *That* it occurs, however, he is quite sure on the grounds (it will be recalled) that, when he asked the Trobriand men whether they wished to have intercourse with their mothers, they ridiculed the very suggestion.

Such a response, he argued, proves that a "repressed Oedipus complex" cannot possibly exist in the Trobriands.

Although I have already dealt with this "proof," it is nevertheless worth repeating because most other critics of the notion that incestuous motives might be repressed adduce exactly the same argument. Briefly, the argument is invalid on three counts. First, although it now seems unlikely that the boy's incestuous wishes in regard to the mother are ever—to use Freud's metaphor—"smashed" in childhood (as a result of castration anxiety), it does seem to be the case that in some individuals and in some societies those wishes do undergo a gradual process of extinction, coordinate with the cessation of childhood sexuality (sexual "latency"). Second, even in those individuals and societies in which incestuous wishes regarding the mother persist into adulthood, it is rare that the adult mother is the object of these wishes. Rather, it is the mother of childhood—or, rather, his mental representation of her—on whom the son's incestuous wishes remain fixated. In the latter event—to come to the third reason—the son's fixation cannot be discovered by the mere asking because, typically, it is not in conscious awareness, which is precisely what is meant—to use Malinowski's expression—by a "*repressed* Oedipus complex." To that extent Westmarck and his followers are correct when they argue that incest taboos do not have the function of prohibiting incest (with mother or anyone else), not because incestuous wishes (as they contend) do not exist, but because typically the implementation of the incest taboos in childhood has achieved its intended function. In short, from this perspective, the function of incest taboos is not to signal to *adults* that their incestuous wishes must be inhibited, but rather to banish such wishes from *children* before they become adults.

If, then, the implementation of the mother-son incest taboo (a subject to which we shall return) typically results in the disappearance of the incestuous attachment to the childhood mother—as a result either of extinction, on the one hand, or of repression and reaction formation, on the other—to challenge the universality of such an attachment on the grounds that in some society (or societies) adults do not consciously experience any sexual feelings for the mother, is clearly misguided. By that criterion, such an attachment does not exist in any society, whether "patriarchal" or matrilineal, not at any rate in its "normal" members. In short the evidence for the universality of a motivational disposition to mother-son incest remains unaffected by this challenge.

Since, then, that evidence is very strong, and since (as we argued above) the existence of the incestuous dimension of the Oedipus complex renders its aggressive dimension all but axiomatic, the only appropriate response to the question, "Is the Oedipus complex universal?" is "How could it possibly not be?" Even in those primate societies in which females have no permanent consorts—the multimale societies of trooping monkeys—and in which, therefore, there can be no rivalry between son and father, powerful rivalry nevertheless exists between the peripheralized young males as a group and the dominant males who monopolize the females (Chance and Jolly 1970). In single-male primate societies, on the other hand, whether those of the monogamous gibbon (Carpenter 1940) or the polygynous hamadryas baboon (Kummer 1968), the rivalry is directly and explicitly between father and son.

In sum, there is only one obvious retort to the above riposte. If there were a human society in which mothers did not have male consorts—so that the son had no adult rival for the love of the mother—in such a society the Oedipus complex (by definition) would not exist. So far as we know, however, no human society of that type exists, or has ever existed. The "matrifocal" households—widely prevalent in the Caribbean (Smith 1956) and among lower class American blacks (Rainwater and Yancey 1967)—do not constitute an exception to that generalization because typically a husband-father is intermittently present or else the mother brings a series of temporary lovers into the household. That being the case, although there is no evidence one way or the other, I would also expect these New World matrifocal households to produce an Oedipus complex. This expectation is supported by the findings of Gough (1953) that an Oedipus complex is found among the Nayar, an Indian caste of the Malabar Coast, despite the fact that Nayar women typically take a series of lovers rather than living with a permanent consort.

That the Oedipus complex, according to this analysis, would be expected to be universal does not imply, I hasten to add, that it would also be expected to be cross-culturally uniform. On the contrary, since we know (from Western data) that the Oedipus complex is variable within societies, we would then expect that it would exhibit a wide range of variability across societies. That is the thesis I want to explore in the following section.

Cross-cultural Variability in the Oedipus Complex

Since the Oedipus complex may be said to have three important dimensions—structure, intensity, and outcome—in principle at least it could be expected to display cross-cultural variability in all three. Let us begin with its structure. By the "structure" of the Oedipus complex

I mean the members—in addition to the boy himself—who make up the Oedipal triangle and who are the objects, therefore, of his sexual and aggressive wishes.

If in the classical Oedipus complex it is the boy's biological parents who are the objects of those wishes, that is not to be explained, surely, by the closeness of their genetic relationship, nor again by some instinctual vectorial dimension of the sexual and aggressive drives. Rather, that particular Oedipal triangle is best accounted for by the sociological fact that the boy and his biological parents, typically constituting a social group and inhabiting a common household, sustain certain modes of social relationships with each other. It is these relationships that account for the biological parents, specifically, becoming the objects of his sexual and aggressive wishes. Hence, variability in these relationships could be expected to result in corresponding and predictable variability in the structure of the Oedipal triangle. Thus, for example, if there were a society in which, rather than belonging to a common residential household, parents and children were distributed in different households, it might then be expected that the child's mother-surrogate (rather than his biological mother) would be the focus of his libidinal wishes, and that her consort (rather than his biological father) would be the focus of his aggressive wishes. At the moment, however, such a society is not known.

If, then, there is no theoretical reason why the adult members of the Oedipal triangle must consist of the boy's biological mother and father, it might well be the case that in some society this triangle consists of the boy, his sister, and his mother's brother. Malinowski's claim that this is the case in the Trobriands was rejected not on theoretical, but on empirical grounds: neither the composition of the Trobriand household nor the social relationships that obtain within the nuclear family display the characteristics that might expectably produce that particular structural variant of the classical Oedipus triangle. For exactly the same reason neither this nor any other structural variant of the classical Oedipus triangle has been reported at a total societal level for any other society, which does not mean that such a variant or variants may not occur in individual cases or in certain subgroups in some societies, or that some variant may not be reported in the future for some (as yet unknown) total society.

Although the structure of the Oedipus complex, while variable in principle, seems to be universal in fact, this is not the case in regard to its two other attributes—its intensity and outcome—in which cross-cultural variability is not only a theoretical expectation but an ethnographic fact. Since variability in the intensity of the Oedipus complex has been discussed elsewhere (Spiro 1982), we shall focus here on variability in its outcome, especially since the latter attribute has important social and cultural consequences. Moreover, since the implementation of the incest taboo is a major determinant of its outcome, we shall limit our discussion to that determinant alone.

Since libidinal desires for the mother may be present, as we have seen, in the nursing infant, the implementation of the incest taboo may be said to begin with weaning, which is also the time when the child is usually banned from the mother's bed and when, in general, he is discouraged from continuing those more intimate forms of physical contact with the mother that she had previously permitted, if not actively encouraged. The diminution, if not cessation, of these intimate forms of bodily contact with the mother during this—the pre-Oedipal—period does not, of course, lead to the extinction of the boy's libidinal desires for her, especially since those desires are intensified when he enters the "phallic" stage of psychosexual development. At the latter stage, therefore, the mother-son incest taboo is implemented in all societies by still other means which (in varying degrees) result in its internalization, i.e., in the acquisition of a motivational disposition on the part of the boy to comply with the prohibition. These means and the process of internalization are conceived of differently by different theorists.

For cognitive theorists, the implementation of the mother-son incest taboo, like the implementation of any other cultural prohibition, is achieved by the usual processes of enculturation, i.e., by verbal instruction, including instruction in the punitive consequences attendant upon its violation. For social learning theorists that kind of instruction is not sufficient to achieve the internalization of the taboo unless it is accompanied by various socialization techniques—techniques of positive and negative reinforcement—which provide the boy with important incentives for complying with the taboo. Psychoanalytic theorists, who also stress the importance of socialization, emphasize the signal importance of castration anxiety as the motivational basis for compliance with the taboo. As they see it, the threats (negative reinforcement) which are used to sever his incestuous attachment to the mother lead to the son's fantasized expectation of castration as the punishment for incest with the mother.

Whether it is achieved by the one means or the other, if the implementation of the incest taboo leads to its internalization, compliance with the taboo is achieved either by the extinction of the boy's incestuous desire for his mother or by its repression, the latter often being accompanied by a reaction formation against the desire, i.e., by an emotional aversion to sexual contact with the mother. In sum, if the taboo is internalized, the boy's incestuous attachment to the mother either disappears entirely (extinction) or, although persisting unconsciously (repression), disappears from conscious awareness. Why the internalization of the taboo results in the one consequence rather than the other is a question concerning which there are many, but few satisfactory, answers.

Extinction and repression, however, are not the only possible outcomes of the incestuous attachment to the mother. If, for example, the implementation of the incest taboo by any of the processes mentioned above is only partially successful in promoting its internalization, the son's libidinal attachment to the mother is not extinguished, and although it may be repressed, it undergoes only weak or incomplete repression. In Bengal, for example, mother and son—so Roy (1975:125) observes—remain "highly cathected libidinal objects [for] . . . a lifetime." (For other parts of India, see also Carstairs 1956 and Kakar 1978.) Similarly, the typical male in the Mexican town of San Juan, according to Hunt (1971:129), "has never been able to transfer his libidinal energies from his mother to an outsider," thereby manifesting a "typical Mediterranean pattern." (For other parts of Mexico, see also Bushnell 1958.) That such an outcome is a "Mediterranean pattern" is readily discerned, for example, from Parson's (1969) description of the mother-son relationship in Italy (Naples). The same pattern is also found, however, in East Asia. In Japan, for example, as Tanaka (1981:16) observes, the mother-son relationship is characterized by the "continuous presence of unresolved libidinality." In many societies in which the incestuous attachment to the mother is incompletely repressed, other means than those mentioned above are used for the implementation of the incest taboo, as we shall see below.

Let us first, however, turn from the incestuous attachment to the mother to comment briefly on the possible outcomes of the boy's hostility to the father, the other dimension of the Oedipus complex. Since, as we have seen, the boy's hostility to the father sustains a correlative relationship with his love for the mother, the outcome of his Oedipal hostility is systematically related to the outcome of his Oedipal love. In short, it is the entire Oedipus complex whose outcome may variously take the form of extinction, repression, or incomplete repression.

While all three outcomes may be found in a single society, as we know from clinical evidence in the West, it is usually the case (as I have been suggesting) that one of them is dominant. Since, however, the dominant outcome (as I have also been suggesting) is not the same in all societies, we may now say that this—the second dimension—of the

Oedipus complex is cross-culturally variable not only in principle but in fact.

Although of some interest in itself, the cross-cultural variability in the outcome of the Oedipus complex is anthropologically important because its outcome has social and cultural consequences. Since, then, the differences in the psychological characteristics of these three outcomes are nontrivial, the differences in their variable social and cultural consequences are likewise nontrivial. The latter differences are especially marked when we compare societies in which extinction and repression are the dominant outcomes with those in which incomplete repression is dominant.

Operationally defined, a "weak" or "incomplete" repression of the Oedipus complex is one in which repression is insufficiently powerful to preclude the conscious arousal of the boy's incestuous wishes for the mother (and hence his hostile wishes toward the father) under conditions of incestuous temptation. Hence, those societies in which incomplete repression is the dominant outcome of the Oedipus complex are societies in which the implementation of the taboos on mother-son incest and father-son aggression by the enculturation and socialization techniques described above is not entirely successful in achieving their internalization. This being the case, rather than relying on the boy's own psychological resources—extinction, repression, and reaction formation—to ensure compliance with those taboos, many of those societies achieve compliance by means of social and cultural resources, as well.

In short, so far as their social and cultural consequences are concerned, the first notable difference between societies in which extinction and repression are the dominant outcome of the Oedipus complex and those in which incomplete repression is its dominant outcome, is that the latter societies (much more often than the former) practice child extrusion and painful initiation rites. These customs ensure compliance with the twin Oedipal prohibitions by reducing the opportunities for incestuous and aggressive temptation or by strengthening the incomplete repression of the boy's sexual and aggressive Oedipal wishes. Let us briefly examine each of these customs, beginning with child extrusion.

When boys—and in some societies, girls too—are extruded from the parental household, their subsequent residence, as the cross-cultural record indicates, is highly variable. It may be an age-graded dormitory, a men's house, a children's village, some other household, a boarding school, or the like. Whatever the conscious motives for these practices may be—depending on the society, they include the reduction of the son's rivalry with the father (Wilson 1949; Spiro 1958), the prevention of his witnessing the primal scene (Elwin 1968), economic apprenticeship (Aries 1962), educational advancement (Gathorne-Hardy 1977), the economic advantage of adoption (Powell 1957), and others—they have the consequence (among others) of separating the son from his parents, thereby reducing the opportunities for the arousal of his sexual and aggressive Oedipal wishes. When, at some later age, more frequent interaction with the parents is once again resumed, his libidinal and aggressive impulses have typically been re-channeled. Son extrusion in human societies has its analogue, it will be recalled, in the peripheralization of male juveniles in primate societies. By the latter process, the juveniles are deprived of the opportunity of acting upon their sexual and aggressive impulses toward their mothers and adult males, respectively.

The second consequence of the incomplete repression of the Oedipus complex—which, like the first, constitutes a cultural resource for enhancing the compliance with the taboos on mother-son incest and father-son aggression—is the practice of painful initiation rites. Although the conscious, culturally constituted explanations for these rites only infrequently relate them to the Oedipal issue we have been addressing here, the ethnographic descriptions of these practices and of the initiates' psychological reactions to them provide strong evidence for the thesis that these rites, like child extrusion, constitute an important cultural resource for ensuring compliance with the taboos on incest with the mother and aggression toward the father.[4]

If, however, child extrusion achieves this end by removing the son from the locus of Oedipal sexual and aggressive temptation, initiation rites achieve the same end (according to some theorists at least) by removing these Oedipal wishes from the son. That is, by hazing, isolation, physical torture, ordeals, and phallic mutilation (circumcision, subincision, and superincision), these rites arouse in the boys intense fear and anxiety—often, in my view, castration anxiety—regarding the father and or the father-figure initiators (Fox 1980:159), thereby serving to break the boys' incestuous attachment to their mothers (Hiatt 1971:81) and inhibit their aggression to their fathers. In sum, these rites, I am suggesting, serve to strengthen the (incomplete) repression of the boys' Oedipal (sexual and aggressive) wishes, and in some cases they might perhaps lead to their extinction. That these painful and often brutal rites also provide a culturally sanctioned (and ritually lim-

4. For four superb descriptions of these rites and of the emotional reactions of the initiates in New Guinea, I especially recomment Herdt (1980, 1982), Poole (1982), Read (1965), and Tuzin (1980).

ited) opportunity for men to express their complementary Oedipal hostility to boys—rationalized, of course, by the ideology of helping them achieve social and cultural maturity—seems equally obvious, as Reik ([1919]1946) suggested some years ago.

I must hasten to say, however, that an Oedipal interpretation of these rites not only is *not* obvious to other commentators, but has typically been rejected by anthropologists (see Langness 1974) and psychoanalysts (see Lidz and Lidz 1977) alike. Since I believe that rituals, like most other cultural activities, have multiple meanings, I have little difficulty in accepting most of the sociological and psychological meanings that other commentators have attributed to these rites. But I have great difficulty in ignoring their Oedipal and complementary Oedipal meanings, which, in the light of recent descriptions (see footnote 4), are just too blatant to overlook. Indeed, from these descriptions I would argue that societies which practice initiation rites of the ferocity found in—and perhaps confined to—New Guinea and Australia are societies in which the incomplete repression of the childhood Oedipus complex is most pronounced.

As an illustration of their "blatant" Oedipal and complementary meanings, consider Herdt's (1982) description of the boy's initiation rite among the Sambia of Papua New Guinea. The first stage of the rite, which consists of forcible nose-bleeding, administered by the men on boys of seven to ten years, is a "violent assault whose effects are probably close to producing authentic trauma," the boys themselves referring to their fright by such expressions as "'I feared they were going to kill me.'" If the boys resist the men and cry, as they often do, the men "have little pity" for them, and they are "severely dealt with by prolonging the action and thereby brutalizing it." Herdt is hardly exaggerating in calling it "an act of raw aggression." Similarly, in the third stage, performed for boys thirteen to sixteen, a line of warriors, appearing as ghosts and enemies, surround them and, plucking bows and arrows, hooting, and shouting, they again forcibly nose-bleed the boys, who are now in a state of "terror."

That this aggression both gratifies the complementary Oedipal complex of the men and is intended to contain the Oedipal wishes of the boys is indicated by Herdt's comments. Nose-bleeding is described by the Sambia as "punishment" for the boys for their insubordination to their fathers and elders. That this insubordination includes Oedipal insubordination is reflected both in the warning given the boys that they may never again so much as touch, hold, talk with, eat with, or look at their mothers and in the conscious and unconscious symbolic equation of nose and penis in Sambia thought and culture. Because of their early and exclusive attachment to them, Herdt comments, the boys "must be traumatically detached from their mothers and kept away from them at all costs." In later stages of the rite, those following puberty, references to the mother drop out, and, instead, the boys are admonished by the initiators to avoid other women, especially married women; should they disobey, they are warned, they will be killed. Indeed, beginning with the separation of the boys from their mothers at the first stage of the initiation rite until their marriage following the last stage, males are never again alone with a woman, and throughout that period ritual aggression is used by the older males to "instill [in them] fear and obedience" so that their avoidance of females will be maintained.

Although the Sambia begin their first stage of initiation in early childhood, it is important to note that there are important cross-cultural differences in the age at which these rites, as well as child extrusion, occur. In some societies they take place in childhood, in others not until puberty. Insofar, then, as these customs are (among other things) cultural resources for the implementation of the taboos on mother-son incest and father-son aggression, it may perhaps be assumed that those societies in which they do not take place until puberty are societies in which the boy's repression of his incestuous and aggressive wishes, though incomplete, is sufficiently strong to prevent them from passing through the repressive barrier throughout childhood, and that it is only at puberty, with the eruption of his sexual urges, that his own psychological resources are inadequate to that task. If that assumption is correct, it then follows that, conversely, those societies in which these cultural resources are already brought into play in childhood are societies in which the boy's psychological resources for coping with his Oedipal wishes are inadequate from the very beginning.

Whether the one or the other, however, if the Oedipus complex is incompletely repressed in childhood, there is a special urgency for containing the boy's Oedipal wishes either before or at the time he reaches puberty, for it is then that he is physiologically capable of acting upon his sexual wishes and physically capable of acting upon his aggressive wishes. That is the time, in short, by which it is especially urgent that cultural resources be brought into play either to strengthen the incomplete repression of his Oedipal wishes (painful initiation rites) or to reduce his opportunities for acting upon them (extrusion).

If, then, son extrusion and painful initiation are most likely to be practiced in societies in which the Oedipus complex is incompletely repressed, and least likely in those which exhibit the two other outcomes, we can now see that differences in the outcome of the Oedipus complex have other important consequences as well. Since, for example, societies in which the Oedipus complex is extinguished or fully repressed are unlikely to practice child extrusion, the family is more likely to remain an intact residential group than in those in which, as a consequence of the incomplete repression of the Oedipus complex, the son is extruded from the household. But not all intact family households are the same; among other things they vary importantly in their emotional texture. Thus, the emotional texture of the family in which the Oedipus complex is extinguished and in which, therefore, children can live together with parents in emotional comfort, without suffering intrapsychic conflicts regarding their sexual and aggressive Oedipal wishes, is very different from the emotional texture of the family in which the Oedipus complex is repressed and in which, therefore, the integrity of the family household is purchased at the cost of persistent unconscious struggles with Oedipal wishes. These differences, of course, are much more pronounced during puberty than during childhood.

Differences of another type distinguish societies which, because of incomplete repression of the Oedipus complex, practice painful initiation rites from those which, because of its extinction or full repression, have no need to practice them. Thus, in many tribal societies, initiation rites can be of unimaginable complexity, extending over a period of many years, and consuming a large proportion of their social and economic resources. Indeed, in many of these societies—most notably those of New Guinea—these rites may be said to dominate the lives of the members of the group, constituting the main focus of their interests and action (see Herdt 1980; Read 1965; Tuzin 1980). A funnel for so many social and economic resources, and for so much emotional energy, a cultural focus of this type has still other consequences. For example, it significantly limits the options of these societies for choosing alternative (and perhaps more productive) cultural means for the investment of emotional energy and the allocation of social and economic resources. Moreover, inasmuch as a cultural focus of this type is both a highly elaborated magical response to unconscious wishes and fears, as well as a stimulus for the arousal of still others, it may serve to reinforce the skewed ratio of magical to realistic thinking found in many of these tribal societies. If so, this would account not only for the high proportion of magical (alternatively, primary-process, prelogical, animistic) thinking that, in my view, is one of their singular psychological characteristics, but also for their seeming inability to evolve an alternative cultural focus (or foci) based on realistic (alternatively, secondary-process, logical, nonanimistic) thinking.

There are, of course, many other social and cultural consequences attendant upon the variability in the outcome of the Oedipus complex which, since their explication would require a separate book, can only be mentioned here. Thus, in societies in which unconscious Oedipal conflicts require persistent repression for their containment, the Oedipus complex may undergo structural transformations as a result of defensively motivated projections and displacements which important-ly affect other social relationships and institutions. That, indeed, is Jones's (1925) contention regarding the boy's hostility toward the mother's brother in the Trobriands, which, so he argues, represents the displacement of his Oedipal hostility for his father. Gough (1953) interprets the nephew's hostility toward the mother's brother among the Nayar in the same manner.[5]

Kin relationships, however, are not the only social relationships in which repressed Oedipal conflicts are projected and displaced. Politi-cal (Lasswell 1960), religious (Erikson 1958), and economic (Brown 1959) institutions, to mention only a few, constitute some of the larger social arenas for the symbolic expression of a repressed Oedipus com-plex. Thus, to advert to its hostility dimension, rebellious attitudes toward authority figures often have their psychodynamic source in re-pressed Oedipal hostility, the former being a vehicle for the displace-ment or sublimation of the latter (see Erikson 1963; Feuer 1969; Rothman and Lichter 1982). The same process occurs in regard to the sexual dimension of the Oedipus complex. Thus, for example, the strong male involvement in the Marian cult in southern Italy (Parsons 1969) and Mexico (Bushnell 1958) is often interpreted as a sublimation of the repressed Oedipal attachment to the mother.

Since religion (because, perhaps, of its frequent use of family idi-oms) like politics (for the same reason) is an especially important cul-tural domain for the expression of repressed Oedipal conflicts, it might be added that other differences between societies in which the Oedi-pus complex is repressed in contrast to those in which it is extinguished may also be seen in such diverse religious phenomena as ritual circum-cision and clitoridectomy, ascetic abstinences and self-torture, sexu-alized goddesses and witches, celibate priests and priestesses, mystical and trance states, and many others.

Although further examples would require a monograph, this brief discussion has perhaps been sufficient to suggest that the continuing

5. Structural transformations in the initial formation of the Oedipus complex are also found in its symbolic expression in myth, as Paul (1980) has shown in his perceptive analysis of the hostility dimension of the Oedipus complex in Greek, Judaic, and Chris-tian Oedipal myths.

debates over the Oedipus complex are debates not merely about a passing episode in the psychological development of the child. Rather, they are debates about a psychological constellation which, as this discussion has attempted to show, has pervasive cultural, social, and psychological consequences.

The Making of a Scientific Myth

In the previous two sections I argued that although the universality of the Oedipus complex is rendered highly likely by the child's potentiality for sexual and aggressive arousal, inasmuch as the intensity and distribution of sexual and aggressive wishes are each a product of the social relationships that the child sustains with those adults who constitute his "significant others," in principle we would expect to find cross-cultural variability in the Oedipus complex as a function of the variability in those relationships. That this expectation is most probably actualized, however, in regard only to the intensity and outcome, but not the structure, of the Oedipus complex is not surprising. Since the classical Oedipal triangle—consisting of mother, father, and son—is determined by the twin facts that the child's early mothering figure is the first and most important object of his sexual wishes, and that his perceived rival for her love is the consequent object of his hostility, cross-cultural variability in this structure would be expected if, but only if, there were some range of variability in the social recruitment to the mothering role. Since at the *societal* level, however, it is the biological mother who is the child's central (if not exclusive) early mothering figure, and the biological father his most salient rival for her love in all known societies, it is understandable that the structure of the Oedipus complex, although cross-culturally variable in principle, is most probably invariant in fact.

This, of course, brings us back to our point of departure, the controversy over the Trobriand Oedipus complex. For the very nub of Malinowski's contention that the structure of the nuclear complex (as he preferred to put it)[6] is culturally variable not only in principle, but also in fact, consists of his claim that although the biological mother is the primary mothering figure in the Trobriands, it is the sister who is the primary object of the boy's libidinal desires. Since that paradoxical

---

6. Since, for Malinowski, the Oedipus complex is a cultural product, he used "nuclear complex" as a cover term for all possible cultural variants, reserving "Oedipus complex" for that particular variant in which mother and father are the objects, respectively, of the child's sexual and aggressive impulses.

claim has already been shown to be refuted by Malinowski's own evidence, there is no need to repeat that demonstration. Rather, in this final section, I wish to address the remarkable fact that this paradoxical claim has been accepted with almost no skepticism or critical inquiry for fifty years.

Given the powerful evidence for the universality of the motivational disposition to mother-son incest, if it were reported that in some society the mother is not an incestuous object for the son, such a report would, of course, be rather surprising. But since the history of science is a history of persistent refutations of well-established generalizations, there would be no reason to greet such a report with special skepticism. In claiming, therefore, that it is a "remarkable fact" that Malinowski's report of such a finding in the Trobriands has not been greeted with sufficient skepticism, it is not because that report challenges an established generalization, but because in the context of Trobriand culture the absence of an incestuous attachment to the mother is twice anomalous.

The first anomaly consists in the fact that of the three types of incestuous desire that might, in principle, be found in any male, the desire of the son for the mother is, alone, reported to be absent in the Trobriands, while that of the father for the daughter is reported to be as strong as it is purported to be in the West, and that of the brother for the sister stronger by far. This gestalt is all the more anomalous since typically the boy's incestuous attachment to the mother is, if anything, much stronger than the other two; and it becomes still more anomalous when it is recalled that the incestuous attachment of the Trobriand daughter to the father, unlike that of the son to the mother, is reported to be of normally expected Oedipal intensity.

In claiming that because it is anomalous Malinowski's report should have been greeted with skepticism, I am by no means suggesting that its truth or accuracy should therefore have been impugned. If "anomaly" is glossed as "puzzle," and if we follow Kuhn (1962:chapter 4) in viewing science as a puzzle-solving enterprise, then, rather than impugning the accuracy of an anomalous finding, scientific skepticism merely signals the existence of yet another puzzle to be solved. In the case of this Trobriand puzzle, one simple solution immediately suggests itself. Since, as has already been observed, it is their physical and emotional intimacy that accounts for the son's incestuous attachment to the mother, part of the Trobriand puzzle would be solved if it were the case that the most intimate relationship of the young boy is with some woman (or women) other than the biological mother. If, moreover, it were also the case that this structural arrangement did not affect the relationship of the male to either his sister or his daughter, the other parts of the puzzle would be solved, as well, and the skepticism could be laid to rest.

Unfortunately, however, the ethnographic facts are the very opposite of this proposed solution. As we have seen, all the conditions that highlight the mother-son relationship as the primary arena for the boy's most intense incestuous struggles in the "normally expectable" family are present in the Trobriands as well—and then some! In short, there is nothing in Malinowski's account that might solve the puzzle of why it is that in a family and socialization system of the Trobriand type the sister and daughter are the objects of the male's incestuous desires, whereas the mother is not. That, indeed, is why I characterized Malinowski's claim as anomalous.

Perhaps, however, the solution to this anomaly might be found by taking another tack. For just as the problem of inflation can be tackled from either the supply or the demand side of the market, the solution to an ethnographically anomalous finding can sometimes be found not in an antecedent, but in a consequent condition. Specifically, if the reported absence of a normally expectable incestuous attachment to the mother were accompanied by the absence of a normally expectable mother-son incest taboo, the former report would not then constitute an anomaly (although the absence of such an attachment would still have to be explained by some as yet unknown, and theoretically unexpected, antecedent condition). Unfortunately, the ethnographic reality is once again the reverse of the proposed solution: the mother-son incest taboo is, in fact, present in the Trobriands. Moreover, the presence of this taboo not only leaves the anomaly unresolved, but creates yet another: if the boy has no incestuous desire for the mother, why should there be a taboo prohibiting incest with her? This second anomaly, of course, could be resolved by simply rejecting the assumption on which it is based, viz., that taboos exist to prevent the practice of the tabooed actions. But that requires at least a brief discussion of the historical debates regarding incest taboos.

It was Frazer ([1887] 1910:vol. 4, p. 97 ff.) who first converted the above assumption about the function of taboos into the generally accepted theory of incest taboos. Since, following from that assumption, the function of incest taboos is the prevention of incest with their stipulated targets, the existence of these taboos, so Frazer argued, implies the existence of incestuous desire for those very targeted persons.[7]

---

7. Why it is that all societies have wanted to prevent incest at least within the nuclear family is a question that has been variously answered, but all the proposed

This theory, however, has had its opponents from its very inception. Most of them, following Westermarck's ([1906–8] 1924:vol. 2, p. 368) view that sexual aversion develops between family members who live in proximity to each other from an early age, argue that incest taboos are merely the institutionalized expression of sexual aversions.

Although the acceptance of this theory would resolve the anomaly of the reported co-occurrence in the Trobriands of a mother-son incest taboo and the absence of an incestuous desire for the mother, there are powerful grounds for rejecting it as invalid. One could point, for example, to the evidence in support of the motivational disposition to nuclear family incest which was summarized earlier in this chapter. Again, one could point to Lindzey's reformulation of Frazer's hypothesis in terms of the adaptive framework of evolutionary biology, a reformulation which, in my view, is unimpeachable. "It seems unlikely that there would have been universal selection in favor of such a taboo if there were not widespread impulses toward expression of the prohibited act" (Lindzey 1967:1055). Rather, however, than evoking these general empirical and theoretical grounds in refutation of Westermarck's theory, it is enough—and in this context much more relevant—to refute it on specific Trobriand grounds.

The latter grounds consist of evidence that proclaims loudly and clearly that at least some Trobrianders who live in close propinquity develop strong sexual feelings for each other, rather than sexual aversion. That is how Malinowski, at any rate, describes the relationship between brothers and sisters in the Trobriands, and (to a lesser degree) between fathers and daughters. At the same time there are taboos in the Trobriands which both prohibit—and (as Malinowski makes quite clear) are intended to prevent—incest between the members of these dyads. For the Trobriands, then, there can be no doubt about the functional relationship between incestuous desires and incest taboos, so far at least as these two dyads are concerned. Hence, for the Trobriands the co-occurrence of the mother-son incest taboo and the absence of incestuous desires for her is clearly an anomaly, not because it violates a (disputed) theoretical assumption, but because in the Trobriand cultural configuration their co-occurence is incongruous.

---

answers point to one or more of the following maladaptive consequences of the widespread practice of nuclear family incest which are precluded by compliance with incest taboos: (1) biological impairment attendant upon inbreeding (see Lindzey 1967), (2) collapse of the family authority structure, because of the sexual rivalry between father and son, with the attendant difficulty of cultural transmission (see Malinowski [1927] 1955:216), (3) structural breakdown of the family attendant upon role confusion (see Parsons 1954), (4) breakdown of social alliances attendant upon family endogamy (see Lévi-Strauss [1949] 1969:chapters 4 and 29).

If, however, it were still contended that this finding is not anomalous—because the anomaly now derives from merely another theoretical assumption, that of pattern consistency—this contention would convert an unresolved anomaly into an unresolved dilemma. For if it were held, on the one hand, that the taboo on incest with the mother does not imply the existence of incestuous wishes for her, what possible explanation might then be offered for the taboos on incest with the sister and daughter which, in fact, do correspond to known incestuous wishes for them? And if it were held, on the other hand, that the taboos on sister and daughter incest are explained by known incestuous wishes for them, how could it then be contended that it is invalid to infer the existence of incestuous wishes for the mother from the taboo prohibiting incest with her?

Malinowski, himself a leading proponent of Frazer's theory of incest taboos, was keenly aware of this dilemma, and, it will be recalled, he attempted to resolve it by holding to both of its horns. That is, while he held that incest taboos are valid measures of incestuous wishes, he also held that in the Trobriands the taboo on mother-son incest is "weak." Hence, he argued, just as the strong incestuous desire for the sister in the Trobriands is reflected in a "strong" brother-sister taboo, the weak desire for the mother is reflected in a "weak" mother-son taboo. Unfortunately, however, the facts (see above) are otherwise: there is simply no evidence for the putative weakness—whether absolute or relative—of the mother-son taboo. In short, despite Malinowski's attempt to resolve it, the second anomaly in his reported absence of an incestuous attachment to the mother in the Trobriands remains—like the first—unresolved.

The fact, then, that neither of these anomalies can be resolved—or, to put it more cautiously, that neither has been resolved thus far—must surely constitute sufficient reason to be skeptical of the report that the Trobriand son has no incestuous attachment to the mother. That this report, then, has not received the skeptical reception that normally greets an anomalous scientific report is not only, as I said above, a remarkable fact, but one which itself constitutes an intriguing intellectual problem. Since its solution could shed important light on the influence of scientific paradigms on the acceptance and persistence of scientific ideas, it is to be hoped that an investigation of the problem might some day be undertaken by an intellectual historian or a historian of science.

Although the causes for the unskeptical reaction to this anomalous report are still to be discovered, its consequence—with some notable exceptions—has been an uncritical acceptance of the putative Trobriand matrilineal complex. I would suggest, then, that if this report had been subjected to the probing scrutiny to which anomalous scientific findings are usually subject, the matrilineal complex would have been rejected as empirically unsupported rather than achieving the status of an incontrovertible finding of anthropological science. Nevertheless, it is not its weak empirical foundation that led me to characterize the Trobriand matrilineal complex a "scientific myth." This characterization stems, rather, from the uncritical acceptance of the reported finding—the absence of an incestuous attachment to the mother—on which its plausibility hangs, despite the fact that this finding is not only once, but twice, anomalous.

A myth, Malinowski taught us, enjoys uncritical acceptance because it serves important functions for those who believe it to be true. It would be well, therefore, if our hoped-for historian were to address yet another question in the course of his investigations: what functions might have been served by the acceptance of *this* myth? Indeed, since the role of the "will to believe" in the acceptance of scientific ideas is as prominent as the role that William James attributed to it in the acceptance of religious doctrines, it is entirely possible that the answer to this second question might simultaneously provide the answer to the first.

References

Aries, Philippe. 1962. *Centuries of childhood.* New York: Alfred Knopf.

Bettelheim, Bruno. 1969. *The children of the dream.* London: Macmillan.

Bischof, Norbert. 1975. Comparative ethology of incest avoidance. In *Biosocial anthropology,* ed. Robin Fox. London: Malaby Press.

Brown, Norman O. 1959. *Life against death.* Middletown: Wesleyan University Press.

Bushnell, John. 1958. La Virgen de Guadalupe as surrogate mother in San Juan Atzingo. *American Anthropologist* 60:261–65.

Buxbaum, Edith. 1970. *Troubled children in a troubled world.* New York: International Universities Press.

Campbell, Donald T., and Raoul Naroll. 1972. The mutual methodological relevance of anthropology and psychology. In *Psychological anthropology,* ed. Francis L. K. Hsu. Cambridge, Mass.: Schenkman Publishing Company.

Carpenter, C. R. 1940. A field study in Siam of the behavior and social relations of the Gibbon (*Hylobatis lar*). *Comparative Psychology Monographs* 16:1–212.

Carstairs, G. Morris. 1956. *The twice born.* Bloomington: Indiana University Press.

Chance, Michael R. H., and Clifford J. Jolly. 1970. *Social groups of monkeys, apes, and men.* New York: Dutton.

Demarest, William J. 1977. Incest avoidance in human and nonhuman primates. In *Primate bio-social development,* ed. Suzanne Chevalier-Skolnikoff and Frank E. Poirier. New York: Garland Publishing.

Elwin, Verrier. 1968. *The kingdom of the young.* Oxford: Oxford University Press.

Erikson, Erik H. 1958. *Young man Luther.* New York: W. W. Norton.

———. 1963. *Childhood and society.* New York: W. W. Norton.

Feuer, Lewis S. 1969. *The conflict of generations.* New York: Basic Books.

Fox, Robin. 1980. *The red lamp of incest.* New York: Dutton.

Frazer, James George. 1910. *Totemism and exogamy* [1887]. London: Macmillan.

Gathorne-Hardy, Jonathan. 1977. *The public school phenomenon, 597–1977.* London: Hodder and Stoughton.

Gough, E. Kathleen. 1953. Female initiation rites on the Malabar coast. *Journal of the Royal Anthropological Society* 85:45–80.

Herdt, Gilbert H. 1980. *Guardians of the flutes: Idioms of masculinity.* New York: McGraw-Hill.

———. 1982. Fetish and fantasy in Sambia initiation. In *Rituals of manhood,* ed. Gilbert H. Herdt. Berkeley: University of California Press.

Hiatt, L. R. 1971. Secret pseudo-procreation rites among the Australian aborigines. In *Anthropology in Oceania,* ed. L. R. Hiatt and C. Jayawardena. San Francisco: Chandler.

Hopkins, Keith. 1980. Brother-sister marriage in Roman Egypt. *Comparative Studies in Society and History* 22:303–54.

Hunt, Robert C. 1971. Component of relationships in the family: A Mexican village. In *Kinship and culture,* ed. Francis L. K. Hsu. Chicago: Aldine.

Jones, Ernest. 1925. Mother-right and the sexual ignorance of savages. *International Journal of Psychoanalysis* 6:109–30.

Justice, Blair, and Rita Justice. 1979. *The broken taboo.* New York: Human Sciences Press.

Kaffman, Mordecai. 1977. Sexual standards and behavior of the kibbutz adolescent. *American Journal of Orthopsychiatry* 47:207–17.

Kakar, Sudhir. 1978. *The inner world.* Delhi: Oxford University Press.

Kuhn, Thomas S. 1962. *The structure of scientific revolutions.* Chicago: University of Chicago Press.

Kummer, Hans. 1968. *Social organization of Hamadryas baboons.* Chicago: University of Chicago Press.

Lancaster, Jane B. 1979. Sex and gender in evolutionary perspective. In *Human sexuality: A comparative and developmental perspective,* ed. Herant A. Katchadorurian. Berkeley: University of California Press.

Langness, L. L. 1974. Ritual power and male domination in the New Guinea highlands. *Ethos* 2:189–212.

Lasswell, Harold D. 1960. *Psychopathology and politics.* New York: Viking.

Lévi-Strauss, Claude. 1969. *The elementary structures of kinship* [1949]. London: Eyre and Spottiswoode.

Lidz, Ruth W., and Theodore Lidz. 1977. Male menstruation: A ritual alternative to the Oedipal transition. *International Journal of Psychoanalysis* 58:17–31.

Lindzey, Gardner. 1967. Some remarks concerning incest, the incest taboo, and psychoanalytic theory. *American Psychologist* 22:1051–59.

Malinowski, Bronislaw. 1955. *Sex and repression in savage society* [1927]. New York: Meridian Books (*SR*).

Money, John. 1980. *Love and love sickness*. Baltimore: Johns Hopkins University Press.

Parsons, Anne. 1969. *Belief, magic, and anomie*. New York: Free Press.

Parsons, Talcott. 1954. The incest taboo in relation to social structure and the socialization of the child. *British Journal of Sociology* 5:101–17.

Paul, Robert A. 1980. Symbolic interpretations in psychoanalysis and anthropology. *Ethos* 8:286–94.

Poole, Fitz John Porter. 1982. The ritual forging of identity: Aspects of person and self in Bimin-Kuskusmin male initiation. In *Rituals of manhood*, ed. Gilbert H. Herdt. Berkeley: University of California Press.

Powell, H. A. 1957. *Analysis of present-day social structure in the Trobriands*. Ph.D. Dissertation, University of London.

Rainwater, Lee, and William L. Yancey. 1967. *The Moynihan report and the politics of controversy*. Cambridge: MIT Press.

Read, Kenneth E. 1965. *The high valley*. New York: Scribners.

Reik, Theodore. 1946. *Ritual: Four psychoanalytic studies* [1919]. New York: Grove Press.

Rothman, Stanley, and S. Lichter. 1982. *The radical impulse*. New York: Oxford.

Rowell, Thelma E. 1972. Female reproduction cycles and social behavior in females. *Advances in the Study of Behavior* 4:69–105.

Roy, Manisha. 1975. *Bengali women*. Chicago: University of Chicago Press.

Shepher, Joseph. 1971. Mate selection among second generation kibbutz adolescents and adults: Incest avoidance and negative imprinting. *Archives of Sexual Behavior* 1:293–307.

Smith, Raymond T. 1956. *The negro family in British Guiana: Family structure and social status in the villages*. London: Routledge and Kegan Paul.

Spiro, Melford E. 1958. *Children of the kibbutz*. Cambridge: Harvard University Press.

———. 1982. *Oedipus in the Trobriands*. Chicago: University of Chicago Press.

Talmon, Yonina. 1964. Mate selection on collective settlements. *American Sociological Review* 29:491–508.

Tanaka, Masako. 1981. *"Maternal" authority in the Japanese family*. Paper presented for the International Symposium on Religion and the Family in East Asia, National Museum of Ethnology, Osaka, August 30–September 7, 1981.

Tuzin, Donald F. 1980. *The voice of the Tambaran*. Berkeley: University of California Press.

Westermarck, Edward. 1924–26. *The origin and development of the moral ideas* [1906–8]. London: Macmillan.

Wilson, Edward O. 1978. *On human nature*. Cambridge: Harvard University Press.

Wilson, Monica. 1949. Nyakyusa age villages. *Journal of the Royal Anthropological Institute* 79:21–25.

Wolf, Arthur P. 1966. Childhood association, sexual attraction, and the incest taboo: A Chinese case. *American Anthropologist* 68:893–98.

————. 1968. Adopt a daughter-in-law, marry a sister: A Chinese solution to the incest taboo. *American Anthropologist* 70:864–94.

————. 1970. Childhood association and sexual attraction: A further test of the Westermarck hypothesis. *American Anthropologist* 72:503–15.

Wolf, Arthur P., and Chich-Shan Huang. 1980. *Marriage and adoption in China, 1845–1945*. Stanford: Stanford University Press.

II FUNCTIONAL ANALYSIS

5   Social Systems, Personality, and Functional Analysis

Introduction

WHEN ANTHROPOLOGY was primarily interested in culture history, the question of how societies get their members to behave in conformity with cultural norms was of small concern. But when anthropology became interested in the problem of how societies operate, this question became—and has remained—salient, not only for culture-and-personality theorists but for other anthropologists as well. "Our great problem as anthropologists," says Firth, is ". . . to translate the acts of individuals into the regularities of social process" (1954: 11).

Since social systems are attributes of society and personality systems are attributes of individuals, it was formerly assumed, both by anthropologists and by psychologists, that there was little relationship between "the acts of individuals" and the "regularities of social process." Before the development of culture-and-personality studies, this assumption seemed reasonable. First, although there is but one social system for a society, there are as many personalities as there are members of society. Secondly, since social systems are normative, their constituent activities are prescribed; but since personality systems are conative, their activities are motivated. Finally, social systems serve social functions, while personalities serve individual functions. In short, although the functions of social systems are served by the activities of individuals, these activities were not seen as serving personal functions. Hence, older theories of cultural conformity[1] and social control ignored personality as an irrelevant variable.

Reprinted with permission of Harper & Row, Publishers, Inc., from *Studying Personality Cross-Culturally*, edited by Bert Kaplan, pp. 93–127. © 1961 by Harper & Row, Publishers, Inc.
  1. The concept, "cultural conformity," is here taken to mean, behavior which is in

Classical cultural determinism, for example, attributed efficient causation to the cultural heritage—people perform this or that activity of the social system "because it's part of their culture." Although this theory represents an advance over still older biologistic theories, it begs the very question which is to be answered. As Nadel has put it: ". . . little is gained [in the study of social control] by adducing the force of custom and tradition, that is, the sheer inertia of habitual behavior and inherited practice" (1953:266). The mere existence of a cultural heritage does not imply that it will be inherited; or, if inherited, that behavior will be in conformity with its requirements. The notion that cultural behavior is inherited automatically from the cultural heritage is probably based on a confusion ultimately derived from Tylor's omnibus definition of culture (1874:1). For it would seem that the model upon which the inheritance of cultural behavior is based is the inheritance of, for example, tools, paintings, and houses—all of which are, of course, inherited automatically, without either effort or motivation. Culture behavior, too, is transmitted from a previous generation; but it is inherited by learning, and not merely by being handed down.

Another answer to the problem of cultural conformity is provided by the social sanctions theory. According to this theory, compliance with cultural norms is achieved through positive and negative sanctions— rewards and punishments—which function as techniques of social control. Although the use of sanctions is probably universal, the thesis that cultural conformity is achieved primarily or exclusively through the use of social sanctions rests, at least implicitly, on two demonstrably false assumptions. These are the Rousseauist assumption that culture is necessarily frustrating, and the super-organistic assumption that cultural norms "exist" in the cultural heritage, but are not internalized by the members of society.

---

conformity with cultural norms. Hence, "cultural conformity," as used in this chapter, is to be distinguished from "social conformity," which refers to behavior which is in conformity with the behavior of others. In a fully integrated and relatively unchanging society it would be difficult to distinguish between these two types of conformity: the behavior of others would be more or less identical with the requirements of the cultural heritage. In a somewhat less integrated and rapidly changing society (such as our own) the distinction between these two types of conformity is clearer; Riesman's (1950) other-directed individuals, for example, represent social conformity rather than (or more than) cultural conformity. In either case, though it might be difficult to distinguish between these types of conformity in overt behavioral terms, it is not at all difficult to distinguish between them in motivational terms. Social conformity is motivated by the desire to conform to the behavior of others; cultural conformity, by the desire to conform to cultural norms. Cultural conformity, as we shall attempt to show, is a requisite for the functioning of human social systems, whereas social conformity is not.

Agreeing with the first, but disagreeing with the second of the above two assumptions, a third theory of cultural conformity views compliance with cultural norms as a function, primarily, of their internalization within personality. Although cultural norms are, indeed, internalized, and although conscience does play an important part in achieving cultural conformity, this theory too is but a partial theory for, as we shall attempt to show, social control is frequently achieved without the necessity for norm internalization.

Culture-and-personality studies suggest that though there is a large measure of truth in these theories, cultural conformity is most frequently achieved because social systems satisfy personality needs. This chapter, then, will attempt to show that there is an intimate relationship between social systems and personality: social systems operate by means of personality, and personality functions by means of social systems. Many of the social functions of social systems can be served only when this intimate relationship obtains.

Human Social Systems: The Problem

Unlike other social animals, the social system of any particular human society cannot be predicted from a knowledge of the species (*Homo sapiens*) of which the society is a member. Nevertheless, since human social systems are rooted in man's biological nature, any discussion of the generic attributes of these systems must take its departure from certain biological dimensions of human existence. From a comparative biological perspective a human social system may be viewed as a functional requirement of human life. Ultimately it stems from the psychobiological needs of what the biologist terms a generalized, fetalized (Bolk 1929), and highly plastic (Montagu 1951:368–75) primate. Here we can only point to the consequences of these biological attributes for human social systems. (But cf. La Barre 1954; Roheim 1943.)

The combination of man's mammalian drives (hunger, sex, etc.) and his plastic hominoid constitution (paucity of instincts) requires that means of drive-reduction be learned. Again, the combination of man's organic needs (protection against weather, predatory beasts, etc.) and his hominoid constitution (generalized and fetalized) requires learned methods of protection and adaptation. Moreover, man's prolonged primate dependency and his primate sexual behavior (lack of a breeding season) combine to produce the relatively permanent biparental family, and—by extension—larger collectivities (societies) consisting of two or more families. In the absence, however, of an instinctual base— shopworn comparisons of human with insect societies (Wheeler 1928) are still much to the point—human social life demands that forms of social interaction, methods of social cooperation, techniques of conflict resolution, and the like be learned. But this is not enough. Social existence is necessarily an orderly and regulated existence. Unless the members of a group are able to predict with some probability far greater than chance the behavior of other members of the group with whom they interact, social action, let alone interaction, would be all but precluded. Hence, man must not only learn the various kinds of behavior patterns mentioned above, but these learned behavior patterns must be prescribed by society and shared with others. The configuration of these socially prescribed, learned, shared and transmitted behavior patterns which mediate and facilitate social relationships constitutes the social system of a human society. We are here only concerned with those characteristics which make social systems necessary for human survival. We are not concerned with those characteristics—a complex brain and central nervous system and the symbolic behavior to which they give rise (White 1940; Mead 1934; Langer 1942; Cassirer 1944; Hallowell 1950)—which make their invention and transmission possible.

To conclude: since man is a generalized, fetalized, and plastic animal and since everywhere he is necessarily social, a typically human existence depends on the existence of socially shared behavior patterns which satisfy his (1) biological needs, (2) those group needs that are an invariant concomitant of social life (Aberle 1950) and (3) those emotional needs that develop in the interaction between biology and society. In this evolutionary perspective a social system may be viewed as an "instrumental apparatus" (Malinowski 1944) for the satisfaction of these needs. Social systems, then, have three types of functions. They promote the physical survival of society and of its constituent members (adaptive functions); they contribute to the persistence of the social structure of a society and, hence, to orderly social interaction (adjustive functions); they promote social solidarity by the reduction of inter- and intra-personal tension (integrative functions).

This is not to say, of course, that all aspects of every social system are functional, or that all social systems are equally functional, or that any social system is functional to the same degree for all the members of, or groups within, a society. The collapse of some social systems, the oppressive means used by powerful groups within a society to preserve others, the repeated history of successful and of unsuccessful rebellions against still others—all these testify to the powerful dysfunctional forces operative in some and potentially in all social systems. But these observations serve to confirm, rather than to confute, the major thesis.

Social systems have vital functions; that these functions be served is their *raison d'être*. If they are not served, to a greater or lesser degree, the social system will, in the long-run, be modified, or the society will not survive.

Before proceeding with this discussion, it is necessary to emphasize an obvious characteristic of human social systems that is frequently obscured by the ambiguity of the word "learned," an ambiguity that sometimes leads to hasty generalizations from small-group experiments to social behavior in society. When it is observed that human social systems, as well as all other aspects of culture, are learned, the word "learned" has one meaning in a phylogenetic, and another in an ontogenetic context. "Learned" in a phylogenetic context means invented or discovered; "learned" in an ontogenetic context means acquired. Thus, the hypothetical *Ur-mensch* of the Paleolithic was, culturally viewed, a *tabula rasa*. The adaptive, adjustive, and integrative requirements of his society had to be satisfied by behavior patterns of his own invention and discovery. Succeeding generations of human societies have also, to be sure, invented and discovered behavior patterns. Their incorporation into the configuration of existing behavior patterns (which comprise their social systems) produces one of the unique dimensions of culture—its cumulativeness. For the most part, however, all generations subsequent to the hypothetical Ur-generation of a society have *acquired* their social systems from a previous generation, rather than inventing or discovering them themselves. In short, the social system of any generation represents, in part, the cultural heritage of the succeeding generation; the social system of the latter, is acquired from the social system of the former.

Social systems, like any other large configuration, can be—and for certain purposes must be—broken down into smaller components. These units, proceeding from the largest to the smallest, are generally termed sub-systems, institutions, roles. Thus, every social system includes an economic system—an organized means for the production, consumption, and distribution of goods and services; a kinship system—an organization of behavior within the family and among kinsmen; a political system—a sanctioned means for the acquisition and use of legitimate power, and so forth. The universality of these subsystems is sometimes referred to as "the universal culture pattern" (Wissler 1923:chap. 5).

Each of these broad categories can usually be classified, in turn, into smaller units. It is rare for any one type of social group within society to perform all the activities which comprise any of these broad subsystems. Thus the kinship system may embrace the activities of nuclear families, lineages and clans; or the economic system may include the activities of trade unions, banks, factories, and accounting firms. In short, since any society is differentiated and, therefore, consists of many types of social groups, and since each type serves different functions, either for its own members or for those of other social groups, each type of group performs different activities. The configuration of activities which characterizes these different types of groups may be termed an "institution." Thus the activities of the members of the family, *qua* family members, may be termed the "family institution"; the activities of the members of the lineage, *qua* lineage members, may be termed the "lineage institution." Since, collectively, these institutions comprise the kinship system of a society, each may be termed a kinship institution.

Although each type of social group within a society is characterized by a different institution, its constituent members do not, *qua* members, perform the same activities. Each type of group, like the entire society of which it is a part, is structurally differentiated so that various members of the group occupy different positions within the group. Within the family, for example, different members may occupy such positions as father, mother, son, or daughter. Since each position ("status") within the group is associated with one (Linton 1936) or more (Merton 1957) sets of activities ("roles"), each institution may be broken down into its constituent roles. Thus the set of activities which comprises the role of father varies from that which comprises the role of mother. Each is a family role; collectively they comprise the family institution. The role, then, is the smallest unit of the social system; the operation of the social system, ultimately and most directly, depends on the proper performance of roles.

To sum up: the survival of a society depends on the operation of its social system; a social system is comprised of subsystems which, in turn, are comprised of institutions; the functions of these institutions are served only if their constituent roles are performed. In turn, this requires the recruitment of individuals for the various statuses which comprise the social structure. If these propositions are valid, we are brought back to the central issue of this chapter—the problem of cultural conformity. How does society induce its members to perform roles—those that are instrumental to the attainment of a status, as well as those that are entailed by the occupancy of a status? (Nadel 1957: chap. 2, has suggested the terms "recruitment roles" and "achievement roles" to refer to these different types of roles.) This problem is best understood against the background of infrahuman societies.

Among lower social animals there is a remarkably high correlation between species and social systems. If the environment is held constant, the description of the social system of one society within a species is more or less descriptive of all other societies within the species. Thus, if one knows the species to which a particular subhuman organism belongs, one can predict with high accuracy and with great detail the social system (assuming that it is social) in which it participates (Hine and Tinbergen 1958; Thompson 1958; Mayr 1958). It is quite meaningful, therefore, to speak of species-specific social systems among lower animals.

But though it is meaningful to speak of the red deer social system (Darling 1937) or the howling monkey social system (Carpenter 1934) it is not at all meaningful, except on the highest level of generality, to speak of *the* human social system. Man differs dramatically from all other social mammals in the great variety of his intraspecies social system differences. Indeed, the magnitude of social system differences within the human species may be as great as the magnitude of difference among animal species. Thus, for example, while the mating pattern of an entire mammalian species may be characterized, and thus distinguished from other species, by monogamy (e.g., gibbons—Carpenter 1940) or polygyny (e.g., baboons—Zuckerman 1932) or group marriage (e.g., howling monkeys—Carpenter 1934), such generalizations apply in the case of humans only to societies within the species and not to the species as a whole. Hence, the fact that one human society practices monogamy, or has patrilineal descent, or is governed by hereditary chiefs, or is stratified by caste, does not enable us to predict that other societies within the species will have the same marriage, descent, political or stratification systems. In short, if one knows that a particular organism belongs to the human species, one cannot predict in any detail the social system in which he participates even if the physical environment is specified. Thus, though paired groups such as California Indians and modern California Americans, precontact Hawaiians and the contemporary inhabitants of Hawaii, Alaskan Eskimos and contemporary modern Alaskans have occupied the same physical environment, their respective social systems are radically different.

It is a reasonable inference, then, that though much of the social behavior of animals is not instinctive (Beach 1955; Lehrman 1953)—as was formerly believed to be the case—so that each generation of social animals may learn a large percentage of its behavior patterns and social roles from a preceding generation, the range of species plasticity is so narrow that any animal has little alternative, if he is to learn at all, but to learn the behavior patterns which he is taught. What he *must* learn in order to participate in his society's social system and what he *can* learn are for the most part identical. Since humans, on the other hand, are highly plastic, what an individual *must* learn in order to participate in the social system of his society is not at all identical with what he *can* learn; for what he is taught represents, as the cross-cultural record clearly reveals, but one alternative among a large number of behavior patterns and roles which he is potentially capable of learning or, at least, of thinking of learning.

Since humans are so enormously plastic it is not enough, if human social systems are to function properly, that social roles and the behavior patterns of which they are comprised be socially learned, shared, and transmitted; it is also necessary that these roles be prescribed (Newcomb 1950:chap. 3). For, since what a person *must* do in order to participate in a given social system is not identical with what he *can* do, it may be inconsistent with what he would *like* to do. Hence in the process of socialization children are not only taught how to behave, but they are taught that the ways in which they are taught to behave are the ways in which they ought to behave. In short, "every human social order," as Hallowell has put it, "operates as a moral order" (1950:169). This normative, or cultural dimension (Spiro 1951:31–36) of the human social system is for humans the functional equivalent of restricted plasticity for lower animals. It is the basis for relatively uniform and, therefore, predictable role behavior. (The psychological basis for the emergence of a moral dimension in experience—the self—is discussed in Hallowell 1954.)

But this analogy cannot be pressed too far, and it is precisely at the point where it breaks down that human societies are uniquely different from animal societies. Since there is always a potential conflict between duty and desire, between cultural heritage and personality, this potentiality—which gives special poignancy to the human situation—sets the problem of our present inquiry: how do human societies get their members to behave in conformity with cultural norms? Or, alternatively, how do they induce their members to perform culturally prescribed roles?

It is at this juncture in the analysis that the concept of personality becomes salient for the understanding of human social systems, for it is in the concept of *role* that personality and social systems intersect. If personality is viewed as an organized system of motivational tendencies, then it may be said to consist, among other things, of needs and drives. Since modes of drive-reduction and need-satisfaction in man must be learned, one of the functions of personality is the promotion of physical survival, interpersonal adjustment, and intrapersonal integration by organizing behavior for the reduction of its drives and the satisfaction of its needs. If some of these needs can then be satisfied by means of culturally prescribed behavior—if, that is, social roles are capable of satisfying personality needs—these needs may serve to motivate the performance of the roles. But if social systems can function only if their constituent roles are performed, then, in motivating the performance of roles, personality not only serves its own functions but it becomes a crucial variable in the functioning of social systems as well. This is the thesis which will be explored in this chapter.

Extrinsic Cultural Motivation

Since role behavior is a subclass of learned behavior we may begin our discussion by asking under what conditions any learned behavior pattern arises. Many—but not all—behavioral scientists[2] seem to agree that behavior occurs when the contemplated action is believed by the actor to be rewarding. An act is performed when a person wants something and when he has reason to expect that the performance of the act will supply his want. A simple ontogenetic model can illustrate how this expectation is established.

The ontogenetic model begins with a "drive"—that is, with some felt tension or discomfort. "Drive" is used here in a psychological, not a physiological, sense, for even the biological drives are significant for behavior only if they function as psychological stimuli; hence, "felt tension or discomfort." Behavior in an infant or in a naïve experimental animal is instigated by the desire to "reduce" the drive. But since the drive is still uncanalized (Murphy 1947:chap. 8)—it has no goal, no cathected object—behavior approaches randomness. By trial-and-error some object or event, which has the property of reducing the drive, is chanced upon; the drive is gratified; homeostasis is restored. If this sequence is repeated a sufficient number of times, the drive-reducing object or event becomes a "goal" and the act which is instrumental to the attainment of the goal becomes a behavior pattern. An expectation of gratifying a drive by means of the goal attained by the behavior pattern has been established.

2. This discussion is based primarily on psychoanalytic (Rapaport 1951) and behavior theory (Miller and Dollard 1941; Tolman 1951). Despite the differences among contemporary psychological theorists, almost all agree that reward—different terms are used to refer to the same concept—is a crucial motivational variable (Nebraska Symposia on Motivation 1953:v. 1, ff.). They differ primarily in their analysis of its referents and its properties. It is with respect to performance, not to learning, that the notion of reward is here held to be crucial.

Using this psychological model two simple questions concerning behavior may be answered. Why does a naïve organism behave at all? Because it has a drive. Why, after experience or training, does it behave in this, rather than in some other, way? Because it has learned that this way attains goals which are rewarding, i.e., drive-reducing. It should be emphasized, of course, that "drive" refers to both innate and acquired drives, and that rewards need not be "physical" nor need they be administered by others. The rewards for exploratory and cognitive activity are frequently—even in the case of lower primates (Harlow 1953)—inherent in the very act of exploration or intrinsic to the solution of a problem. It should also be emphasized that no assumption is made concerning fixed homeostatic states such that the achievement of drive-reduction leads to relative quiescence until the drive is reactivated. It is assumed, on the contrary, that there is always some discrepancy between achievement and aspiration levels (Lewin et al., 1944) so that present goal achievement may become but a temporary way-station for contemplated further and different goal achievement. It *is* assumed, however, that drives *are* motivational variables and, although not every act is instigated by the anticipation of drive-reduction, that every drive must eventually be reduced, either directly or indirectly.

Can this psychological model help us to understand cultural behavior, in general, or the performance of the constituent roles of a social system, in particular? At first, the answer might appear to be negative. For social roles, it will be remembered, are not discovered at random by each individual, and social systems are not invented *de novo* by each generation. On the contrary, since the social system of any generation is in the main acquired from its cultural heritage, from a previous generation, the goals which are attained by the performance of roles are either sanctioned or prescribed.[3] The roles which are instrumental for the attainment of these goals are prescribed. In short, since social systems are normative systems, social roles—unlike other learned behavior patterns—very likely are performed not because they are rewarding but because they are mandatory.

It is this imperative dimension of human social systems that has led

3. "Sanctioned" goals are goals which are culturally approved; "prescribed" goals are goals which are culturally mandatory. Thus, though all prescribed goals are sanctioned, not all sanctioned goals are prescribed. The goal of achieving the status of physician, for example, is a sanctioned, not a prescribed, goal in our culture. That is, we approve of those who aspire to achieve the goal, but we do not expect everyone to aspire to it. On the other hand the goal of curing patients is not only a sanctioned, but a prescribed goal for physicians. From now on the expression, "culturally stipulated" will be used to embrace both "sanctioned" and "prescribed."

many social theorists to interpret cultural conformity as a function, primarily, of special techniques of social control. Since social systems have vital social functions, which are served only if their constituent roles are performed, their operation requires that individuals behave in culturally desirable, rather than in personally desired, ways. The proponents of this theory see little relationship between personal motivation and cultural behavior. Conformity to cultural norms, they believe, is not a matter of personality drives primarily, but of social sanctions.

All societies, of course, employ social sanctions as a means of achieving social control, though the specific techniques and agents of control may differ from society to society. Thus, the sanctions may consist in quite different kinds of rewards or punishments. Similarly the agents who administer these sanctions (agents of control) may be one's peers who exercise control through the ubiquitous (informal) techniques of public opinion—shame and praise. This may be termed "alter-ego" control. Alternatively, the agents may be one's superiors, who exercise control through numerous (formal) techniques of public recognition and punitive sanctions available to constituted authority. This may be termed "super-alter" control. These superiors, it might be added, may be natural or supernatural authority.

It should be obvious, however, that even a social sanctions theory of social control, despite the antipsychological bias of many of its proponents (Radcliffe-Brown 1957:45–52), is essentially a motivational theory. No social sanction can *compel* a person to conform; it can only *motivate* him to do so. As Radcliffe-Brown himself observes (1933: 531), "The sanctions existing in a community constitute motives in the individual for the regulation of his conduct in conformity with usage." Thus the positive sanction of material reward does not *compel* a person to perform an economic role; rather, it *motivates* him to perform it because the material reward serves as a goal to reduce some drive such as hunger or prestige. Similarly malicious gossip or a jail sentence can induce a person not to steal only if either of these negative sanctions are painful to him; if incarceration or gossip were not painful, they could not compel him to conform to the injunction. Unless the members of society have certain personality drives which can be reduced by acquiring positive, and avoiding negative, sanctions, it is unlikely that these sanctions would serve as techniques of social control. In short, social sanctions serve as techniques of social control because they function as motivational variables.

If social sanctions become incentives for action because of their cathexes as personal (positive or negative) goals, their efficacy may be

explained in terms of our psychological model. They function as anticipated rewards or punishments. Since these rewards and punishments
are extrinsic to the performance of a role, and since they are administered by persons other than the actor, this type of cultural motivation[4]
may be termed "extrinsic cultural motivation," and this type of social
control may be termed "extrinsic social control."

To the extent that all societies employ extrinsic social control in
some degree as a means of achieving cultural conformity, personality
motivation enables the social system to serve its vital social functions.
Though the performance of roles may be motivated by the fear of
punishment or the desire for rewards, their social functions are served
regardless of the personal motives for their performance. Even if social
sanctions were the primary technique of social control, analysis of cultural conformity could not avoid the concept of personality.

Although extrinsic social control is universal, it does not follow that
its importance in achieving cultural conformity is paramount. Social
sanctions may be necessary in order to achieve the conformity of some
individuals in some societies almost all of the time, and of most individuals in any society some of the time. Moreover, they are necessary
to resolve those conflicts that frequently arise between two persons or
groups, both of whom are behaving in conformity with the cultural
norms. It is probably safe to assume, however, that this type of control
is only rarely the primary type in any society; it is most prevalent in
those historical periods of a society which are characterized by anomie.
Thus, it is typically found as a primary type of control in transitional
periods in which changes, either in tension-producing or tension-re-
ducing social institutions seriously restrict the possibility of satisfying
personality needs by culturally stipulated techniques (Sapir 1924,
"Spurious culture"). In the long run, however, further changes in the
social system will restore its tension production-reduction balance
(Henry 1953: 154), so that extrinsic control is no longer primary; or the
psycho- and sociopathology that result from this cultural pathology will
become so extensive that social life is no longer viable.

Intrinsic Cultural Motivation

Personal Motives and Manifest Social Functions

If social sanctions are not the primary means of achieving cultural conformity, it is because social roles, though prescribed, satisfy personality
needs. Fromm is undoubtedly correct when he writes:

4. The motivation for the performance of social roles is termed "cultural motivation"
because these roles are *culturally* sanctioned and prescribed.

In order that any society may function well, its members must acquire the kind of character which makes them *want* to act in the way they *have* to act as members of the society . . . They have to *desire* what objectively is *necessary* for them to do. (1944:381)

In order to understand this transformation of duty into desire we must first understand how the normative dimension of human social systems serves to qualify our psychological model. In this model, it will be recalled, behavior is instigated initially by the desire to reduce a drive, and any object or event which serves this end will do. Subsequently those objects or events which gratify the drive may become cathected so that they function as goals. When this happens behavior is motivated by the desire not merely to gratify a drive, but to gratify it by attaining a particular goal. Canalization, as Murphy (1947:chap. 8) has termed this process of drive-goal connection, is characteristic of much motivation. But cultural motivation is unique in that these canalizations are ordained by the cultural heritage prior to individual experience instead of arising in the context of individual experience. By stipulating that only a limited, out of a potentially large, number of objects or events may serve as goals for drives, and by prohibiting all others, the cultural heritage insists that if a drive is to be gratified at all, it must be gratified by means of these stipulated prescribed or sanctioned goals. Thus, though a New Guinea headhunter must bring home a head if he is to gratify his prestige drive, an Ifaluk must not; and though an American is permitted to gratify his hunger drive by eating roast beef, a Hindu is not.

If the goal of a behavior pattern is distinguished from its drive, much of the dramatic diversity found in the cross-cultural record reflects the diversity, not of man's "nature," but of his history and of his cognitive ingenuity. Since man is enormously plastic, a large variety of goals may, potentially, reduce the same drive. In the absence of biologically rigid drive-goal connections, different societies, as a function of their unique histories and ecologies, have "chosen" different goals for the same drives as well as different roles for the attainment of these goals. The resultant diversity in goals has led some anthropologists to insist that each culture is not only *sui generis* but that cross-cultural generalizations are impossible to achieve. Such a position is, functionally viewed, wide off the mark. Although cultural goals are parochial, most human drives—because of their rootedness in a common biology and in common conditions of social life—are probably universal. Hence, it is generally not too difficult to demonstrate (on a fairly high level of generality, of course) that the quite diverse goals of different societies, as well as the roles which are instrumental for their attainment, are functionally equivalent; they serve to gratify the same drives (Murphy 1954:628–31).

But the fact that goals are prescribed does not imply—as some theorists take it to imply—that they do not or cannot gratify drives. On the contrary, culturally prescribed goals may be as rewarding as nonprescribed goals. By prescribing goals the cultural heritage does not frustrate drives, it merely limits the number of ways in which they may be gratified. To be sure, since man has few instincts, he must learn to perceive the prescribed goals as rewarding. But this is the function of child-training. In the process of socialization, children acquire not only drives, but they acquire goals as well; they learn which objects or events—the culturally prescribed goals—are drive-reducing. In short, socialization systems—by techniques which cannot be described here—are institutionalized means for transforming culturally-stipulated goals into personally-cathected goals (Erikson 1950; Whiting and Child 1953). If the personal cathexis of a stipulated goal is termed a "need," it is apparent that a need-satisfaction model is more appropriate than a drive-reduction model as a description of cultural motivation. For in general once a prescribed goal is sufficiently cathected, that goal which is culturally viewed as the only desirable, if not the only possible, goal for the gratification of a drive, becomes personally viewed as the most desired goal. Indeed, in some instances it, and no other, is perceived as drive-reducing, so that drive-frustration may be preferred to drive-reduction by noncathected goals. An Orthodox Hindu, for example, refuses to eat beef, not only because it is prohibited, but because it is not desired; the very notion of eating beef may be disgusting to him. Hence the paradox: although evolution has produced a species characterized by the absence of drive-goal invariants, culture produces personalities who behave as if there were. For after cultural goals are cathected, human beings sometimes behave as if *their* drive-goal connections were the only ones possible.

To conclude: social roles, like other types of learned behavior, are performed if they are rewarding. But if the culturally stipulated goals, which are attained by their performance, are cathected, behavior is motivated by the expectation of attaining a goal, not by the desire to reduce a drive. To be sure, the goal is desired because its attainment produces drive-reduction; if it did not, it would not, in the long run, continue to be desired. But this is precisely the point of the "need" concept: it looks, so to speak, in two directions. On the one hand it affirms that drive-reduction is rewarding, so that acts that do not reduce drives are not performed. On the other hand, it denies that the desire to reduce a drive is a sufficient explanation of cultural motivation; for when culturally stipulated goals are sufficiently cathected, action is motivated (with the possible exception of extreme deprivation) by the expectation of attaining these cathected goals.[5]

It is now perhaps clear how cultural imperatives can become personal desires—how, in short, people can want to perform social roles. If the performance of social roles does in fact attain those culturally stipulated goals for whose attainment they are intended by the cultural heritage, and if these goals have been cathected by the members of society, these roles are performed because of the desire to attain these goals. In short, although social roles are prescribed by the cultural heritage, their performance is motivated by the expectation of satisfying personality needs. Though these roles must be performed so that their functions for society can be served, individuals desire to perform them because personal functions are thereby served.[6] Thus, for example, the American army serves an important adaptive function for American society by defending its people against foreign enemies. Should an individual American become identified (in the psychoanalytic sense) with his society, he will internalize this function as a personal drive and, therefore, he might cathect this stipulated goal as a personal goal. Should this happen he may be motivated to become a soldier and to perform its prescribed role because its performance satisfies a personality need. In short, if the social function of a role is internalized as a personal drive, its performance, which is intended to serve a social function, serves a personal function—albeit unintentionally—as well. Diagrammatically, this can be represented thus:

need ————→performance of role ⟨ personal function (unintended)
                                  social function (intended)

But if cultural goals are cathected as personal goals only when social functions are internalized as personal drives, the number of roles whose performance can serve personal functions would be small in-

5. This notion of "need" is almost identical with the notion of "need-disposition" in Parsons' action theory (Parsons and Shils 1951:114–20). There are other points of convergence, as well, between the limited formulations of this chapter and those of Parsons (Parsons and Shils 1951: parts 1 and 2; Parsons 1951: chaps. 1–3, 6–7). The serious student of the relationship between social system and personality is urged to read these two important volumes.

6. For a preliminary typology of functionalism, see Spiro 1953. For a detailed analysis of functionalism as "functional consequence," see Merton 1949. For illuminating discussions of functionalism, based on Merton's analysis, see Nagel 1957: chap. 10, and Hempel 1959. For a general review of recent functionalist theory and research, see Firth 1955.

deed. Indeed, it is precisely because the social functions of roles only rarely become personal drives that some theorists have stressed the importance of social sanctions as a means, par excellence, of assuring cultural conformity. And surely the argument is plausible. For if a role has a social function, and if the serving of its function is not a personality need, how can its performance be motivated by the expectation of satisfying a personality need?

This argument, however plausible, neglects to consider still another possibility. Stipulated goals may be cathected, and therefore social roles performed, although social functions are not internalized; and social functions may be served, although they are unintended. As Kroeber, generalizing from his analysis of religious change among the Kota, has put it: "In manipulating their culture for their personal ends, the participants often produce a cultural effect that may be enduring, as well as attaining their individual goal or tension reliefs" (1948:507).

This can happen in two ways: when personal and social functions are members of the same functional class, and when they are members of different functional classes. Both of these ways, beginning with the first, can be illustrated by returning to the soldier role and the motives for its performance. Since individuals exist qua members of society as well as qua individuals, their welfare is frequently dependent upon the welfare of society. Thus, though an individual may not internalize the adaptive (social) function of the soldier role as a personal drive, he may nonetheless, if he believes that his personal survival depends on the survival of his society, cathect its goal of national defense; and he may then be motivated to perform the role in order to satisfy this personality need. But since the social (adaptive) function of the soldier role consists in the summation of its personal (adaptive) functions for individuals, the performance of the role not only serves a personal function, but it serves its social function as well—albeit unintentionally.

There is still another way in which culturally stipulated goals can become personality needs. Not everyone who becomes a professional soldier, for example, is motivated to achieve or to perform this role in order to defend either himself or his society from enemy attack. Since the promotion of national defense is, at least in our society, one means for the attainment of prestige and power, this culturally stipulated goal may become the cathected goal for the reduction of these drives. The performance of the soldier's role may then be motivated by the expectation of satisfying power and prestige needs. Nevertheless though the personal functions (integrative and adjustive) and social function (adaptive) of the role are members of different functional classes, and though its performance is intended to serve personal functions, its social function—although unintended—is served as well. Diagrammatically, these last two cases can be represented thus:

need ⟶ performance of role ⟨ → personal function (intended)
                                → social function (unintended)

To sum up, any act may be viewed from at least two perspectives: motive and function. The motive of an act is the consequence, either for the actor or for society, which is intended by its performance; its function is the actual consequence of its performance, either for the actor or for society. Functions may be positive or negative; that is, the consequence of an act may contribute to the welfare of the actor or of society or it may detract from their welfare. (We are here concerned with positive functions only, and the generic term, "function," refers to positive function exclusively.) Finally acts have intended and unintended functions. That is, the consequence of an act may be the consequence which was intended by its performance, or it may be one which was not intended by its performance. Since social roles have social functions, and since acts are performed only if they have personal functions, it has often been assumed that there is little intrinsic relationship between personality needs and the performance of roles except in those few instances in which an act is intended to serve both personal and social functions. A soldier, for example, might be motivated to play his role because he intended to serve both himself and his country.

But if acts can have unintended as well as intended consequences, it is possible for personal and social functions to be served in the performance of the same acts or roles. And this can happen in two ways: when their personal functions are intended and their social functions are unintended, and when their personal functions are unintended and their social functions intended. In either event since the performance of the roles serves personal as well as social functions, their performance is motivated—without the operation of social sanctions—because they satisfy personality needs. Since these needs consist in the personal cathexes of culturally stipulated goals, the performance of social roles is effected by, what may be termed, "intrinsic cultural motivation." Alternatively, the cultural conformity which results from this type of motivation is achieved by "intrinsic social control," for the control function is, as it were, built into the very fabric of the role. By satisfying personality needs, its performance is assured, and its social functions performed, without the necessity for sanctions extrinsic to the role or for agents external to the actor.

Personal Motives and Latent Social Functions

Thus far it has been contended that personality plays an important part in the operation of social systems because, by motivating the performance of social roles, it enables the social system to serve its social functions. The discussion, however, has dealt with the manifest functions of roles exclusively, that is, with those social functions which, whether intended or unintended by the members of society, are recognized by them. But social systems, have latent functions as well, and sometimes their latent functions are more important for society than their manifest functions. It is here, moreover, that personality is uniquely important for the functioning of society.

If manifest functions are those consequences of role performance which are recognized by the members of society, latent functions are those consequences which—whether intended or unintended—are not recognized by them.[7] That the paradox of an intended but unrecognized function is apparent rather than real, becomes clear when one considers that motives may be unconscious, as well as conscious. In short, manifest (recognized) functions are served by the performance of roles when at least one of the motives for their performance is conscious; latent (unrecognized) functions are served when at least one of the motives for their performance is unconscious. Hence, before analyzing latent functions, it is necessary to examine the concept of unconscious motive.

If the motive for behavior consists in an intention to satisfy a need by performing a particular act (and if a need consists in a drive and a goal), a motive may be unconscious, i.e., unrecognized, in any one or all of these three dimensions. Thus a drive, its goal, and the desired means for the attainment of the goal may all be unconscious. With the exception of neurotic, i.e., idiosyncratic, repression, if any or all of these dimensions of a motive are unconscious in a typical member of a society, the motive has generally been rendered unconscious because of a cultural prohibition or because of its systematic frustration. In the latter case, since need-frustration as well as the memory of need-frus-

---

7. Merton (1949), whose now-classic analysis of functionalism remains the incisive treatment of this subject, and who first introduced the terms "manifest" and "latent" into functional analysis, ignored a potentially powerful mode of analysis by merging "intention" and "recognition." As he defines them, manifest functions are those which are both intended and recognized, while latent functions are those which are neither intended nor recognized. Since manifest functions—as we have seen—may be unintended, and since latent functions—as we shall see—may be intended, intention and recognition may vary independently.

tration are painful, repression of the frustrating experience as well as of the need is one possible defense against pain. We shall confine the discussion to the former basis for repression. Thus, for example, the cultural heritage may prohibit any reduction of the sex drive, as in sacerdotal celibacy; or it may prohibit a desired goal for its reduction, such as intercourse with kinsmen who fall within the boundaries of the incest taboo; or it may prohibit a desired means for the attainment of the goal, such as some "perverted" technique of sexual relations. In short the cultural heritage not only provides means of need-satisfaction for an animal without instinctive means for drive-reduction, but—by prescribing these means—it prohibits other means which this relatively plastic and imaginative animal may come to prefer. Moreover it may completely prohibit any conceivable (manifest) expression or reduction of certain drives.

But motives do not disappear simply because they are prohibited. Even if the cultural prohibition is internalized as a personal norm, the culturally prohibited canalization may continue to persist as a personally preferred canalization, and the culturally prohibited drive may continue to seek expression. The resultant incompatibility between internalized norm and personal desire leads to inner conflict which must be "handled" in some way. If these personally preferred, but culturally prohibited, canalizations are stronger than the internalized cultural prohibition, they may be expressed directly. If, then, the resultant behavior is categorically prohibited, it is deemed criminal or psychologically aberrant (depending on the culture) by the members of society. Alternatively, if the behavior is culturally aberrant, but not clearly prohibited, it may be viewed as a cultural innovation—that is, as a new, but culturally acceptable, behavior pattern.

On the other hand, should the internalized cultural prohibition be stronger than the personal desire, the inner conflict may be resolved by repressing the desire. The prohibited motive, in short, becomes unconscious. But unconscious as well as conscious motives seek expression and satisfaction. They may be expressed (and satisfied) in neurosis and psychosis; in private fantasy (day-dreams and night dreams); in symbolic, but culturally creative, ways (artistic and scientific work); or, and more germane to this chapter, in the performance of culturally prescribed roles. Since unconscious motives cannot be satisfied directly—if they could they would not be unconscious—they may thus seek indirect satisfaction in the performance of culturally sanctioned behavior. In short, in addition to its conscious motivation, culturally sanctioned behavior, including role behavior, may be unconsciously motivated as well. Since, in the latter case, the performance of a role is motivated by an unconscious as well as by a conscious intention of satisfying a need, the role may have unrecognized though intended personal functions; and these, in turn, may produce unrecognized and unintended social functions. This thesis may be illustrated by examples from two societies: warfare among the Sioux Indians of the American Plains, and religion among the Ifaluk of Micronesia.

Diagrammatically, the relationship between the motives for the performance of the Sioux warrior role and its various personal and social functions can be represented thus:

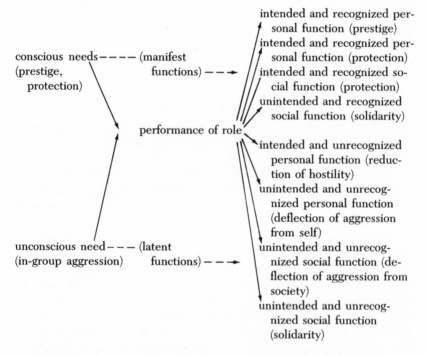

intended and recognized personal function (prestige)

intended and recognized personal function (protection)

intended and recognized social function (protection)

unintended and recognized social function (solidarity)

intended and unrecognized personal function (reduction of hostility)

unintended and unrecognized personal function (deflection of aggression from self)

unintended and unrecognized social function (deflection of aggression from society)

unintended and unrecognized social function (solidarity)

conscious needs — — — — (manifest
(prestige,   functions) — — →
   protection)

performance of role

unconscious need — — — (latent
(in-group aggression)   functions) — — →

Sioux warfare was motivated by two conscious needs: prestige and protection from enemies. In satisfying these needs for prestige and protection, warfare served manifest personal (integrative) and social (adaptive) functions. It may be assumed, it served an unintended (integrative), but manifest social function, as well—the promotion of social solidarity by the creation of *esprit de corps* among the warriors.

But the "choice" of warfare as a preeminent institutionalized means of obtaining prestige leads us to suspect that the conscious motives for the performance of the warrior role, though genuine, were not its only motives. Warfare is an aggressive activity. why did the Sioux act aggressively when the objective threat from the enemy was slight? Sioux war parties, it will be recalled, attacked rather than defended; they preferred to attack when their "enemies" were least prepared, that is, when they constituted no threat; young bucks had to be restrained from going on the warpath, rather than having to be encouraged to do so. And why did they seek prestige through aggression when, as the cross-cultural record reveals, there are many nonaggressive roles through which prestige can be obtained? Sioux warfare apparently was motivated not only by the conscious needs of prestige and protection, but by yet another, unconscious, motive—hostility against their fellows.

As is the case in most societies, Sioux socialization, as well as the conditions of adult Sioux social life, created in each new generation a motive for aggression against their fellows (Erikson 1939, 1945). Like most societies, moreover, the cultural heritage of the Sioux prohibited physical aggression against the in-group. However, only one of the three dimensions of this motive was prohibited. Neither the drive itself (hostility) nor the means of its reduction (physical aggression), but only its object (the in-group), was prohibited. It was assumed, then, that the specific dimension of physical aggression against *fellows* was repressed, i.e., rendered unconscious. But by displacing hostility from the in- to the out-groups, this motive could now be expressed. This motive, one may suggest, sought satisfaction in, and was therefore important in the motivation of, Sioux warfare. In addition to their motives of prestige and protection, Sioux war parties were also motivated by aggression. In satisfying this motive, the warrior role served a latent personal function (integration), as well as its manifest personal and social functions.

When the performance of roles is motivated by unconscious needs, it serves unintended and unrecognized social functions as well as intended but unrecognized personal functions. What possible unintended and unrecognized function for society was served by the Sioux institution of warfare? By displacing hostility, and its subsequent aggression, in warfare against the outgroup, the warrior role protected Sioux society from the aggression of its own members (adaptive function). Had the original hostility not been displaced and subsequently gratified in socially sanctioned aggression, it might have sought undisguised and, therefore, socially disruptive expression. It might have sought expression in other ways as well. Indeed, Erikson interprets the sun dance, and its painful consequences for its participants—staring into the sun and tearing of skewers from their flesh—as the turning of aggression inward. It might be suggested, then, that in the absence of war, even more aggression would have been turned against the self.

Hence, the performance of the warrior role served a latent, unintended personal function, as well as its latent unintended social function.

But to return to the social functions of Sioux warfare: by deflecting hostility from in- to out-group, the preponderance of positive over negative sentiments concerning the members of the group was increased, thereby promoting in-group solidarity (integrative function). Neither of these unintended and unrecognized social functions would have been served had the performance of the warrior role been motivated exclusively by the motives of prestige and protection. Moreover, those anthropologists who are unaware of, or uninterested in, the latent personal functions of roles—because unaware of, or uninterested in, unconscious motives—would remain ignorant of the important latent social functions which are served by this role, and of the general functional significance of Sioux warfare within the total social system.

The second example of the relationship between unconscious motives and social functions not only illustrates the importance of unconscious motivation in the functioning of social systems, but it also illustrates how a society and its social system may be affected by the intrinsic motivation of another cultural system—religion. Most public religious rituals in the Micronesian atoll of Ifaluk are either therapeutic or prophylactic in nature; they are designed to maintain or restore health by exorcising malevolent ghosts (who cause illness by possessing their victims), or by preventing these ghosts from executing their intentions in the first place. It is not within the province of social science to decide whether one of the manifest, intended, functions of these rituals—defeat of the ghosts—is served; the Ifaluk, of course, believe that it is. But these rituals serve other manifest functions to which the behavioral scientist can testify. By their performance the twin fears of illness and of attack by ghosts are reduced (manifest intended personal function), and by assembling and acting in concert for the achievement of a common end, good fellowship is strengthened (manifest unintended social function).

But the performance of these rituals requires another motive in addition to its therapeutic motive. These are aggressive rituals in which malevolent ghosts are attacked and, it is hoped, routed. It requires little insight to infer that hostility, as well as fear, motivates the performance. Indeed, the Ifaluk are quite consciously hostile toward the ghosts. But though consciously hostile to ghosts, the Ifaluk, like all people, have occasion to be hostile to their fellows, particularly to their close kinsmen. By displacing hostility from fellows to ghosts, their hostility is acceptable, and their subsequent aggressive motive can be gratified in a socially sanctioned manner in the performance of these rituals (Spiro 1953a). A latent personal function (integrative) of these rituals, then, consists in the opportunity which their performance affords for the satisfaction of this aggressive need.

As in the Sioux example, however, the performance of these rituals also serves a latent (unintended) social function, one which is vital for this society. The Ifaluk social system, based on the strongly held values of sharing, mutual aid, and kindliness, is highly cooperative. If the Ifaluk were unable to express aggression symbolically in ritual, it is not improbable that their hostility would eventually seek direct expression. If this were to happen, the probability of physical survival on an atoll, six-tenths of a mile square, would be effectively reduced. By serving to deflect aggression onto malevolent ghosts, the performance of these rituals effectively increases the chances for survival. Moreover, as in the case of the Sioux, the belief in malevolent ghosts, which permits the displacement of hostility from the in-group to the wicked out-group, assures the persistence of the warm sentiments which the Ifaluk harbor towards each other. Hence the psychological basis for their cooperative social system—probably the only kind of system which is viable in this demographic-ecological balance—is preserved. In short, by serving its latent personal function, this ritual is also able to serve the latent social functions of promoting the group's survival and of preserving the viability of its social system (Spiro 1952).

Diagrammatically, the relationship between the motives for the performance of Ifaluk rituals, which attack and exorcise malevolent ghosts, and their personal and social functions can be represented in the following way:

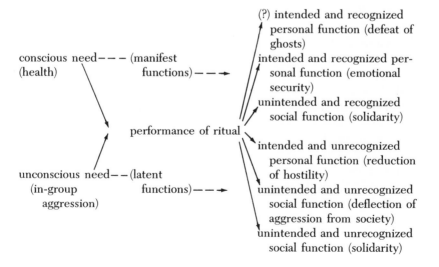

This discussion of unconscious motives, and of the latent social functions served by social roles (and other types of cultural behavior) whose performance is motivated by them, has been somewhat extended because, with the exception of culture-and-personality research, they are ignored in most analyses of social systems. Unconscious motives are frequently dismissed by social scientists as irrelevant to an understanding of society. "Oh," it is often said, "these unconscious motives may be important for personality, but we're interested in the study of society." This analysis has attempted to demonstrate that anyone interested in society should also be interested in unconscious motives. They are as important for the student of society as for the student of personality, not only because they motivate the performance of social roles but because the latent social functions which they enable these roles to serve are often more important than those which are served under conscious motivation. It should be emphasized, however, that unconscious motives, however important, are not the only motives of behavior, that conscious motives are not merely rationalizations. Though this may sometimes be the case, the assumption that only unconscious motives are genuine is as fallacious as the contrary assumption. If the conscious motives of Sioux warfare and Ifaluk ritual are not sufficient explanations for their performance, neither are the unconscious motives: both are necessary, both are genuine, neither is sufficient. To assume that only unconscious motives are genuine is to perpetuate that vulgar interpretation of psychoanalytic theory in which schoolteaching, for example, is "nothing but" the sublimation of an unconscious sexual motive, or surgery is "nothing but" the displacement of unconscious aggression.

Theories of social systems that ignore unconscious motives are not only truncated, but when social analyses which are based on such theories are applied by administrators, they often lead to unfortunate results. If we were to assume, for example, that Sioux warfare or Ifaluk religious rituals are means merely for obtaining prestige or reducing anxiety concerning illness respectively, and that by achieving these ends they also promote social solidarity—the typical social anthropological functionalist analysis—then it is a fair administrative conclusion that these "savage" and "superstitious" practices can be abolished without harm to society as long as the "civilized" practices with which they are replaced are their functional equivalents, as long, that is, as the new practices are also means for obtaining prestige, for reducing anxiety concerning illness, and for promoting social solidarity. But despite these good intentions, the new practices are *not* the functional equivalents of the old if they do not serve, as well, the latent personal function of displacing unconscious hostility. Unless this function is achieved, substitutes cannot serve the latent social function of deflecting aggression from the in-group. Hence, this unconscious motive may seek expression in numerous dysfunctional ways—dysfunctional both for individuals and society. It may be expressed directly, leading to crime, or indirectly, leading to drunkenness, etc.; it may be inverted, leading to anxiety and depression ("race suicide"), and so forth. By ignoring the importance of unconscious motivation in social behavior, the attempt of well-intentioned administrators (acting upon the findings of psychologically uninformed researchers) to substitute "unobjectionable" for "objectionable" native practices has often been a history of grave disappointments to the administrator and sordid results for the natives.

It should be strongly emphasized that although personality needs are satisfied in and therefore motivate the performance of social roles, a person's personality cannot necessarily be inferred from a knowledge of the roles he performs. In the first place, although this chapter is concerned with the relationship between personality and the social system, it is obvious that only part of the personality is relevant to and is expressed through the social system. The relationship between personality and other cultural systems (religion, art, science, etc.), as well as those private aspects of personality that are not caught up in the sociocultural net (Murphy 1958:part 3), are deliberately ignored. In short, a description of a person's various social roles would not lead to an exhaustive description of his personality.

More important, however, for our purposes, a knowledge of a person's social roles would not even lead to an accurate prediction of those aspects of his personality that are caught up in their performance. For, as this section has attempted to show, since different goals may be cathected by the same drive and since different roles may be instrumental for the attainment of the same goal, "a high degree of role differentiation," as Kaplan has put it, does not necessarily require "a similar degree of differentiation at the personality level" (1957: 100). At the same time, since the same goal may be cathected by different drives, and since the same role may be instrumental for the attainment of different goals, a high degree of personality differentiation does not necessarily require a similar degree of differentiation at the social system level. Thus, (1) different drives may be canalized by the same goal, which is attained by the performance of the same role; (2) the same drive may be canalized by different goals, which are attained by the performance of different roles; and (3) different drives may be canalized by the same goal which is attained by the performance of different roles. These alternatives are shown in the following diagrams.

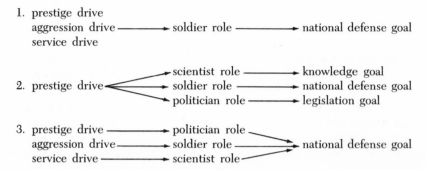

1. prestige drive
   aggression drive ⟶ soldier role ⟶ national defense goal
   service drive

2. prestige drive ⟨ scientist role ⟶ knowledge goal
                     soldier role ⟶ national defense goal
                     politician role ⟶ legislation goal

3. prestige drive ⟶ politician role
   aggression drive ⟶ soldier role ⟶ national defense goal
   service drive ⟶ scientist role

But if this is true within a society, it is equally true across societies. Since there are fewer drives in man than there are goals in all his societies, and since there are fewer goals in all human societies than there are roles in their social systems, it is reasonable to expect fewer modal personality systems than social systems. On the other hand, since drives, goals, and roles may vary independently of each other, it is possible for different modal personality systems to be associated with similar social systems, and for similar modal personality systems to be associated with different social systems.

If this is so the student of social systems, who is interested in their motivational well-springs, must at the same time be a student of personality; and statements about the relationships between personality and social systems must be based on personality investigations, and not inferred from a description of social systems (Inkeles and Levinson 1954). Personality investigation may entail the use of psychological instruments, such as projective tests (Hallowell 1955), the analysis of dreams (Eggan 1952), the collection of life histories (Kluckhohn 1945), and depth interviewing. It may also be based, however, on the observation of behavior when viewed from the perspective of, and interpreted in terms of, psychodynamic personality theory. For if the same set of activities can serve both personal and social functions, the same set of activities may be viewed from a personality perspective (as a means for serving personal functions) or from a social system perspective (as a means for serving social functions). If one's focus is on society and on those adaptive, adjustive, and integrative prerequisites of a viable social life, a given set of activities is analyzed as a role within the social system. If, on the other hand, one's focus is on an individual and on the adaptive, adjustive, and integrative prerequisites of a viable individual life, the same set of activities is analyzed as a means for satisfying the needs of the personality system. This last technique uses a powerful, but rare instrument—a sensitive observer.

Internalized Cultural Motivation

Since intrinsic cultural motivation is based on the personal cathexis of culturally stipulated goals, it obviously cannot serve as a technique of social control when these goals are not cathected. There are various conditions which reduce the probability of goal cathexis. The following are probably most important: (a) the goals of many taboos and prohibitions, since they lead to frustration, may increase rather than reduce the intensity of drives (Freud 1930); (b) in societies undergoing rapid culture change, many new goals will not reduce extant drives (Hallowell 1945); (c) a similar situation will obtain in the case of subordinate groups, whose culture has largely been imposed by a dominant group; (d) cathexis may be withdrawn from previously cathected goals because of the realization that they cannot be achieved (Merton 1938).

Even when goals are cathected it does not necessarily follow that the culture patterns or roles that attain them will be performed. There are other possibilities. Though the goal is desired, the role which is prescribed for its attainment may be odious. Thus, though everyone may desire clean public latrines, no one may desire to perform the role of latrine attendant. Again, a nonsanctioned means for the attainment of a desired goal may be perceived as more efficient or as less burdensome than the sanctioned role. Similarly, the cultural goal may be scarce, so that not all who strive for its attainment can be successful. Hence, competitive anxiety may motivate the performance of proscribed, but more efficient, techniques. Finally, the social structure, particularly in a stratified society, may effectively preclude certain categories of persons from performing the roles which attain the goals (Merton 1938).

In all of these situations social conformity will be achieved only by some technique of social control other than—or in addition to—intrinsic cultural motivation. Extrinsic social control is one such technique; but it is not the only one. For the importance of personality needs in the motivation of social roles is not restricted to intrinsic cultural motivation. The latter type of motivation is ultimately based on two kinds of personality needs—id and ego needs, in psychoanalytic vocabulary. But personality has superego needs as well; and many roles may be performed (though id and ego are not satisfied, and may even be frustrated) because their performance satisfies superego needs.

If the performance of roles is motivated by the expectation of satisfying superego needs, social control is achieved by, what we may term, "internalized cultural motivation." For cultural conformity in this instance is achieved, not through external sanctions (extrinsic control), nor by intrinsic goals (intrinsic control), but by internalized norms. To put it in terms we have been employing, if extrinsic control is achieved (in the case of positive sanctions) by the cathexis of the social sanction, and if intrinsic control is achieved by the cathexis of the cultural goal, internalized control is achieved by the cathexis of the cultural norm.

There has been a great deal of discussion concerning the internalization of norms. Some writers, following Ruth Benedict (1946: 222–27, 288–89), have suggested that norm-internalization is a phenomenon restricted to certain types of societies and absent from others. Cultures which give rise to norm-internalization are termed "guilt-cultures," for cultural conformity is motivated by guilt. Those which do not produce norm-internalization are termed "shame-cultures," for the members of society conform to cultural norms only when their fellows are present to shame them. Hence, in societies with shame cultures extrinsic control is necessary to ensure cultural conformity—assuming that the performance of roles is not intrinsically motivated.

Although shame obviously operates as a control technique in any society, the validity of this shame culture—guilt culture dichotomy is open to question (Piers and Singer 1953). Since social systems are, to a great extent, normative—many of their constituent roles and goals are prescribed by the cultural heritage—it is improbable for the members of any society not to have internalized these norms. If norms were not internalized, parents would have none to transmit to their children because, *ex hypothesi*, they would not have internalized any in the course of their own socialization. Further, if no one has internalized the norms, who, in societies with shame cultures, would do the shaming? The existence of agents of shame implies that at least some members of society have internalized at least some norms.

In short, one may argue that although in any society there may hypothetically be some individuals who have internalized very few norms (the so-called psychopaths), and many individuals who have not internalized some of the norms, in all societies most individuals not only (a) learn *about* their cultural norms, but they also (b) accept them, (c) evaluate their own acts in accordance with them, and (d) experience anxiety ("moral anxiety") should they desire to violate them. This anxiety serves as an important deterrent to norm violation. Indeed, even in societies whose cultures correspond most closely to the description of the ideal shame culture, ". . . blame, ridicule, or holding up to shame are controls only if they express commonly accepted values and correspond to the promptings of the superego" (Nadel 1953:272).

How does this moral anxiety develop? And what does it represent?

To answer the second question first, this anxiety presumably represents the largely unconscious expectation of punishment, as distinguished from the rational, conscious fear of being punished. This distinction must be explained.

The individual who has internalized a norm, and not merely learned about it, perceives his anticipated violation of it as a transgression and hence as deserving of punishment. This perception induces anxiety (the anticipation of punishment). The mere intention of committing an act which he himself labels as a "transgression," or of not performing an act which he deems compulsory, leads him to expect that his behavior (which in his eyes is deserving of punishment) will in some way be punished. Where the individual believes that punishment is his due, "expectation of punishment" is but another term for "moral anxiety."

On the other hand, the individual who has merely learned about the norm, but has not internalized it, suffers no moral anxiety as a consequence of his anticipated violation of it. Because he himself has not internalized the norm, he does not (though others may) consider his anticipated violation to be deserving of punishment, since he does not consider his act to be "wrong." In short, he experiences no moral anxiety. He may, of course, experience considerable anxiety about the punishment which would be meted out to him were he caught. In moral anxiety, however, it is not the fear that one might be punished if caught, but the belief that one merits punishment that evokes anxiety.

Moral anxiety, therefore, has both drive and cue properties. It informs the individual that his anticipated behavior is wrong (worthy of punishment), and that its performance will lead to punishment; and it motivates him to reduce the anxiety by refraining from transgression. Hence, the anxiety serves as a motive for conformity.

Since moral anxiety is not innate, how is it acquired? So far as our present knowledge permits, we may suggest that it arises out of certain universal features of human socialization systems. In all societies, agents of socialization are not only trainers, but they are also nurturers, satisfying the child's most important need—the need for love. To the extent that these agents employ rewards and punishments as part of their training methods, and to the extent that such rewards and punishments are, for the child, symbolic of their love, the child is motivated to comply with the demands of these "significant others" (Mead 1934) in order to obtain their love or, conversely, to preclude its withdrawal. Through their ability to give and withhold love, the child not only learns what the agents of socialization judge to be good and bad behavior, but he also learns to concur in their judgment; in short, he models his behavior in accordance with their norms. He learns to ac-

cept their judgment as his own because behavior which these significant others judge to be bad is indeed "bad" *for him*—it leads to the
withdrawal of love (punishment) by those whose love he so strongly
desires. Since he agrees that certain acts are "bad," and therefore deserving of punishment, his mere intention to transgress leads to the
anticipation of punishment (moral anxiety). He has developed a superego, or a conscience.

But having questioned the validity of one distinction—that between
shame and guilt cultures—it is necessary to introduce another. The
superego has been implicitly defined operationally as the configuration
of those expectations of punishment, experienced as anxiety (either
conscious or unconscious) that are evoked by the anticipated violation
of an internalized cultural norm. But we have not yet specified the
agent of punishment, the "significant other" from whom punishment
(withdrawal of love) was originally expected. Two types of superego,
based on the agent of anticipated punishment, can be distinguished.
This agent may be outside the individual or "within" him. It is our
hypothesis that societies in which the child is trained by only a few
agents of socialization, who themselves administer punishments, produce individuals who not only internalize the norms of the socializing
agent but who "introject" the agent as well. This introjected figure,
then, is the significant other for such individuals and it is withdrawal of
its "love" that constitutes the anticipated punishment. Since this
punishment, when it comes—and it comes after the transgression is
committed—is experienced as guilt ("pangs of conscience"), this type
of superego may be termed "guilt-oriented."

Other societies, we believe, in which the child is trained by a
number of socializing agents, or in which the trainers discipline the
child by claiming that other agents will punish him, do not produce
individuals with "guilt-oriented" superegos. For, though these individuals internalize the norms of the socializing agents, they do not
introject the agents themselves. Since the significant others continue
to remain external, it is withdrawal of the love of others that constitutes
the anticipated punishment. Because this punishment, when it comes,
is experienced as shame, this type of superego may be termed "shame-
oriented." Of course, these two types of superego represent the polar
extremes, conceived as ideal types, of a superego continuum. Most
superegos would represent admixtures of the two, weighted toward
one or the other end of the continuum.

A shame- no less than a guilt-oriented superego constitutes a conscience. By producing anxiety concerning anticipated punishment,
both types inform the individual that his anticipated behavior is wrong,

and both motivate him to refrain from transgressing a norm, whether others are present or not. Nevertheless, they function differently after a transgression has occurred. A person with a guilt-oriented superego suffers guilt when he transgresses, even if no one perceives his transgression, because the agent of punishment (the introjected figure) is always with him. However, a person with a shame-oriented superego does not suffer shame when he transgresses unless others witness his transgression, for no agent of punishment (the external others) is present. Instead of experiencing *actual* punishment (shame), he continues to anticipate punishment; he suffers from anxiety.[8] This anxiety may be so painful that it may lead some persons who live in societies with so-called shame-cultures to commit suicide. Incidentally, this fact is sufficient to cast doubt on the validity of the shame-culture guilt-culture dichotomy. The Japanese, who allegedly have a shame-culture, may be driven to suicide when they perceive themselves to have lost face, even in the absence of any other perceiver. In the terms we have been employing, the Japanese would be said to have shame-oriented superegos; they experience anxiety when they anticipate performing a forbidden act or not performing a prescribed act. After committing the transgression, they continue to anticipate punishment, anxiety mounts, and suicide represents the last desperate attempt to remove the anxiety.

To conclude, then, regardless of the type of superego that is preponderant in the personalities of the members of any society, cultural conformity is frequently achieved by means of internalized cultural motivation. Though the goal attained by the performance of a role may not be cathected, and though a means other than the prescribed role may be preferred, the role may nevertheless be performed (and its social functions thereby served) without the necessity for extrinsic control. If the members of society have cathected and internalized their cultural norms, conformity with these norms serves to reduce the drive of moral anxiety. In short, in internalized, as well as in intrinsic, cultural motivation the members of society have acquired "the kind of character which makes them *want* to act in the way they have to act . . ."

Conclusions

In the past, when the behavioral sciences were still reacting against instinctivist theories of social behavior, the relationship between social

---

8. For an empirical demonstration of this process, see Spiro 1958: chap. 15, from which part of this discussion, with permission of the publisher, is taken.

system and personality was viewed as primarily asymmetrical. Personality was viewed as a relatively passive agent—affected by, but not affecting, the social system. Faris (1937:ch. 3), for example, refers to personality as the "subjective aspect of culture." Recent work in culture-and-personality, however, has tended to conceive of the social system—personality relationship as more nearly symmetrical. These studies have suggested that although personality is, indeed, affected by the social system, the social system, in turn, is affected by personality.

This changing conception of the relationship between personality and social system has had its influence on the study and analysis of social systems by culture-and-personality theorists. Instead of merely asking how the social system influences the development and structuring of personality, we are now equally interested in how personality affects the functioning of social systems. And, in general, it seems to be agreed that there is feedback between social system and personality such that the social system creates those personality needs which, in turn, are satisfied by and motivate the operation of the social system (Kardiner 1939). Since society has but one social system, while the component members of society have different personalities, this feedback is effected because the component roles of the social system can satisfy different needs, and its socialization system produces common needs, or a modal personality (DuBois 1944).

This chapter has been exclusively concerned with the impact of personality on the social system, and specifically on the importance of personality for the motivation of role performance. Since the social system can serve its functions for society only if its component roles are performed, every society is confronted with the problem of social control—the problem of getting people to behave in conformity with cultural norms. By supplying the psychological basis for cultural motivation, personality is a vital instrument in society's attempt to achieve social control. It serves as such an instrument in three ways.

In the first place, although society provides sanctions as a means for achieving social control, these sanctions are effective only if the members of society have drives which can be reduced by the attainment of these goals. If this is the case these sanctions are cathected, and thereby become personality needs which motivate role performance. Second, if the cultural norms, which prescribe the performance of the role, are internalized by the members of society, nonconformity induces anxiety. Since this anxiety can be reduced by the performance of the role, conformity with these norms becomes a need which motivates role performance. Finally, the prescribed goals which are attained by role performance are, themselves, cathected and, hence, serve as personality needs to motivate the performance of roles.

These three types of control have been termed, extrinsic, internalized, and intrinsic, respectively. We may summarize their differences and similarities, as follows: (a) In extrinsic control which is based on positive social sanctions, and (b) in intrinsic control which is based on manifest personal functions, the performance of roles is motivated by the desire to obtain a rewarding goal—either the cathected social sanction or the cathected goal of the role. (c) In extrinsic control which is based on negative social sanctions, (d) in internalized control, and (e) in intrinsic control which is based on latent personal functions, the performance of roles is motivated by the desire to avoid pain—in the forms of physical or social punishment, moral anxiety, or unrelieved needs, respectively.

References

Aberle, D. F., *et al.* 1950. The functional prerequisites of a society. *Ethics* 9:100–111.

Beach, F. 1955. The descent of instinct. *Psychological Review* 62:401–10.

Benedict, R. 1946. *The chrysanthemum and the sword.* Boston: Houghton Mifflin.

Bolk, L. 1929. Origin of racial characteristics in man. *American Journal of Physical Anthropology* 13:1–28.

Carpenter, C. 1934. A field study of the behavior and social relations of the howling monkeys (*Alouatta paliata*). *Comparative Psychology Monographs*, vol. 10.

Carpenter, C. 1940. A field study in Siam of the behavior and social relations of the Gibbon (*Hylobates lar*). *Comparative Psychology Monographs*, vol. 16.

Cassirer, E. 1944. *An essay on man.* New Haven: Yale University Press.

Darling, F. 1937. *A herd of red deer.* London: Oxford University Press.

DuBois, C. 1944. *The people of Alor.* Minneapolis: University of Minnesota Press.

Eggan, D. 1952. The manifest content of dreams: A challenge to social science. *American Anthropologist* 54:469–85.

Erikson, E. H. 1939. Observations on Sioux education. *Journal of Psychiatry* 7:101–56.

———. 1945. Childhood and tradition in two American Indian tribes. *Psychoanalytic Study of the Child* 1:319–50.

———. 1950. *Childhood and society.* New York: Norton.

Faris, E. 1937. *The nature of human nature.* New York: McGraw-Hill.

Firth, R. 1954. Social organization and social change. *Journal of the Royal Anthropological Institute* 84:1–20.

————. 1955. Function. *Yearbook of Anthropology* 1:237–58.

Freud, S. 1930. *Civilization and its discontents.* New York: J. Cape and H. Smith.

Fromm, E. 1944. Individual and social origins of neurosis. *American Sociological Review* 9:380–84.

Hallowell, A. 1945. Sociopsychological aspects of acculturation. In *The science of man in the world crisis,* ed. R. Linton. New York: Columbia University Press.

————. 1950. Personality structure and the evolution of man. *American Anthropologist* 52:159–73.

————. 1954. The self and its behavioral environment. *Explorations* 2:106–65.

————. 1955. The Rorschach test in culture and personality studies. In *Developments in the Rorschach technique,* vol. 2, ed. B. Klopfer *et al.* Yonkers-on-Hudson: World Book Company.

Harlow, H. 1953. Motivation as a factor in the acquisition of new responses. *Nebraska Symposia in Motivation* 4:24–49.

Hempel, C. 1959. The logic of functional analysis. In *Symposium on sociological theory,* ed. G. Gross. Evanston: Row, Peterson and Co.

Henry, J. 1953. Towards a system of socio-psychiatric invariants: A work paper. *Journal of Social Psychology* 37:133–61.

Hilgard, E. 1956. *Theories of learning.* New York: Appleton-Century-Crofts.

Hine, R., and N. Tinbergen. 1958. The comparative study of species-specific behavior. In *Behavior and evolution,* ed. A. Roe and G. Simpson. New Haven: Yale University Press.

Inkeles, A., and D. Levinson. 1954. National character: The study of modal personality and sociocultural systems. In *Handbook of social psychology,* ed. G. Lindzey. Cambridge: Addison-Wesley.

Kaplan, B. 1957. Personality and social structure. In *Review of sociology, analysis of a decade,* ed. J. Grittler. New York: John Wiley and Sons.

Kardiner, A. 1939. *The individual and his society.* New York: Columbia University Press.

Kluckhohn, C. 1945. The personal document in anthropological science. In *Use of personal documents in history, anthropology, and sociology,* ed. L. Gottschalk, C. Kluckhohn, and R. Angel. Social Science Research Council, Bull. no. 53.

————, and H. Murray, with the collaboration of D. Schneider. 1953. *Personality in nature, society, and culture.* New York: Knopf.

Kroeber, A. L. 1948. *Anthropology.* New York: Harcourt, Brace.

La Barre, W. 1954. *The human animal.* Chicago: University of Chicago Press.

Langer, S. 1942. *Philosophy in a new key.* Cambridge: Harvard University Press.

Lehrman, D. 1953. A critique of Konrad Lorenz' theory of instinctive behavior. *Quarterly Review of Biology* 28:337–63.

Lewin, K., T. Dembo, L. Festinger, and P. Sears. 1944. Level of aspiration.

In *Personality and the behavior disorders,* ed. J. Hunt. New York: Ronald Press.

Linton, R. 1936. *The study of man.* New York: Appleton-Century.

Malinowski, B. 1944. *A scientific theory of culture.* Chapel Hill: University of North Carolina Press.

Mayr, E. 1958. Behavior and systematics. In *Behavior and evolution,* ed. A. Roe and C. Simpson, New Haven: Yale University Press.

Mead, G. 1934. *Mind, self, and society.* Chicago: University of Chicago Press.

Merton, Robert K. 1949. *Social theory and social structure.* New York: Free Press.

————. 1957. The role set. *British Journal of Sociology* 8:106–20.

Miller, N. E., and J. Dollard. 1941. *Social learning and imitation.* New Haven: Yale University Press.

Montagu, A. 1951. *An introduction to physical anthropology.* Springfield, Ill.: Thomas.

Murphy, G. 1947. *Personality: A biosocial approach to origins and structure.* New York: Harper.

————. 1954. Social motivation. In *Handbook of social psychology,* ed. G. Lindzey. Cambridge: Addison-Wesley.

————. 1958. *Human potentialities.* New York: Basic Books.

Nadel, S. F. 1953. Social control and self-regulation. *Social Forces* 31:265–73.

————. 1957. *The theory of social structure.* London: Cohen and West.

Nagel, E. 1957. *Logic without metaphysics.* Glencoe, Ill: The Free Press.

Nebraska symposia on motivation, ed. M. R. Jones. 1953. Lincoln: University of Nebraska Press.

Newcomb, T. M. 1950. *Social psychology.* Dryden: New York.

Parsons, T. 1951. *The social system.* Glencoe, Ill.: The Free Press.

————, and E. Shils. 1951. *Toward a general theory of action.* Cambridge: Harvard University Press.

Piers, G. and M. B. Singer. 1953. *Shame and guilt: A psychoanalytic and a cultural study.* Springfield: Charles C. Thomas.

Radcliffe-Brown, A. R. 1933. Sanctions, social. *Encyclopedia of the social sciences* 13:531–34.

————. 1957. *A natural science of society.* Glencoe, Ill.: The Free Press.

Rapaport, D. 1951. The conceptual model of psychoanalysis. *Journal of Personality* 20: 56–81.

Riesman, D. 1950. *The lonely crowd.* New Haven: Yale University Press.

Roheim, G. 1943. *The origin and function of culture.* New York: Nervous and Mental Disorder Monograph Series, vol. 63.

Sapir, E. 1924. Culture, genuine and spurious. *American Journal of Sociology* 29:401–29.

Spiro, M. E. 1951. Culture and personality: The natural history of a false dichotomy. *Psychiatry* 14:19–46.

————. 1952. Ghosts, Ifaluk, and teleological functionalism. *American Anthropologist* 54:497–503.

————. 1953a. Ghosts: An anthropological inquiry into learning and perception. *Journal of Abnormal Social Psychology* 48:376–82.

————. 1953b. A typology of functional analysis. *Explorations* 1:84–95.

————. 1958. *Children of the kibbutz*. Cambridge: Harvard University Press.

Thompson, W. 1958. Social behavior. In *Behavior and evolution*, ed. A. Roe and G. Simpson. New Haven: Yale University Press.

Tolman, E. C. 1951. *Collected papers in psychology*. Berkeley and Los Angeles: University of California Press.

Tylor, E. B. 1874. *Primitive culture*. Chicago: Brentano.

Wheeler, W. M. 1928. *The social insects—their origin and evolution*. New York: Harcourt, Brace.

White, L. 1940. The symbol: The origin and basis of human behavior. *Philosophy of Science* 7:451–63.

Whiting, J. W. M., and I. Child. 1953. *Child training and personality*. New Haven: Yale University Press.

Wissler, C. 1923. *Man and culture*. New York: Thomas Y. Crowell.

Zuckerman, S. 1932. *The social life of monkeys and apes*. New York: Harcourt, Brace.

6   Religious Systems as Culturally Constituted Defense Mechanisms

Since the range of beliefs, values, and rituals related to super-natural beliefs and events is enormous, it is obvious, as Durkheim observed long ago, that no belief, value, or ritual is intrinsically identifiable as "religious." Since the "religious," on the contrary, is a quality capable of being attached to almost any instance of these three dimensions of religious systems, the latter, to use a modern idiom, are in large measure projective systems. It is this characteristic of religion that poses a problem which has long confronted its students, and which comprises the problem of this chapter: If religious systems are indeed projective in character, how can we be sure that religious behavior is not abnormal behavior, requiring psychiatric, rather than sociocultural, analysis?

Anthropology, as is well known, has adopted a fairly uniform stance with respect to the cross-cultural variability which characterizes notions of the good, the true, and the beautiful. This stance, so far as the normal-abnormal distinction is concerned, was given classic expression by Benedict (1934), who maintained that judgments concerning abnormality are necessarily relative to intracultural standards. What is judged to be abnormal in one cultural setting may be properly characterized as normal in other cultural settings. This relativistic approach continues to provoke somewhat heated controversy, not only within the anthropological fraternity, but within the social sciences in general.

In a series of seminal papers Professor Hallowell has offered us important conceptual vehicles by which we can avoid the Scylla of nihilistic relativism and the Charybdis of ethnocentric absolutism. His concept of a "culturally constituted behavioral environment" (Hallowell 1955:chapter 8) allows us to view behavior relative to its cultural

Reprinted with permission of The Free Press, a division of Macmillan, Inc., from *Context and Meaning in Cultural Anthropology*, edited by Melford E. Spiro, pp. 100–113. © 1965 by The Free Press.

setting and, at the same time, to assess its functional consequences in terms of pancultural scientific criteria. I should like to examine the relationships between religion, abnormality, and relativism in the light of these conceptual tools. Although only these concepts are explicitly taken from Hallowell, this entire paper is heavily indebted to his work. Indeed, it is difficult to say when his ideas end and mine begin.

The persistent controversy over cultural relativism has been confounded by implicit disagreements concerning its proper antithesis. Some scholars conceive of (what I shall term) "universalism" to be the antithesis of relativism, while others take (what may be termed) "absolutism" to be its antithesis. The logic of relativism is quite different, depending upon which of these two alternative conceptions is taken to be its antithesis; indeed consensus concerning one or the other antithesis would mitigate, if not resolve, the controversy. I should like to propose absolutism as the valid antonym for relativism, and universalism as the antonym not for relativism, but for what might be called "particularism."

Universalism vs. Particularism

The question entailed by this distinction is whether a particular belief or behavior pattern found in our society—and which a clinician would characterize as pathological—occurs in all societies, in some societies, or only in our own society. This is an empirical question, concerned exclusively with the *occurrence* and relative *incidence* of a certain type of behavior. Correspondingly, the answer to this question must also be empirical, rather than judgmental. Whatever the answer to this question may be, the research task—once the answer is provided—is to identify those causal or antecedent conditions which produce the behavior or which account for its differential occurrence. In the older arguments for relativism, in which sociocultural variables were adduced as foils for, or as antidotes to, biological variables (usually, but not always, associated with racism), relativistic theorists turned to sociocultural determinants in order to explain the differential occurrence of different types of behavior. Particularism, as I shall label this variety of relativism, interprets the differential occurrence of a certain type of behavior as relative to, because determined by, differential sociocultural conditions.

Anthropological data—and, one might add, historical and sociological data as well—are unambiguous so far as the universalistic-particularistic dichotomy is concerned. The occurrence and relative incidence of certain types of behavior which, when occurring in our society, are labeled as schizophrenic, hysterical, paranoid, etc., vary not only from society to society, but they vary as well within the same society at different periods in its history, and among different social groups (class, ethnic, religious, etc.) within the same historical period. This empirical finding is independent of any judgment by which these types of behavior may be evaluated.

Absolutism vs. Relativism

This, rather than the former, dichotomy raises the genuine relativistic question, viz., can certain types of behavior which are designated as pathological when they occur in our society be properly designated by the same label when they occur in other societies? The concern here is not with the question of the differential occurrence of beliefs and practices—this is taken for granted—but with their clinical assessment. Absolutism holds that certain types of behavior are properly designated as pathological wherever and whenever they occur. Relativism holds that judgments concerning pathology are necessarily relative. There are different types of relativism, however, differing according to what these judgments are conceived to be relative to. One type, which we may label "social relativism," holds that judgments concerning pathology are relative to intrasocietal criteria, because there are no panhuman criteria by which cross-cultural judgments can be made. A second type, which may be termed "cultural relativism," holds that the criteria for judging pathology are panhuman, but that judgments based on these criteria are relative to the cultural context in which the action occurs. I should like to examine these two types of relativism, and their respective subtypes.

Social Relativism—Social relativism holds that judgments concerning pathology can only be based on intrasocietal—and, as we shall see, quantitative—criteria. One subtype, which might be termed "objective social relativism," insists that judgments concerning the pathology of some type of behavior must be relative to its incidence in the society (or some social group within a society) in which it occurs. Hence, behavior is properly judged to be pathological if (but only if) it is statistically rare; if, that is, it deviates from the statistical norms for that society. According to this subtype, "schizophrenic" behavior is pathological in our society because it characterizes a minority; if schizophrenics were to become a majority, schizophrenia would be normal. For this subtype, then, the abnormal represents social deviation.

"Subjective social relativism" holds that behavior may be judged to be pathological if it is deemed to be pathological by the members of the society in which it is found; it is not pathological if they deem it to be normal, or, at least, if it is positively rather than negatively evaluated by them. If, according to objective social relativism, judgments concerning pathology are relative to the incidence of some type of behavior within a society, according to subjective social relativism they are relative to its evaluation by the members of society. For the former, pathology represents deviation from statistical norms discovered by the anthropologist; for the latter it represents deviation from evaluative norms held by the society.

Although their criteria differ, both subtypes of relativism agree that there can be no panhuman criteria by which judgments concerning pathology can be established. Hence, behavior which is properly labeled "paranoid" when found in our society is "normal" if found among the Kwakiutl; hysteria is normal in the case of St. Theresa, but abnormal in a contemporary middle-class woman; the belief that most of mankind is doomed to eternal hell-fire is normal for a Calvinist, but abnormal for a Buddhist, and so on.

In my opinion both subtypes of social relativism are untenable. In the first place, since man (even *homo religiosus*) is a biological organism, there are, I would suggest, panhuman *biological* criteria by which behavior may be judged. If the majority in a given society have cancer, are we to say that they, the majority, are biologically normal, while those who do not have cancer, the minority, are biologically abnormal? This crude analogy suggests the fallacy inherent in the first subtype of social relativism. Judgments concerning biological normality or abnormality (health and illness) are indeed relative; but they are relative to specified criteria for the functioning of healthy organisms, criteria which are—or, at least, biological science takes them to be—universally applicable. Only two of the criteria which are relevant for the problem of behavioral pathology need be mentioned here: adaptation and optimum functioning.

Any organic characteristic which, like cancer, produces death, and which, if generalized, precludes the survival of the group—i.e., any maladaptive characteristic—is biologically abnormal. Furthermore, any characteristic which reduces efficient functioning—efficient relative to the potentiality of either the organ or the organism—is biologically abnormal. Thus, impaired vision or hearing, let alone blindness or deafness, are abnormal because they reduce the optimum functioning of these organs and, ultimately, of the organism. In short, maladaptive and inefficient functioning are, for the physician and biologist, panhuman criteria by which the presence of biological abnormality may be assessed; this assessment is independent of the incidence of these characteristics in a society or of their evaluation by its members.

If we are prepared to accept these criteria it would seem to follow that any condition which produces these effects—whether it be a characteristic of the organism or a characteristic of behavior—is pathological. Hence, if it is the case that a religious belief or a religious ritual is maladaptive and/or reduces optimum biological functioning, such a belief is, biologically viewed, abnormal.

But man is not only a biological, he is also a psychological and a social animal. For psychological, as for biological processes, the homeostatic principle, tension→tension-reduction, holds: tension stimulates action which is intended to reduce tension. Hence the persistence of tension is abnormal. Most psychological tension stems from conflict, either between one's moral values and/or one's self-image, or between those desires which violate the one or the other (or both). Since the tension induced by such conflict is painful, the typical actor—in accordance with the homeostatic principle enunciated above—attempts to resolve the conflict and, hence, to reduce tension. This is usually accomplished by a number of maneuvers, termed "mechanisms of defense," which defend the ego against the pain induced by the tension. Although these defense mechanisms may reduce the tension, thereby satisfying the homeostatic criterion of normality, they may have other pathological consequences. Any resolution of conflict, however successful in reducing tension, which results in the impairment of psychological, social, or cultural functioning may be taken to be a universal index of pathology.

"Impairment of psychological functioning" refers to distortions of three important modes of action: (1) Cognitive distortion: this refers to any cognitive behavior in which a demonstrably false belief is held to be true; (2) Perceptual distortion: this refers to any perceptual behavior in which stimuli are perceived to be other than what they are; (3) Affective distortion: this refers to any emotional behavior which, relative to the stimulus condition, is characterized by hyper- or hypoaffectivity. "Impairment of social functioning" refers to any condition of the actor which precludes the performance of social roles. "Impairment of cultural functioning" refers to any condition of the actor which precludes compliance with cultural norms and rules.

The three psychological criteria of pathology are panhuman because, if satisfied, the reality-testing function of the ego, the agent of man's adaptation (to nature) and adjustment (to society), is impaired, and the consequence of such impairment may be either individual or social disruption. The last two sociocultural criteria of pathology are panhuman because, in the absence of adequate social and cultural functioning, the survival of the individual—and, if generalized, the survival of the group—is jeopardized. No society could persist if the behavior of its members was characterized, for example, by genuine schizophrenia or genuine paranoia. Hence any religious belief or religious ritual which is characterized by, or which leads to, these three types of impairment is properly characterized as abnormal, regardless of its incidence and regardless of its evaluation by the members of society.

Cultural Relativism—Despite these animadversions on social relativism, its rejection does not entail the acceptance of absolutism. According to absolutism certain forms of behavior and certain kinds of beliefs are pathological wherever or whenever they may be found. Thus, for example, if a religious belief or ritual in a non-Western society is phenotypically similar to a belief or behavior pattern characteristic of a Western psychotic, the former, according to absolutism, is also abnormal. This position is as untenable as social relativism. Although the criteria by which behavior is judged may be universally applicable, it does not follow that all instances of phenotypically identical behavior or belief, when evaluated by these criteria, will lead to the same judgment. Although the criteria are panhuman, the judgments based on these criteria are necessarily relative to the sociocultural context within which behavior occurs. Distortion, for example, implies the existence of some reality relative to which a cognition is false, a perception is skewed, an affect is misplaced. But this reality, as Professor Hallowell has so cogently shown, is not a universal "given." Different cultures structure reality in different ways. For any actor reality is mediated through the world view and behavioral environment constructed by his culture. Hence, judgment concerning the existence of distortion must be based on the culturally constituted world view and the behavioral environment of the actor whose behavior is being assessed. For a Western man to believe that he is the reincarnation of some ancestor is to commit severe cognitive distortion; a Buddhist who holds the same belief commits no distortion. In short, the same criterion, applied to two identical acts, yields different judgments because the judgment—but not the criterion—is relative to the sociocultural context within which action occurs.

Social and cultural inadequacy must be assessed in the same manner. Whether a particular condition does or does not permit normal social and cultural functioning is necessarily relative to the repertory of social roles and the set of cultural norms which are found in the actor's, not the observer's, society.

If the preceding discussion is sound, it may then be concluded that beliefs and rituals which characterize the behavior of religious actors in non-Western societies, although phenotypically identical with beliefs and behavior which may characterize abnormal individuals in our society, are not necessarily (or even usually) abnormal when sanctioned or prescribed by the religious systems of the former societies and taught to the actors as part of their cultural heritage. There are a number of reasons for this conclusion: (a) The religious actor acquires his beliefs and rituals, as he acquires other aspects of his cultural heritage, through the usual techniques of instruction and imitation. Hence these beliefs and rituals are expressions, rather than distortions, of (his culturally constituted) reality. They are consistent with, rather than obstacles to, social and cultural functioning. Psychotic beliefs and behavior, on the contrary, are devised by the actor himself, as an attempt to reduce the painful tension induced by inner conflict. This attempt is necessarily based on his private distortion of (culturally constituted) reality, resulting in serious impairment of his social and/or cultural functioning; (b) Since religious beliefs and practices are derived from tradition, they are frequently compulsory; but since they are not created by the actor himself to defend against forbidden or shameful impulses, they are not compulsive. Psychotic beliefs and practices, on the contrary, are not compulsory—indeed they are usually prohibited—but as attempts to reduce tension, they are compulsive; (c) Although not devised by the actor to resolve conflict, religious beliefs and ritual may be used for that end. When so used they may not only resolve conflict, but as "culturally constituted defenses" (Spiro 1961:472–97) they are consistent with, rather than distortions of, reality; they comprise culturally sanctioned, rather than culturally prohibited, behavior; they protect the individual and his society from the disruptive consequences both of his shameful and/or forbidden needs and of his private defensive maneuvers. Conflict may also be resolved by psychotic beliefs and practices; but these idiosyncratic resolutions produce those psychological distortions and socio-cultural impairments which, as I have argued, are properly characterized as abnormal. I should like to examine these propositions in the context of one empirical situation—Burmese Buddhist monasticism.

Burmese Monasticism[1]

In Burma, one of the centers of Theravada Buddhism, the monastic vocation is the most venerated of all patterns of life. Almost every vil-

1. Materials in this section are based on field work carried out during 1961–62; I am grateful to the National Science Foundation for a fellowship which made the research possible.

lage contains at least one monastery with at least one resident monk. The monk, in theory at least, lives an exclusively otherworldly existence. His monastery is outside the village gates, and his interaction with the layman is confined to occasional ritual situations. The monk is prohibited from engaging in any form of physical labor, including any economic activity. All of his wants are attended to by the laymen, who provide his daily meals, his robes, and other necessities. Except for teaching young children, the monk's official responsibilities to the laymen are restricted to chanting of "prayers" at funerals and to public recitation of the Buddhist precepts on the "Sabbath" and other sacred days. His primary responsibility is to himself and to his attempt to attain nirvana. The latter goal is achieved through the study of Scripture and through various techniques of Buddhist meditation. These activities are believed to be instrumental to the attainment of Release from the round of rebirths because they lead to ultimate comprehension of the true characteristics of existence, viz., impermanence, suffering, and the absence of an ego. This comprehension, in turn, is believed to lead to the severance of all desire for, and cathexis of, the world. With the destruction of desire or "clinging" (tanha), the basis for rebirth is destroyed. Nirvana, whatever else it may be, is the cessation of rebirth.

The true monk, then, is completely absorbed in his own "salvation." Although living in a state of absolute dependence on the laymen, he has withdrawn both physically and psychologically from the physical and social world, and even—in states of trance (dhyānas)—from his own self. This extreme withdrawal from reality is similar to that withdrawal behavior which, in our society, would be taken as symptomatic of severe pathology, most certainly schizoid, if not schizophrenic. Is the Burmese monk to be similarly characterized? Such a judgment, in my opinion, would be grossly in error. Phenotypically, the behavior of the monk and that of the schizoid or schizophrenic patient may be very similar. Genotypically and functionally, however, they are importantly dissimilar. All of the criteria suggested in the previous section for assessing pathology are applicable to the schizophrenic; none is applicable to the monk.

In the case of the schizophrenic the actor resolves his inner conflict by constructing private fantasy and action systems; in the case of the monk, however, the actor uses culturally constituted fantasy and action systems (Buddhism) to resolve his inner conflicts. This difference not only provides the primary basis for a differential diagnosis of monk and schizophrenic, but it also provides, parenthetically, an important insight into the nature of religion. Culturally constituted religious behavior not only is not a symptom of pathology but, on the contrary, it serves to preclude the outbreak of pathology. The schizophrenic and the Burmese monk, alike, are characterized initially by pathogenic conflict, and schizophrenia and monasticism may each be interpreted as a means for resolving conflict. But this is where the similarity ends. Although schizophrenia and monasticism are both symptomatic of pathogenic conflict, the former represents a pathological, whereas the latter represents a nonpathological, resolution of the conflict. Let us examine these claims.

An analysis of monastic personality, based on the Rorschach records of a sample of Burmese Buddhist monks, and without reference to their (monastic) behavioral environment, would surely lead to a diagnosis of severe pathology. Dr. James Steele (1963), who has analyzed these records, finds the following "pathological" features, among others: (1) a very high degree of "defensiveness"; (2) "pathologically regressed" expression of aggressive and oral drives; (3) cautious avoidance of "emotionally laden" situations as a means of obviating the necessity of handling affect, for which there are no adequate resources; (4) a "hypochondriacal self-preoccupation" and "erotic self-cathexis," instead of a cathexis of others; (5) latent homosexuality; (6) above-average fear of female- or mother-figures.

One of the significant characteristics of the Rorschach protocols of these monks, according to Steele, is their similarity to the records of Burmese laymen. It is not that the monastic records do not differ from those of the laymen; but the difference is one of degree, not of kind. Monks differ from laymen, not because they have different problems, but because they have more of the same problems. The monk, in other words, is a Burman *in extremis*. Burmese laymen (like Burmese monks) are constricted, ruminative, defensive, anxious about females, distrustful of others, and, perhaps, latently homosexual. The monks differ from the laymen only in that, for all these characteristics, they are *more so*. Monks are *more* constricted, *more* ruminative, *more* . . . , etc. For other characteristics, however, monks are *less so*. Compared to laymen, monks are ". . . less phallic, less self-confident, less striving, and less impulsive." In summary, Burmese monks not only appear to have "more of the basic problems" which characterize Burmans in general, but they also seem to be characterized by a "more constricted adjustment." It is the latter feature, still quoting Steele, which makes them "less accessible to social interaction with the protection that this provides."

This picture of the Burmese monks is surely a picture of pathology. Are we to conclude then—holding in abeyance a specific psychiatric

diagnosis, and assuming that the Rorschach test is a reliable instrument—that these monks are abnormal? If personality existed in a social and cultural vacuum, the answer would be an unqualified "yes."
Acute psychological conflicts and attendant intrapersonal tensions are
marked. That these conflicts have produced defensive distortions of
various kinds—perceptual, cognitive, affective—is clearly indicated.
That social impairment is a most likely consequence of these conflicts,
tensions, and distortions can hardly be doubted. In brief, if personality
existed *in vacuo* one would probably conclude that Burmese monks
resolve their conflicts in a manner which issues in severe pathology
(perhaps paranoid schizophrenia).

But the proviso, "if personality existed *in vacuo*," is crucial. Although Steele's analysis of their Rorschach records is remarkably similar to my clinical impressions of these monks, impressions derived
from intensive participant-observation in a score of monasteries, and
from personal interviews with more than twenty-five monks—thus
providing a dramatic test of the reliability of the instrument and of
Steele's skill in its use—I did not ever feel that these monks, with but
one exception, were pathological or, specifically, schizophrenic. Nor is
this a paradox. The psychological analysis (based on Rorschachs and
clinical impressions) provides a set of statements concerning the emotional problems of the subjects; it also provides, to a somewhat lesser
extent, a picture of their idiosyncratic defenses, i.e., of those defenses
which the subjects have constructed for themselves, in an attempt to
resolve their problems. That these defenses are hardly adequate to the
task is obvious from the Rorschach analysis. Left exclusively to their
own inner resources many of these subjects would have become, I
believe, genuine psychotics.

But personality does not exist *in vacuo*, and Burmese males, characterized by the problems described, are not confronted with the necessity of solving these problems by means of their own resources. In
addition to their private resources, they are able to utilize a powerful
cultural resource for their solution, i.e., they can solve their problems
by recruitment to the monastic order. By utilizing the role-set prescribed for this institution as a culturally constituted defense, Burmese
monks can resolve their conflicts with a minimum of distortion. Since,
moreover, the performance of the roles comprising this role-set satisfies their prohibited and/or shameful needs and reduces their painful
fears and anxieties, these potentially disruptive psychological variables, rather than provoking socially disruptive behavior, provide the
motivational basis for the persistence of the most highly valued institu-

tion—monasticism—in Burmese society. As a culturally constituted defense, the monastic institution resolves the inner conflicts of Burmese males, by allowing them to gratify their drives and reduce their anxieties in a disguised—and therefore socially acceptable—manner, one which precludes psychotic distortion, on the one hand, and criminal "acting-out," on the other. Hence, the monk is protected from mental illness and/or social punishment; society is protected from the disruptive consequences of antisocial behavior; and the key institution of Burmese culture—Buddhist monasticism—is provided with a most powerful motivational basis. Space permits only a brief examination of these assertions.

The monastic rules which interdict *all* labor, and those Buddhist norms which guarantee that the laity provide monks with *all* their wants, combine to satisfy the monk's "regressed oral drives." The monastic life, moreover, makes no demands, either social or psychological, which might render the monk's weak "phallic-orientation," his low degree of "striving and impulsivity," and his lack of "self-confidence" nonviable modes of adjustment. Quite the contrary, the physical isolation of the monastery, and the monastic norms proscribing social participation, preclude the stimulation of "disruptive affect." At the same time, the monk's "self-preoccupation" and "erotic self-cathexis" is wonderfully expressed and institutionalized in the prescribed techniques of Buddhist meditation. Latent "homosexual" needs can be satisfied in the exclusively male setting in which the monks live. Finally, the strong interdiction on interaction with females provides little opportunity for encounters with them and for the consequent fear attendant upon such encounters. Buddhist monasticism, then, is a highly efficient means for coping with the psychological problems of many Burmese men. The differences between a monastic and a psychotic resolution of these problems are instructive.

1. In general the genesis of the psychotic's conflict is idiosyncratic, while the genesis of the monk's problem is rooted in modal features of his society. That is, the source of the monk's conflict—which we cannot discuss here—is to be found in culturally constituted experiences which the monk shares with many other members of his social group. The monk differs from other Burmans in one of three ways: his potentially pathogenic experiences are more intense than those of other males; other Burmans utilize alternative, non-Buddhist, institutions for the resolution of equally intense problems; still others (a minority) develop idiosyncratic methods of conflict-resolution (in extreme cases, these take the form of mental illness or criminal behavior).

2. The psychotic resolves his problems by means of idiosyncratic, private, defenses; the monk resolves his problems in an institutionalized manner, by utilizing elements of his religious heritage as a culturally constituted defense. The difference between these two types of defense accounts for the following differences between the psychotic patient, on the one hand, and the normal monk, on the other.

3. The behavior of the psychotic is incompatible with any normal social role within his society, and inconsistent with important cultural norms of the larger society. The psychotic is *psychologically incapable* of performing social roles or of complying with those cultural norms which he violates. The behavior of the monk, on the other hand, is entirely appropriate to—indeed, it is the enactment of—a most important and honorific social role. The monk may be psychologically incapable of performing nonmonastic roles, but he is ideally suited for performing the monastic role.

4. As a corollary of the above, the behavior of the psychotic is bizarre in the eyes of, and disapproved by, his fellows. The behavior of the monk is not only approved by the other members of his society, but it is most highly valued.

5. Following from the last point, the behavior of the psychotic alienates him psychologically from his fellows. The behavior of the monk, on the contrary, though isolating him physically from his group, serves to integrate him psychologically into the group; for in his behavior he expresses the most cherished values of Burmese culture.

6. The world view constructed by the psychotic represents a dramatic distortion of reality, as the latter is structured by the world view of his culture; and the cognitions and perceptions that are derived from his idiosyncratic world view are highly distorted, relative to the behavioral environment in which expected social interaction of his society takes place. The world view of the monk, on the other hand, rather than being constructed from his private fantasies, is taught to him as an integral part of the cultural heritage of his society. The private world view of the monk corresponds to the public world view of his society; his world view, in brief, is a culturally constituted world view. The Buddhist world view, of course, may be false, a distortion of reality, relative to the world view of modern science; but it is true, relative to the knowledge available to Burmese society. True or false, however, the monk's cognitions and perceptions are consistent with, rather than distortions of, reality, as the latter is structured by the world view and behavioral environment of his society. The perceptions and cognitions, the fantasies and emotions experienced by the monk in the course of

Buddhist meditation and concentration may never be experienced by other Burmans—because the latter do not meditate or concentrate—but they are experiences consistent with the conception of reality which all Burmans hold, and they are vouchsafed to any Burman who is prepared to enter into these spiritual disciplines.

7. The psychotic sustains social relationships neither with the normal members of his society, nor with other psychotics. Psychotics, in short, do not participate in the society of which they are members, nor do they comprise a social group, distinct from the larger society, but nevertheless viable for its constituent members. Burmese monks, on the other hand, although socially isolated from Burmese society, are yet psychologically part of it. Moreover, although the monk may find difficulty in participating in the larger society, and in forming social relationships within it, he does enter into social relationships with other members of the monastic order. Monks are members of increasingly larger concentric groups, beginning with other members of the local monastery and extending to the entire order of monks. In short, while psychotics comprise a typological class, the monks constitute a social group. The psychotic cannot live as a member of a social group, even if it be but a subgroup of the larger society.

8. Finally, and as a corollary of the last point, the behavior of the psychotic is anomic; it violates many of the rules of his society. The monk, on the other hand, not only exemplifies the rules of Burmese society, but he must, in addition, comply with the 227 rules of the monastic order (as outlined in the *Vinaya*). Should he violate these rules, he is expelled from the order as a charlatan, regardless of whatever wondrous visions he is alleged to have had, or miraculous powers he is supposed to possess.

In summary, then, a psychiatrically diagnosed psychotic is not only incapable of participating in his own society, he is incapable of participating in any society. An American psychotic would function no better in a Buddhist monastery than in an American city. A Buddhist monk, to be sure, while not capable of functioning in every cultural environment, functions very well indeed within *his* cultural environment. This is hardly surprising, since the latter environment is so structured that it satisfies his needs and resolves his conflicts. That he cannot function in a radically different environment does not render him "sick," nor his adjustment precarious. Typically, differential sets of human needs are differentially satisfied in different types of cultural milieux. It is doubtful if the typical Burmese peasant could adjust to an American urban environment, or a typical American to a Buddhist monastery. For neither is the new environment capable of satisfying the needs and resolving the conflicts which were produced by the old.

Summary and Conclusions

Burmese monks, as Rorschach data and clinical observations agree, are characterized by serious emotional conflicts. Their religious heritage, however, provides them with institutionalized means for resolving conflicts, and, moreover, for resolving them in a manner which satisfies none of the five criteria suggested in the first section of this chapter as panhuman indices of abnormality (psychological distortions and sociocultural impairments). Employing the monastic system as a culturally constituted defense obviates the necessity for Burmese males to erect private defenses which, necessarily, would lead to one or more of these distortions and impairments. Monasticism, in short, has important psychological functions for individual actors. By the same token, however, the psychological problems of these actors have the important cultural function of helping to perpetuate the monastic system; that is, these conflicts are not only resolved by means of the monastic system, but they provide the motivational basis for recruitment to the monastery and, hence, for the persistence of the system. The existence of the monastic system, moreover, not only permits the resolution of emotional conflict (the latent psychological function of the monastery), but by serving this function it reduces the probability of the occurrence of other, nonsanctioned means by which these conflicts might be expressed and resolved (latent social function of the monastery). If this culturally constituted defense were not available for the resolution of conflict, the consequent persistence of tension might lead to defenses of a psychotic nature, psychosomatic disorders of various kinds, or many types of antisocial, i.e., criminal behavior. I would suggest that a study of Burmese crime, including dacoity and insurgency—both of which are, and have been, endemic in Burma—would reveal that a large percentage of dacoits and insurgents are recruited from the ranks of those for whom the monastic life is not (for reasons still to be determined) a psychologically viable means for resolving emotional conflict.[2]

The monastic system, in short, not only serves the important personal function of precluding psychotic breakdown, but it also serves

2. This generalization excludes those—and I have met them—for whom insurgency and dacoity are romantic, adventurous activities to be given up when the adventure palls. It also excludes those whose emotional conflicts are idiosyncratic, rather than culturally patterned, and for which there are no cultural institutions by which conflict can be resolved.

the important social function of allowing potentially disruptive, anti-social drives to be channeled into culturally approved (institutional) behavior. Since the monastery, moreover—for reasons beyond the scope of this paper—is the most integrative institution in Burmese society, the social function of psychological conflict, when resolved in this fashion, cannot be overestimated.

If the foregoing analysis is correct, then—to return to the more general problem of this chapter—abnormal behavior can be expected to appear under one of three conditions: (1) when emotional conflict is idiosyncratic, so that cultural means are not available as potential bases for culturally constituted defense mechanisms; (2) when emotional conflict is modal, and cultural means are available for conflict resolution, but these means have been inadequately taught or inadequately learned; (3) when, under conditions of rapid social change, culturally constituted defense mechanisms are unavailable, either because older institutions have been discarded or because the new situation creates a new set of conflicts. These three conditions, however, are necessary, but not sufficient, conditions for abnormal behavior. Although emotional conflict is potentially pathogenic, it need not produce pathology. Emotional conflict issues in pathology only if it is not resolved, or if it is resolved in a manner which is characterized by psychological distortion and/or sociocultural impairment. The latter resolutions are characteristic of neurotic and psychotic resolutions.

But neurosis and psychosis are not the only means for resolving conflict. Other private defense mechanisms may be constructed which are perceptually, cognitively, and affectively consistent with the behavioral environment of the actors, and which, moreover, constitute no obstacle to adequate sociocultural functioning. Finally, there is a third category of defense mechanisms—culturally constituted defenses— which are not only not disruptive of, but rather serve to perpetuate, the sociocultural system. Conflict, in short, may indeed produce pathological defenses; but it may also produce normal defenses, either private or culturally constituted.

In most traditional societies, where religious beliefs and practices continue to carry conviction, religion is the cultural system *par excellence* by means of which conflict-resolution is achieved. In such societies, in which religious behavior is appropriate to, rather than disruptive of, the behavioral environment of the actors, and in which a religious world view is consistent with, rather than a distortion of, "reality," religion serves as a highly efficient culturally constituted defense mechanism.

References

Benedict, R. 1934. *Patterns of culture*. Boston: Houghton Mifflin.

Hallowell, A. I. 1955. *Culture and experience*. Philadelphia: University of Pennsylvania Press.

Spiro, M. E. 1961. An overview and a suggested reorientation. In *Psychological anthropology*, ed. F. L. K. Hsu. Homewood, Ill.: Dorsey Press.

Steele, J. 1963. *A preliminary analysis of the Burmese Rorschachs*. Unpublished ms.

7 Collective Representations and Mental Representations in Religious Symbol Systems

IN THIS chapter I want to address the relationship between statements of the following two types: "The omnipotence of God is a basic doctrine of Christianity," and, "As a Christian, John holds the doctrine of the omnipotence of God to be true." To put it more abstractly, I want to address the relationship between religious doctrines as they are found in the collective representations of a social group, on the one hand, and in the mental representations of the religious actors, on the other. Divested of jargon, I want to ask why it is that religious actors believe in the doctrines that comprise the religious system of their culture. If this question seems trivial, or if the answer seems obvious, it is only because we have for too long—certainly since Durkheim—accepted the coercive power of cultural symbols on the human mind to be a self-evident truth.

I have at the outset introduced the mind as one of the key terms of our discussion because one of the unexamined assumptions of much of anthropology is that any attempt to understand culture by reference to the mind is at best to confuse levels of analysis, if not levels of 'reality,' and at worst, to perpetuate the intellectual sin of reductionism. Although I oppose the confusion and abjure the sin, I will argue that inasmuch as cultural doctrines, ideas, values, and the like exist in the minds of social actors—where else *could* they exist?—to attempt to

Reprinted from *On Symbols in Anthropology: Essays in Honor of Harry Hoijer*, edited by Jacques Maquet (Malibu: Udena Publications, 1982), pp. 45–72. © 1982 by Melford E. Spiro.

I am indebted to Jacques Maquet and Walter Goldschmidt for inviting me to participate in the second series of lectures in honor of Harry Hoijer, and to Roy G. D'Andrade, Fitz John Poole, Theodore Schwartz, Marc J. Swartz, and Donald F. Tuzin for their valuable criticisms of an earlier draft of this paper. I wish to acknowledge my gratitude to the National Institute of Mental Health for its support of a research project on the comparative study of culturally-constituted defense mechanisms, some of whose findings are incorporated in this paper.

understand culture by ignoring the human mind is like attempting to understand *Hamlet* by ignoring the Prince of Denmark. To be sure, cultural doctrines and the like are encoded in those public and visible signs (cultural symbols) which, following Durkheim, we call 'collective representations'; but since the latter neither possess nor announce their meanings, they must be found in the minds of social actors. If this is not so, then to understand culture it is not sufficient to attend to cultural symbol systems and how they work; it is also necessary to attend to the mind and how *it* works. That, at any rate, is the thesis I wish to explore here.

In referring to the mind, I am not only referring to those intellectual and information-processing functions which are often exclusively associated with that concept. Rather, I am referring to all of those psychological processes—cognitive, affective, and motivational—which underlie any type of complex behavior. Such a broad notion of 'mind' is especially important if we are to deal adequately with the complex problem with which we are concerned in this chapter. Its complexity is a function of the fact that although religious systems are cognitive systems, they persist because of powerful motivational dispositions and affective needs of the social actors to which they are responsive. Moreover, although the culturally constituted meanings of the symbols in which religious doctrines are encoded are consciously held by the actors, the latter also invest them with private, often unconscious meanings, whose cognitive salience is no less important for their understanding. This being the case, in order to explain why social actors believe in the religious doctrines of their culture we must attend to the motivational and affective, as well as the cognitive properties of the mind; and in attending to these properties, we must be concerned with their unconscious, as well as their conscious dimensions.

In an important sense, this chapter may be viewed as a long, and somewhat extended and delayed commentary on an observation I made eleven years ago as a discussant at a symposium on symbolic anthropology. "If symbolic behavior is even half as important as Freud, for example, suggested, symbolic anthropology is the custodian of the richest of all the mines which are worked by the science of man. To be sure, we have not yet produced our Freud, but until we do, perhaps we would be wise to reread *The Interpretation of Dreams*" (Spiro 1969:214).

Before embarking on this inquiry, I should perhaps define its basic terms. By "belief" I will mean any proposition concerning human beings, society, and the world that is held to be true. By "religious belief" I will mean any belief that, directly or indirectly, relates to beings who possess greater power than human beings and animals, with whom human beings sustain asymmetrical relationships (interactions and transactions), and who affect human lives for good or for ill. In short, "religious" beliefs comprise that subset of beliefs which, directly or indirectly, are concerned with 'superhuman' beings. Not all beliefs, of course, are culturally-constituted, and since the distinguishing feature of "culture," as I shall use that term, is tradition, a "culturally-constituted" belief—religious or any other—is a *traditional* belief. That is, it is one which is acquired by learning a cultural doctrine—a proposition about man, society, or nature—that originates and develops in the history of a social group, and is transmitted from generation to generation by means of those social processes that are denoted by such terms as "education" and "enculturation." Our definition of "symbol" will be deferred until later.

With these definitions in mind, and considering what I have already said about the need to study culture in its relationship to the social actors—the culture-bearers, as they used to be called—the investigation of a culturally-constituted belief involves—or at least it ought to involve—a six-fold task. First, the cultural doctrine which is the basis for the belief must be described. Second, its traditional meanings must be ascertained. Third, its relationship to the other doctrines comprising the system of which it is a part must be delineated. Fourth, the structure of the system must be explicated. Fifth, the grounds for the actors' accepting the doctrine as their own belief must be uncovered. Finally, the functions of holding this belief—the consequences, for either the social actors or their society—must be discovered.

In referring above to the "meanings" of cultural doctrines, I was, of course, speaking elliptically; for their meanings, as I have already said, are "located" not in the doctrines themselves, but in the minds of the actors who hold and transmit them. Thus, when we ask, "what does the Christian doctrine in the omnipotence of God mean?" we are really asking, "what does this doctrine mean to Christians?" But since cultural doctrines are acquired through social transmission (rather than constructed from personal experience), the answer to questions of this type is far from obvious, as it depends on the cognitive salience with which the doctrines are acquired as personal beliefs.

Briefly, and in ascending order of importance, we may delineate a hierarchy comprising five levels of cognitive salience: (a) The actors *learn about* the doctrines; as Bertrand Russell would say, they acquire an "acquaintance" with them; (b) The actors not only learn about the doctrines, but they also *understand* their traditional meanings as they are interpreted in authoritative texts, for example, or by recognized specialists; (c) The actors not only understand the traditional meanings of the doctrines, but understanding them, they *believe* that the doctrines so defined are true, correct, or right. That actors hold a doctrine to be true does not in itself, however, indicate that it importantly effects the manner in which they conduct their lives. Hence (d) at the fourth level of cognitive salience, cultural doctrines are not only held to be true, but they inform the behavioral environment of social actors, serving to structure their perceptual worlds and, consequently, to *guide* their actions. When cultural doctrines are acquired at this level we may say that they are genuine beliefs, rather than cultural clichés; (e) As genuine beliefs the doctrines not only guide, but they also serve to *instigate* action; they possess motivational as well as cognitive properties. Thus, one who has acquired, for example, the doctrine of hell at this—the fifth—level of cognitive salience, not only incorporates this doctrine as part of his cosmography, but he also internalizes it as part of his motivational system; it arouses strong affect (anxiety) which, in turn, motivates him to action whose purpose is the avoidance of hell.

Although, in general, anthropologists have assumed that cultural doctrines are acquired at the fourth, if not the fifth level of this hierarchy, this assumption is all too often unwarranted, and it has led to erroneous interpretations of the importance of particular cultural doctrines, as well as to extravagant claims concerning the importance of culture in general in human affairs. Thus, for example, many key features of the social structure, political system, and economic organization of the Buddhist societies of Southeast Asia have often been explained as a function of the putative 'otherworldly' orientation of Buddhist actors, an orientation which is inferred from the Buddhist doctrine of nirvana. This explanation, however, is typically invalid because, as recent anthropological studies of these societies have shown, except for a few monastic virtuosi, this doctrine has not been internalized by Buddhist actors as a culturally-constituted belief, but is rather a cultural cliché.

My point, then, is that in order to explain a cultural doctrine—that is to account for its existence—we must first interpret it; we must discover its 'meaning' for the actors. This requires that we ascertain at which of the five levels of cognitive salience adumbrated above it has been acquired as a belief. On the premise that cultural doctrines have been acquired as personal beliefs at the fourth or fifth level of that hierarchy, anthropologists have typically adopted two complementary intellectual modes in their attempts to explain and interpret them.

One mode is concerned with culturally particular analysis and the other with trans-cultural analysis.

Conceived in the first mode, the analysis of cultural beliefs focuses on the local ethnographic setting in all of its uniqueness. For this mode, the question of why the Burmese, say, believe in cultural doctrines related to gods, demons, and the Buddha evokes an unambiguous answer: as part of the cultural heritage of their society, these doctrines have been acquired as beliefs by each successive generation of Burmese from previous generations. Hence, this mode is especially interested in discovering how these doctrines are related to other aspects of Burmese culture and society such that, together, they comprise an integrated "system." To the extent that this mode presses its analysis further, it turns in one of two directions. One direction, culture history, is concerned with diachronic 'explanation,' and attempts to discover the socioeconomic and political conditions which might have led to the invention or borrowing of these doctrines. The other, symbolic anthropology, is concerned with symbolic 'interpretation,' and attempts to discover the meanings of the symbols by means of which the Burmese express and represent their doctrines. In both cases, anthropologists who operate exclusively in this mode usually contend that cultural beliefs can be understood only in the historical context and the conceptual terms of the culture in which they are embedded. For, so they claim, in as much as the history which produced them and the symbols which represent them are unique, their meanings cannot be conveyed nontrivially by transcultural concepts.

The analysis of cultural beliefs conceived in the second mode goes beyond the first mode in that it seeks explanations not only of a culturally parochial, but also of a transcultural provenance. This mode is necessary to explain certain phenomena which are difficult, if not impossible to explain in the first mode. Why, to take one example, do cultural doctrines sometimes die out or sufficiently transform over time as to become unrecognizable? Or, to take another example, why are some cultural beliefs no more than clichés, while others are held with strong conviction and emotional intensity? In the second mode, explanations for such questions are usually not sought in parochial culture history, but in generic human experience. Moreover, those analysts who employ the second, as well as the first mode, usually disagree with the contention of those who employ the first mode exclusively that the cross-cultural diversity in symbols and symbol systems implies that the meanings of cultural beliefs are unique and incommensurable. They contend, rather, that underlying the wide range of variability in the 'surface' meanings of cultural symbols, there is a narrow range of variability—if not universality—at some 'deep' level of meaning, and that their interpretation must attend to the latter, as well as the former, meanings.

Since it is this second intellectual mode whose application to the analysis of religious symbol systems I wish to explore in this chapter, it is necessary to examine the set of assumptions—at least as I see them—on which it rests. First, despite the diversity of human cultures, the minds of culture-bearers everywhere share panhuman characteristics ("psychic unity of mankind"); second, these characteristics are the product of a shared biological phylogeny, on the one hand, and a similar social ontogeny on the other; third, the diversity of cultures represents variable attempts of the human mind to cope with the existential and adaptive problems of individual and social living, which vary as a function of diverse historical experiences and ecological conditions; fourth, the diversity which is found at the 'surface' meanings of cultural beliefs is associated with panhuman regularities in their 'deep' meanings; fifth, these regularities are transformed, by processes to be described below, into the historically conditioned, and therefore culturally parochial, meanings of the symbols by which these beliefs are represented and conveyed. It is primarily in their surface meanings that the much heralded diversity and relativity of human cultures, whose proclamation has become the hallmark of anthropology, is to be found.

Just as the first mode in the study of cultural beliefs can be divided into culture history and symbolic anthropology, the second mode can likewise be divided into two types: structuralism and culture-and-personality. Structuralism, whose founder and most eminent figure is Lévi-Strauss, is wholly concerned with the cognitive, and more particularly, the intellectual dimension of the psychic unity of mankind. Hence, it views the resolution of intellectual puzzles and paradoxes as the crucial feature of the mind, so far, at least, as its relationship to religious beliefs and mythic themes is concerned. In their interpretation of myth, for example, structuralists not only can (and do) ignore all other characteristics of the mind, but they also exclude from their purview the social actors who acquire and transmit the myths, focusing their attention on the myths themselves, as they are recorded in texts.

Culture-and-personality theory, insofar at least, as it takes its departure from the psychoanalytic conception of the mind, is concerned not only with the intellectual dimension of cognition, but also with its other dimensions, as well as with the affective characteristics of the social actors, as on the structural characteristics of religion and myth, in order to arrive at an adequate interpretation and explanation for them. It is this approach to religion that I shall explicate in this chapter. First, however, we must delineate those characteristics of the mind that are relevant for understanding religious symbols.

That human beings attempt to maximize pleasure, and that pleasure involves the gratification of needs, wishes, and desires— whether these be biological, social, emotional, or intellectual—are two propositions concerning the human mind which, I take it, would evoke fairly wide assent. That, typically, wishes and desires can be gratified only by transactions with the external environment—both physical and social—and that these transactions are based on specifiable perceptual and mental processes whose characteristics are universal are also (I expect) widely accepted assumptions. Thus, with respect to perceptual processes, if there ever was a society whose members could never distinguish fantasy from reality, or hallucinatory from veridical perception, such a society, surely, is part of the fossil record of human history. The same consideration holds with respect to mental processes. Societies whose members were typically unable to assess causal relationships, to grasp logical connections, to construct valid inductive generalizations, or to make valid deductive inferences—these are societies in which even the simplest of subsistence activities would have little chance of success. In a word, such societies would not have survived.

The perceptual and mental processes alluded to above—which, taken jointly, I shall label as "cognitive"—comprise a type (in the Weberian sense) in which mentation is governed by normally accepted rules of logic, and in which ideas and thoughts are represented by *verbal* signs which are combined and manipulated by conventional rules of grammar and syntax. It is a type, moreover, in which the perception of internal stimuli is distinguished from that of external stimuli. In the study of dreams, fantasy, and related phenomena, however, we encounter yet another type of cognition. So far as mentation is concerned, it is a type in which ideas and thoughts are typically represented by *visual* signs (both iconic and symbolic) and whose logic, as we shall see below, is analogous to that exhibited in metaphor, metonymy, and other tropes. So far as perception is concerned, it is a type in which stimuli originating in the inner world are taken as objects and events in the outer world. Following Freud, this type may be termed the "primary process" mode of cognition, in contrast to the first type which may be termed the "secondary process" mode.

In this chapter, we shall be primarily concerned with the primary process mode of cognition. For it, to turn from the individual to the sociocultural level, economic and technological systems, for example, may be said to be based more-or-less on the secondary process mode, then I would claim that mythicoreligious and ritual systems are based to a much greater extent on the primary process mode. In considering the above discussion of the latter mode, this claim means, first, that religion and myth possess a logical structure which differs importantly from that found in the technicoeconomic domain, strictly conceived; second, it means that they are the cultural domains, *par excellence*, in which fantasy is taken for reality. In short, they are the domains in which the adaptive constraints on the satisfaction of wishes and desires find an important exception. We shall begin this discussion with the second claim, deferring the discussion of the first to the following section.

To better understand the claim that in religion and myth fantasy is taken for reality, it is instructive to compare these cultural phenomena with dreams; those psychological phenomena in which this dimension of the primary process is most obvious and best understood. The dream world is a *reified* world. That is, although dreams consist of images of persons and events, these images are believed by the dreamer to *be*, rather than to *represent*, the persons and events they signify. In short, in the dream the mental representation of a thing is taken for the thing itself. Similarly, based on culturally acquired religious doctrines and rituals, as well as mythic narratives, the religious believer constructs a mental representation—also in the form of images—of a special and wondrous world of beings and events. Unlike the dreamer, however, the religious believer does not confuse the mythicoreligious world with his mental representation of it. Except in trance and other altered states of consciousness, the images in his mind, as well as the cultural symbols from which they are constructed, are not believed to *constitute* the beings and events that comprise that world; rather, they are believed to *represent* them. In short, unlike the world of the dream, the mythicoreligious world is believed to exist independently of the mental images and public symbols by which it is represented. In this sense, the images and symbols of the mythicoreligious world are like the images of the dream-as-recalled, rather than those of the dream-as-dreamt. For when the dreamer awakens from his nocturnal slumber, he recognizes (in many societies at least) that the persons and events comprising his dream-as-dreamt had, in fact, consisted of his mental representations of them.

Nevertheless, the analogy between religion and the dream-as-dreamt still holds. In the latter, the images in the mind are not only reified, they are *externalized,* that is, these images of persons and events are not only taken for actual persons and events, but they are located in the external world, outside of the dreamer. In his waking life, however, the dreamer recognizes not only that the dream consists of images in his representational world, but that these images are representations of fantasied events, constructions of his mind, which occur not in the external, but in his internal world. In short, he recognizes that the dream is a hallucination.[1] The case of the religious believer, however, is rather different. Although distinguishing between the mythicoreligious world, on the one hand, and the private images and public symbols by which it is represented, on the other, he nevertheless believes (in accordance with the teachings of his religious tradition) that these images and symbols signify real, rather than fantasied, beings and events which, as in the dream-as-dreamt, he locates in the external world.

Since, then, except for those who enter into trance and similar experiences, there is no experiential ground for believing in the external reality of the mythicoreligious world, but the authority of tradition, the first problem posed by the analogy between religion and dreams is why the religious believer does not (like the awakened dreamer) awaken from his religious slumber and recognize that the mythicoreligious world exists not in some external reality, but rather in the inner reality of the mind. The explanation, I think, is twofold. First, there are obvious differences between the images and symbols of the mythicoreligious world and those of the dream world. Second, there are certain characteristics of the mind which predispose human actors to believe in the external reality of the mythicoreligious (but not of the dream) world.

Before examining the first explanation, something must be said about that slippery word, 'symbol,' which I have thus far been skirting. Following Charles Peirce, I use 'symbol' as one type of sign, a 'sign' being any object or event which represents and signifies some other object and event, or a class of objects and events. A symbol, then, is

---

1. There are some primitive societies, of course, in which the dream-as-recalled is taken as a memory not of a nocturnal hallucination, but of an actual happening. For them, in short, the line between fantasy and reality (so far at least as dreams are concerned) is blurred. This does not mean that they are "pre-logical" in a wholesale sense, for the boundary between fantasy and reality is confined to a restricted domain. Nevertheless, it does mean that the primary process mode is a more prominent feature in the mental functioning of these societies than in those that do recognize the hallucinatory quality of the dream. It also means, moreover, that for such societies the reality of the mythicoreligious world poses a problem of a much smaller magnitude than those in which the boundary between fantasy and reality is drawn much more sharply.

that type of sign in which (to shift from Peirce to Saussure) the relationship between the signifier and the signified is arbitrary. It is this dimension of the symbol which distinguishes it from Peirce's other two types of signs: the 'index,' in which there is a factual *contiguity* between signifier and signified, and the 'icon,' in which there is a factual *similarity* between them. By these definitions, a relic of the Buddha is (or is believed to be) an index of him; a sculpture of the Buddha is (or is believed to be) an icon of him; and the word "Buddha," is a symbol for him. Icons and symbols (but not indices) may be internal (i.e., we may have iconic or symbolic mental representations of objects or events) or they may be external (i.e., objects and events may be represented by physical icons and symbols in the external world). Cultural symbols and icons are, of course, external signs whose meanings are public (or shared) and conventional (handed down by tradition). With some few exceptions, of the kind already mentioned, cultural signs are symbols.

On the basis of this brief definitional excursus—I shall have more to say about icons and symbols below—we may now turn to the first difference between the dream world and the mythicoreligious world which, as suggested above, might account for the belief in the external reality of the latter world, and its repudiation in the case of the dream world.

In reference to the dream world, it is necessary to distinguish between the dream-as-dreamt and the dream-as-recalled. (These two versions of the dream—in both versions I am concerned with the manifest content only—must also be distinguished, of course, from the dream-as-reported; but the latter version, important as it is for other purposes, is tangential to the purpose of this paper.) The dream-as-dreamt is a fantasy world which, represented in *private* and *internal* images (iconic and symbolic signs), is the dreamer's own creation. In constructing this world, the dreamer of course calls upon the memories of his own social experiences, the history of his group, cultural performances and traditions, and the like; but whatever its social and cultural inspirations, it is a representation of his own wishes and fears, hopes and anxieties. The dream-as-recalled is a representation, in memory (whether fragmentary or complete, distorted or veridical) of the dream-as-dreamt. Unlike the latter, however, which is experienced as an actual event, the dream-as-recalled is usually taken to be a memory of what the dream really is—a fantasied event. That it might, rather, be a memory of an actual event is usually contradicted by other events in the dreamer's waking life, as well as by the testimony of those of his fellows who may have comprised the *dramatis personae* of the dream.

Although the mythicoreligious world is also a fantasy world, rather than invented by himself, it is *acquired* by the religious believer from his cultural traditions. These traditions, which proclaim the historicity and factuality of that world, are transmitted by means of cultural signs—the verbal symbols of religious doctrine and myth, and the visual symbols of ritual and sacred drama. Hence, unlike the dream world, the mythicoreligious world is represented not only by the private and internal images of the religious believer, but also by the *public* and *external* symbols of his culture. Indeed, it is from these collective representations of the mythicoreligious world that the dreamer constructs his mental representation of it.

In short, one possible explanation for religious believers holding to the external reality of the mythicoreligious world, while denying such reality to the dream world, is that the latter is constructed from private thoughts, the former from cultural traditions. This difference has three important consequences. First, the reality of the mythicoreligious world is not only *proclaimed* by the full authority of tradition, but it is *confirmed* by the ever-present (and psychologically compelling) cultural symbols from which the believer's representation of this world is constructed in the first place. Second, the fantasy quality which characterizes any mental representation consisting of images, is blunted in the case of the mythicoreligious world because of its simultaneous representation in verbal symbols. Hence, unlike the dream-as-dreamt whose reality, upon awakening, is challenged by its chaotic, fragmentary, and often bizarre quality, the relatively systematic and coherent character of religious belief systems and myth narratives presents less of a challenge to the reality of the mythicoreligious world. Third, since culturally-constituted symbols are public (and their meanings are therefore widely shared), the actor's belief in the correspondence between the mythicoreligious world and his mental representation of it is confirmed by the consensual validation of his fellow.

Important as they are, these formal differences between the private images of the dream and the public symbols of religion are not, in my view, a sufficient explanation for the belief in the reality of the mythicoreligious world. They do not explain, for example, why religious doctrines persist even in the face of competing, and often compelling, counter-claims of fact or reason, nor why cognitive dissonance is resolved not by abandoning the doctrines, but rather by resting their truth in faith. These facts (and others) suggest, as William James pointed out long ago, that religious belief ultimately rests on the actors' "will to believe," an intellectual posture which perhaps finds its extreme expression in Tertullian's precept *credo quia absurdum est*, I believe because it is absurd.

This brings us to the second explanation for the belief in the reality of the mythicoreligious world mentioned above, for to speak of the will to believe is, of course, to shift our attention from the belief, and its representational medium, to the believer and his mind. In introducing this shift, I should like to distinguish "religion-as-a-doctrinal structure" from "religion-in-use," a distinction analogous to Saussure's distinction between 'langue' and 'parole.' By "religion-as-a-doctrinal structure" I refer to the organization of religious doctrines taken as a cognitive system, that is, a system of propositions together with their constituent meanings. In affirming these doctrines, the religious actor, unlike the religious philosopher, is concerned not only with their meanings, but also with what James termed their 'cash value.' That is, the religious actor is not so much interested in theory as in praxis (to employ a much over-worked distinction), and it is the latter dimension of religion to which I refer by the expression, "religion-in-use." As the expression indicates, this dimension refers to the purposes to which the religious actor puts his beliefs.

To say that religious actors are primarily concerned with religion-in-use is to say that although religious systems are cognitive systems, they persist not only because of the cognitive basis for the belief in the reality of the mythicoreligious world, not even because its symbols are good to think, but because the belief in its reality satisfies some powerful human needs. In referring to the satisfaction of needs, I am of course alluding to the functions of religion—not, however, to its social functions, but to those which it serves for the religious actors themselves. Here I would follow Max Weber's contention that religion serves two universal functions, both of which are related to the vexatious problem of suffering—illness, death, drouth, loss, bereavement, madness, and so on. First, it provides answers to the intellectual problem of the *existence* of suffering and its seemingly unfair and inequitable distribution (the theodicy problem). Second, it provides various means for *overcoming* suffering, both as a temporary achievement and a permanent victory (salvation).

If, despite the remarkable cross-cultural diversity in its structure and content, religion universally serves (at least) these two functions, then it follows that the latter are related to two corresponding need-dispositions of the human mind which preadapt social actors to believe in the reality of their mythicoreligious worlds. These comprise the need to explain and find 'meaning' in that which is otherwise inexplicable and meaningless, and the need to conquer the intolerable anxiety attendant upon painful and frightening situations that are beyond human ability to effect or control. If this proposition seems banal, it is nevertheless important to state as a reminder that even the most radical cultural relativist can hardly begin to understand the persistence of religion—or much else about human culture—without postulating some set of need-dispositions as a universal characteristic of the human mind.

Powerful as it might be, however, motivation alone is not a sufficient explanation for the belief in the reality of the mythicoreligious world. Such a belief persists, I would suggest, because social actors are preadapted cognitively, as well as motivationally, to believe in its reality. Furthermore, I would suggest, this cognitive preadaptation is derived from two biological (hence universal) characteristics of childhood—prolonged helplessness and extended dependency—as a result of which cultural systems, when viewed ontogenetically, are not the first resource from which social actors construct their representational world.

Beginning from birth—hence prior to the acquisition of language and the *culturally-constituted* conceptions of the world which language makes possible—children develop what might be called *socially-constituted* conceptions as a consequence of (prelinguistic) transactions with parents and other parenting figures. Hence, long before they are taught about the powerful beings who inhabit the mythicoreligious world young children have persistent and prolonged experiences, often accompanied by intense affect, with these powerful beings who inhabit their family world. Entirely helpless from birth, and absolutely dependent on these beings, young children form highly distorted, exaggerated, and even bizarre representations of these parenting figures. To be sure, as they grow older most (but not all) children relinquish these representations—often, however, after considerable struggle—in favor of more realistic conceptions of them. At first, however, these bizarre and distorted images, the products of primary process cognition, are unconstrained by the secondary process cognition characteristic of mature ego-functioning; that type of cognition which depends on the achievement of 'object constancy,' language competence, and 'reality-testing.' Let us examine each of these in turn.

Prior to the attainment of the developmental cognitive stage of object constancy, the representations of different types of experience with one and the same person are not yet integrated by the child so as to form an organized, albeit differentiated, representation of him; rather, each type of experience produces a separate representation. Hence, although the actual parent is typically both good *and* bad, helpful *and* harmful, dependable *and* undependable, the young child, by a process known as 'splitting' forms separate images of a helping figure, a harming figure, a frustrating figure, and so on.

But even with the achievement of object constancy, it is difficult to form an integrated representation of one and the same person until the acquisition of language. For when images, rather than words, constitute the representational medium, the portrayal of different, but especially opposing, attributes of the same person—nurturant and punitive, good and bad, etc.—in a single image is difficult, if not impossible to achieve by means of such a medium, as any dreamer or sculptor knows. Hence, typically, the prelinguistic child forms different and opposing representations of the same parent, rather than one, conceptually integrated representation of him or her.

In addition to this cognitive basis, however, there is an equally important affective basis for the young child's splitting the opposing characteristics of his parents into separate representations. The integration of the loving and loved parent and the frustrating and hated parent into a single representation presupposes a degree of emotional maturity not yet attained by the young child. The inner conflict resulting from hating the person he loves, and is dependent upon, is beyond his emotional capacity to tolerate. Moreover, given the child's lack of reality testing, to hate someone is to destroy him, and since he both needs and loves the parent, this potentially intolerable conflict is obviated by splitting these opposing mental representations of the parent.

Having mentioned the concept of 'reality testing,' we may now explore its relevance for our thesis in greater detail. In order to do so, we shall once again return to the dream. I have already noted certain ways in which, with respect to their mental functioning, the cognitive *stage* of the prelinguistic child is similar in some respects to the cognitive *state* of the dreamer. I now wish to examine yet another similarity. The dream, I have already observed, is a nocturnal hallucination in which the dreamer, whose reality-testing is impaired, does not distinguish fantasy from reality, nor does he distinguish the fantasies themselves from the images by which they are represented, with the result that these images are reified.

Clinical data suggest that these same cognitive confusions may be found in the mental functioning of the prelinguistic child, not because his reality-testing is impaired, but because it is still undeveloped. Thus, for example, the young child's mental images of his parenting figures, just like dream images, may be reified, and thereby experienced as autonomous agents. Since, moreover, the boundary between inner and outer experience is blurred at this age, these reified agents

may be experienced as located within himself (whence they are labeled, in the terminology of psychoanalysis, 'introjects'), or they may
be externalized and located in the outer world (in which case they are
labeled 'projections'). Although as the ego develops reifications are
gradually given up, they are nevertheless not relinquished easily, as is
indicated by the projections which form the basis for the imaginary
playmates of children, and by the introjects which are the basis for
spirit possession. (Those few adults who never give up these reifications suffer severe psychopathology; for example, psychotic depression, in the case of persistent introjects, and paranoid delusions, in the
case of persistent projections.) Rather than being relinquished, however, the externalized reifications of the early parental images may instead undergo a transformation, and it is this vicissitude of these
projections with which we are concerned here.

In societies in which there is a high degree of integration between
social and cultural systems, the child's early experiences with his parents may lead him to construct mental representations of them which,
structurally, at least, are isomorphic with the mental representations of
the superhuman beings of the mythicoreligious world whose characteristics are only subsequently conveyed through the verbal and visual
symbols of his culture. If one considers the typical mythicoreligious
world—with its gods and demons, saviors and satans, redeemers and
destroyers—then it becomes apparent that the *socially-constituted* images which young children form of the powerful beings comprising
their family world are highly similar to the *culturally-constituted* images which, at a later age, they form of the powerful beings comprising
the mythicoreligious world. Since, then, the former images, with all
their bizarre distortions and exaggerations, represent and signify actual
beings whose reality they have personally experienced, we may say
that children are cognitively preadapted to believe in the reality of the
superhuman beings that are represented and signified in the external
collective representations of mythic narratives and religious ritual, as
well as in the mental images which children form of them.

But given the fact that the child's early mental images of his parenting figures are reified and externalized, I would claim even more. For,
I would suggest, when the child constructs his mental representations
of the superhuman figures of the religious world, they may be merged
(identified) with the corresponding representations he had previously
constructed of the parenting figures of his family world, thereby forming a single representational world. When this occurs, the child's projections of his parental images may be retained without any
psychopathological entailments, for they are then assimilated to his

images of the superhuman beings whose existence is taught by religion and myth. At the same time, this process assures the belief in the external reality of these superhuman beings, for they are now merged with the reified and externalized images of those powerful human beings whose external reality he has himself experienced. (In rapidly changing societies, or in any other in which there is only minimal integration between social and cultural systems, the self-evident belief in the reality of the mythicoreligious world is maximally jeopardized, with the result that the belief may be relinquished, or—as I have already observed—proclaimed as an article of faith.)

Thus, to take an example near home, when God is referred to as "Our Father who art in heaven," the cultural symbol, "Father," may be said to have two simultaneous meanings for the religious believer, one at the 'surface' level, the other at a 'deep' level. Since it is God who is designated as "Father," and since He is not literally conceived by the religious believer to *be* his father—whether genitor or pater—the surface meaning of "Father" is obviously a metaphorical one. That is, with respect to certain of His attributes—justice, mercy, love, etc.—God, who resides in heaven, is conceived to be *like* his father (pater) or, at any rate, like the normative conception of father, as that conception is informed by Western values regarding fatherhood. If, however, his mental representations of superhuman beings are merged with the religious believer's projections of his mental representation of the parents of childhood, then, in its deep meaning, "Father" is taken literally. For although God is not conceived by the believer to be his actual father (the one who is, or at least was, on earth), He is conceived, according to this explanation, as one of the reified and externalized representations of his childhood father—or a composite representation of some of them—which, in accordance with religious doctrine, the believer locates in heaven. Since in this sense, but in this sense only, God is indeed his father who is in heaven, in its deep meaning, "Father" is taken literally.

Let me summarize my argument thus far. My main point has been that the belief in the reality of the mythicoreligious world, a belief in which culturally-constituted fantasy is invested with the appearance of reality, may be explained to a large extent as a function of the primary process mode of cognition. The cultural conceptions of the superhuman beings who inhabit that world are conveyed, of course, by the external cultural symbols by which they are represented—words, icons (sculpture and painting), and ritual—and from these collective representations the believer forms his mental representations of them.

That these beings are believed to exist independently of the collective, as well as the mental, representations which signify them is best explained by the correspondence that exists between these representations and the mental representations that the young child previously forms of those actual powerful beings whose reality he has personally experienced—his parenting figures. These representations are based on the primary process mode of cognition because, in the absence of language, the representational medium consists of images; in the absence of object constancy, these images are formed by the process of splitting; and in the absence of reality testing, they are reified and externalized. It is the merging of the believer's mental representations of the parents of early childhood that constitutes the *cognitive* basis for the belief that the mythicoreligious world exists independently of the collective representations by which it is both represented and signified.

By this explanation for the belief in the reality of the mythicoreligious world, religious symbols have both 'surface' and 'deep' meanings, and no interpretation of any particular religion is complete unless its symbols are interpreted at both levels.[2] For this reason, the interpretation of religion (and other cultural systems) is similar to the interpretation of a dream in that the knowledge of its manifest content alone can be highly misleading without knowledge of its latent content.

According, then, to this explanation, the external and public symbols of religion—its collective representations—represent and signify at their 'surface' level the superhuman beings whose existence is affirmed by the various culturally parochial, religious traditions—Jahweh, Allah, Siva, the Madonna, Durga, and the like. These are their conscious and culturally variable meanings. At their 'deep' level, however, these symbols represent and signify the projections of the mental representations of the parents of early childhood. These are their unconscious, and culturally universal meanings. (Such an interpretation of the collective representations of religion might be contrasted with that of Durkheim who, it will be recalled, viewed them—in their 'deep' meanings—as signifying society.)

---

2. The current interest in cultural hermeneutics persistently distinguishes between interpretation and explanation, interpretation being viewed as a humanistic endeavor, concerned with intentions' purposes, goals, and the like, while explanation is viewed as a scientific or positivistic endeavor, concerned with the search for causal and functional 'laws.' In my view, this is a false dichotomy. If the former endeavor is concerned with producing valid, rather than just any kind of interpretations, it must be no less concerned with 'laws,' than the former, because, of course, the cogency, if not validity of the idiographic interpretation is dependent on the nomothetic theory from which it is implicitly or explicitly deduced.

In sum, I have argued thus far that underlying the cross-cultural diversity in the surface meanings of culturally parochial religious symbols, there are universal deep processes and meanings. If this is so, these cultural symbols effect three important psychological transmutations in the religious actors: transmutation of infantile into adult conceptions, of individual into public meanings, and of unconscious into conscious concerns. The satisfaction of these adult, public, and conscious concerns—especially those related to the explanation and conquest of suffering—constitutes, so I have argued, the most important manifest function of religion, providing a powerful motivational basis for the belief in the reality of the mythicoreligious world.

However, if religious symbols also have deep meanings, then religion not only has manifest functions related to the surface meanings of these symbols, but it must also have latent functions related to their deep meanings. Hence in this, the concluding section of this paper, I wish to argue that religion attends not only to the conscious and public concerns of the actor's adult-like experience, but also to the unconscious and private concerns of his child-like experience. For if religious symbols are associated with unconscious infantile mental representations, it can only be because in addition to their conscious, adult concerns, social actors retain unconscious, infantile concerns, and it is their satisfaction that constitutes the latent function of religion. The intention of satisfying these concerns constitutes yet another—an unconscious—motivational basis for the belief in the reality of the mythicoreligious world.

Since dreams constitute the most important private symbol system for the gratification, in fantasy, of infantile needs, I shall turn once again to the dream to help us understand the motivational aspects of unconscious symbolic processing. Since in this context, however, we are interested not in the hallucinatory, or ontological dimension of primary process cognition, but in its "logical" dimension, we shall seek assistance from poetry as well. (The argument of this section of the paper is similar to, but also differs to some extent from one I have previously developed elsewhere. See Spiro 1977:xix–xxx.)

Should a poet wish to represent a conception of a friend—his bravery for example—he may convey this conception in a simple prose sentence, "John is brave"; in a figure of speech, such as the simile, "John is like a bull"; or in a trope, such as the metaphor, "John is a bull." In the metaphor, the intended meaning of the verbal symbol, "bull," is figurative rather than literal, for it is intended to represent the poet's conception of John, rather than to signify the brave bull in Madrid's corrida.

Unlike the poet, the dreamer has fewer degrees of freedom to express his thoughts because a representational medium consisting of images cannot directly represent qualities, such as bravery, which in language are represented by adjectives, adverbs, and similar parts of speech. In such a medium, which only contains the structural equivalents of nouns and verbs, the thought, "John is brave," cannot be represented in a form analogous to a simple sentence, let alone a simile. Rather, given the constraints of his medium, the dreamer, just like the painter or sculptor, can only represent such a thought in a form analogous to a trope. Hence, to represent the thought that John is brave, he may dream of a bull. Like the verbal trope of the poet, the visual trope of the dreamer can be misleading to one who does not understand the code. Thus, though the consciously intended meaning of the bull is figurative, rather than literal, inasmuch as an image of a bull is conventionally taken to be a representation of a certain species of bovine, it is a conventionally inappropriate sign for a human being. To put it in Peirce's classification of signs, although the image of the bull is intended as a *symbol* for John, its meaning will be misunderstood if it is taken as an *icon* for a bull. And this potential confusion is precisely one of the difficulties that is posed by the interpretation of dreams, as well as one of the reasons for their seemingly bizarre qualities. For although in the sleeping code by which he constructs his dream, the dreamer consciously intends the bull to be a symbolic representation of John, in his waking code by which he interprets the dream, it is taken by him to be an iconic representation of a bovine. In short, in the dream-as-recalled, the image of the bull is taken literally, though in the dream-as-dreamt it was intended figuratively.

The poet, of course, does not have an analogous problem—though his reader may—because he uses the same code in reading his poem that he had used when composing it. On both occasions, the conventionally inappropriate verbal symbol, "bull," is consciously understood by him to be a metaphor, a form which he chose in the first place in order to convey his conception of John more effectively, forcefully, or artistically than might have been achieved by a simple prose sentence. In short, both in the case of the poem and of the dream-as-dreamt, the figurative meaning of the sign—the word in the former, the image in the latter—is its consciously intended, and only, meaning.

In addition, however, to the representational constraints of his medium, the dreamer may set forth his thoughts in conventionally inappropriate images for yet another reason: the wish to disguise them. All of us have thoughts that are repugnant to our moral values, and since such thoughts are painful—they arouse moral anxiety—we often repress them, i.e., eliminate them from conscious awareness. Let us suppose, then, that in his waking state a dreamer has a repressed thought concerning his friend, John—the thought, for example, that he would like him to die. Let us further suppose that this thought continues in his sleep. If the dreamer were to distort this thought, by substituting a bull for John as the object of his wish, then he might, with moral impunity, gratify this disguised wish in a dream in which he kills a bull. In such a dream, the image of the bull has two meanings simultaneously—one literal, the other figurative. Its literal meaning (bull) is *consciously* intended, while its figurative meaning (John) is *unconsciously* intended. Since in this dream, unlike the first, the image is an unconscious symbol for John—consciously, of course, it is taken as an icon of a bull—the substitution of a bull for John is an example not of a trope, but of a defense mechanism; that is, it is a cognitive maneuver in which a forbidden wish undergoes unconscious symbolic distortion in the service of a disguise.

Let me now summarize very briefly the formal characteristics of defense mechanisms, in contrast to tropes, in somewhat more technical terms: (a) In a defense mechanism the symbolic distortion of the wish is *overdetermined,* that is, it is based on multiple and simultaneous motives, including the motives to gratify and—since it is forbidden—to disguise a wish; (b) Disguise and gratification alike are achieved by *displacement,* an unconscious process in which a conventionally inappropriate sign is substituted for an appropriate one. (Displacement is based on the same criteria—similarity or contiguity between the original and substituted objects signified by the two signs—that are employed in the symbolic substitutions found in metaphor, metonymy, synecdoche, and other tropes.); (c) Hence, the substitute sign is characterized by *condensation,* i.e., it has two or more simultaneously intended meanings, at least one of which is unconscious; (d) The conscious, or *manifest* meaning of the sign is its literal meaning; its unconscious, or *latent* meaning is its figurative meaning.

Let us now apply this analysis of the defensive use of the private symbols comprising the dream to the cultural symbols comprising religion. As a cultural system, religion attends in the first instance, as I have stressed more than once, to the public and conscious concerns of the believers' adult experience, especially their concern with suffering in both its intellectual and existential dimensions. That is, it attends to the needs to both explain and overcome suffering. To achieve the latter end, the religious actor engages in ritual transactions with the superhuman beings comprising the mythicoreligious world. Some of these beings, kindly and benevolent, he turns to for assistance and aid in his attempt to cope with suffering. Others of them, aggressive and malevolent, are often viewed as the cause of suffering, and these he attempts to drive out or drive off. The former type arouse his wishes for and emotions of dependency and succorance; the latter type arouse his aggression, fear, and hatred.

Although such postures of dependency and aggression—whether expressed in the form of wishes, emotions, or actions—are culturally appropriate for adults in the religious contexts in which they are aroused and displayed, they are usually considered inappropriate for them in other contexts. There is one context, in particular, in which they are especially inappropriate; that context, of course, is the family. As the child's most significant others, his parents are at once his most important frustrating figures (consequently, the targets of his most intense aggressive feelings and wishes) and his most important nurturant figures (consequently the objects of his most intense dependency feelings and wishes). Parents are also, however, the very persons concerning whom, following an initial, culturally variable period of indulgence, the cultural prohibitions against dependency and aggression are most severe. The reasons are obvious. Social survival requires that children eventually outgrow their dependency on their family of origin, and that, having achieved independent status, they establish their own families and become objects for the dependency of their own children. Similarly, since aggression within the family is entirely disruptive of its integration, if not survival—hence inimical to its vital individual and social functions—it too must be prohibited.

This being so, every social actor and every society are confronted with an acute existential dilemma. Although his parents are the objects of the child's most intense dependency and aggressive needs and wishes, they are also the persons concerning whom their gratification is eventually most strongly frustrated. For although as children grow older and become adults, they learn to comply with the cultural norms prohibiting the overt display of aggression toward and dependency upon parents, this does not mean that these infantile needs are extinguished. That the contrary is the case is indicated not only by an abundance of clinical evidence, but also by commonplace observations of everyday life which indicate that these emotions and wishes are capable of arousal—and not only in a displaced form—in certain contexts, at least, and under certain provocations.

In sum, then, I am arguing that the intense dependency and aggressive wishes of children concerning parents, though seemingly extinguished, continue to exist in a repressed state in adults. Like all repressed wishes, these too seek gratification, and like them they are typically gratified—if they are gratified at all—in symbolic disguise. In addition to dreams, repressed wishes may be represented and (partially) gratified in the many privately constructed symbolic forms (including symptoms) which have been described and classified by psychiatrists. Typically, however, such wishes, particularly if they are widely shared, are represented and gratified in culturally-constituted rather than privately-constructed symbolic forms. Although many cultural systems—from games through politics—can be and have been used for this purpose, I would argue that religion is the system, *par excellence*, which is used for the disguised representation and gratification of the repressed wishes with which we are concerned here— dependency and aggressive wishes with regard to the parents of childhood. This is certainly the case in traditional societies, and if newspaper reports and television broadcasts can be taken as evidence, it is also the case, to a larger extent than we usually credit, in certain strata of modern society as well. That religion should be a focal system for the gratification of these wishes is hardly surprising if the explanation which I have offered for the meaning of its symbols is valid. For if the cultural symbols which represent the superhuman beings of the mythicoreligious world signify, in their 'deep' meaning, the reified and externalized mental representations of the parents of childhood, what better way to express and gratify unconscious rage toward and dependency longings for these parents than through the vehicle of religious beliefs and rituals?

My thesis, then, is that when religious actors invoke the assistance of benevolent superhuman beings, or exorcise malevolent superhuman beings, they are not only *consciously* gratifying dependency and aggressive needs in regard to beings who are their *culturally appropriate* objects and targets, but they are also doing more than that. For if the actors' mental representations of these benevolent and malevolent superhuman beings are merged with the reified and projected representations of their kindly and hateful parents of childhood, then, they are simultaneously, but *unconsciously*, gratifying their dependency and aggressive needs in regard to their childhood parents, their *culturally inappropriate* objects and targets. That religion-in-use serves this (latent) function explains at least one of the unconscious motivational bases for the belief in the reality of the mythicoreligious world. I might add that if this argument is valid, religion also serves an equally important latent function for society. For if religion-in-use is a means for the symbolic gratification of these powerful infantile needs, society is thereby spared the highly disruptive consequences of their direct gratification. But that is a topic for another paper.

We may now summarize the implications of this paper, with respect to both its specifically religious argument and its more general cultural-symbolic argument. The former argument has been concerned with only one problem related to the explanation of religious systems, the problem of why religious actors believe in the reality of the mythicoreligious world. Whether or not the particular solution offered here is correct is less important, however, than its underlying thesis that a comprehensive explanation for such a belief must attend to at least three dimensions of the problem: (a) the private, as well as public meanings of religious symbols; (b) their 'deep,' or socially acquired meanings, as well as their 'surface,' or culturally transmitted meanings; and (c) the latent, as well as the manifest functions of the actor's belief that these symbols signify a real, and not merely a representational world. An explanation that ignores any of these dimensions is, I have tried to show, incomplete.

To arrive at such a comprehensive explanation, I further attempted to show, we must be as much concerned with the properties and processes of the human mind as with the properties of cultural symbols and the doctrines which they represent. Although Durkheim's insistence that collective representations constitute the focus of anthropological investigation marked a giant leap forward in the study of sociocultural systems, he made a serious error in ruling out the study of mental representations as irrelevant to their study. For, as this paper has attempted to show, any cultural system is a vital force in society so long as there is a correspondence between the symbols in which cultural doctrines are represented and their representation as beliefs in the minds of social actors. When such a correspondence does not obtain, a cultural system may yet survive, but it survives as a fossil—as a set of clichés—rather than as a living force. If this is so, then the study of mental representations is no less important than that of collective representations for the anthropological enterprise.

My argument makes an even more radical claim, namely, that in attending to the human mind it is as important to understand its unconscious, as well as its conscious processes. Although a knowledge of conscious cognitions and motives can help us to understand the 'surface' meanings and manifest functions of cultural symbols, knowledge of unconscious cognitions and motives is required to understand their 'deep' meanings and latent functions. Lest I be misunderstood, I have not argued, as an older generation of psychoanalytic theorists was sometimes prone to do, that the latter meanings and functions are more important for the understanding of symbols (whether cultural or noncultural) than the former. I have argued, however, that they are no less important.

References

Spiro, Melford E. 1969. Discussion. In *Forms of symbolic action*, ed. Robert F. Spencer. Seattle: University of Washington Press (for the American Ethnological Society), 208–14.

———. 1977. *Kinship and marriage in Burma*. Berkeley: University of California Press.

———. 1978. *Burmese supernaturalism*. Expanded edition. Philadelphia: Institute for the Study of Human Issues.

III   RELIGION AND MYTH

8   Religion: Problems of Definition and Explanation

Introduction[1]

BEFORE EXAMINING various approaches to the explanation of religion, we must first agree about what it is that we hope to be able to explain. In short, we must agree on what we mean by 'religion'. Anthropology, like other immature sciences—and especially those whose basic vocabulary is derived from natural languages—continues to be plagued by problems of definition. Key terms in our lexicon—'culture', 'social system', 'needs', 'marriage', 'function', and the like—continue to evoke wide differences in meaning and to instigate heated controversy among scholars. Frequently the differences and controversies stem from differences in the *types* of definition employed.

Logicians distinguish between two broad types of definition: nominal and real definitions (Hempel 1952:2–14). Nominal definitions are those in which a word, whose meaning is unknown or unclear, is defined in terms of some expression whose meaning is already known. We all engage in such an enterprise in the classroom when we attempt to define, i.e. to assign meaning to, the new terms to which we expose our untutored undergraduates. Our concern in this case is to communicate ideas efficiently and unambiguously; and, in general, we encounter few difficulties from our students, who have no ego-involvement in alternative definitions to our own. We do have difficulties with our colleagues, however, because they—unlike us!—are ego-involved in their immortal prose and, intransigently, prefer their nominal definition to ours. Despite their intransigence, however, the problem of

Reprinted from *Anthropological Approaches to the Study of Religion*, edited by Michael Banton (London: Tavistock Publications, 1966), pp. 85–126.

1. Work on this paper is part of a cross-cultural study of religion supported by research grant M-2255 from the National Institutes of Health, U.S. Public Health Service.

187

achieving consensus with respect to nominal definitions is, at least in principle, easily resolved. We could, for example, delegate to an international committee of anthropologists the authority to publish a standard dictionary of anthropological concepts, whose definitions would be mandatory for publication in anthropological journals.

The problem is more serious, and its resolution correspondingly more difficult, in the case of real definitions. Unlike nominal definitions which arbitrarily assign meaning to linguistic symbols, real definitions are conceived to be true statements about entities or things. Here, three difficulties are typically encountered in anthropology (and in the other social sciences). The first difficulty arises when a hypothetical construct—such as culture or social structure—is reified and then assigned a real definition. Since that which is to be defined is not an empirically observable entity, controversies in definition admit of no empirical resolution.

A second difficulty is encountered when real definitions are of the kind that stipulate what the definer takes to be the 'essential nature' of some entity. Since the notion of 'essential nature' is always vague and almost always nonempirical, such definitions are scientifically useless. Kinship studies represent a good case in point, with their—at least so it seems to a nonspecialist—interminable controversies concerning the essential nature of marriage, descent, corporality, and the like.

Sometimes, however, real definitions are concerned with analyzing a complex concept—which has an unambiguous empirical referent—by making explicit the constituent concepts which render its meaning. These are known as analytic definitions. Thus, the expression 'X is a husband' can be defined as 'X is a male human, and X is married to some female human'. But the possible objections which such a definition would evoke among some anthropologists, at least, exemplifies the third definitional difficulty in anthropology: what might be called our obsession with universality. Since there are instances in parts of Africa of a phenomenon similar to what is ordinarily termed 'marriage', but in which both partners are female, some scholars would rule out this definition on the grounds that it is culturally parochial. This insistence on universality in the interests of a comparative social science is, in my opinion, an obstacle to the comparative method for it leads to continuous changes in definition and, ultimately, to definitions which, because of their vagueness or abstractness, are all but useless. (And of course they commit the fallacy of assuming that certain institutions must, in fact, be universal, rather than recognizing that universality is a creation of definition. I am also at a loss to understand why certain institutions—marriage, for example—must be universal, while others—such as the state—need not be.)

The Problem of Definition in Religion

An examination of the endemic definitional controversies concerning religion leads to the conclusion that they are not so much controversies over the meaning either of the term 'religion' or of the concept which it expresses, as they are jurisdictional disputes over the phenomenon or range of phenomena which are considered to constitute legitimately the empirical referent of the term. In short, definitional controversies in religion have generally involved differences in what are technically termed ostensive definitions. To define a word ostensively is to point to the object which that word designates. In any language community, the fiery ball in the sky, for example, evokes a univocal verbal response from all perceivers; and a stranger arriving in an English-speaking community can easily learn the ostensive definition of the word 'sun' by asking any native to point to the object for which 'sun' is the name. Similarly the empirical referent of 'table' can be designated unequivocally, if not efficiently, by pointing to examples of each subset of the set of objects to which the word applies.

The community of anthropologists, however, is not a natural language community—more important, perhaps, it does not share a common culture—and although there is little disagreement among anthropologists concerning the class of objects to which such words as 'sister', 'chief', 'string figure'—and many others—properly *do* apply, there is considerable disagreement concerning the phenomena to which the word 'religion' *ought* to apply. Hence the interminable (and fruitless) controversies concerning the religious status of coercive ritual or an ethical code or supernatural beings, and so on. From the affect which characterizes many of these discussions one cannot help but suspect that much of this controversy stems, consciously or unconsciously, from extrascientific considerations—such as the personal attitudes to religion which scholars bring to its study. Since I am concerned with the logic of inquiry, I must resist a tempting excursion into the social psychology of science.

The scientific grounds for disagreement are almost always based on comparative considerations. Thus Durkheim rejects the belief in supernatural beings as a legitimate referent of 'religion' on the grounds that this would deny religion to primitive peoples who, allegedly, do not distinguish between the natural and the supernatural. Similarly, he rejects the belief in gods as a distinguishing characteristic of 'religion' because Buddhism, as he interprets it, contains no such belief (1954:24–36). Such objections raise two questions; one factual, the other methodological. I shall return to the factual question in a later section, and confine my present remarks to the methodological question. Even if it were the case that Theravada Buddhism contained no belief in gods or supernatural beings, from what methodological principle does it follow that religion—or, for that matter, anything else—must be universal if it is to be studied comparatively? The fact that hunting economies, unilateral descent groups, or string figures do not have a universal distribution has not prevented us from studying *them* comparatively. Does the study of religion become any the less significant or fascinating—indeed, it would be even more fascinating—if in terms of a consensual ostensive definition it were discovered that one, or seven, or sixteen societies did not possess religion? If it indeed be the case that Theravada Buddhism is atheistic and that, by a theistic definition of religion, it is not therefore a religion, why can we not face, rather than shrink, from this consequence? Having combatted the notion that 'we' have religion (which is 'good') and 'they' have supersitition (which is 'bad'), why should we be dismayed if it be discovered that society *x* does not have 'religion', as we have defined that term? For the premise 'no religion' does not entail the conclusion 'therefore superstition'—nor, incidentally, does it entail the conclusion 'therefore no social integration', unless of course religion is defined as anything which makes for integration. It may rather entail the conclusion 'therefore science' or 'therefore philosophy'. Or it may entail no conclusion and, instead, stimulate some research. In short, once we free the word 'religion' from all value judgments, there is reason neither for dismay nor for elation concerning the empirical distribution of religion attendant upon our definition. With respect to Theravada Buddhism, then, what loss to science would have ensued if Durkheim had decided that, as he interpreted it, it was atheistic, and therefore not a religion? I can see only gain. First, it would have stimulated fieldwork in these apparently anomalous Buddhist societies and, second, we would have been spared the confusion created by the consequent real and functional definitions of religion which were substituted for the earlier substantive or structural definitions.

Real definitions, which stipulate the 'essential nature' of some phenomenon are, as I have already argued, necessarily vague and almost always nonempirical. What, for example, does Durkheim's 'sacred'—which he stipulates as the essential nature of religion—really mean? How useful is it, not in religious or poetic, but in scientific discourse?

It is much too vague to be taken as a primitive term in a definitional chain, and it is useless to define it by equally vague terms such as 'holy' or 'set apart'. But if such real definitions are unsatisfactory when the phenomenal referent of the *definiendum* is universally acknowledged, they are virtually useless when, as in this case, it is the phenomenal referent which is precisely at issue. If there is no agreement about what it is that is being defined, how can we agree on its essential nature? Durkheim, to be sure, circumvented this problem by arguing that the sacred is whatever it is that a society deems to be sacred. But even if it were to be granted that one obscurity can achieve clarity by the substitution of another, real definitions of this type—like functional definitions to which I now wish to turn—escape the trap of overly narrow designata only to fall into the trap of overly broad ones.

Most functional definitions of religion are essentially a subclass of real definitions in which functional variables (the promotion of solidarity, and the like) are stipulated as the essential nature of religion. But whether the essential nature consists of a qualitative variable (such as 'the sacred') or a functional variable (such as social solidarity), it is virtually impossible to set any substantive boundary to religion and, thus, to distinguish it from other sociocultural phenomena. Social solidarity, anxiety reduction, confidence in unpredictable situations, and the like, are functions which may be served by any or all cultural phenomena—Communism and Catholicism, monotheism and monogamy, images and imperialism—and unless religion is defined substantively, it would be impossible to delineate its boundaries. Indeed, even when its substantive boundaries are limited, some functional definitions impute to religion some of the functions of a total sociocultural system.

It is obvious, then, that while a definition cannot take the place of inquiry, in the absence of definitions there can be no inquiry—for it is the definition, either ostensive or nominal, which designates the phenomenon to be investigated. Thus when Evans-Pritchard writes that 'objectivity' in studies of religion requires that "we build up general conclusions from particular ones" (1954:9), this caution is certainly desirable for discovering empirical generalizations or for testing hypotheses. But when he tells us that "one must not ask 'what is religion?' but what are the main features of, let us say, the religion of one Melanesian people . . . " which, when compared with findings among other Melanesian peoples, will lead to generalizations about Melanesian religion, he is prescribing a strategy which, beginning with the study of that one Melanesian people, cannot get started. For unless he knows, ostensively, what religion is, how can our anthropologist in his Melanesian society know which, among a possible n, observations constitute observations of religious phenomena, rather than of some other phenomenal class, kinship, for example, or politics?

Indeed, when the term 'religion' is given no explicit ostensive definition, the observer, perforce, employs an implicit one. Thus, Durkheim warns that in defining religion we must be careful not to proceed from our "prejudices, passions, or habits" (1954:24). Rather, " . . . it is from the reality itself which we are going to define" (ibid.). Since any scientist—or, for that matter, any reasonable man—prefers 'reality' to 'prejudice', we happily follow his lead and, together with him, " . . . set ourselves before this reality" (ibid.). But since, Durkheim tells us, "religion cannot be defined except by the characteristics which are found wherever religion itself is found," we must " . . . consider the various religions in their concrete reality, and attempt to disengage that which they have in common" (ibid.). Now, the very statement of this strategy raises an obvious question. Unless we already know, by definition, what religion is, how can we know which 'concrete reality' we are to 'consider'? Only if religion has already been defined can we perform either this initial operation or the subsequent one of disengaging those elements which are shared by all religions.

In sum, any comparative study of religion requires, as an operation antecedent to inquiry, an ostensive or substantive definition that stipulates unambiguously those phenomenal variables which are designated by the term. This ostensive definition will, at the same time, be a nominal definition in that some of its designata will, to other scholars, appear to be arbitrary. This, then, does not remove 'religion' from the arena of definitional controversy; but it does remove it from the context of fruitless controversy over what religion 'really is' to the context of the formulation of empirically testable hypotheses which, in anthropology, means hypotheses susceptible to cross-cultural testing.

But this criterion of cross-cultural applicability does not entail, as I have argued above, universality. Since 'religion' is a term with historically rooted meanings, a definition must satisfy not only the criterion of cross-cultural applicability but also the criterion of intracultural intuitivity; at the least, it should not be counter-intuitive. For me, therefore, any definition of 'religion' which does not include, as a key variable, the belief in superhuman—I won't muddy the metaphysical waters with 'supernatural'—beings who have power to help or harm man, is counter-intuitive. Indeed, if anthropological consensus were to exclude such beliefs from the set of variables which is necessarily designated by 'religion', an explanation for these beliefs would surely continue to elicit our research energies.

Even if it were the case that Theravada Buddhism postulates no such beings, I find it strange indeed, given their all-but-universal distribution at every level of cultural development, that Durkheim—on the basis of this one case—should have excluded such beliefs from a definition of religion, and stranger still that others should have followed his lead. But this anomaly aside, is it the case that Buddhism contains no belief in superhuman beings? (Let us, for the sake of brevity, refer to these beings as 'gods'.) It is true, of course, that Buddhism contains no belief in a creator god; but creation is but one possible attribute of godhood, one which—I suspect—looms not too large in the minds of believers. If gods are important for their believers because—as I would insist is the case—they possess power greater than man's, including the power to assist man in, or prevent him from, attaining mundane and/or supermundane goals, even Theravada Buddhism—Mahayana is clearly not at issue here—most certainly contains such beliefs. With respect to supermundane goals, the Buddha is certainly a superhuman being. Unlike ordinary humans, he himself acquired the power to attain Enlightenment and, hence Buddhahood. Moreover, he showed others the means for its attainment. Without his teachings, natural man could not, unassisted, have discovered the way to Enlightenment and to final Release.

The soteriological attributes of the Buddha are, to be sure, different from those of the Judaeo-Christian-Islamic God. Whereas the latter is living, the former is dead; whereas the latter is engaged in a continuous and active process of salvation, the former had engaged in only one active ministry of salvation. But—with the exception of Calvinism—the soteriological consequences are the same. For the Buddhist and the Western religionist alike the Way to salvation was revealed by a superhuman being, and salvation can be attained only if one follows this revealed Way. The fact that in one case compliance with the Way leads directly to the ultimate goal because of the very nature of the world; and, in the other case, compliance leads to the goal only after divine intercession, should not obscure the basic similarity: in both cases man is dependent for his salvation upon the revelation of a superhuman being. (Indeed, there is reason to believe—I am now analyzing field data collected in a Burmese village which suggest that this might be the case—that Buddhist worship is not merely an expression of reverence and homage to the One who has revealed the Way, but is also a petition for His saving intercession.)

But superhuman beings generally have the power to assist (or hinder) man's attempts to attain mundane as well as supermundane goals, and when it is asserted that Buddhism postulates no such beings, we must ask to which Buddhism this assertion has reference. Even the Buddhism of the Pali canon does not deny the existence of a wide range of superhuman beings who intervene, for good and for ill, in human affairs; it merely denies that they can influence one's salvation. More important, in contemporary Theravada countries, the Buddha himself—or, according to more sophisticated believers, his power—is believed to protect people from harm. Thus Burmese peasants recite Buddhist spells and perform rites before certain Buddha images which have the power to protect them from harm, to cure snake bites, and the like. And Buddhist monks chant passages from Scripture in the presence of the congregation which, it is believed, can bring a wide variety of worldly benefits.

There are, to be sure, atheistic Buddhist philosophies—as there are atheistic Hindu philosophies—but it is certainly a strange spectacle when anthropologists, of all people, confuse the teachings of a philosophical school with the beliefs and behavior of a religious community. And if—on some strange methodological grounds—the teachings of the philosophical schools, rather than the beliefs and behavior of the people, were to be designated as the normative religion of a society, then the numerous gods and demons to be found in the Pali canon—and in the world-view of most Theravadists, including the monastic virtuosos—find more parallels in other societies than the beliefs held by the numerically small philosophical schools.

Finally—and what is perhaps even more important from an anthropological point of view—the Pali canon is only one source for the world-view of Buddhist societies. Indeed, I know of no society in which Buddhism represents the exclusive belief system of a people. On the contrary, it is always to be found together with another system with which it maintains an important division of labor. Whereas Buddhism (restricting this term, now, to Canonical Buddhism) is concerned with supermundane goals—rebirth in a better human existence, in a celestial abode of gods, or final Release—the other system is concerned with wordly goals: the growing of crops, protection from illness, guarding of the village, etc., which are the domain of numerous superhuman beings. These are the *nats* of Burma, the *phi* of Laos and Thailand, the *neak ta* of Cambodia, etc. Although the Burmese, for example, distinguish sharply between Buddhism and *nat* worship, and although it is undoubtedly true—as most scholars argue—that these nonBuddhist belief systems represent the pre-Buddhist religions of these Theravada societies, the important consideration for our present discussion is that these beliefs, despite the long history of Buddhism in these countries, persist with undiminished strength, continuing to inform the world-view of these Buddhist societies and to stimulate important and extensive ritual societies and to stimulate important and extensive ritual activity. Hence, even if Theravada Buddhi*sm* were absolutely atheistic, it cannot be denied that Theravada Buddhi*sts* adhere to another belief system which is theistic to its core; and if it were to be argued that atheistic Buddhism—by some other criteria—is a religion and that, therefore, the belief in superhuman beings is not a necessary characteristic of 'religion', it would still be the case that the belief in superhuman beings and in their power to aid or harm man is a central feature in the belief systems of all traditional societies.

But Theravada Asia provides only one example of the tenacity of such beliefs. Confucianist China provides what is, perhaps, a better example. If Theravada Buddhism is somewhat ambiguous concerning the existence and behavior of superhuman beings, Confucianism is much less ambiguous. Although the latter does not explicitly deny the existence of such beings, it certainly ignores their role in human affairs. It is more than interesting to note, therefore, that when Mahayana Buddhism was introduced into China, it was precisely its gods (including the Boddhisatvas), demons, heavens, and hells that, according to many scholars, accounted for its dramatic conquest of China.

To summarize, I would argue that the belief in superhuman beings and in their power to assist or to harm man approaches universal distribution, and this belief—I would insist—is the core variable which ought to be designated by any definition of religion. Recently Horton (1960) and Goody (1962) have reached the same conclusion.

Although the belief in the existence of superhuman beings is the core religious variable, it does not follow—as some scholars have argued—that religious, in contrast to magical, behavior is necessarily other-worldly in orientation, or that, if it is otherworldly, its orientation is 'spiritual'. The beliefs in superhuman beings, other-worldliness, and spiritual values vary independently. Thus, ancient Judaism, despite its obsession with God's will, was essentially this-worldly in orientation. Catholicism, with all its other-worldly orientation is, with certain kinds of Hinduism, the most 'materialistic' of the higher religions. Confucianism, intensely this-worldly, is yet concerned almost exclusively with such 'spiritual' values as filial piety, etc. In short, superhuman beings may be conceived as primarily means or as ends. Where values are worldly, these beings may be viewed as important agents for the attainment and/or frustration of worldly goals, either 'material' or 'spiritual'. Where values are materialistic, superhuman beings may be viewed as important agents for the attainment of material goals, either in this or in an after life. Where values are other-worldly, mystical union with superhuman beings may be viewed as an all-consuming goal; and so on.

Although the differentiating characteristic of religion is the belief in superhuman beings, it does not follow, moreover, that these beings are necessarily objects of ultimate concern. Again, it depends on whether they are viewed as means or as ends. For those individuals whom Weber has termed 'religiously musical' (Gerth & Mills 1946:287), or whom Radin (1957:9) has termed 'the truly religious', superhuman beings are of ultimate concern. For the rest, however, superhuman beings are rarely of ultimate concern, although the ends for which their assistance is sought may be. Hence, though their benevolent ancestral spirits are not of great concern to the Ifaluk, restoration of health—for which these spirits are instrumental—most certainly is. Similarly, while the Buddha may not be of ultimate concern to a typical Burmese peasant, the escape from suffering—for which He is instrumental—can certainly be so designated.

Conversely, while religious beliefs are not always of ultimate concern, nonreligious beliefs sometimes are. This raises a final unwarranted conclusion, viz. that religion uniquely refers to the 'sacred', while secular concerns are necessarily 'profane'. Thus, if 'sacred' refers to objects and beliefs of ultimate concern, and 'profane' to those of ordinary concern, religious and secular beliefs alike may have reference either to sacred or to profane phenomena. For the members of Kiryat Yedidim, an Israeli kibbutz, the triumph of the proletariat, following social revolution, and the ultimate classless society in which universal brotherhood, based on loving kindness, will replace parochial otherhood, based on competitive hostility, constitutes their sacred belief system. But, by definition, it is not a religious belief system, since it has no reference to—indeed, it denies the existence of—superhuman beings.

Similarly, if communism, baseball, or the stock market are of ultimate concern to some society, or to one of its constituent social groups, they are, by definition, sacred. But beliefs concerning communism, baseball, or the stockmarket are not, by definition, religious beliefs, because they have no reference to superhuman beings. They may, of course, serve many of the functions served by religious beliefs; and they are, therefore, members of the same functional class. Since, however, they are substantively dissimilar, it would be as misleading to designate them by the same term as it would be to designate music and sex by the same term because they both provide sensual pleasure.

(Modern American society presents an excellent example of the competition of sports, patriotism, sex, and God for the title, perhaps not exclusively, of 'the sacred'. Indeed, if the dictum of Miss Jane Russell is taken seriously—God, she informs us, is a "livin' doll"—I would guess that, whichever wins, God is bound to lose.)

A Definition of 'Religion'

On the assumption that religion is a cultural institution, and on the further assumption that all institutions—though not all of their features—are instrumental means for the satisfaction of needs, I shall define 'religion' as 'an institution consisting of culturally patterned interaction with culturally postulated superhuman beings'. I should like to examine these variables separately.

Institution. This term implies, of course, that whatever phenomena we might wish to designate by 'religion', religion is an attribute of social groups, comprising a component part of their cultural heritage; and that its component features are acquired by means of the same enculturation processes as the other variables of a cultural heritage are acquired. This means that the variables constituting a religious system have the same ontological status as those of other cultural systems: its beliefs are normative, its rituals collective, its values prescriptive. This, I take it, is what Durkheim (1954:44) had in mind in insisting that there can be no religion without a church. (It means, too, as I shall observe in a later section, that religion has the same methodological status as other cultural systems; i.e. religious variables are to be explained by the same explanatory schemata—historical, structural, functional, and causal—as those by which other cultural variables are explained.)

Interaction. This term refers to two distinct, though related, types of activity. First, it refers to activities which are believed to carry out, embody, or to be consistent with the will or desire of superhuman beings or powers. These activities reflect the putative *value system* of these superhuman beings and, presumably, they constitute part—but only part—of the actors' value system. These activities may be viewed as desirable in themselves and/or as means for obtaining the assistance of superhuman beings or for protection against their wrath. Second, it refers to activities which are believed to influence superhuman beings to satisfy the needs of the actors. These two types of activity may overlap, but their range is never coterminous. Where they do overlap, the acfion in the overlapping sphere is, in large measure, symbolic; that is, it consists in behavior whose meaning, cross-culturally viewed, is obscure and/or arbitrary; and whose efficacy, scientifically viewed, is not susceptible of ordinary scientific 'proof'. These symbolic, but definitely instrumental, activities constitute, of course, a *ritual*, or symbolic *action, system*. Unlike private rituals, such as those found in an obsessive-compulsive neurosis, religious rituals are culturally patterned; i.e. both the activities and their meaning are shared by the members of a social group by virtue of their acquisition from a shared cultural heritage.

Superhuman beings. These refer to any beings believed to possess power greater than man, who can work good and/or evil on man, and whose relationships with man can, to some degree, be influenced by the two types of activity described in the previous section. The belief of any religious actor in the existence of these beings and his knowledge concerning their attributes are derived from and sanctioned by the cultural heritage of his social group. To that extent—and regardless of the objective existence of these beings, or of personal experiences which are interpreted as encounters with them—their existence is culturally postulated. Beliefs concerning the existence and attributes of these beings, and of the efficacy of certain types of behavior (ritual, for example) in influencing their relations with man, constitute a *belief system*.

This brief explication of our definition of 'religion' indicates that, viewed systemically, religion can be differentiated from other culturally constituted institutions by virtue only of its reference to superhuman beings. All institutions consist of *belief systems*, i.e. an enduring organization of cognitions about one or more aspects of the universe; *action systems*, an enduring organization of behavior patterns designed to attain ends for the satisfaction of needs; and *value systems*, an enduring organization of principles by which behavior can be judged on some scale of merit. Religion differs from other institutions in that its three component systems have reference to superhuman beings.

Having defined 'religion', our next task is to examine the types of explanation that have been offered to account for its existence. First, however, we must answer some elementary questions concerning the nature of anthropological explanation.

Explanation in Social Anthropology

What do anthropologists attempt to explain? Of what do explanations consist? How do these explanations differ from each other? Once we penetrate beneath our jargon, it appears that always the phenomenon to be explained is (a) the *existence* of some social or cultural variable, and (b) the *variability* which it exhibits in a cross-cultural distribution. These statements of course are really one, because the variable 'exists' in the range of values which it can assume. If a theory purports to explain the existence of religion, but its concepts are so general or so vague that it cannot explain the variability exhibited by its empirical instances, it is disqualified as a *scientific*, i.e. a testable, theory.

'Existence' is an ambiguous term. In asking for an explanation for the existence of religion, we might be asking how it came to exist in the first place—this is the question of religious origins—or how it is that it exists (i.e. has persisted) in some ethnographic present. Since a testable, i.e. scientific, theory of religious origins will probably always elude our explanatory net, this chapter will be concerned with the persistence, not the origin, of religion.

In all of our explanations, to answer the second question, we stipulate a condition or a set of conditions in whose absence the variable to be explained would not exist. Now, to say that any sociocultural variable—religion, for example—'exists' is, in the last analysis, to say that in some society—or, in one of its constituent social groups—a proposition is affirmed, a norm complied with, a custom performed, a role practiced, a spirit feared, etc. In short, the 'existence' of a sociocultural variable means that in any sense of 'behavior'—cognitive, affective, or motor—there occurs some behavior in which, or by which, the variable in question is instanced. Hence, a theory of the 'existence' of religion must ultimately be capable of explaining religious 'behavior'.

In general, theories of the existence—in the sense of persistence—of sociocultural variables are cast in four explanatory modes: historical (in the documentary, not the speculative, sense), structural, causal, and functional. When analyzed, the first two can be reduced to either the third or the fourth. Thus historical explanations are either no explanation at all, or they are causal explanations. Surely, the mere listing of a series of events which are antecedent to the appearance of the variable in question does not constitute explanation—unless it can be shown that one or more of these events was a condition, either necessary or sufficient, for its appearance. If this can be demonstrated, the explanation is based on a causal theory, the fact of its having originated in the past being incidental to the theoretical aim of explaining a certain type of social or cultural innovation.

The key term here is 'innovation'. Although a causal explanation of the historical type may account for the existence of some sociocultural variable during the period in which it made its appearance, it is not a sufficient explanation for its persistence into a later period—no more than a genetic explanation for the birth of an organism is a sufficient explanation for its persistence. Thus while a historicogenetic explanation is necessary to account for Burma's adoption of Buddhism, it cannot account for its persistence nine hundred years later. Alternatively, historical data explain why it is that the Burmese, if they practice any religion at all, practice Buddhism rather than, for example, Christianity; but they do not explain why they practice any religion at all—and, therefore, they do not explain why they practice Buddhism.

Structural explanations, too, can be reduced either to causal or to functional modes. Those structural accounts which delineate the configuration in, or relationships among, a set of sociocultural variables are essentially descriptive rather than explanatory—unless of course some theory, causal or functional, is offered to explain the configuration. Structural explanations which purport to explain some variable by means of a structural 'principle'—such as the principle of the unity of the sibling group—are either verbal labels which at best order a set of data according to a heuristic scheme; or they are phenomenological 'principles' of the actors (cognitive maps), in which case they comprise a cognitive subset in a set of causal variables. Similarly, structural explanations which stipulate some variable as a "structural requirement' of a system, on the one hand, or as a 'structural implication', on the other, can be shown to be either causal or functional respectively.

This brings us, then, to causal and functional explanations. Causal explanations attempt to account for some sociocultural variable by reference to some antecedent conditions—its 'cause'. Functional explanations account for the variable by reference to some consequent condition—its 'function'. (For a detailed analysis of the logic of causal and functional explanation, cf. Spiro 1963).

How, then, is the existence of religion to be explained, causally or functionally? The answer depends, I believe, on which aspect of a religion is to be explained.

Typically, explanations for the existence of religion have been addressed to one or both of two questions. (a) On what grounds are religious propositions believed to be true? That is, what are the grounds for the belief that superhuman beings with such-and-such characteristics exist, and that ritual is efficacious in influencing their behavior? (b) What is the explanation for the practice of religion? That is, what is the basis for belief in superhuman beings, and for the performance of religious rituals? These questions, though clearly related—religious practice presupposes religious cognitions—are yet distinct; and they probably require different types of explanation.

The 'Truth' of Religious Beliefs

Every religious system consists, in the first instance, of a cognitive system; i.e. it consists of a set of explicit and implicit propositions concerning the superhuman world and of man's relationship to it, which it claims to be true. These include beliefs in superhuman beings of various kinds, of rituals of a wide variety, of existences—both prior and subsequent to the present existence—and the like. To the extent that documentary evidence is available, it is possible to discover a testable explanation for their origin and their variability. Since, for most of man's religions, however, such evidence is lacking, explanations are necessarily speculative. I shall be concerned, therefore, with explanations for their persistence.

This cognitive system, or parts of it, is of course acquired by the members of a group, and, on the individual level, it becomes a 'culturally constituted belief system'. It is a 'belief' system because the propositions are believed to be true; and it is 'culturally constituted' because the propositions are acquired from this culturally provided religious system. But the latter fact, surely, is not a sufficient basis for the belief that these propositions are true. Children are taught about many things which, when they grow up—often, before they grow up—they discard as so much nonsense. The fact that my personal belief system is acquired from my society explains why I might believe in the existence of the Lord Krishna rather than that of the Virgin Mary; it does not explain the grounds on which I believe in the existence of superhuman beings of any kind, whether Krishna or the Virgin.

The notion of 'need' fares no better as an explanation. A need, in the sense of desire, may provide the motivational basis for the acquisition of a taught belief, but it cannot establish its truth. Similarly, a need, in the sense of a functional requirement of society, may explain the necessity for some kind of religious proposition(s), but—even if this need is recognized and its satisfaction is intended—it does not explain why the proposition is believed to be true.

Most theorists seem to agree that religious statements are believed to be true because religious actors have had social experiences which, corresponding to these beliefs, provide them with face validity. Thus Durkheim and Freud, agreeing that the cognitive roots of religious belief are to be found in social experience, disagree only about the structural context of the experience. Durkheim (1954) argues that the two essential attributes of the gods—they are beings more powerful than man, upon whom man can depend—are the essential attributes of society; it is in society that man experiences these attributes. These attributes are personified in superhuman beings, or imputed to extra-social powers, because of highly affective collective experiences in which the physical symbols of the group are taken to be symbolic of the one or the other. Freud (1928), emphasizing man's helplessness in a terrifying world, stresses the importance of personifying these terrifying forces so that, on a human analogy, they can be controlled. These personifications—the gods—reflect the child's experience with an all-powerful human being, his father.

In both Freud and Durkheim, then, society is the cause for the fixation of religious belief. It is ironical to observe, however, that it is Freud rather than Durkheim who anchors this experience within a specified structural unit, the family. In general, I believe that Freud has the better case. To be sure, his ethnocentric conception of patriarchal fathers, and of gods reflecting this conception of 'father', is entirely inadequate for comparative analysis: but the general theory which can be generated from this ethnocentric model is both adequate and, I believe, essentially correct. The theory, briefly, states that it is in the context of the family that the child experiences powerful beings, both benevolent and malevolent, who—by various means which are learned in the socialization process—can sometimes be induced to accede to his desires. These experiences provide the basic ingredients for his personal projective system (Kardiner 1945) which, if it corresponds (structurally, not substantively) to his taught beliefs, constitutes the cognitive and perceptual set for the acceptance of these beliefs. Having had personal experience with 'superhuman beings' and with the efficacy of 'ritual', the taught beliefs reenforce, and are reenforced by, his own projective system (Spiro 1953).

This theory is superior to Durkheim's, first, in its ability to explain these latter two nuclear religious variables. It is difficult to see how they can be deduced from Durkheim's theory. More important, even if they were deducible, it is difficult to see how Durkheim's theory can explain their cross-cultural variability. Since the antecedent condition—a power greater than man upon which man can rely—is a constant, how can it explain the consequent condition—religious belief—which is a variable? Hence, although the general theory may be true, there is a serious question concerning what empirical operations, if any, would permit us to decide whether it is true or false. The Freudian-derived theory, on the other hand, *is* capable of explaining cross-cultural differences and, therefore, it can be tested empirically. If personal projective systems, which form the basis for religious belief, are developed in early childhood experiences, it can be deduced that differences in religious beliefs will vary systematically with differences in family (including socialization) systems which structure these experiences. A number of anthropological field studies have been able to test—and have confirmed—this conclusion. And one need not go so far astray as personality-and-culture studies to find the evidence. In his illuminating analysis of Tallensi religion, Fortes (1959:78) concludes that, "All the concepts and beliefs we have examined are religious extrapolations of the experiences generated in the relationships between parents and children."

As important as they are, case studies do not constitute rigorous proof of theories. The cross-cultural method in which large samples can be used for statistical testing of hypotheses is more rigorous. A fairly large number of hypotheses, predicting religious variables—the character of supernatural beings, the means (performance of rituals or compliance with norms) which are believed to influence them, the conception of ritual (coercive or propitiatory) and the like—from child-training variables have been tested by this method, and many of them have been confirmed. (These studies are summarized in Whiting 1961.)

Despite the differences between Freud and Durkheim, both propose causal explanations of the credibility of religious cognitions, in which society, as cause, produces a religious (cognitive) effect by means of psychological processes—in one case, in the *feeling* of dependency; in the other, in the feeling of dependency combined with the personal *projection* of nuclear experiences. For both theorists the independent, sociological, variable may be said to 'cause' the dependent, religious, variable by means of a set of intervening, psychological, variables.

Before passing to the next section it is necessary to counter one assumption which is often linked to this type of explanation, but which is not entailed by it. From the hypothesis that the antecedent condition for belief in superhuman beings is to be found in specified sociological variables, it does not follow that for the believer these beings are identical with, have reference to, or are symbolic of these variables. To put it bluntly, the fact that conceptions of God have their roots in society does not mean that *for the believer* society is God, or that God is merely a symbol of society, or that society is the true object of religious worship. Freud never said this, nor—despite some claims to the contrary—did Durkheim. Hence, it is no refutation of Durkheim's sociological hypothesis—as Horton (1960:204) believes it to be—that for the Kalabari—and, I would add, for every other people—the statement " 'I believe in God' " does not imply, " 'I subscribe to the system of structural symbolism of which this belief statement is part.' "[2]

Similarly it is not only among the Kalabari that a person who uses belief or ritual "merely to make a statement about social relations or about his own structural alignment" is viewed as one who " 'does not really believe' " (ibid.:203). Indeed the contrary notion is so absurd that it is difficult to believe that it could be proposed by anyone who has personally observed a Micronesian exorcising a malevolent ghost, a Catholic penitent crawling on hands and knees to worship at the shrine of Our Lady of Guadalupe, an Orthodox Jew beating his breast on Yom Kippur to atone for his sins, a Burmese spirit-medium dancing in a trance before a *nat* image. And yet, Leach, writing of Kachin spirits, insists (1954:182) that "the various nats of Kachin religious ideology are, in the last analysis *nothing more* than ways of describing the formal relationships that exist between real persons and real groups in ordinary Kachin society" (italics mine). For Leach, then, not only are religious beliefs derived from social structure, but the only referent of these beliefs, even for the believer, is social structure. Since Leach has, I am sure, observed as many manifestations of religious belief as I have, what are we to make of this extraordinary statement? I should like to suggest that this assertion reflects a confusion between the *practice* of religion and its *manipulation;* and although the former may be of as much interest to the student of religion as the latter, not to recognize this distinction is to sow confusion.

Leach, it will be recalled, interprets Kachin religion as almost exclusively an instrument in the political struggle for power and prestige. That theology, myth, or ritual may be manipulated for prestige and power, and that the latter drives may provide motivational bases for their persistence are documented facts of history and ethnology. But the manipulation of religion for political ends tells us more about politics than about religion. In the former, religion is used *as a means*, in the latter *religious means* are used, for the attainment of certain ends. (Indeed, they may both be instrumental for the same end.) This is an

2. In any case, Durkheim's sociology of religion is unconcerned with structural symbolism. It is concerned with society as a collectivity, not as a configuration of structural units; with collective representations, not with social structure.

essential distinction. The differential characteristic of religious, compared with other types of instrumental, behavior consists in an attempt to enlist the assistance, or to execute the will, of superhuman beings. Indeed, by what other criterion *could* religious be distinguished from nonreligious behavior? Surely not in terms of ends: with the exception of mysticism (confined to religious virtuosos) the range of mundane ends for which religion, cross-culturally viewed, is conceived to be instrumental is as broad as the range of all human ends. My argument, then, is not that political power is disqualified as a *religious end*, but that any attempt to achieve this end by means which do not entail a belief in the existence of superhuman beings is disqualified as *religious means*. A Kachin headman may attempt to manipulate myths and *nats* in order to validate his, or his clan's claim to power and authority; but this political behavior is to be distinguished from his religious behavior, which consists in his belief in the existence of the *nats*, and in his propitiation of them, both at local shrines and during *manaus*. Indeed, only because Kachins do believe that the verbal symbol 'nat' has reference to an existential being—and is not merely a social structural symbol—is it possible to manipulate this belief for political ends.

The Practice of Religious Belief

The religious actor not only believes in the truth of propositions about superhuman beings, but he also believes in these beings—they are objects of 'concern': he trusts in God, he fears and hates Satan. Similarly, he not only believes in the efficacy of ritual, but he performs rituals. Explanations for religion, then, are addressed not only to the truth of religious propositions but also—and more frequently—to certain practices. In order to explain the practice of religion, we must be able to explain the practice of any sociocultural variable.[3]

3. The notion that religion necessarily eludes the net of naturalistic explanation, though implicit in certain recent anthropological writing, is beginning to find explicit expression. Thus, Turner (1962:92) claims that "one has to consider religious phenomena in terms of religious ideas and doctrines, and not only, or principally, in terms of disciplines which have arisen in connection with the study of secular institutions and processes. . . . Religion is not *determined* by anything other than itself, though the religious find *expression* in sensory phenomena. . . . We must be prepared to accept the fruits of simple wisdom with gratitude and not try to reduce them to their chemical constituents, thereby destroying their essential quality as fruits, and their virtue as food."

To say that religion is determined by religion is surely as meaningless as to say that tables are determined by tables, or that social structure is determined by social structure. But even if this statement is an ellipsis for a meaningful one, I would have thought that the

All human behavior, except for reflexive behavior, is purposive; i.e. it is instigated by the intention of satisfying some need. If a given response is in fact instrumental for the satisfaction of the need, this 'reinforcement' of the response ensures its persistence—it becomes an instance of a behavior pattern. The motivational basis for the practice of a behavior pattern, then, is not merely the intention of satisfying a need, but the expectation that its performance will in fact achieve this end. Institutional behavior, including religious behavior, consists in the practice of repeated instances of culturally constituted behavior patterns—or customs. Like other behavior patterns they persist as long as they are practiced; and they are practiced because they satisfy, or are believed to satisfy, their instigating needs. If this is so, an explanation for the practice of religion must be sought in the set of needs whose expected satisfaction motivates religious belief and the performance of religious ritual.[4]

Needs

As a concept in the social sciences, 'need' has been borrowed from two sources: biology and psychology. Its ambiguity as a social science concept stems from a confusion in its two possible meanings. In biology 'need' refers to what might be termed a 'want', i.e. to some requirement which must be satisfied if an organism is to survive. In psychology, on the other hand, it refers to what might be termed a 'desire', i.e. a wish to satisfy some felt drive by the attainment of some goal. These two meanings may, of course, overlap. Thus water satisfies an

---

determinants of religion are to be established empirically rather than by verbal assertion. I would have thought, too, that to 'reduce' religion to its 'chemical constituents'—which, I take it, refers to the discovery of its social and psychological bases—is precisely the task of the student of culture. I would not have thought that for the religionist—and the anthropologist, *qua* anthropologist, is of course neither a religionist nor an anti-religionist—the 'reduction' of religion to its social and psychological 'constituents' destroys its 'essential quality', any more than the 'reduction' of a Brandenburg concerto to its physical 'constituents' destroys its 'essential quality' for the lover of Bach.

4. There is, of course, no convincing evidence for the existence of a distinctively 'religious need'. That the belief in superhuman beings corresponds to and satisfies a 'need' for a belief in them is an unfounded instinctivist assumption. Nor is there any evidence for the assumption that the motivational basis for religious action, or the affect which it arouses, are unique. The meager evidence from religious psychology suggests that any drive or affect connected with religious behavior is also found in such activities as science, warfare, sex, art, politics, and others. The 'religious thrill' which Lowie (1924) and others have pointed to as a differentiating characteristic of religion is still to be documented. A clinical psychologist, commenting on still another set of data remarks: "Some of our tests seem able to tap fairly deep levels of personality functioning, and yet we rarely encounter a clearly religious response to our Rorschach and Thematic Apperception tests. . . . For the psychology of religion this means that the clinical psychologist will not readily be able to furnish new data" (Pruyser 1960:122).

organic want and it may also be the object of desire. Just as frequently, however, they do not overlap. The circulation of the blood is a want, but—for most animals, at any rate—it is not the object of desire. In sociological and, especially, in functionalist discourse, much confusion has resulted from not distinguishing these two meanings of 'need' when it is applied to society. In this paper I shall, when clarity does not suffer, use the generic 'need' to refer both to sociological wants and to psychological desires. Otherwise, I shall use 'sociological want' to refer to any functional requirement of society; and I shall use 'desire' in its motivational sense. I hasten to add that desires are not necessarily 'selfish', oriented to the welfare of the self. The goal, by whose attainment a drive is satisfied, may be—and, obviously, it often is—the welfare of an entire group, or of one or more of its constituent members.

We may now return to our question. If the practice of religion is instigated by the expectation of satisfying needs, by which set of needs—desires or wants—is its practice to be explained? It should be perfectly obvious that although behavior can *satisfy* both wants and desires, it is motivated by desires, not by wants. Wants in themselves have no causal properties. The absorption of moisture, for example, is a functional requirement of plants; but this requirement cannot cause the rains to fall. Human behavior, to be sure, is different from the growth of plants. A social group may recognize the existence of some, at least, of its functional requirements, and these recognized wants may constitute a set of stimulus conditions which evoke responses for their satisfaction. Notice, however, that it is not the functional requirement—even when it is recognized—which evokes the response, but rather the wish to satisfy it. A functional requirement of society becomes a stimulus for a response, i.e. it acquires motivational value if, and only if (a) it is recognized, and (b) its satisfaction becomes an object of desire. If the functional requirement of social solidarity, for example, is not recognized, or, if recognized, it is not an object of desire, or, although both recognized and desired, it is not the desire whose intended satisfaction motivates the practice of the variable to be explained, it cannot be used to explain behavior, even though need-satisfaction may be one of its consequences. If social solidarity is a consequence—an unintended consequence—of the practice of religion, social solidarity is properly explained by reference to the religious behavior by which it is achieved; but religion, surely, is improperly explained by reference to social solidarity. An unintended consequence of behavior—however important it may be—can hardly be its cause. If religious behavior is to be explained by reference to those functions which it serves—and, indeed, it must be—the functions must be those

that are intended, not those that are unintended (and probably unrecognized). We must, therefore, remind ourselves of some elementary
distinctions among functions.

Functions

I should like, first, to distinguish between 'psychological' and 'sociological' functions. The psychological functions of behavior consist in
the satisfaction of desires,[5] its sociological functions consist in the satisfaction of functional requirements.

Second, I should like to distinguish between 'manifest' and 'latent'
functions. In his now-classic analysis of functional explanation, Merton
(1957) distinguished between intended and recognized functions—
which he termed 'manifest'—and unintended and unrecognized functions—which he termed 'latent'. Merton's dichotomous classification
can be shown to yield a four-class functional typology. In addition to
intended-recognized and unintended-unrecognized functions, we can
also distinguish intended-unrecognized and unintended-recognized
functions (Spiro 1961a). The latter is a simple concept to grasp; social
solidarity may be a recognized function of religious ritual, for example,
although the intention of satisfying this functional requirement may
not motivate its performance. An intended-unrecognized function,
however, seems paradoxical. Assuming that intentions may be conscious as well as unconscious, this paradox is more apparent than real;
if a behavior pattern is unconsciously motivated—or, more realistically, if its motivational set includes both conscious and unconscious
intentions—one of its functions, although intended, is unrecognized.

The final distinction I should like to make is between real and apparent functions. 'Real functions' are those which, in principle at least, can
be discovered by the anthropologist, whether or not they are recognized by the actors. 'Apparent functions' are those which the actors
attribute to the sociocultural variable in question, but which cannot be
confirmed by scientific investigation.

With these distinctions in mind, we may now attempt to answer the
question with which we began this section. If institutional behavior in
general is motivated by the expectation of satisfying desires, to what

5. That a function 'psychological' does not mean that the object of desire is psychological. The object of desire may be political, meteorological, economic, nutritional,
sexual—and all other goals known to man. These goals are cathected because they satisfy
some drive, acquired or innate. The attainment of the goal reduces the drive or, alternatively, satisfies the desire. The satisfaction of the desire—or, more realistically, the set
of desires—whose intended (conscious or unconscious) satisfaction instigates behavior is
its 'psychological' function.

extent can religious behavior, specifically, be explained within this framework? That is, what desires are satisfied by religion? Since this question remains one of the unfinished tasks of empirical research, I can only make some tentative suggestions. As I interpret the record, I would suggest that there are at least three sets of desires which are satisfied by religion and which—for lack of better terms—I shall call cognitive, substantive, and expressive. The corresponding functions of religion can be called adjustive, adaptive, and integrative.

Cognitive

I believe that it can be shown that everywhere man has a desire to know, to understand, to find meaning;[6] and I would suggest—although this is a terribly old-fashioned nineteenth-century idea—that religious beliefs are held, and are of 'concern', to religious actors because, *in the absence of competitive explanations,* they satisfy this desire. Religious belief systems provide the members of society with meaning and explanation for otherwise meaningless and inexplicable phenomena.

'Meaning', of course. is often used in two senses. It may be used in an exclusively cognitive sense, as when one asks for the meaning of a natural phenomenon, of a historical event, of a sociological fact. In this sense, it has the connotation of 'explanation', as that word is typically used. But 'meaning' is also used in a semantic-affective sense, as when one asks for the meaning of unequal life-fates, frustration, or death. The phenomena for which religion provides meaning, in this second sense of 'meaning', have been classified by Weber under the general rubric of 'suffering' (Gerth & Mills 1946:ch. 11). The main function of the higher religions, he argues, is to provide meaning for suffering (and some means to escape from or to transcend it).

Although the range of phenomena for which religious beliefs provide meaning in the first, explanatory, sense of 'meaning', occupies a broad spectrum, some structuralists hold to the peculiar notion that man's curiosity is so limited that religious explanations, regardless of their ostensible meaning, are concerned almost exclusively with phe-

6. The most striking evidence, on the simplest perceptual level, of this 'need' for meaning is provided by the cross-cultural use of the Rorschach test. As Hallowell has observed (1956:476–88), the most dramatic finding of cross-cultural Rorschach investigations is that at every level of technological and cultural development in which this test has been administered, subjects have attempted to offer 'meaningful' responses to what are, objectively, 'meaningless' ink-blots. The insistence, even on the part of 'primitive' peoples, on finding meaning in what is for them an exotic task—something concerning which many anthropologists had been skeptical—is certainly consistent with the assumption concerning a universal need for meaning.

nomena of social structure. Again I should like to use an example from Leach—although the example concerns magical rather than religious belief—because, with his usual verve, he adopts what I would think to be an extreme position.

In his highly critical evaluation of Frazer, Leach (1961) tells us that Frazer (and Roth, too) is naïve in interpreting Australian explanations for conception as in fact referring to conception—and, therefore, as reflecting ignorance of physiological paternity. According to the 'modern interpretation', their notions of conception are to be seen, not as biological, but as sociological, statements. Let us examine the ethnographic facts, as Leach (p. 376) quotes them from Roth. Among the Tully River Blacks,

> A woman begets children because (a) she has been sitting over the fire on which she has roasted a particular species of black bream, which must have been given to her by the prospective father, (b) she has purposely gone a-hunting and caught a certain kind of bull-frog, (c) some man may have told her to be in an interesting condition, or (d) she may dream of having the child put inside her.

Both Frazer and Roth agree—and, I may add, I agree with them—that these statements are addressed to the problem to which they appear to be addressed—the problem of conception; and they agree that from these statements it may validly be deduced that the aborigines are ignorant of physiological paternity, believing rather that conception is the result of four kinds of 'magical' causation. Leach will have none of this. For him (ibid.) it is not

> a legitimate inference to assert that these Australian aborigines were ignorant of the connection between copulation and pregnancy. The modern interpretation of the rituals described would be that in this society the relationship between the woman's child and the clansmen of the woman's husband stems from public recognition of the bonds of marriage, rather than from the fact of cohabitation, which is a very normal state of affairs.

The logic of this 'modern interpretation' is certainly not evident to me. Ignoring the fact that only two of the four explanatory beliefs have reference to a male—so that they, at least, are hardly susceptible of this modern interpretation—by what evidence or from what inference can it be concluded that the other two statements mean what Leach claims that they mean? Is this the interpretation which the aborigines place on these beliefs? There is certainly no evidence for this assumption. Perhaps, then, this is the meaning which they intended to convey, even though they did not do so explicitly? But even if we were to grant that, for some strange reason, aborigines prefer to express structural relationships by means of biological symbolism, how do we *know* that this was their intention? Perhaps, then, the symbolism is unconscious, and the structural meaning which Leach claims for these beliefs, although intentional, is latent? This interpretation is certainly congenial to other 'modern interpretations'. Again, however, we are hung up on the problem of evidence. From what ethnographic data, or from what psychological theory of the unconscious, can this meaning be inferred? If, then, there is no way of *demonstrating* that either the manifest or the latent content of these symbols has reference to the structural relationship between a woman's children and the clansmen of her husband, I am compelled to discard this interpretation as not only implausible but false. I shall insist, instead, that the aborigines are indeed ignorant of physiological paternity, and that the four statements quoted in Roth are in fact proffered explanations for conception.

Substantive

The most obvious basis for religious behavior is the one which any religious actor tells us about when we ask him—and, unlike some anthropologists, I believe him. He believes in superhuman beings and he performs religious ritual in order that he may satisfy what I am calling substantive desires: desires for rain, nirvana, crops, heaven, victory in war, recovery from illness, and countless others. Everywhere man's mammalian desires (those which can be satisfied by naturalistic goals) must be satisfied, and *in the absence of competing technologies which confer reasonable confidence,* religious techniques are believed to satisfy these desires. Almost everywhere, moreover, the human awareness of the cessation of existence and/or of the unsatisfactory character of existence, produces anxiety concerning the persistence of existence (in some cases, it is desired; in others, it is not desired), and *in the absence of competing goals for the reduction of anxiety,* belief that one is successfully pursuing these religious goals (heaven-like or nirvana-like states) serves to reduce this anxiety.

Most, if not all, of these substantive desires, then, can be classified as attempts to overcome or transcend suffering. The religious actor wishes to overcome specific suffering—economic, political, physical, and the like; and he wishes to transcend more general suffering induced by some conception of life and the world as being evil, frustrating, sinful, and so on. Religion, as Weber (1930) points out, not only provides an explanation for, but it also promises redemption from, suffering. Religious techniques—performance of ritual, compliance with morality, faith, meditation, etc.—are the means by which this promise is felt to be fulfilled.

For the religious actor, if we can believe him, the expectation of realizing this promise is the most important motivational basis for religous behavior; the realization of this promise is its function. For him, it is an intended and recognized function. Believing in its reality, he clings tenaciously to his religious beliefs and practices—however irrational they may seem, and however dysfunctional with respect to other ends their consequences may be. From the anthropologist's point of view—and this is what presents such a knotty problem to many classical functionalists—these functions are apparent; they are not real. Ritual cannot effect rainfall, prayer cannot cure organic diseases, nirvana is a figment of the imagination, etc. It is this seeming irrationality of religion and, therefore, the apparent—rather than real—nature of its intended functions, that has given rise, I believe, to misplaced emphases on the importance of its sociological functions. Thus, despite Merton's incisive analysis of functional theory, it is highly questionable if the persistence of Hopi rain ceremonies is to be explained by the social integration to which *he* (Merton) thinks their performance is conducive (their real, but latent, functions), rather than by the meteorological events to which *Hopi* think they are conducive (their manifest, but apparent, functions).

The Hopi belief in the efficacy of their rainmaking ritual is not irrational—although it is certainly false—because the conclusion, rain ceremonies cause the rains to fall, follows validly from a world-view whose major premise states that gods exist, and whose minor premise states that the behavior of the gods can be influenced by rituals. That the premises are false does not render them irrational—until or unless they are disconfirmed by evidence. But all available 'evidence' confirms their validity: whenever the ceremonies are performed it does, indeed, rain. Hence, given their 'behavioral environment' (Hallowell 1955:75–110), Hopi beliefs are not irrational; and given their ecological environment, the apparent function of these ceremonies is surely a sufficient explanation for their persistence. (For further argument, see Spiro 1964).

If it is not sufficient, however, no appeal to unintended sociological functions will provide us with a better explanation—indeed, as we have already seen, it can provide us with no explanation at all. For how can the function of social solidarity explain the practice of these—or of any other—rituals? Notice that the objection to such an explanation is not that social solidarity may not be an object of desire—there is no reason why it cannot; and it is not that social solidarity is not achieved by the practice of these rituals—it often is. The objection, rather, is that the achievement of this end is *not* the desire which the practice of *these* rituals is intended to satisfy. Surely, not even the proponents of this type of explanation would suggest that Hopi rain ceremonies, sacrifices to Kali, exorcism of demons, celebration of the Mass, and the like are practiced with the conscious intention of achieving social solidarity. Is it suggested, then, that this is their unconscious intention? I would doubt that anyone would make this suggestion, for this suggests that if the efficacy of these rituals for the attainment of their designated ends were to be disbelieved, they would nevertheless be performed so that their solidarious functions might be served. This argument surely cannot be sustained. I can only conclude, then, that the persistence of these rituals is explicable by reference to what, for anthropologists, are their apparent, rather than their real, functions.[7]

Even if it were to be conceded that institutions must have real, rather than apparent, functions, anthropologists must surely be aware of those real functions of ritual which *are* recognized by religious actors and which may, therefore, reenforce their practice. For although religious ritual may not, in fact, be efficacious for the elimination of poverty, the restoration of health, the bringing of rain, and the like, the belief that it does achieve these ends serves the important psychological (real) function of reducing hopelessness—and its attendant anxiety—concerning their otherwise impossible attainment.

Expressive

A third set of desires which, I would suggest, constitutes a motivational source of religious behavior consists of painful drives which seek reduction and painful motives which seek satisfaction. By 'painful drives' I refer to those fears and anxieties concerning which psychoanalysis has taught us so much: fears of destruction and of one's own destructiveness, castration anxiety, cataclysmic fantasies, and a host of other infantile and primitive fears which threaten to overpower the weak and defenseless ego of the young child and which, if they become too overwhelming, result in schizophrenic and paranoid breakdown. By 'painful motives' I refer to those motives which, because culturally forbidden—prohibited forms of aggression, dependency, (Oedipal) sexuality, and the like—arouse feelings of shame, inadequacy, and moral anxiety.

---

7. One might, of course, wish to defend the weaker thesis, viz. that if these practices were sociologically dysfunctional, they would eventually disappear. Even this thesis is somewhat doubtful, however, when applied to multi-religious societies in which the practice of religion, however solidarious it may be for each religious group, has important dysfunctional consequences for the total social system. Still these religions persist, and with undiminished vigor, despite—one is tempted to say, because of—these consequences.

These drives and motives are much too painful to remain in consciousness and they are generally rendered unconscious. Although unconscious, they are not extinguished; they continue to seek reduction and satisfaction.

In the absence of other, or of more efficient means, religion is the vehicle—in some societies, perhaps, the most important vehicle—by which, symbolically, they can be handled and expressed. Since religious belief and ritual provide the content for culturally constituted projective, displacement, and sublimative mechanisms by which unconscious fears and anxieties may be reduced and repressed motives may be satisfied, these drives and motives, in turn, constitute an important unconscious source of religious behavior. Because the range of painful drives and motives which find expression in religion remains to be discovered by empirical research, I shall merely comment on two motives which I believe to be universally—but not exclusively—satisfied by religion; and since I have already attempted to deal with this problem elsewhere (Spiro 1961b), I shall be brief.

Forbidden dependency needs inevitably seek satisfaction in religious behavior, in that the religious actor depends on superhuman beings for the gratification of his desires. Repressing his desire to remain in a state of childlike dependency on powerful adult figures, he can still satisfy this desire, symbolically, by his trust in and reliance upon superhuman beings.

Similarly, since all religions of which I am aware postulate the existence of malevolent, as well as of benevolent, superhuman beings, repressed hostility motives can be displaced and/or projected in beliefs in, and rituals designed for protection against, these malevolent beings. Prevented from expressing his hostility against his fellows, the religious actor can satisfy this desire symbolically through religion (Spiro 1952).

These, then, are three sets of desires whose satisfaction partially explains the persistence of religion. But though the persistence of religion is to be found in motivation—a psychological variable—the sources of motivation are to be sought, in part, in society. For just as the sociological causes (social structural variables) of the truth of religious beliefs achieve their effects through mediating psychological processes—feelings, projections, perceptions, and the like—so too the psychological causes (desires) of religious behavior may be explained by reference to those sociocultural (and biological) variables by which they are produced. With few exceptions, human drives are acquired rather than learned; and all human goals, it is probably safe to assume, are acquired. Since the crucial context for the learning of human drives and goals is social, and since most religious drives—but not most goals—are acquired in the child's early experiences, it is the family that once again is the nuclear structural variable.

Indeed, because these motivational variables are acquired within specified structural contexts, and because these contexts exhibit a wide range of variability, differences in the kinds and/or intensity of desires which constitute the motivational basis for religious behavior should vary systematically with differences in family systems (including socialization systems), *as well as with the alternative, nonreligious means for their satisfaction.* The latter qualification is important. I have stressed, with respect to the three sets of desires which have been discussed, that in the absence of alternative institutional means, it is religion which is the means *par excellence* for their satisfaction. If cognitive desires, for example, are satisfied by science; if substantive desires are satisfied by technology; or if expressive desires are satisfied by politics or art or magic, religion should, by that extent, be less important for their satisfaction. In short, the importance of religion would be expected to vary inversely with the importance of other, projective and realistic, institutions.[8]

Holding other institutions constant, then, the kinds and intensity of drives which are satisfied by religion, the means by which they are believed to be satisfied, and the conceptions of the superhuman beings that are the agents of satisfaction should vary with variations in childhood experiences in which drives (and their intensity) are acquired, the means by which children influenced parents (and surrogates) to satisfy their drives, and the degree to which parents (and surrogates) do, in fact, satisfy them (Spiro & D'Andrade 1958).

In short, a motivational explanation of religious behavior can, in principle, explain variability in behavior and, hence, can be tested empirically. A great deal of culture-and-personality research, too extensive to cite here, has been devoted to this very problem. Indeed, much of the research concerned with the structural bases for religious cognitions has, simultaneously, been devoted to the motivational bases for religious behavior. Unfortunately, however, cognitive desires have received less attention than expressive and substantive desires, possibly because we know comparatively little about how they are acquired.

---

8. This does not imply, as some nineteenth-century thinkers believed, that as other institutions assume more of the traditional functions of religion, the latter will disappear. So far, at least, there has been no viable alternative to religion in providing a solution to the problem of 'suffering': and the malaise of modern man, on the one hand, and the persistence of religion among many modern intellectuals, on the other, seem to suggest that a viable functional alternative is yet to be discovered.

Causal and Functional Explanations

We may now return to the question with which we began this paper: is the existence of religion to be explained causally or functionally? I have suggested that the acquisition of religious beliefs is to be explained causally, and that the practice of these beliefs is to be explained in terms of motivation—which means that it is explained both causally and functionally. Religion persists because it has functions—it does, or is believed to, satisfy desires; but religion persists because it has causes—it is caused by the expectation of satisfying these desires. Both are necessary, neither is sufficient, together they are necessary and sufficient. The causes of religious behavior are to be found in the desires by which it is motivated, and its functions consist in the satisfaction of those desires which constitute its motivation.

Classical functionalist theory has, of course, tended to dismiss motivation and other psychological variables as being outside the domain of anthropology. Firth, for example (1956:224), writes that in the study of ritual the anthropologist is not concerned with " . . . the inner state as such of the participants," but rather with "the kinds of social relations that are produced or maintained."9 If 'inner states' were irrelevant for an explanation of religion, one might wish to defend the thesis that anthropology, whose central concern is the explanation of social and cultural institutions, should ignore them. But if by ignoring 'inner states', and other psychological variables, we cannot adequately explain religion, or, for that matter, the 'kinds of social relations' which it produces, we ignore them at our peril. Let me, beginning with the first proposition, take up each in turn.

An explanation of religion, or of any other sociocultural variable, consists in the specification of those conditions without which it could not exist. If religion is what is to be explained, if religion, that is, is the dependent variable, it can be explained only in terms of some independent variable, some condition by which it is maintained or sustained. I have argued that motivation is the independent variable. That religion, like other sociocultural variables, has sociological functions—it produces or maintains certain kinds of 'social relations'—is undeniable; and it is one of our tasks to study these sociological functions. Indeed, these sociological functions may be crucial for the maintenance of society. If, for example, social solidarity is a functional requirement of

9. I should hasten to add that, in a later publication (1959:133), Firth changed his view and stressed the importance of the individual for a complete explanation of religion.

society, and if religion—as it is frequently argued—is one of the institutions that satisfies this requirement, religion is necessary (a cause) for the maintenance of society. Notice, however, that if religion does produce solidarious social relations, solidarity provides us with an explanation of society, not of religion. In this case, in short, social solidarity does not explain religion; religion explains social solidarity. For social solidarity is the dependent, and it is religion that is the independent, variable. In sum, if we are interested in the 'kinds of social relations' that are produced by religion, we are interested in explaining society; and religion—it is assumed—can supply us with an entire, or a partial, explanation.

But the functionalist argument sometimes assumes a different form. Religion, it is argued, not only satisfies certain functional requirements of society, but it is a necessary condition for their satisfaction. Since society cannot exist unless these requirements are satisfied, and since religion is a necessary condition for their satisfaction, these requirements 'cause' the existence of religion. It is not that the desire to satisfy some requirement motivates religious behavior—the latter may be accounted for by numerous other desires of the kind suggested, perhaps, in this paper. Rather, since religion is a necessary condition for the satisfaction of this requirement, the need for its satisfaction can explain the existence of religion. This argument, I think, is implicit in most functionalist interpretations of the Radcliffe-Brown variety. Thus Radcliffe-Brown himself (1948:324) writes that religious ceremonies "are the means by which the society acts upon its individual members and keeps alive in their minds a certain system of sentiments. Without the ceremonial these sentiments would not exist, and without them the social organization in its actual form could not exist."

Notice, before we examine this type of explanation, that it is not a functionalist explanation at all; it is a causal explanation in which the cause happens to be a functional requirement. Notice, too, that despite the present tense of the predicates, this is really an explanation of the origin, not the persistence, of religion: the practice of religion—which is the only means by which religion persists—is not motivated by a desire to keep these sentiments alive, although the persistence of these sentiments is its consequence. But these questions aside, as an explanation of religion, this theory suffers from three defects: technical, methodological, and theoretical. Technically, no mechanism is specified by which the need for solidarity—and, therefore, the need for religion—gives rise to, or 'causes', religion. Methodologically, it cannot explain the variability of religion—how is it that the need to sustain social sentiments produces such a bewildering range of religious beliefs and rituals?—and, therefore, there is no way by which it can be tested. Theoretically, it is based on an unwarranted functionalist assumption, which Merton (1957) has aptly termed the assumption of 'indispensability'. What does this mean?

For some functional requirements any number of variables may be adequate for their satisfaction. Since none is necessary, although each may be sufficient, they are called 'functionally equivalent alternatives'. These are to be distinguished from a variable which is necessary or indispensable for the satisfaction of a requirement—without it the requirement could not be satisfied. The cross-cultural evidence strongly suggests that there are few, if any, indispensable variables; that, rather, for almost any sociocultural variable there are functional equivalents. Hence, even if it is the case that religion is the means by which Andamanese 'sentiments' are kept alive, it does not follow that religion is the only means by which this end could be accomplished, or that in other societies other institutions do not or cannot serve the identical function. [10]

In sum, from the fact that religion is a sufficient condition for the satisfaction of a requirement, it is invalidly deduced that it is a necessary condition. And, if it is not a necessary condition, its existence cannot be explained by arguing that without it society could not survive.

Although it is society, rather than religion, which is explained by the sociological consequences of religion, social anthropology—as the comparative study of social and cultural systems—is most certainly concerned with these functions; and psychological variables are not only necessary for the explanation of religion, but without them certain of its sociological functions would go unrecognized. (The classic example, of course, is Weber's [1930] analysis of the rise of capitalism, but it deals with the change in, rather than the persistence of, a social system.) Thus, the adjustive (real) function of religion, by satisfying the need for explanation, provides a society with a common 'behavioral environment' which, as Hallowell (1955) observes, satisfies a set of minimal requirements for the existence of any society: the requirement for

10. To cite but two counter-instances. First, there are the more than 150 atheistic *kibbutzim* in Israel, in which religious ceremonial does not exist (Spiro 1956). Second, there are societies in which the important social sentiments are supported by secular rather than religious institutions. It would be difficult, for example, to discover even one sentiment important for the maintenance of capitalist democracy which is conveyed by the paramount Christian ceremony, the Eucharist. National celebrations, however, especially as interpreted by Warner (1959), serve this function *par excellence*.

a common object orientation, spatiotemporal orientation, motivational orientation, and normative orientation. It would be difficult to conceive of the possibility of social integration without a minimum level of such shared orientations.

The adaptive (apparent) function of religion, in satisfying the desire for the attainment of goals, provides—as Marxism has stressed—a most important basis for social stability. Disbelief in the efficacy of superhuman means for the achievement of this-worldly goals could certainly become a potential basis for social discontent and socioeconomic change. At the same time, the (real) function of religion in reducing anxiety concerning the attainment of goals—especially those for whose attainment available technological skills are ineffective—and, thus, in providing a minimum level of psychological security, serves to release energy for coping with the reality problems of society.

Finally, the integrative (real) function of religion, in allowing the disguised expression of repressed motives, serves a number of sociological functions. By providing a culturally approved means for the resolution of inner conflict (between personal desires and cultural norms), religion (a) reduces the probability of psychotic distortion of desires, thereby providing a society with psychologically healthy members,[11] (b) protects society from the socially disruptive consequences of direct gratification of these forbidden desires, (c) promotes social integration by providing a common goal (superhuman beings) and a common means (ritual) by which the desires may be gratified.

Conclusion

It would appear from the foregoing discussion that an adequate explanation for the persistence of religion requires both psychological and sociological variables. If the cognitive bases for religious belief have their roots in childhood experience, their explanation must be found in social structural and, more specifically, family structure variables. Here religion is the dependent variable, and family structure is the independent sociological variable which effects religious belief by means of such intervening psychological variables as fantasies, projections, perceptions, and the like.

11. Nadel, recognizing the 'defensive' function of religion, writes that in providing rituals by which forbidden impulses may be expressed, religion " . . . anticipates as well as canalizes the working of psychological mechanisms, which might otherwise operate in random fashion or beyond the control of society, in the 'private worlds' of neurosis and psychopathic fantasies" (1954:275).

If religion persists because of its gratification of desires, explanations for the bases of religious behavior must be found in psychological and, specifically, motivational variables. Here, again, religion is the dependent, and motivation is the independent, variable. Since, however, motivation consists in the intention of gratifying desires, and since desires are rooted either in organic or in acquired drives, the motivational roots of religious behavior can, ultimately, be found in those biological and social structural variables, respectively, by which they are produced and/or canalized. Again, it is the family which emerges as the crucial sociological variable. Religion, then, is to be explained in terms of society and personality.

Many studies of religion, however, are concerned not with the explanation of religion, but with the role of religion in the explanation of society. Here, the explanatory task is to discover the contributions which religion, taken as the independent variable, makes to societal integration, by its satisfaction of sociological wants. This is an important task, central to the main concern of anthropology, as the science of social systems. We seriously err, however, in mistaking an explanation of society for an explanation of religion which, in effect, means confusing the sociological functions of religion with the bases for its performance.

In this paper, I have been concerned almost exclusively with the latter aspect of religion. I have not, except incidentally, dealt with its sociological functions or, what is perhaps more important, with how these are to be measured. I have not dealt, moreover, with the problem of religious origins because—despite the fact that numerous speculations have been proposed (and I have my own, as well)—these are not testable. Nor have I dealt with the problem of the cross-cultural variability in religion, except to suggest some motivational bases for the persistence of different types of belief and ritual. But the crucial problems—to which Max Weber has most importantly contributed—I have not even touched upon. If, for example, religion is centrally concerned with the problem of 'suffering', why is it that explanations for suffering run such a wide gamut: violation of ethical norms, sin of ancestors, misconduct in a previous incarnation, etc.? Or, if religion promises redemption from suffering, how are the different types of redemption to be explained? And, moreover, what is the explanation for the different means by which the redemptive promise is to be achieved? These are but a few of the central problems in the study of religion with which this chapter, with its limited focus, has not been concerned.

Acknowledgments

Thanks are due to the author, the editor, and the American Academy of Arts and Sciences for permission to quote the passage from "Golden Bough or Gilded Twig?" by E. R. Leach, in *Daedalus*, 1961.

References

Durkheim, E. 1954. *The elementary forms of the religious life.* Glencoe, Ill.: Free Press.

Evans-Pritchard, E. E. 1954. *The institutions of primitive society.* Oxford: Blackwell.

Firth, R. 1956. *Elements of social organization.* London: Watts; New York: Philosophical Library.

——— 1959. Problem and assumption in an anthropological study of religion. *Journal of the Royal Anthropological Institute* 89.

Fortes, M. 1959. *Oedipus and Job in West African religion.* Cambridge: Cambridge University Press.

Freud, S. 1928. *The future of an illusion.* London: Hogarth Press.

Gerth, H. H., and Mills, C. W., eds. 1946. *For Max Weber: Essays in sociology.* New York: Oxford University Press.

Goody, J. 1961. Religion and ritual: The definitional problem. *British Journal of Sociology* 12.

Hallowell, A. I. 1955. *Culture and experience.* Philadelphia: University of Pennsylvania Press.

——— 1956. The Rorschach technique in personality and culture studies. In *Developments in the Rorschach technique,* vol. 2, ed. B. Klopfer. Yonkers-on-Hudson, N.Y.: World Books; London: Harrap.

Hempel, C. G. 1952. *Fundamentals of concept formation in empirical science.* Chicago: University of Chicago Press; London: Cambridge University Press.

Horton, R. 1960. A definition of religion and its uses. *Journal of Royal Anthropological Institute* 90.

Kardiner, A. 1945. *The psychological frontiers of society.* New York: Columbia University Press.

Leach, E. R. 1954. *Political systems of highland Burma.* London: Bell.

——— 1961. Golden bough or gilded twig? *Daedalus.*

Lowie, R. 1924. *Primitive religion.* New York: Boni & Liveright.

Merton, R. K. 1957. *Social theory and social structure.* rev. ed., Glencoe, Ill.: Free Press.

Nadel, S. F. 1954. *Nupe religion.* Glencoe, Ill.: Free Press.

Pruyser, P. 1960. Some trends in the psychology of religion. *Journal of Religion* 40.

Radcliffe-Brown, A. R. 1948. *The Andaman islanders.* Glencoe, Ill.: Free Press.

Radin, P. 1957. *Primitive religion.* New York: Mayflower & Vision Press.

Spiro, M. E. 1952. Ghosts, Ifaluk, and teleological functionalism. *American Anthropologist* 45.

―――― 1953. Ghosts: An anthropological inquiry into learning and perception. *Journal of Abnormal and Social Psychology* 48.

―――― 1956. *Kibbutz: Venture in Utopia.* Cambridge: Harvard University Press.

―――― 1961a. Social systems, personality, and functional analysis. In *Studying personality cross-culturally,* ed. B. Kaplan. Evanston, Ill.: Row, Peterson.

―――― 1961b. An overview and a suggested reorientation. In *Psychological anthropology,* ed. F. L. K. Hsu. Homewood, Ill.: Dorsey Press.

―――― 1963. Causes, functions, and cross-cousin marriage: An essay in anthropological explanation. *Journal of Royal Anthropological Institute* 97.

―――― 1964. Religion and the irrational. In *Symposium on new approaches to the study of religion,* Proceedings of the American Ethnological Society, Seattle.

Spiro, M. E., and D'Andrade, R. G. 1958. A cross-cultural study of some supernatural beliefs. *American Anthropologist* 60.

Turner, V. W. 1962. *Chihamba: The white spirit.* Manchester: Manchester University Press.

Warner, W. L. 1959. *The living and the dead.* New Haven: Yale University Press.

Weber, M. 1930. *The protestant ethic and the spirit of capitalism.* London: Allen & Unwin; New York: Scribner's.

Whiting, J. W. M. 1961. Socialization process and personality. In F. L. K. Hsu (ed.), op. cit.

9 Virgin Birth, Parthenogenesis, and Physiological Paternity: An Essay in Cultural Interpretation

Introduction

IN HIS CLASSIC report, W. E. Roth (1903:22) described the conception beliefs of the Tully River Blacks. None assigns a procreative role to the father.

Although sexual connection as a cause of conception is not recognized among the Tully River blacks so far as they are themselves concerned, it is admitted as true for all animals:—*indeed this idea confirms them in their belief of superiority over the brute creation.* A woman begets children *because* (a) she has been sitting over the fire on which she has roasted a particular species of black bream, which must have been given to her by the prospective father, (b) she has purposely gone a-hunting and caught a certain kind of bullfrog, (c) some man may have told her to be in an interesting condition, or (d) she may dream of having a child put inside her.

By whichever of the above *methods the child is conceived,* whenever it eventually appears, the recognized husband accepts it as his own without demur. (My emphasis.)

In 1961 Edmund Leach (1961:376) wrote "[It is not] a legitimate inference to assert that these Australian aborigines were ignorant of the connexion between copulation and pregnancy." Instead,

The modern interpretation of the rituals described would be that in this society the relationship between the woman's child and the clansmen of the woman's husband stems from the public recognition of the bonds of marriage, rather than from the facts of cohabitation, which is a very normal state of affairs.

Reprinted from *Man: The Journal of the Royal Anthropological Institute,* vol. 3, no. 2 (June 1968):224–61.

This article was written while I was a Research Fellow in the Social Science Research Institute, University of Hawaii. It has importantly benefited from the criticisms of Robert I. Levy and David M. Schneider.

In 1966 I wrote (Spiro 1966:112) that since, on the face of it, I found this interpretation implausible, and since Dr. Leach had not supported it (either with data or with theory), I would hold, instead, that:

. . . the aborigines are indeed ignorant of physiological paternity, and that the four statements quoted in Roth are in fact proffered explanations for conception.[1]

In 1967, "provoked" by my "critical comments," Leach returned to the problem of aborigine conception beliefs in his Henry Myers Lecture (Leach 1967). Stripped of its many and tedious *ad hominem* arguments—the impugnations of his opponents' scholarship,[2] their scientific integrity,[3] and even their "normality,"[4] the gratuitous imputation to them of motives and attitudes,[5] the obsessive imputation to

1. Since my entire contribution to the present controversy is confined to this brief statement, it is rather intriguing to know by what modes of inference Dr. Leach was able to conclude in his most recent contribution that (to take some examples at random):

Professor Spiro believes that explanation consists of postulating causes and ultimate origins for the facts under observation (Leach 1967:39).

He is positively *eager* to believe that the aborigines were ignorant and he accepts their assertion as a fact without investigating the evidence at all (1967:41, original emphasis).

He displays an *extreme reluctance* to believe that the products of aboriginal thought can be structured in a logical way (1967:41, my emphasis).

Professor Spiro (and all the neo-Tyloreans who think like him) *desperately wants* to believe . . . that dogma and ritual must somehow correspond to the inner psychological attitudes of the actors concerned (1967:40, my emphasis).

As ostensible characterizations of my position, these—and *every* other position which Leach *imputes* to me—have one thing in common. They are all false.
    2. One or two instances will suffice. Thus according to Leach, I am "quite unaware that almost identical questions have been asked many times before" (1967:39); I am ignorant of the fact "that a huge literature of commentary surrounds Roth's original ethnographic report," and so on.
    3. For example, the proponents of physiological ignorance " . . . have shown themselves willing to accept even the flimsiest evidence *for* the fact of ignorance, while evidence *against*, even when it is most meticulously recorded, is repeatedly rejected . . . " (1967:46, original emphasis).
    4. Thus, convinced in his own mind that when her informants spoke to Kaberry about birth and pregnancy they could not have been ignorant of physiological paternity since—according to Leach—they were really speaking of metaphysical matters, Leach comments: "That a distinguished anthropologist [Kaberry] should once have thought otherwise displays the oddity of anthropologists rather than the oddity of the aborigines" (Leach 1967:47). Leach's comment is all the more gratuitous since, contrary to the implication of this quotation, Kaberry goes out of her way (Kaberry 1939:ch. 2) to emphasize the rational and empirical bases for aboriginal belief.
    5. For example, if certain groups "have persuaded" their ethnographers that they were "ignorant of the facts of life," and if the ethnographer "believed what he was told it was because such belief corresponded to his own private fantasy of the natural ignorance of savages" (1967:41). Again, the motivation for this "fantasy" is that these ethnographers "seem to gain reassurance from supposing that the people they study have the simple minded ignorance of small children" (1967:45).

them of a racist ideology[6]—this lecture might be summarized in the following propositional form. 1) If a cultural belief in Australia states that a woman conceives when a spirit-child enters her womb, 2) it may not be inferred from this belief that the natives are ignorant of physiological paternity, because 3) only "idiots" would believe this conception theory, and 4) only those anthropologists who view the natives as "childish," "stupid," "superstitious," and so on, would believe that the natives would believe in such a theory. Hence 5) although this belief seems to be about conception, it is really not about conception at all; rather 6) it is about patrilateral filiation. 7) Moreover, even if it is about conception this belief must be viewed as a cultural "dogma," i.e., as a "kind of religious fiction," which, though asserted, is not really believed to be true.

Before examining this argument, it is important to set one fact straight. Although the question of whether it is possible to draw valid conclusions about the personal beliefs of social actors from their cultural beliefs is an important theoretical question—and one to which we shall return—Dr. Leach begs the empirical question by posing it as the central problem in this controversy. For contrary to Leach's claim, Sharp and Malinowski, Kaberry and Austin, and most of the others who contend that the natives are ignorant of physiological paternity, do not claim it to be an *inference* based on the Australian cultural belief which they recorded; they claim, rather, that—the cultural belief aside—it is an *empirical finding.* And they support this claim with a great deal of field data. Based on their interviewing, probing, inquiring, and challenging of informants, they concluded that the personal beliefs of the social actors corresponded to the cultural beliefs which they had been taught. If, then, it can be assumed that the quality of Australian fieldwork is no worse, on an average, than field work conducted in other parts of the world, Austrlian ignorance of physiological paternity is an anthropological finding whose empirical status—until refuted—is no worse (and no better) than most anthropological findings. (The meaning of "ignorance," however, is not simple, as we shall see below.) Having structured the controversy, then, as involving ethnographical inference (rather than ethnographical fact[7]) it must be

---

6. This is examined below.

7. All "facts," to be sure, are inferences. "Facts" obtained through anthropological interviews rest on a number of inferences concerning the reliability of our interviewing instruments, the motivation and veracity of our informants, and so on. But to the extent that this is so, the factual basis for Australian conception beliefs is no less suspect than most other anthropological "facts."

stressed that Dr. Leach nowhere confronts, let alone refutes, this finding.

Given Leach's premise, that the controversy concerns ethnographical inference, his argument (as summarized above) contains two main theses: the cultural belief concerning conception does not *mean* what it says, and, even if it does, the natives do not *believe* what it says. There are, then, two distinct issues in this controversy. First, what is the meaning of the cultural belief? Second, whatever its meaning, can it be inferred from this belief that the natives are ignorant of physiological paternity? Since it is impossible to examine all of Leach's arguments, I shall confine my discussion to those which seem to be salient. With respect to the issue of physiological paternity, I shall examine three of his arguments, viz.: 1) Only "idiots" could be ignorant of physiological paternity, and only those who view natives as "idiots" would argue that they are ignorant of the relationship between copulation and conception. 2) The Australian evidence supports his thesis that the aborigines are not ignorant of this relationship. 3) The comparative—and especially the Christological—evidence supports this thesis. With respect to the meaning of the cultural belief, I shall examine two of Leach's arguments, viz.: 1) Both the Australian and 2) the Christological evidence support the sociological meaning which he attributes to the belief.

The Issue of Physiological Paternity

1. The Argument of Alleged Intellectual Inferiority

Although Leach's attribution of a racist ideology to his opponents is, like all *ad hominem* arguments, irrelevant to the substantive issues of this controversy, it must nevertheless be examined because it looms so large in his lecture: it is, he claims, the "crux" of the controversy (1967:45). Leach's argument is simply stated. That Australians are ignorant of physiological paternity is not a scientific finding, but a personal prejudice based on the conviction that primitive peoples are intellectually inferior and incapable of logical thought.

To say that a native is *ignorant* [notice the escalation of the specific, "ignorant of physiological paternity," to the generic, "ignorant"] amounts to saying that he is childish, stupid, superstitious. Ignorance is the opposite of rationality; it is the quality which distinguishes the savage from the anthropologist (1967:41, original emphasis).

But surely the premise of this argument is false. None of Leach's opponents—neither Roth nor Malinowski, neither Kaberry nor Ashley

Montagu—holds that "ignorance is the opposite of rationality." For, of course, ignorance is the opposite not of rationality, but of knowledge; irrationality, not ignorance, is the opposite of rationality. To be ignorant of something, i.e., to have no knowledge (or false knowledge) is not necessarily to be irrational (or, for that matter, childish, stupid, superstitious, etc.). Indeed, if it were, Leach's efforts to salvage their "rationality" by insisting that the natives are aware of physiological paternity would be in vain. For they would still be ignorant of the fact that the earth is round, that it moves around the sun, that genes are the physical basis of heredity, that man evolved from a lower primate, etc., etc. And not only the Australians! On this premise, Europeans were irrational until the nineteenth century because they were ignorant of human evolution; until the fifteenth century, because they did not believe in a heliocentric universe; and so on.[8] In short, the premise—ignorant=irrational—is not only semantically false, but it is culturally and historically absurd.

If knowledge (rather than rationality) is the opposite of ignorance, the question can then be posed: is it irrational for Australians to be ignorant of physiological paternity and to believe, instead, that women conceive because they are entered by spirit-children? The answer to this question clearly depends on what we might mean by "irrational." When we characterize a belief as "irrational" we can mean, so far as I can tell, one or more of the following things. 1) The belief is a conclusion invalidly deduced from some axiom or premise; to hold the belief is irrational because it rests on a fallacy in deductive logic. 2) The belief is an empirical generalization which is invalidly derived from available evidence; to hold the belief is irrational because it rests on a fallacy in inductive logic. 3) The belief asserts some proposition which is inconsistent with, or in contravention of, some other belief; to hold the belief is irrational because it violates the law of contradiction. 4) The belief asserts something about the universe which is inconsistent with, or in contravention of, reliable knowledge; to hold the belief is irrational because it is empirically absurd (cf. Spiro 1964).

If I am correct in assuming that these are the criteria we use for judging the irrationality of belief, Australian ignorance of physiological

---

8. Malinowski's statement concerning this matter is as apposite today as it was thirty-five years ago:

> I think it is rather inconsistent to get excited about the faulty knowledge of the Trobrianders when it comes to processes of sexual fertilisation, while we are perfectly satisfied that they possess no real knowledge as to processes of nutrition, or metabolism, the causes of disease and health, or any other subject of natural history . . . (Malinowski 1932:ii).

paternity can scarcely be taken as a measure of irrationality. Of all the possible reasons—too numerous to detail here, but superbly summarized by Ashley Montagu (1937:235–76)—which have been offered for the limitation in their knowledge of the relationship between coitus and conception, none includes faulty logic. Moreover, using the above criteria, for the aborigines to believe in their spirit-children theory of conception is entirely rational: it explains all the facts, it accounts for all the anomalies rendered inexplicable by a procreation theory (cf. Malinowski 1932:184–94), it is contradicted by no available knowledge, and it leads to valid deductive and inductive conclusions (cf. Ashley Montagu, 1937:ch. 14). To be sure, this conception theory is false; but to hold a false belief is not in itself irrational, unless it violates the four criteria mentioned above. For, although judgments concerning the *truth* of a belief are relative to the latest developments in science, judgments concerning the *rationality* of holding that belief must be relative to the state of knowledge of the society in which it is found. The cultural heritage of any group provides its members with a weltanschauung which is based on (among other things) the level of knowledge found in that society. This weltanschauung includes a set of assumptions concerning the nature of the world which not only comprise the major premises for any argument or discourse, but which constitute the parameters of their "behavioural environment" (Hallowell 1955:ch. 4). Hence, given *their* major premises—and they have no access to alternative premises—and given *their* behavioral environment (is any other available to them?) the Australians would exhibit none of the four types of logical fallacy alluded to above in holding their conception beliefs to be true (cf. Spiro:1964). Holding them does not render them childish, stupid, superstitious or idiotic; and for anthropologists to believe that they hold these beliefs does not mean that they view them in this manner.

Indeed, Leach's allegation that his opponents do, in fact, take ignorance of physiological paternity to be a sign of childish, irrational mentality is simply untrue. Since it would be tedious to take up each of his opponents in turn, I shall confine my comments to Ashley Montagu, whose monograph (1937) remains the classic statement of the controversy, and who, after an examination of the entire ethnographical literature, concludes that nowhere in Australia can one find true knowledge not only of physiological *paternity*, but of physiological *maternity* as well. Now, for Ashley Montagu—whether his conclusion is right or wrong—to be included among those who believe in the inferiority of any group is nothing short of extraordinary.

Thus, at the very beginning of his study, Ashley Montagu (1937:10–

11) dismisses any possible notion that ignorance of physiological paternity implies

. . . that the Australian aboriginal is a being mentally inferior to ourselves, or that he is incapable of our particular kind of reasoning, or that he has a pre-logical mentality, or what not. The facts point clearly in the opposite direction, namely, that the Australian aboriginal native endowment is quite as good as any European's, if not better. In support of the latter statement that exists a certain amount of evidence of the weightiest kind . . .

He concludes his study (1937:308) with a similar statement.

The mind of the Australian is no more pre-logical than that of the modern educated man or woman. Essentially the mind of the savage functions in exact-ly the same way as our own does, the differences perceptible in the effects of that functioning are due only to the differences in the premises upon which that functioning is based, premises which represent the logical instruments of the native's thought, and have their origin in categories and forms of judgment which are to some extent different though quite as rigorously organised as our own.

Although space forbids the citation of similar statements by, for example, Roth (1903:23), Malinowski (1932:ii sqq), Kaberry (1939:ch. 2), Spiro (1964:109–10), etc., the conclusion is inescapable. It is not true that those anthropologists who believe that the aborigines are ignorant of physiological paternity either view their ignorance as childish, or view them as intellectually inferior.

2. The Argument from the Australian Evidence

Since those who hold that the Australians are ignorant of physiological paternity base their conclusion, according to Leach, on prejudice, an objective examination of the ethnographical data, so he argues, supports his thesis that the Australians are not ignorant of physiological paternity. I submit that, with one exception, none of the data which Leach cites support this conclusion.

Leach's first argument is that there is a "classically established reason" for supposing that the Tully River Blacks were not ignorant: "They freely admitted to Roth that the cause of pregnancy in animals other than man is copulation" (Leach 1967:40). Since that is the entire argument and the full quotation, it is rather difficult to divine precisely what the force of this argument might be:[9] that we can best know about

9. In order to forestall Leach's penchant for impugning the scholarly knowledge of his opponents, I would only comment that know the arguments of Roheim, Warner, and Thomson on the subject. It is Leach's that I am unaware of.

a people's beliefs about themselves from their beliefs about animals? But then Dr. Leach would have to concede that the Trobrianders and the Arunta, for example, are indeed ignorant of physiological paternity because they, like many other groups, deny any procreative basis for animal pregnancy. (For the Trobriands, cf. Malinowski 1932:162; Austin 1934:112; for the Arunta, cf. Spencer & Gillen 1899:84, v. 2.) Moreover, people everywhere make distinctions between themselves and animals, sometimes invidious to themselves, sometimes invidious to the animals. In the Tully River case the latter is the case, as Roth tells us: "This idea confirms them in their belief of superiority over the brute creation."

Leach's second argument is that the data of the more recent ethnographers, working in other parts of Australia, show that Australian conception beliefs are cultural dogmas, "a kind of religious fiction"; hence the "formally expressed ignorance" reflected in the dogmas does not correspond to the attitudes of the social actors (Leach 1967:40). Ignoring the debatable methods by which data from other parts of Australia are used to refute the Tully River data, or (even conceding that) by which data collected thirty to fifty years after the original report are used (considering the variety of ensuing acculturative forces) to interpret its meaning, my reading of these data is rather different from his.

Of the six ethnographies which Leach says support his position Warner's alone (1937) can be claimed; the others are either unclear, or else they refute it. Thus, Stanner (1933) argues that the "confused version" of physiological paternity, which is found side by side with a "mystical theory" among the Daly River tribes, is a result of acculturation. Meggitt, although certainly stressing that the *contemporary* Walbiri (especially the females) emphasise both spiritual *and* physical causes of pregnancy, is cautious, in view of Spencer and Gillen's data, about drawing conclusions conerning the beliefs of former generations from contemporary data. "Although it is clear," he writes, "that people in the past recognized the fact of physiological maternity, we cannot be sure to what extent they were aware of physiological paternity" (Meggitt 1962:272). Roheim, although arguing that the Australians are indeed aware of physiological paternity, yet admits that following initiation, the knowledge is repressed, i.e., it is rendered unconscious (Roheim 1932:97); on a conscious level, adults are ignorant.

Thus far, then, Leach's contention that his position is supported by recent ethnographers, is rather misleading. When, however, he includes Sharp and Thomson (1933) among those whose data allegedly support him, his contention is not only misleading, it is untrue. Lauriston Sharp (in letters written from the field to Ashley Montagu) states repeatedly that the Yir-Yiront are literally ignorant of physiological paternity. Moreover, after three years of fieldwork he expresses astonishment that their ignorance " . . . should by some be considered as an indication that they must be moronic" (Sharp, in Ashley Montagu 1937:162–65). As for Thomson, although he reports that the Koko Ya'o believe in the procreative function of semen, their procreative knowledge remains as "magical" as—and, from Leach's view, even more "irrational" than—that of the other Australian tribes. For, while affirming physiological *paternity*, they strongly deny physiological *maternity*: "Informants . . . treated contemptuously any suggestion that the mother has any part in conception" (Thomson 1933:506). [10]

Leach's last argument in support of his thesis that the Tully River Blacks believe in physiological paternity is that the alleged ignorance of physiological paternity in the Trobriands is seriously to be questioned. Thus, Leach claims that 1) by 1932 Malinowski had seriously qualified

10. Leach concedes that the data of at least one "modern" ethnographer—Phyllis Kaberry—do not support his thesis; but he attributes this fact to her faulty interpretation. When properly interpreted, he argues, her data support him. Thus, he claims, Kaberry's finding concerning the belief in a spirit-child theory of conception means that the entry of a spirit-child into a woman is a *sign* of pregnancy, not its *cause*. Commenting on Kaberry's report, he writes (1967:47). "In other words, a woman *recognizes* that she is pregnant when she experiences 'morning sickness'—which is true also of European women" (my emphasis). Now, in addition to his misreading of European ethnoscience—European women recognize pregnancy by the stopping of their menses, an event which occurs before morning sickness—Leach has misread Kaberry as well. For, in the passage quoted by Leach, Kaberry writes: "Conception *occurs* when one of these [spirit children] enters a woman. Its presence in the food given her by her husband makes her vomit . . . " (Leach 1967:47, my emphasis). I submit that "conception occurs" does not mean " . . . a woman recognises that she is pregnant. . ." Exegesis aside, however, although Kaberry herself interprets this belief as referring to the cause of conception, not its recognition, Leach's only rebuttal is to state that it is not so.

Again, to Kaberry's comment that, "Questioned on the function of intercourse natives admitted that it prepared the way for the entry of the spirit child" (Leach 1967:47). Leach is "very puzzled as to how anyone [i.e. Kaberry] could interpret such data as indicating 'ignorance of physiological paternity.'" But I am puzzled by Leach's puzzlement. It is one thing to say that sexual intercourse opens the vagina so that the spirit child can enter the woman—a frequently recorded belief in Australia; it is quite another to say that it impregnates the woman, especially when the conception belief states explicitly that only the spirit-child does *that*. The issue, in short, is whether intercourse is believed to be the *cause* of pregnancy, and this the natives deny. As Ashley Montagu (1937:200), summarizing all of the data on this question, remarks: [When the anthropologist] inquires whether intercourse has any connection with pregnancy or childbirth he is in most cases informed that intercourse serves to prepare the woman for the entry of a spirit child into her, but that this preparation is not in itself the cause of pregnancy or of the entry of the child into the woman . . . In other words, intercourse prepares the way for that factor to become operative which is the cause of pregnancy [spirit child entry], but intercourse is not either alone or in conjunction with other factors the cause of pregnancy.

his original position; 2) Powell and Austin, independently, had recorded observations "strikingly similar" to those of Meggitt on the Walbiri; 3) Fortune showed that Trobriand "ignorance" reflected religious dogma, rather than the state of their knowledge. Ignoring again the methodological problem, the fact is that all of these claims (with the exception of the one concerning Powell) are demonstrably false.

1. It is true that in his "Special foreword," Malinowski (1932) (good contextualist that he is) cautions his readers to view Trobriand conception beliefs within the total context of Trobriand culture. Nowhere in this foreword, however, does he *retract* anything he had previously written about their beliefs. More important, five years later, Malinowski (1937:xxiv) writes:

[The verdict of Ashley Montagu] that in Australia practically universally, according to orthodox belief, pregnancy is regarded as causally unconnected with intercourse will, I think, remain the ultimate conclusion of science. It is supported by an irrefutable body of solid fact.

2. Since Powell's thesis is not available to me, I cannot comment. Austin's report, however, is available, and, contrary to Leach's claim, everything in his report explicitly and unambiguously confirms Malinowski's findings. The following samples will have to suffice. "The Trobriand Island native does *not* know of the fertilizing agency of the male seed. In my interviews with some fifty intelligent natives, drawn from all parts of the Trobriand group of islands, not one believed that male semen, or any part of it, entered the uterus" (Austin 1934:105, original emphasis). Again, when asked about precautions taken by women to prevent conception by ridding themselves of semen, they would answer in these terms: "Why should our girls do this? *Momona* [semen] does not cause pregnancy. It is like water" (106). Austin also reports that although most informants held to the *baloma* theory of conception, a minority—"not at all considered the prevailing opinion"—did not consider this the controlling principle. Even they, however, did not place any credence in sexual intercourse as a cause of pregnancy. On the contrary, for them, " . . . the child was merely formed out of the mother's blood" (107). As Austin says (108), "In both cases, however, there was no doubt that 'man's contribution towards the new life in the mother's body' was nil." In short, "there was no doubt that the father was *not* thought to be a contributor towards the formation of the foetus . . . " (112; original emphasis).

3. From an anecdote in Fortune (1963:239), Leach (1967:48) infers that the debate reported between the Trobrianders and the Dobuans over the former's conception theory " . . . was plainly about doctrine

not about knowledge." Aside from the gratuitous assumption that doctrine cannot be about knowledge, the logic of Leach's inference eludes me. His inference is based on the fact that when Fortune, who had accompanied a party of Dobuans to the Trobriands, arranged for the debate, the Dobuans became angry with him and turned their heads to the wall. On the basis of this rather strange *inference* Leach then concludes that the *"evidence* for [Trobriand belief being] 'dogma' [rather than knowledge] is very clear" (my emphasis). Fortune himself, incidentally, whose interpretation Leach ignores, provides no support for Leach's interpretation. In his original report Fortune attributed the Dobuan behaviour to the fact that the two parties had quarrelled about their respective theories in the past and had no desire to revive the dispute (Fortune 1963:329). In his new preface (1963:xiv–xv) and new appendix (1963:311–12), he suggests that the more basic reason for Dobuan anger is to be found in their taboo against asking to hear legends while on an outward-bound voyage or in a port of call. This interpretation, too, is ignored by Leach.

In summary, then, the Australian data cited by Leach are, for the most part, the reverse of what he purports them to be. 1) That Tully River Blacks admit that sexual intercourse is the cause of animal pregnancy is true, but its implication for the issue at hand is unclear. 2) Contrary to Leach's argument, the modern ethnographies cited by him refute his claims that as cultural "dogmas" Australian conception beliefs are not taken seriously. 3) Contrary to Leach's argument, Malinowski's data on the Trobriand remain unchanged by either what he, or any of the other scholars cited by Leach (with the possible exception of Powell) have written.

3. The Argument from the Christian Evidence

Referring to the numerous European folk tales which recount the magical conception of gods and heroes, Leach (1967:40) observes that "some of these stories resemble very closely indeed the account given to Roth by the Tully River Blacks of how *ordinary* human births occur" (original emphasis). He then asks, rhetorically:

But if the existence of European tales about ladies who became pregnant after eating magical fish is not now held to imply that Europeans are, or were, ignorant of the facts of physiological paternity, why should such stories have this implication in the case of the Tully River Blacks?

This same rhetorical question, phrased in different ways, and directed especially to his trump card—the Virgin Birth—is repeated a number of times: if the magical birth of heroes and gods in the religions and myths of higher (and especially Christian) civilization does not imply ignorance of physiological paternity in Christendom, why—except to reinforce Western belief in the ignorance of "natives"—should such an inference be drawn from reports of magical conception among Australians? Hence, if we do not accord these two cases the same status it can only be, according to Dr. Leach, because of Western prejudice, viz.: "If *we* believe such things, we are devout; if *others* do so they are idiots" (1967:45, original emphasis).

That Leach should not have recognized the obvious fallacy in his analogy is especially surprising since his own statement underscores the basis for the fallacy. In the passage quoted above he stresses that he is comparing *ordinary* births among the Australians with the births of gods and heroes—*extraordinary* births—among Europeans.[11] And there's the rub! If—to take Leach's *pièce de résistance*—the dogma of the Virgin Birth is not held to imply that Christians are or were ignorant of physiological paternity, it is because this cannot possibly be its implication. Far from claiming that the virginal conception of Jesus typifies a general norm of virginal conception, this dogma, by holding that His birth was a miracle, makes precisely the reverse claim; it denies that the norm of procreative conception applies in His case. Indeed, Leach's entire argument is misconceived because, unlike the spirit-child belief, the Virgin Birth does not assert that Jesus had no genitor, it asserts that he had no *human* genitor; and unlike the Christian dogma, the Australian belief is not about virgin births, but about nonprocreative births. In referring to the Christian and Australian beliefs as "virgin birth" doctrines, Leach confuses virgin birth with parthenogenesis. Although both of these former beliefs—like parthenogenesis itself—share the notion that conception occurs without copulation, the similarity stops there. The Australian case is not strictly analogous to nonhuman parthenogenesis because, paradoxically, it is nonvirgins who conceive parthenogenetically; in the Christian case, a Virgin (the first paradox) conceives procreatively (the second paradox).

In both cases, however, the paradox is only apparent. In Australia, conception does not result from copulation, but from the entry of an already formed spirit-child into the vagina. Hence, though the mother is a nonvirgin, there is no genitor. In the Christian myth there is a

---

11. For this reason, Leach's more telling argument would have been the Western secular belief that children are brought by storks. Like the Australian conception belief this belief explains all—not merely extraordinary—births, and it is even more "irrational" than the former: it reflects ignorance of physiological *maternity* as well as paternity. Moreover, we know that it was transmitted (to children), though not believed (by adults).

genitor, and conception does result from fertilization; but the mother remains a Virgin because fertilization occurs without copulation—procreation is aural, not vaginal; semen is spiritual, not physical; genitor is nonhuman (God), not human. For only on the assumption that normal conceptions are nonvirginal can the dogma claim that the virginal conception of Jesus is a miracle (which is why His birth is not just another virgin birth, but *the* Virgin Birth). And it is precisely because it is a miracle that the Virgin Birth is a dogma of the church, i.e. an article of faith. For, like all miracles, the Virgin Birth is not normal but abnormal, not ordinary but extraordinary, not rational but irrational—in a word (as Tertullian put it), absurd! And to believe in the absurd requires a leap into faith: *credo quia absurdum est.*

In sum, Leach's analogical argument is invalid. Whatever else it can imply, the Virgin Birth cannot imply ignorance of physiological paternity; it *must* imply knowledge of physiological paternity. [12]

But Leach's analogical argument does not stop there. If, as he argues, the dogma of the Virgin Birth is not held to imply ignorance of physiological paternity it is because, being a dogma, its biological message is not taken very seriously; rather it serves to "reinforce the dogma that the Virgin's child is the son of God" (1967:32). Now ignoring the logical difficulty posed by this argument—since the "dogma" that the Virgin's child is the son of God is one and the same dogma, it is difficult to understand how a dogma can reinforce itself—of course (as I would prefer to put it) the theological function of the Virgin Birth is to *legitimize* the Christian claim that Jesus is the son of God. It is not clear, however, why this implies that the dogma of the Virgin Birth does not have a biological message, or—since it explicitly states that Jesus was not begotten of Joseph—that this message is not taken seriously. Indeed, how else, except by denying to Joseph a procreative role in the conception of Jesus, can the dogma then assign that role to the third person of the Trinity? And how else can Jesus be divine unless He is God's—not Joseph's—only begotten Son? In short, were it not for its biological message—Jesus did not have a human genitor—

---

12. The identical logical critique renders invalid yet another of Leach's Christological arguments. "Theologians who debate the doctrine of transubstantiation," Leach (1967:48) informs us, "cannot usefully be accused of ignorance of the elementary facts of chemistry." Not only "usefully," but "logically." For, of course, it is only because these theologians *are* aware of the elementary facts of chemistry that transubstantiation is, for them, a supernatural, not a natural, event—a Mystery. By the laws of nature, it could not happen. It is precisely because it violates what they believe to be the laws of nature—"the elementary facts of chemistry"—that transubstantiation must be an article of faith.

and were this message not taken seriously, the theological function of the dogma of the Virgin Birth could not be served.

Having examined Leach's arguments on behalf of his first thesis, viz., that from Australian conception beliefs it may not be inferred that the natives are ignorant of physiological paternity, we may now turn to his arguments on behalf of his second thesis, viz., that these beliefs are not about conception but about patrilateral filiation.

The Issue of the Meaning of Australian Conception Beliefs

1. The Argument from the Australian Evidence

According to Dr. Leach, the "modern interpretation" of the Tully River conception beliefs is that "the relationship between the woman's child and the clansmen of the woman's husband stems from the public recognition of the bonds of marriage." The meaning of this interpretation is unclear. Does it refer to the cognitive meaning of the beliefs (and, if so, to their conscious or unconscious meaning)? Or does it refer, rather, to their sociological function (and, if so, to their manifest or latent function)? Or does it refer to their sociological implication, i.e., to the sociological message which they convey, not to the natives, but to the anthropologists? However, I shall ignore the conceptual difficulties entailed by each of these possible meanings of the interpretation, and, instead, restrict my comments to Leach's arguments on its behalf.

Whatever construction we might wish to place on Leach's interpretation it is not (to say the least) self-evident that the proper interpretation of "a woman begets children because she may dream of a child put inside her," is that "the relationship between the woman's child and the clansmen of the woman's husband stems from the public recognition of the bonds of marriage." Hence, since this belief, according to Leach's interpretation, does not mean what it seems to mean— i.e., it is not about conception but about patrilateral filiation—we should like to know something about the evidence (or theory) upon which this symbolic interpretation is based. Is there anything in Roth's ethnography which suggests that this is what the natives themselves take this belief to mean? Short of that, are there any data on Tully River symbolism from which it might be inferred that this is its meaning? Short of that, can it be deduced from a cross-cultural theory of symbolism that this (whether conscious or unconscious) is its meaning?

It is rather disappointing, then, to discover that Leach presents no evidence for his interpretation. Instead he offers one argument,[13] to

13. Although Leach professes to offer four arguments in support of this interpreta-

wit: his interpretation is not original with him—it is found in Frazer, Malinowski, Radcliffe-Brown, Ashley Montagu, "and elsewhere." Disappointment rapidly changes to surprise when it is realized that even this argument (slim as it is) is misconceived: for, in fact, the authorities cited by Leach do not support his interpretation. All of them agree, to be sure, that in Australia, fatherhood (and by implication, patrilateral filiation) is sociological rather than biological; it is this, presumably, that Leach takes to be support for his position. For them, however, this is not the meaning of the Australian conception beliefs, but the implication of the natives' ignorance of physiological paternity. Since the mother's husband is pater, and yet—being ignorant of physiological paternity—he is not believed to be genitor, it must be, so they argue, because fatherhood (and, by implication, patrigroup filiation) is grounded in sociology, not in biology.

2. The Argument from the Christian Evidence

Leach's real concern, however, is not with the Australian evidence, but with the Christian analogy, the Virgin Birth. The basic message of the Virgin Birth—and so, too, the basic message of Australian conception beliefs—is, according to Dr. Leach, neither biological nor theological, but sociological. Moreover, it is identical with his interpretation of the Australian conception beliefs. Thus, from the fact that although the dogma of the Virgin Birth asserts that God is His father, two of the synoptic Gospels (Matthew and Luke) provide Jesus with a pedigree which places him "in the direct line of patrilineal descent from *David through Joseph*" (Leach 1967:42, original emphasis), Leach concludes:

In other words the kind of interpretation which I put on Roth's evidence . . . has been orthodox among Christians for about 1600 years. The myth, like the rite, does not distinguish knowledge from ignorance. It establishes categories and affirms relationships.

For Leach, then, the message of the key dogma of Christianity—the Incarnation—and, hence, the central message of Christianity is that Jesus's relationship to Joseph is sociological rather than biological! Although Dr. Leach must be admired for his consistency—in order to defend his thesis he not only does not shrink from, but he is even "positively eager" to embrace, its *reductio ad absurdum*—his logic

---

tion, three of the four speak to the separate issue of physiological paternity (we have examined them above). If, so Leach seems to argue, the natives can be shown to believe in physiological paternity, it then follows that his interpretation of their conception beliefs is true. This conclusion, needless to say, does not follow.

and theology are rather less deserving of admiration. For, on both accounts, the argument from Jesus's Davidic pedigree refutes, rather than supports, this thesis.

Granted that the Gospels, concerned to provide Jesus with Davidic descent, establish his pedigree on the sociological paternity of Joseph, the dogma of the Virgin Birth denies physiological paternity to Joseph not to enunciate a banal sociological principle, but to proclaim an audacious theological truth, viz.: God, in order to save mankind, became flesh—in the person of Jesus. If, then, the dogma of the Virgin Birth claims that God is Jesus's genitor, it is not to announce that Joseph is His pater, but to proclaim that He is Saviour. But Jesus is not only Saviour (=God), he is also Christ (=Messiah); and in the context of ancient Judaism these distinct claims created an urgent theological dilemma for Christianity. For although, *qua* Saviour, Jesus cannot (being God) have a human genitor, *qua* Christ, He must have a human genitor for—according to Judaism—the Messiah is a patrilineal descendant of David. In short, the dogma of the Virgin Birth solved one theological problem only to create another: the very criterion by which it established the claim that Jesus is Saviour disqualified Him for the claim that He is Messiah. Hence, even leaving aside Leach's aberrant interpretation of its meaning, the structural consequence of the Virgin Birth is precisely the reverse of what he claims it to be. Rather than "establish[ing] categories and affirm[ing] relationships" so as to provide Jesus with a Davidic pedigree, it destroyed the only recognized (Jewish) basis for such a pedigree—genealogical relationship.

Although, contrary to Leach, the consequence of the Virgin Birth was to deprive Jesus of the possibility of a Davidic pedigree, both Mark and Luke—tracing his descent, generation by generation, from David through Joesph—provide him with a Davidic genealogy. This genealogy, however, is not only extrinsic to the dogma of the Virgin Birth, but, as all Biblical critics (from the earliest Church Fathers) have realized, it is clearly incompatible with it. Troubled by this obvious inconsistency and, especially, by the uses made of it by anti-Christian writers—who, accepting the genealogy, rejected the Virgin Birth, or who, having always rejected the Virgin Birth, viewed the genealogy as an attempt to rescue Mary from charges of sexual immorality—the Church Fathers (and later Christian theologians) offered a variety of solutions for it.[14] One (but only one) of these attempted solutions pro-

14. For summaries of the controversies surrounding this problem of Jesus's putative Davidic genealogy, cf., "Genealogy (Christ)," in *The interpreter's dictionary of the Bible;* "Genealogies of Jesus Christ," in *Catholic Biblical encyclopedia, New Testament;* "Genealogies of Jesus Christ," in *Hastings dictionary of Christ and the gospels.*

posed that, although Joseph is not His biological father, the Gospels' genealogy (as well as Jesus's claim to Messiahship) can be justified on the grounds that Joseph is his sociological father. This interpretation was proposed, however, not as the message of the genealogy, let alone as the message of the Virgin Birth—for the Church Fathers (and for all Christians) nothing could be more absurd than the suggestion that the function of Jesus's Davidic genealogy (let alone the Virgin Birth) is to affirm this structural principle—but as a solution to the theological difficulty which it poses. For the Biblical commentators (and for all Christians) the function of the Davidic genealogy, however it be reconciled with the dogma of the Virgin Birth, was (and is) clear: it legitimizes the Christian claim that Jesus is the Messiah. In sum, the Christological argument once again refutes, rather than sustains, Leach's position.[15]

In summary, it may be concluded that none of Dr. Leach's arguments stands up under scrutiny. His spurious racist argument aside, the Australian-based evidence is the reverse of what he purports it to be, and the conclusions to be drawn from his Christological evidence are the reverse of what he believes them to be. Since, then, his arguments are refuted by his own evidence, his contentions—that the Australians are not ignorant of physiological paternity, and that their conception dogmas enunciate a structural principle—remain unsupported.

Alternative Models of Culture and Cultural Interpretation

1. Leach's Structural Interpretation

If this controversy were primarily concerned with the proper interpretation of arcane ethnographical facts, this article would have reached its conclusion in the previous section. But this controversy is not primarily a disagreement over fine points of Australian ethnography (although, to be sure, it stems from such a disagreement): over-

---

15. Because of space limitations, I shall forbear to comment on Leach's other interpretations of the Christian myth, especially his speculations on the type of society which finds it most congenial. They are irrelevant to the central issue of this controversy (and set beside the historicoeconomic interpretations of Kautsky, the historical interpretations of Harnack, the psychoanalytic interpretations of Freud and Fromm, and the cultural interpretations of Warner, they are, to say the least, unconvincing). Leach himself is not unaware of their irrelevance; in the midst of these speculations he says— quite correctly—"Professor Spiro will be wholly unimpressed. He will ask: But how can you *prove* that these associations of facts are relevant?" (Leach 1967:44, original emphasis). Surprisingly, he does not attempt to indicate their relevance; indeed, he is disarmingly frank about their irrelevance. Thus, he writes, "Well, quite frankly, I don't claim to prove anything at all" (1967:43); and, "How do I *know* that such patterns are significant? I don't. I find them interesting" (1967:45, original emphasis).

shadowing this is a much more important controversy, for which the ethnographical facts are merely a medium of intellectual exchange. The latter controversy is theoretical and methodological in character. It involves such issues as the nature of culture, how it works, what its functions are, what explanatory variables must be attended to in attempting to interpret any of its manifestations. The better to deal with these issues, let us assume that the ethnographical reports are silent on what the *natives* believe concerning physiological paternity; let us assume, rather, that our only datum concerning this matter is the *cultural* belief in spirit-children. On this assumption, then, let us turn from Leach's arguments on behalf of his interpretation, and examine, instead, its conceptual structure, comparing it with the conceptual structure of its rival interpretation.

Placed in the context of Leach's lecture, it is somewhat difficult to decide whether his interpretation—the basis for patrilateral filiation is the public recognition of the marriage of the child's parents—of the Australian spirit-child belief refers to the cognitive meaning of this belief, or to its sociological implication. Sometimes, depending on his specific arguments, it seems to refer to the one; sometimes to the other. Nevertheless, however it be construed, this interpretation encounters serious conceptual difficulties. If, for example, his interpretation has reference to the *cognitive meaning* of the belief, it obviously cannot refer to the meaning of its *manifest* content, for the latter is patently concerned with conception. Since the manifest content, moreover, enunciates a nonprocreative explanation for conception, this interpretation is inconsistent with Leach's claim that the natives are not ignorant of physiological patebnity. Hence, if his interpretation refers to the cognitive meaning of the belief, it must have reference to the meaning of its latent content. If so, it poses some difficult functional and motivational problems.

First, why is not this sociological message expressed directly? What function can possibly be served in expressing it by means of a symbolic circumlocution? Moreover, if structural principles (for some unknown reason) are best expressed (or enunciated) symbolically, what function can be served by enunciating this particular principle in the symbolism of conception? Second, since *ex hypothesi*, the natives are not ignorant of physiological paternity, what can possibly be the function of expressing this message by means of symbolism, the meaning of whose manifest content is the opposite of what they really believe? To say that the natives transmit, generation upon generation, a conception belief in whose manifest meaning they do not believe, so that they may enunciate a structural message contained in its latent content, and in which they do believe—this can only make sense on the assumption that the latter message, being painful, has undergone repression, and can only be expressed by means of unconscious symbolism. If, then, Leach's interpretation of the belief refers to its cognitive meaning, does he mean to say that this structural message is indeed unconscious? If so, he must explain why such an innocuous message is repressed.

Even if these functional problems were resolved, this interpretation, when combined with Leach's claim that the natives are not ignorant of physiological paternity, raises a serious motivational problem. For observe: if the natives are ignorant of physiological paternity, then, in default of any knowledge concerning the biological basis for paternity, father, in this cultural context, can only be pater. Consequently there is no alternative to a sociological basis for patrilateral filiation: like the sociological basis for the relationship between mother's son and mother's husband, the sociological basis for the latter relationship, too, is a necessary consequence of biological ignorance. But if, as Leach holds, the natives are not ignorant of physiological paternity, the culturally designated basis for paternity and for patrilateral filiation is the consequence not of default, but of choice: the choice represents a culturally designated preference between two equally known alternative bases—patership or genitorship (or any combined weighting of these). Hence, if Leach holds that his postulated sociological basis for patrilateral filiation is the structural consequence of the sociological basis for fatherhood, then since, *ex hypothesi*, the natives know that father is genitor, what could possibly be their motive for rejecting genitorship as the basis for fatherhood? (Moreover, if it is the consequence of this rejection, the cultural belief enunciates a superfluous message; the message necessarily follows from the rejection.) If he holds, on the other hand, that genitorship is rejected as the basis for fatherhood in order to establish paterhood as the basis for filiation, what could possibly be the motive for that choice?

Perhaps, in view of these unresolved difficulties, Leach's interpretation refers not to the cognitive meaning of the cultural belief, but to its *sociological implication:* that patrilateral filiation is based on the father's role as pater is not, then, the *message* of the belief, but its *function.* Hence, on the basis of this cultural belief, the anthropologist can infer that one of the structural features of the society in which it is embedded (and which it reflects) is that patrilateral filiation is sociological. Aside from the fact that we are then left without a cognitive meaning for the belief—and unless we know its meaning how can we assess its sociological implications?—this interpretation, like the first, is incompatible with Leach's claim that the natives are not ignorant of physiological paternity.

If (because its manifest content enunciates a nonprocreative explanation for conception) the conception belief is taken to imply ignorance of physiological paternity, father is necessarily pater, and the basis for patrilateral filiation in such a society is necessarily sociological. (Since this conclusion is entailed by the premise, if the premise is true, the probability of the conclusion being true approaches certitude.) If, however, following Leach, it is assumed that the natives are not ignorant of physiological paternity, then (even when descent is matrilineal) how can this belief possibly imply that in such a society patrilateral filiation is sociological? If the natives are aware of physiological paternity, there is no basis for arguing that the conception belief implies that fatherhood and, therefore, patrilateral filiation are sociological. *From this cultural belief alone,* there is no basis whatsoever for contending that this is its implication. (If, in fact, the premise were true—i.e., if the natives were not ignorant of physiological paternity—the probability of the conclusion being true would be no greater than chance. For, when physiological paternity is known, the culturally assigned basis for fatherhood might be either biological or sociological.)

No explanation, of course, is required to deal with all of the difficulties raised by its critics. But any explanation which merits a serious hearing must, at the very least, be free from internal logical contradictions. And any explanation of culture, which is more than a private assertion, must be consistent (if not derived from) those principles which are believed to govern human behavior. Leach's explanation is vulnerable on both scores. This being so, I should like to examine its rival explanation which, I submit, obviates both difficulties.

2. An Alternative Functional Explanation

As in the case of my examination of Leach's explanation, I am concerned, not with the truth of its alternative—so far as I know the evidence is lacking for testing the truth of either—but with its conceptual structure. Is it internally consistent? Is it consistent with what we know about human society and personality? The present explanation rests on three assumptions.

Since the Australian conception belief states that conception is caused by the entry of a spirit child into the mother, and since—in the absence of any evidence which indicates the contrary—it is gratuitous to assume that this cultural belief does not mean what it says, it would seem not unreasonable to assume that it enunciates a theory of conception. Since, moreover, it is a nonprocreative theory, and since—in the absence of any evidence which indicates the contrary—it is gratuitous to assume that the natives do not believe what it says, it would seem not injudicious to assume that the belief implies that the natives are ignorant of physiological paternity. On the basis of these two assumptions, and on the basis of the further assumption that the Australian natives are as intelligent as any other natives—the Americans for example—the Australian conception belief is amenable to two different but equally valid interpretations. Although sharing these three assumptions, these interpretations disagree on the basis for the natives' ignorance, the motive for their belief in the conception theory, and the psychological function of the theory.

The first interpretation, deriving from Malinowski, holds that the basis for the natives' ignorance of physiological paternity is cultural: for a variety of perfectly rational reasons (both logical and empirical)—and spelled out by Malinowski and Ashley Montagu—knowledge of the causal relationship between sexual intercourse and conception is absent from their cultural inventory of biological knowledge. Hence, *in default* of a procreative explanation, the conception belief enunciates a nonprocreative theory of conception. This being so, the function of the message is cognitive-explanatory, and the motivational basis for the natives' belief in the message is intellectual curiosity concerning an otherwise inexplicable phenomenon, and one which is of central concern.

This interpretation poses no conceptual difficulties. The interpretation of the message of the belief is consistent both with its manifest content and with the inference that the natives are ignorant of physiological paternity; and all three are consistent with the postulated function of, and the motive for belief in, the message. From this interpretation, moreover, it may be deduced that patrilateral filiation is sociological (without falling into the logical traps entailed by Dr. Leach's interpretation): since, *ex hypothesi*, the natives are ignorant of physiological paternity, there is no alternative to a sociological basis for patrilateral filiation. According to this interpretation, however, the sociological basis for paternity (and hence for filiation) is neither the message nor the function of the spirit-child theory (although it is its sociological implication); it is, rather, the unintended (though recognized) function of the natives' ignorance of physiological paternity.

Although this interpretation poses no conceptual difficulties, it raises a serious ethnographical problem. Since most peoples seem not to be ignorant of physiological paternity, it is somewhat difficult to understand why the Australians, too, have not discovered the causal link between sexual intercourse and conception.[16] This difficulty is the point of departure for a possible second interpretation. Distinguishing between two kinds of ignorance—one based on the absence of knowledge, the other based on its rejection—this interpretation, deriving from Jones (1924), argues that the basis for the natives' procreative ignorance is not cultural, but psychological; i.e., it is based not on the absence of biological knowledge, but on its rejection. If so, the natives' procreative ignorance is *motivated*—motivated by the wish to deny physiological paternity; and the spirit-child belief enunciates a non-procreative theory of conception, not *in default*, but *in lieu*, of a procreative explanation.[17] This rather strange interpretation must be explicated.

That a son should wish to reject knowledge of the fact that his father is his genitor is not, of course, a strange notion in the annals of child development. One explanation for this frequently found wish is based on the assumption—derived from psychoanalytic theory, and supported by a great deal of empirical evidence—that fathers are both loved and hated, and that the latter emotion derives from one or both of the following conditions: resentment over their punitive authority, and/or jealous rivalry for the love (sexual and/or affectionate) of the

16. Dr. Leach, quite properly, raises this same problem. For Leach, however, the reported evidence for such ignorance does not constitute a scientific problem, but a problem, rather, in the psychology of science. "If," he argues, "certain peoples have persuaded their ethnographers that they were ignorant of the facts of life then it is because 'ignorance' was for these people a kind of dogma. And if the ethnographer in question believed what he was told, it was because such belief corresponded fo his own private fantasy of the natural ignorance of savages" (Leach 1967:41).

Since I do not share his psychological assessment of a large group of anthropologists, I do not believe that the scientific problem is so easily dismissed. Thus, if the natives really believe that women conceive because they are entered by spirit-children, the psychological problem is not, *pace* Leach, why are they so stupid and idiotic? It is, rather, on what grounds, which *they* accept as evidential, do they believe it to be true? And if, in all deference to Malinowski *et al.*, we have reason to suspect that the natives do not "really" believe that this is the cause of conception, then the psychological problem is not, *pace* Leach, on what motivational grounds were the ethnographers "taken"? It is, rather, on what functional or motivational grounds do the natives perpetuate a theory which, on some level, they believe to be false?

17. That the natives are (on some level) aware of physiological paternity might be argued from a symbolic interpretation of some of the ethnographical data. Thus, for example, the spirit-child is typically an ancestor; and ancestors, of course, are fathers two or three times removed. Again, the Trobriand child, Malinowski informs us, is believed to look like his father—but never like his mother. Trobrianders, too, are filled with embarrassment should the discussion of parental intercourse be touched upon. More important than these symbolic interpretations, however, is the report of Roheim (1932) that the procreative awareness which he found explicitly in young children is "repressed" following initiation.

mother. But hatred of the father leads to a typical Oedipal conflict. On the one hand, the child, motivated by resentment or by rivalry, wishes to harm, to be rid of, the father. On the other hand, whether from a *talion* fear ("I want to harm him, therefore he wants to harm me") or from guilt ("Since he loves me and/or since I love him, how can I wish to harm him?") this wish is extremely painful. In the absence of institutional or cultural assistance in dealing with this conflict, the child must cope with it by his own internal resources, of which I shall mention only two. He can *repress* his hatred, which is the typical (and normal) technique found in Western society, or he can express it symbolically by *denying* in fantasy that his father is his genitor. (The latter is often accomplished, both in private fantasy as well as in hero myths, by the substitution of grandiose fathers—gods, kings, and so on—for the real father.) Sometimes, it should be added, rather than denying that his father is genitor, the child denies that he had any genitor: his conception was not caused by procreation. (For a discussion of the mechanism of denial, cf. Freud 1946:chaps. 5–7.) Both of these defense-mechanisms resolve the conscious conflict, but in different ways—the former by rendering the child's hatred unconscious, the latter by expressing it by means of a symbolic short-circuit.

Not all conflicts, however, find resolution by the unaided, intrapsychic, efforts of the individual. Many conflicts, expecially those which are shared by social actors, are resolved by means of social institutions and cultural beliefs. Indeed, just as culture has cognitive-explanatory functions, so it has (among others) affective-integrative functions. My second, alternative, interpretation of the Australian conception theory views *it* as having such a function. This interpretation holds that the spirit-child theory, whatever the basis for its origin might have been, now serves (this at least would be one of its functions) to resolve the natives' Oedipal conflict by providing them with the cognitive (cultural) basis for denial. By believing in the traditional conception theory, each Australian is implicitly, but necessarily, denying that *his* father is *his* genitor. For since, according to this cultural theory, all conceptions are caused by a nonprocreative method, then he too was conceived without parental intercourse. Hence, his father is not his genitor, although he is his mother's husband.

This conception belief not only enables the Australian to deny that his father is his genitor; it enables him to do so by means of a wish-fulfilling fantasy. For since, according to this belief, conception is caused by the entry of a spirit-child into a woman's womb, he too was a spirit-child, and he too was conceived by entering the womb of *his* mother. Hence, since he not only came out of, but also went into, his mother's womb, it was his entry, not his father's, that caused her to become pregnant. By believing in this cultural theory, then, the boy takes his father's place, for, according to this theory, the son is literally the father of the man—and of the child; he is his own genitor. By believing in this conception theory, then, the boy both denies the painful fact that his conception was caused by the sexual intercourse of his parents, and he fulfills his wish that he take his father's place.

If, then, according to the first of these functional interpretations, belief in the conception theory is motivated by curiosity concerning the cause of conception, it is motivated according to this second interpretation, by the child's pain-induced hatred of his father; and if, according to the first interpretation, the function of belief is cognitive—it satisfies an intellectual need—according to the second, its function is ego-integrative—it resolves emotional conflict. For both interpretations, however, this conception belief has the same microsociological implication, viz., it implies that father is pater (either because, according to the first interpretation, genitorship is unknown; or because, according to the second, it is denied); and for both, therefore, it has the same macrosociological implication, viz., the basis for patrilateral filiation is sociological. (For the first explanation these implications are the unintended—but recognized—functions of ignorance of physiological paternity; for the second they are the unintended—but recognized—functions of denial of physiological paternity.)

According to the second interpretation, finally, belief in the conception theory has an (unintended) interpersonal adaptive function whose importance exceeds these (adaptively neutral) sociological functions: it promotes a high degree of amity between father and son. Whether the culturally assigned basis for the father-son relationship is the father's paterhood or his genitorship, the emotional quality of this relationship depends on (among other things) how the son copes with his hostility to his father. If the hostility-induced conflict is not resolved, father is, at best, the affectively neutral mother's husband, at worst the hated Oedipal figure. It can be resolved, as we do, intrapsychically, by the repression of the hatred; or it can be resolved—as suggested by this second interpretation of the spirit-child belief—culturally, by institutionalized denial. Both techniques of conflict resolution have their respective advantages and disadvantages. The second technique can serve to transmute a hated genitor, not merely into a mother's husband—a sociological pater—but, if we can believe Malinowski, into a warm and nurturant father—a psychological pater.

Here, then, is a second functional interpretation of the Australian conception belief which, like the first, is faithful to the manifest meaning of the belief, whose internal structure creates no logical difficulties; and whose sociological and psychological consequences pose no conceptual problems. Which of these interpretations—if either—is true, cannot be decided from the available data. Both are consistent with the reported data that the natives are—or, at least, were—ignorant of physiological paternity, but they interpret these data differently: and from the data, alone, it cannot be known whether ignorance is—or, at least, was—based on absence of knowledge or on denial. Theoretically, there is little to choose between them. The first explanation is by far the more parsimonious; the second copes with the ethnographical problem raised by procreative ignorance.

Both explanations, finally, are derived from the same model of culture, a model whose assumptions are, if I understand him correctly, precisely the reverse of Leach's. In this model, to mention only those of its assumptions that are relevant to this controversy, culture serves a number of functions—not only sociological, but psychological (cognitive and emotional) as well; cultural theories attend not only to the functional requirements of society, but also to the functional requirements of social actors—hence, their messages may relate to nature and human nature, as well as to social structure; belief in these theories is motivated (by cognitive and/or emotional needs)—hence their functions and meaning, alike, are often inexplicable without an awareness of the possible motivational bases for beliefs; finally, culture is man's most important means of adapting to the condition of being human— hence, since psychological tension (including cognitive curiosity and emotional conflict) is a persistent feature of that condition, cultural beliefs represent, among other things, the attempts of social groups to cope with these tensions.[18]

18. After receiving proofs, my attention was called to still a third possible basis for ignorance of physiological paternity (at least among the Trobrianders) in a suggestion made by Dorothy Lee. In her ingenious reconstruction of Trobriand thought (Lee 1940), she suggests that Trobriand conceptual categories do not allow for the perception of teleology, in any strict sense of that term; that the cultural emphasis is on the "essential, rather than the accidental or relational" (361); that, given this conceptual set, events are viewed as "self-contained and essentially unrelated" (360); and that serial events are perceived to exhibit "simple sequence" rather than causal relationship. If this be so, then—as Lee herself observes (358)—Trobriand ignorance of physiological paternity might be a function of their (culturally based) nonteleological, cognitive set.

If her reconstruction is sound, this epistemological hypothesis—that Trobriand cognition is concerned with *things* (objects, events, essences) rather than with *relationships* among things—is consistent with either of the two hypotheses advanced in the text to

References

Austin, L. 1934. Procreation among the Trobriand islanders. *Oceania* 5:102–18.

Fortune, R. F. 1963. *Sorcerers of Dobu* (new ed.). London: Routledge & Kegan Paul.

Freud, A. 1946. *The ego and the mechanisms of defense*. New York: International Universities Press.

Genealogies of Jesus Christ 1917. In *Hastings dictionary of Christ and the gospels*. New York: Scribners.

Genealogies of Jesus Christ 1956. In *Catholic Biblical encyclopedia: New Testament*. New York: Joseph T. Wagner.

Genealogy (Christ) 1962. In *The interpreter's dictionary of the Bible*. New York: Abingdon Press.

Hallowell, A. I. 1955. *Culture and experience*. Philadelphia: Univ. of Pennsylvania Press.

Jones, E. 1924. Mother-right and the sexual ignorance of savages. *International Journal of Psycho-Analysis* 6:109–30.

Kaberry, P. M. 1939. *Aboriginal woman*. London: Routledge.

Leach, E. R. 1961. Golden bough or golden twig? *Daedalus* (Spring) 1961:371–87.

———— 1967. Virgin birth. *Proceedings of the Royal Anthropological Institute* 1966:39–50.

Lee, D. 1940. A primitive system on values. *Philosophy of Science* 7:355–78.

Malinowski, B. 1932. *The sexual life of savages in northwestern Melanesia* (3rd ed., with special foreword). London: Routledge.

———— 1937. Foreword. In *Coming into being among the Australian aborigines*, by M. F. Ashley Montagu. London: Routledge.

Meggitt, M. J. 1962. *Desert people*. Sydney: Angus & Robertson.

Montagu, M. F. Ashley 1937. *Coming into being among the Australian aborigines*. London: Routledge.

Roheim, G. 1932. Psycho-analysis of primitive cultural types. *International Journal of Psycho-Analysis* 13:1–224.

Roth, W. E. 1903. *Superstition, magic and medicine* (N. Queensl. Ethnogr. Bull. 5). Brisbane: Vaughan.

Spencer, B. & F. J. Gillen 1899. *The native tribes of Central Australia*. London.

Spiro, M. E. 1964. Religion and the irrational. In *Symposium on new approaches to the study of religion*, ed. J. Helm (Proceedings of the American Ethnological Society 1963). Seattle: Univ. of Washington Press.

----

account for ignorance of physiological paternity. The cultural hypothesis becomes, then, a theorem which is deducible from the epistemological axiom; and the psychological hypothesis becomes a subset of a more comprehensive theory which would attempt to discover the psychodynamic function of a cultural epistemology that emphasizes things over relationships.

———— 1966. Religion: Problems of definition and explanation. In *Anthropological approaches to the study of religion*, ed. M. Banton (Ass. Social Anthrop. Monogr. 3). London: Tavistock Publications.

Stanner, W. E. H. 1933. The Daly River tribes: The theory of sex. *Oceania* 4:26–28.

Thomson, D. F. 1933. The hero cult, initiation and totemism on Cape York: The knowledge of physical paternity. *Journal of the Royal Anthropological Institute* 63:505–10.

Warner, W. L. 1937. *A black civilization*. New York: Harper.

10   Whatever Happened to the Id?

There has been a strong tendency in structural and symbolic anthropology to assume that sex and aggression are of no concern to cultural symbol systems. Even when cultural beliefs, myths, or rituals are explicitly and preponderantly sexual or aggressive in content, they are typically interpreted as metaphors for social structural themes. This thesis is illustrated with respect to aggression by an analysis of Lévi-Strauss' interpretation of a Bororo myth, after which the assumptions that structural theory makes concerning the place of aggression in cultural symbol systems are contrasted with the opposing assumptions of psychoanalytic theory [STRUCTURALISM, PSYCHOANALYSIS, CULTURAL SYMBOL SYSTEMS, MYTH].

I HAD INTENDED, when asked to address the subject of anthropology and psychoanalysis for this symposium, to write on the problem of hermeneutics, which I see as the important meeting ground for anthropological and psychoanalytic theorizing. Despite my intention, I have instead addressed an old war-horse, the relationship between nature and culture. I have chosen this subject because, in reviewing the literature on structural and symbolic anthropology in preparation for the hermeneutic paper, I came increasingly to realize that the received opinion in many quarters of cultural anthropology holds that the body, or its drives, or the affects and motives to which they give rise— but most especially those related to sex and aggression—are seldom the concern of cultural symbol systems. If the latter appear to be con-

Reprinted from *American Anthropologist* vol, 81, no. 1 (Mar. 1979):5–13, by permission of the American Anthropological Association. Not for further reproduction.

This paper was prepared for, and a shorter version was read at, the 1977 annual meetings of the American Anthropological Association, as a part of a symposium entitled "Psychological Anthropology: a Perennial Frontier?" organized by Professor Theodore Schwartz. The preparation of this paper was assisted by a grant from the National Institute of Mental Health.

cerned with sex or aggression, it is the job of the anthropologist to uncover the reality behind the appearance. Although examples are abundant, I can here mention only a few.

I would instance, for example, Leach's contention (Leach 1967) that the denial of physiological paternity in Australia and parts of Melanesia, or the denial of a human genitor to Jesus in parts of Christendom, are statements not about biological sex but about rules of descent. Again, I would instance the contention of Mary Douglas that the (widely held) belief that males are endangered by the vagina and vaginal fluids is not a belief about the "actual relation of the sexes" but is, rather, a symbol of the hierarchical structure of the social system (Douglas 1966:4), or that rituals concerning excreta, breast milk, saliva, and other bodily emissions are concerned not with the body but with the "powers and dangers credited to the social structure," for which the body is a symbol (1966:115); or that rituals of genital bleeding, such as subincision rites, are concerned not with sex, or blood, or the penis but with society: "What is being carved in human flesh [the penis] is an image of society," and when they are performed by tribes with moieties these genital mutilations "are concerned to create a symbol of the symmetry of the two halves of society" (1966:116).

Now, what is even more remarkable than the Leach-Douglas theory itself is that it is widely accepted as received anthropological wisdom. It is all the more remarkable because this counterintuitive theory is presented by its proponents as a self-evident truth requiring no support other than that of assertion. Consider the following examples, taken at random from Douglas. Item: the notion that beliefs concerning sexual pollution may actually be concerned with sexual pollution is simply "implausible" (1966:3). Item: "we cannot possibly" take rituals concerning excreta, milk, and the like to be in fact concerned with these bodily fluids and emissions (1966:115). Item: "I insist" that the seeming "obsession" of the Yurok with notions of pollution must be related to the "fluid formlessness" of their social structure (1966:127). That is all. No argument or evidence is offered in support of those contentions.

It used to be that one had to be a Freudian to believe that nonsexual themes in ritual and myth might possibly be viewed as disguised expressions of sexual concerns. It now appears that only a Freudian might believe that undisguised sexual themes might be expressions of sexual concerns. And not only sexual. For the wide influence of Lévi-Strauss' theory of myth also suggests that only a Freudian might believe that explicitly aggressive themes in myth are really concerned with aggression. Indeed, it was my recent reading of that marvelous book *The Raw and the Cooked* that finally stimulated me to change the topic of this paper from hermeneutics to the cultural relevance of sex and aggression. Since, however, I have dealt elsewhere (Spiro 1968a,b) with the Leach-Douglas denial of sex as a relevant variable in belief systems, I shall concentrate here on Lévi-Strauss' denial of aggression in myth.

Although most readers will doubtless recall the Bororo myth (Lévi-Strauss 1969:35–37) that constitutes the key text for *The Raw and the Cooked*, I shall briefly summarize it. One day, when the women went into the forest to gather palms, a certain youth secretly followed his mother and raped her. Discerning what had happened, and "anxious to avenge himself," the youth's father sent his son on a series of dangerous undertakings intended to cause his death, but the son repeatedly eluded the traps (with the assistance of helpful animals). Finally, the father acted more directly. After ordering his son to climb to the top of a cliff to capture some birds, he overturned the pole by which the son had ascended, abandoning him to death. After many tribulations the son managed, however, to return to the village. One day, when his father was hunting, the son "full of thoughts of revenge," saw his opportunity. Donning some false antlers and transforming himself into a deer, he "rushed at this father with such ferocity that he impaled him on the horns." He then galloped to a lake inhabited by carnivorous fish, and dropped his father into the lake, where he was devoured by the fish. Returning to the village, the son then "took his revenge" on his father's wives, including his mother. (We are not told what form the "revenge" took, and we can only guess that it was either rape or murder.)

According to Lévi-Strauss, that myth, the central text of the book, is an etiological myth that explains the origin of cooked food. Conceding that "to all intents and purposes" that theme appears to be absent from the myth, Lévi-Strauss contends (1969:64) that it is nevertheless "concealed" in it, and in a remarkable *tour de force*, combining staggering erudition with astonishing brilliance, he attempts in the remaining 300 pages of his book to demonstrate the truth of this startling interpretation. Briefly, since an older version of this myth ends with the son's declaring that he will take revenge on the entire clan of his father by sending cold, wind, and rain, this indicates, so Lévi-Strauss claims, that on its surface the myth deals with the origin of storms and rain.[1]

1. In fact, the text itself does not support that contention. When the son, following abandonment by his father, returns to the village, he reveals his identity to his grandmother (who had consistently befriended him against his father) and on that night there

On the premise, then, that water is (on a number of dimensions) the inversion of fire, he then proceeds to show, by means of a succession of complex and ingenious structural analyses of a corpus of South American myths, that this Bororo myth can be interpreted as a transformation by inversion of a set of Ge myths that explicitly explain the origin of cooking fire.

Now, even granting the validity of that transformational hypothesis,[2] I would nevertheless have thought that violent Oedipal conflict was the central theme of a myth that begins with a son's raping his mother, continues with the father's numerous attempts to kill the son, proceeds to the son's brutally killing his father, and ends with his killing or raping (depending on correct interpretation of the ambiguous term "revenge") his mother and stepmothers. That its central theme is taken instead to be the origin either of cooking fire or of rain—even granting that an etiological theme is one of its elements—is surely a remarkable reversal of figure and ground.[3] At least it seems to be re-

---

occurred a "violent wind, accompanied by a thunder storm which put out all the fires in the village except the grandmother's" (Lévi-Strauss 1969:36). Now, if wind and thunderstorm already occur in the *middle* of the myth (and their occurrence is not attributed to the boy's creation), it is difficult to understand how the older version, which *ends* with the boy taking his revenge by sending cold and rain, can be interpreted as their origin. This would seem to signify, rather, that the boy had the power to control the rains, not that this was their origin. Implicitly aware of this criticism, Lévi-Strauss defends his interpretation by noting (1969:137) that (in their commentary) the collectors of the myth state that the natives themselves claim that the rain that falls in the middle of the myth was the origin of rain. This hardly proves, however, that the origin of rain is the central concern of this myth.

Indeed, to the extent that the text itself has any etiological reference, it has to do with the origin of a certain type of aquatic plant. Thus, after the boy's father was devoured by the carnivorous fish, "All that remained," the text continues, "were the bare bones which lay on the bottom of the lake, and the lungs which floated on the surface in the form of aquatic plants, whose leaves, it is said, resemble lungs" (1969:37).

2. If, as I suggest in the note above, the Bororo myth is not concerned with the origin of rain, the transformational hypothesis is invalid, since it rests on a set of putative structural relationships that obtain between fire and water (rain), Lévi-Strauss, perhaps anticipating this problem, contends (1969:137) that, even without the transformational argument, the Bororo myth in itself can be seen as dealing with the origin of fire. Since the storm extinguished all the fires in the village except that of the boy's grandmother, the boy "becomes the master of fire, and all the inhabitants of the village must apply to him to obtain firebrands with which to kindle the lost fire. In this sense the Bororo myth also relates to the origin of fire, but by a process of omission.". That interpretation seems to be adventitious, however, because, even assuming that the boy was living with his grandmother, there is no indication that the villagers applied to him for fire, rather than to his grandmother; indeed since he was still uninitiated, the former hypothesis would seem unlikely. Nevertheless, fifty pages later, Lévi-Strauss escalates his claim: "The Bororo myth creates water in order to destroy fire or, more precisely, to allow the hero [the boy] to become the master of fire" (1969:188).

3. It is remarkable for at least three reasons. First, the occurence of the rain is a

markable until one comes to realize that the code constructed[4] by Lévi-Strauss for the translation of these myths precludes the possibility that violence of any kind might be taken as a mythic concern; instead, the code converts all acts of violence into metaphors for nonviolent social structural relationships.

Take, for example, the son's rape of his mother. In the first step in code switching, that episode is classified by Lévi-Strauss as "incest," i.e., its sexual dimension remains but its violence dimension disappears. In the second step the sexual dimension also disappears, for "incest" becomes a metaphor—*voila!*—for the boy's dependent attachment to his mother. Thus, since the palms collected by the women in the myth are of the type used for penis sheaths, that signifies that the son had reached the age of initiation, when boys are expected to transfer from their mother's hut to the men's house. In such a sociocultural context, the mother-son "incest" (the code word for the boy's rape of his mother) signifies the son's objection to the "loosening of the maternal bonds" and his "return to the mother's bosom at a time when other sons are about to be weaned for good" (1969:56).

As if to emphasize that this translation is not a structuralist spoof, Lévi-Strauss clinches his argument with the following *pièce de résistance*. Since the adult hero of a cognate myth, the putative homologue of the boy in the present myth, is nicknamed "Secluded," and since, by structuralist assumptions, the boy can be assumed to have had the same nickname, and since a secluded boy in the sociocultural context alluded to above is one who "refuses to be separated from female society," it follows that the son is "the sort of boy who, as we say, 'clings to his mother's apron strings'" (1969:57).

---

minor (two-line) episode in a very long myth concerned primarily with the relationship between the boy and his parents. Second, even if we accept that the natives say that the rain in the myth was the origin of rain, the commentators do not contend that they take the myth to have an etiological aim. Third, even the *pro forma* "And this is the origin of x" (often appended to a myth as a device for attributing didactic import to an otherwise nondidactic narrative) is not found in this case.

4. I say "constructed" because it is important to emphasize that this code is not discovered by structural analysis of the myths but is an invention of Lévi-Strauss. Although clearly ambivalent about the issue, Lévi-Strauss admits that this may be so. Thus, in addressing the problem, he begins by claiming that his code "has neither been invented nor brought in from without. It is inherent in mythology itself where we simply discover its presence" (1969:12). (That is reminiscent of Michelangelo's modest claim that, rather than creating a sculpture *ex nihilo*, he merely reveals the sculpture that is inherent in the uncarved marble—which, of course, is true, except that for *n* sculptors there are *n* sculptures inherent in the marble.) In a later passage, however, Lévi-Strauss concedes that that may not be the case: "It is in the last resort immaterial whether in this book the thought processes of the South American Indians take shape through the medium of my thought, or whether mine take place through the medium of theirs" (1969:13).

And what about the behavior of the boy's parents? By a similar technique of code switching, the violent acts in which the mother and father are respectively involved with their son signify the polar differences in their "attitudes" toward him. Thus, having classified the son's rape of his mother as incest, the mother's "incestuous" relationship with the son is taken to be indexical of her "close" attitude to the son, while the father's "murderous" relationship is indexical of his "remote" attitude to him (1969:138–39).

Thus it is that, by the alchemy of code switching, aggression is simply abolished as a mythic category: the son's sexual assault on his mother is transmuted into his dependency upon her, while the mother's victimization by the son's assault as well as the father's assaults upon the son are transmuted into positions on a scale of psychological distance from the son.

Lest I be misunderstood, I hasten to emphasize that I am not unmindful of the fact that Lévi-Strauss is not so much interested in the content of myths, per se, as in their logical structure—"the system of interrelationships to which we reduce them" (1969:12)—and that, since that aim is achieved by the structural comparisons of a large corpus of myths, it must be pursued by means of a code whose concepts are sufficiently abstract to subsume the concrete concepts of the codes employed by the myths themselves. Since, however, his code consists not of the formal and content-free symbols of mathematics and symbolic logic, but of concepts only slightly more abstract than those of the myths he analyzes, the fact that Lèvi-Strauss chooses concepts that systematically eliminate every theme of violence from these myths indicates that this consequence is principled rather than fortuitous. An excellent case in point is the conversion of rape ("incest") and murder in the Bororo myth into the attitudes "close" and "remote."

The attitudes "close" and "remote" are attributed to the parents in the Bororo myth in order to show that "family attitudes" is one variable in a set of variables by which this myth can be inferred to be the inversion (and hence the transform) of the Ge myth. In the latter myth, a young boy who is left by his brother-in-law to die in the wilderness is rescued by a jaguar, who then brings him to his own home (thereby becoming his "adopted father"). The jaguar's wife (therefore, the boy's "adopted mother") dislikes the boy and tries to kill him, but, encouraged by the jaguar, the boy kills her instead. As Lévi-Strauss sees it, the parental attitudes exhibited in the Bororo myth are an inversion of those exhibited in the Ge myth: in the former the mother is "close" and the father "remote," whereas in the latter the father is "close" and the mother "remote." The dimension close/remote is a perfectly good dimension for describing attitudes, but there are at least three reasons for rejecting the assumption that this is the dimension along which the opposite-sex parents in these myths sustain the logical relation of binary opposition within each myth and that of identity across the myths.

(a) That the attitudes of the (adopted) Ge parents toward their son exhibit a relation of binary opposition is self-evident: the father saves the boy's life, while the mother attempts to kill him. Nevertheless, even on the dubious assumption that "close" is an appropriate term to characterize the attitude expressed in a father's rescue of a son's life, to characterize as "remote" the attitude expressed in a mother's attempt to kill her son is surely to distort the meaning of the text beyond recognition. These designations not only distort the meaning of the text but are not necessary in order to show that binary opposition in the parents' attitudes. Thus, for example, the dimension life-giving/life-destroying (or some such terms) is not only faithful to the text but denotes much more effectively the relation of opposition that characterizes the attitudes of the Ge father and mother to their son.

(b) The dimension close/remote is even less applicable to the Bororo parents than to the Ge parents. If "remote" which converts lethal intentions into indifference, is an inappropriate designation for the murderous father, "close" is entirely misplaced when applied to the mother. For, whether we remain faithful to the text (and describe the mother as the victim of her son's rapacious assault) or distort the text (and describe her as the object of the son's "incest"), how can the attitude "close" or any other attitude be applied either to an *involuntary victim* (rape) or a *passive object* (incest)? If, nevertheless, the close/remote dimension is still held to be applicable to the mother, I would have thought that "remote" would be the more appropriate term because, presumably, one is raped only after resisting (= "remote") seduction. But if the mother is "remote," the Bororo parents cannot be contrasted along the close/remote dimension unless we are prepared to designate the father as "close." Rejecting such sophistry, a relation of binary opposition can be validly attributed to the Bororo parents only by comparing them (as I suggested in the case of the Ge parents) along some dimension that is faithful to the violent themes of the myth itself. That can be done in one of two ways. Restricting the comparison to the episodes described in the myth, we can draw a contrast between the mother, as the *victim* of violent (sexual) assaults *by* her son, and the father, as the *agent* of violent assaults *on* his son. Or, going beyond the episodes described in the myth. we can contrast the parents along the same dimensions employed in characterizing the Ge parents: the mother (having borne the son) is life-giving and the father (being murderous) is life-destroying. From a structuralist point of view, and consistent with Lévi-Strauss' aim of showing that the Bororo myth is a transformation of the Ge, that has the additional advantage of demonstrating that the attitudes of the parents in the Bororo myth are an inversion of those exhibited by the parents in the Ge myth.

(c) Contrary to Lévi-Strauss, a comparative analysis of the two myths does not permit the conclusion that the Bororo mother and Ge father sustain the logical relation of identity on the close/remote dimension. For, even granting the dubious classification of incestuous rape as "incest," by what logical criterion is the attitude "close" attributed both to a *passive object* of incest (the Bororo mother) and an *active agent* of nurturance (the Ge father)? If, moreover, the classification of incestuous rape as "incest" is invalid (as I deem it to be), the attribution of an identity relation to the Bororo mother and Ge father would seem to be fallacious. How can the same attitude ("close") be attributed to two parents of which one is the victim of a son's rapacious assault and the other a protector of the son against assault? On either account, when they are compared with respect to the close/remote dimension, it must be concluded that, rather than sustaining a relation of identity, the relation of the Bororo mother and Ge father is one of binary opposition. If they are to be attributed instead with a relation of identity— and if, therefore, the parents of the Bororo myth are to be seen as an inversion of those in the Ge myth—that can only be accomplished by concepts that are faithful to the violent themes found in these myths. Thus, for example, use of the dimension violent/nonviolent (restricting the comparisons to the episodes described in the myths themselves) or the dimension life-giving/life-destroying (going beyond the episodes described in the myths) makes it apparent that the opposite-sex parents sustain a relation of binary opposition within the myths and one of identity across the myths: hence, the relation of the parents in the Bororo myth is an inversion of that of the parents of the Ge myth.

By this time the reader may be wondering why I stated at the outset that I had changed my topic from hermeneutics to the relationship between nature and culture when, thus far, this chapter has been devoted entirely to the interpretation of cultural symbol systems. The paradox is more apparent than real, however. It should be evident by now that the two codes examined (one that systematically and totally denies that sex and aggression in ritual and myth really signify sex and aggression and one that allows that they may indeed signify sex and aggression) may seem to differ in hermeneutic assumptions about the role of metaphor in cultural symbol systems, but actually differ in psychological assumptions about the importance of sex and aggression in human nature following the transition to culture.

What might be the assumptions of a code that interprets the Bororo myth (which on its surface explaines why it is that a boy became a vicious parricide) to be an origin myth, whether of cooking or of rain, a code by which a boy's rape of his mother signifies his dependent attachment to her, the mother's being the victim of his rape signifies her close attitude to him, and the father's attempts to murder his son signify his (the father's) remote attitude to him? Such a code, I would suggest, can be based only on an assumption that, in a state of culture, aggressive motives of this type are either transcended or markedly muted so that they cannot possibly be the real concern of myths.[5] Hence it is that, if aggression seems to be the dominant theme of the Bororo myth, its aggressive episodes must be interpreted to mean something other than (if not the very opposite of) what they seem to mean.

In making this suggestion, I am aware, of course, that Lévi-Strauss contends (1969:12) that his interpretations of myths refer to their "unconscious formulations." That contention, however, does not affect the validity of my suggestion, because, for Lévi-Strauss, the "unconscious" meaning of a myth or a mythic episode is not its trivial meaning, but its most fundamental meaning. Hence, when he interprets a myth of Oedipal violence as (unconsciously) signifying the origin of cooking fire, he is not making the trivial claim that the latter element is also to be found in the myth; rather, he is making the important claim that this myth, which *seems* to be about violence, is *really* about something else. Consider, then, that in Lévi-Strauss' code, aggression is systematically and gratuitously precluded as the (unconscious) meaning of any of the violent episodes in these myths. Consider, too, that alternative codes (such as those suggested above), whose (unconscious) interpretations are faithful to the violent content of the myths, achieve the aims of structural analysis without the dubious logic and textual distortions often required by Lévi-Strauss' interpretations. Consider, also, that for Lévi-Strauss, their unconscious meanings are the fundamental meanings of myths. Considering all of this, it seems reasonable to conclude that Lévi-Strauss' elimination of violence as a mythic category, although applying to the unconscious meaning of myths, is based on the assumption that violent motives of the type exhibited in the Bororo and Ge myths cannot be their *real* concern.

5. The same assumption underlies Douglas' (though not necessarily Leach's) elimination of sex as a concern of cultural belief systems.

That conclusion is supported by his contention (1969:164)—although he attributes the notion to native thought—that cooking marks the transition from nature to culture and that the Bororo myth therefore explains the origin not merely of cooking but also (and by that very same fact) of culture. That is not only, he argues, because of the analogy raw:cooked: :nature:culture but also because in the Ge myths both useful and ornamental objects are manufactured from the inedible parts of the cooked plants and animals. That he, therefore, interprets all of the aggressive episodes in the Bororo myth metaphorically suggests that this exegetical maneuver is a solution to a painful dilemma. It is as if he were saying that, if this myth is really concerned with filial rape, parracide, and filicide, the origin of cooking cannot represent the transition to culture, because aggressive motives of this kind, although found perhaps in a state of nature, cannot possibly persist in a state of culture; but, on the other hand, if this myth does not explain the origin of cooking, and if cooking does not represent the transition to culture, the entire argument of the book would collapse. It is this dilemma that is resolved by a code that interprets all aggression in the myth as a metaphor.

It will come as no surprise—turning finally to the psychoanalytic dimension of this paper—that the assumptions of Freud concerning the relationship between aggression and culture are the polar opposite of those of Lévi-Strauss. In Freud's view, aggressive motives are as strong in a state of culture as in a state of nature. Given that assumption, the themes of parricide, filicide, and the like, although *really* signifying parricide and filicide, would not in themselves disqualify the Bororo myth from being interpreted by Freud as a myth of the origin of culture. Nevertheless, even granting that this myth explains the origin of cooking fire, Freud would never agree that it depicts the origin of culture, as can easily be seen from even a cursory glance at Freud's own origin myth. That myth (Freud 1971a), although remarkably similar to the Bororo myth (both are concerned with violent conflicts between father and son over the sexual possession of the wife-mother), is its structural inversion. In Freud's myth (which, however, he took to be history), the sons desire the father's wives, and since he will not share them, the sons kill the father in order to take possession of them. Following their patricide, however, the sons experience feelings of remorse that lead them to atone for their deed by renouncing their claims on the women and to institute prohibitions against further parricide, fratricide, and incest.

For Freud, then, it is not the acquisition of cooking fire, nor even the manufacture of useful and ornamental objects attendant upon the cooking of food, that marks the transition from nature to culture, but the institution of norms for the control and regulation of aggression (first, within the sibling-group and subsequently to increasingly larger groups). For Freud, moreover, the transition to culture does not mean the transcendence of nature. Hence, although aggressive behavior, regulated as it is by cultural norms, may be inhibited in a state of culture, aggressive motives are not extinguished. Indeed, it is precisely because these motives (including parricide and filicide) persist in and are even exacerbated by culture (Freud 1971b) that the existence of norms for their regulation is a necessary condition for the existence of culture. Necessary, although not sufficient. For, as Freud views it, it is the internalization of these norms (as a result of the infant's prolonged attachments to nurturant parenting figures) that produces the moral anxiety and guilt that, by inhibiting expression of aggressive motives, preclude the return to a state of nature.[6]

We can now see why Freud would never characterize the Bororo myth as marking the transition from nature to culture—not because the son desired his mother, or the father wished to kill his son, or the son wished to kill his father, nor even because they acted upon their wishes, but because they experienced neither moral anxiety about their desires nor guilt about their deeds.[7] Since absence of anxiety and guilt implies an absence of cultural norms prohibiting aggressive behavior, in Freud's view this myth could not possibly represent a transition from nature to culture, even if it were granted that it represents the origin of cooking.

For Freud this myth would, however, represent something else. Holding that the transition to culture, although marking the control of aggressive behavior, does not mark the disappearance of aggressive affects and motives. Freud assumed that aggression is a matter of important concern to social actors in a state of culture. And since, so he further assumed, their important concerns are inevitably represented in their fantasies—the privately constituted fantasy of dreams and the culturally constituted fantasy of myth and religion—it follows that the manifestly aggressive themes in the Bororo myth, like the manifestly

6. That Freud is the (unacknowledged) spiritual descendant of Hobbes, just as Lévi-Strauss is the (acknowledged) spiritual descendant of Rousseau, would seem to be obvious. Freud differs from Hobbes in that the latter believed that the physical authority of the state is necessary to assure compliance with the cultural prohibition on aggression, while Freud believed that the key to the problem is the moral authority of the parents, internalized as the superego and reflected in moral anxiety and guilt.

7. Indeed, rather than experiencing guilt and, thereby, atoning for killing his father by renouncing his claims on his mother and stepmothers, the son continues to take his "revenge" on them.

sexual themes in the rituals and beliefs analyzed by Leach and Douglas, are just that: aggressive and sexual themes. In short, for Freud, the myths, rituals, and beliefs discussed in this paper are concerned with those very sexual and aggressive wishes and fears that these anthropologists and their many followers, denying that they are of concern to cultural symbol systems, interpret out of existence. It is rather startling that this simpleminded view (which, of course, is hardly original with Freud or restricted to Freudians) must be reiterated to an anthropological audience in 1977.

References

Douglas, Mary. 1966. *Purity and danger.* New York: Praeger.

Freud, Sigmund. 1971a. Totem and taboo. In *The standard edition of the complete psychological works of Sigmund Freud,* vol. 13. London: Hogarth Press.

―――― 1971b. Civilization and its discontents. In *The standard edition of the complete psychological works of Sigmund Freud,* vol. 21. London: Hogarth Press.

Leach, Edmund. 1967. Virgin birth. *Proceedings of the Royal Anthropological Institute for 1966*:39–49.

Lévi-Strauss, Claude. 1969. *The raw and the cooked.* New York: Harper and Row.

Spiro, Melford E. 1968a. *Review of purity and danger. American Anthropologist* 70:391–93.

―――― 1968b. Virgin birth, parthenogenesis, and physiological paternity. *Man* 3:224–61.

11   Some Reflections on Family and Religion in East Asia

Introduction

THE FAMILY and religion were among the core interests of anthropological inquiry from its very inception, and they have remained among its most perduring subjects of investigation. There are, I believe, at least two reasons why this should have been so.

In the first place, although like the family and religion other sociocultural systems are also universal, none is as easily recognizable across all the etic types which are employed by anthropologists to classify the wide array of sociocultural systems as are family and religious systems. In the case of economic and political systems, for example, those which fall at the polar extremes of any of the recognized typologies by which they are classified are often identifiable as members of the same series only because of their similarities to the intermediate types comprising the typologies. We need only remind ourselves of the differences between nomadic-gathering economies and industrial-bureaucratic economies, or between small, acephalous band organizations and large-scale centralized empires in order to grasp this rather simple point. For both comparisons it is difficult to identify an invariant sociocultural core that cuts across all the types comprising a formal typology, or that persists from the earliest manifestation of an evolutionary typology to the most recent of its manifestations.

The contrary, however, is the case in regard to the family or religion, or so it would seem, if I am correct in claiming that the nuclear family is the invariant core of every family system, and that the worship of superhuman beings comprises the invariant core of every religious

Reprinted from *Religion and Family in East Asia*, edited by George DeVos and Takao Sofue. Senri Ethnological Studies, no. 11. Presented at the Fifth International Symposium, National Museum of Ethnology, Sept. 1981. (Osaka: National Museum of Ethnology, 1984), pp. 35–54. © 1987 The Regents of the University of California.

system. Indeed, the founders of nineteenth century evolutionary thought in Europe were as perplexed by the similarities between their own (Victorian) family and religious systems and those of the non-European societies that they studied as they were intrigued by (and sometimes contemptuous of) the differences.

The second reason, I believe, for the perduring anthropological interest in the family and religion is that these two systems are related to one another in a systematic relationship which holds for no two other sociocultural systems. At first blush, this statement seems paradoxical because while the human family marks man's affinity with the rest of the animal kingdom—especially the class of mammals—religion marks his uniqueness. That is, the family (whether uniparental or biparental) is a generic mammalian institution, and since man evolved from a mammalian (more particularly a primate) species, it is hard to escape the assumption that the human family is phylogenetically rooted in the family system of our prehominid ancestors.

Since religion, however, is found (as far as we can tell) in our species alone, if religious systems are also universal it is because (as Robertson Smith and Freud pointed out a long time ago) they are rooted in, and may be viewed as metaphorical expressions of family (including kinship) relations. If that is so, then religion and the family (in contrast, say, to religion and economics or religion and politics) sustain a special relationship with each other, the existence of religion being in large part a function of the existence of the family.

To say that religious systems may be viewed as a metaphorical expression of family relations is to say that while the existence of the family may be explicable in terms of biological characteristics and needs which we share with other mammals, religion is explicable only in terms of the uniquely human capacity for symbolization, for it is in the symbolic process that the privately-constituted world of fantasy, the wellspring of religious belief, is transformed into the culturally-constituted world of religion. That is so because the symbol creates Being (spirits and gods) out of non-Being, and it invests words and gestures with the instrumental power that is imputed to religious ritual. In short, religious symbols often represent the transformation and elaboration, at the *cultural* level, of fantasies and cognitions that are found at the *psychological* level, which in turn, are produced by family relations at the *social* level.

Although there is nothing new in this, its implications for the universal dimensions of the family and religion have not always been spelled out by anthropologists who, in their special concern with variation, have more often concentrated on the cross-cultural differences in family and religious systems than in their regularities. Although there can be no denying the importance of these differences, their regularities are equally important, and it is the recognition of the cross-cultural regularities in the family, viewed as a system of social relationships, that enables us to understand its connection with religion, viewed as a system of symbolic relationships.

Cross-Cultural Regularities in Human Family Systems

The panhuman roots of the regularities in human family systems are not hard to discover, for however much these systems must adapt to and are conditioned by variations in ecology, economy, demography, the polity, and the like, every family (and kinship) system is a response to certain irreducible biological characteristics of human existence, among which I would stress the following.

(1) Human reproduction is bisexual, and conception is effected by means of sexual intercourse.

(2) Human beings are born helpless, and they remain dependent both physically and emotionally for a prolonged period on their caretakers.

(3) Human beings are also born instinctless, so that their caretakers attend not only to their dependency needs but also to their need to acquire the cultural traditions of the group into which they are born.

(4) Since relatively permanent pair-bonding, brought about both by the absence of estrus and the need for economic cooperation, has been a human characteristic since at least the origin of hunting, the core caretakers are parents, together with whom children comprise a domestic group.

(5) Dependency being the child's prepotent need, he develops feelings of affectionate attachment toward his caretaking parents who, to a greater or lesser degree, gratify that need.

(6) Gratification, however, is always relative to frustration, and caretakers not only gratify, but they also frustrate children's needs.

Caretakers are frustrators, willy-nilly, in a number of ways. First, since they are agents of socialization and enculturation, they impose restrictions, constraints, and prescriptions on their offspring which are almost always frustrating if not downright painful. Second, since there is no incompatibility between lactation and sex in human beings, as there is in infrahuman mammals (in which the female does not enter estrus until her infant is weaned), caretakers are simultaneously both parent and spouse. Hence, since the mother, for example, is simultaneously mother and wife, the child must share her attention and love with the husband-father. Third, since humans are dependent for a highly prolonged period, their dependency does not cease with the birth of a sibling—as it does in infrahuman mammals, who either leave or are driven from the domestic group by the time the new infant arrives—which means that the attention and love of the mother must be shared with siblings as well as father. The sharing of love and attention is frustrating enough for adults, as the ubiquity of jealousy and envy indicates; for children, however, the frustration is even stronger.

Given, then, that caretakers both gratify and frustrate children's dependency needs, parents are not only the first and most important objects of their children's affection, but they are also, together with siblings, the first and most important objects of their hostility.

In sum, so far as their emotional texture is concerned, we would expect that in any society the relationships among all of the dyads comprising the family would be characterized by strong ambivalence, and that children would develop both an Oedipus complex (Spiro 1982a) and sibling rivalry. That these expectations also hold for East Asian families is abundantly evidenced in the papers that have been prepared for this conference—those at least that deal with the social relationships of the family. That these characteristics are symbolically expressed in the religious systems of East Asian cultures is no less evident from those reports. I shall return to these points later in my discussion.

These general observations concerning the cross-cultural regularities in the human family have important implications for our understanding of its variability. For if these observations are correct, the biological characteristics enumerated in the foregoing discussion comprise a set of parameters, or invariant conditions, which all societies have had to cope with in the historical development of their family systems. On the one hand, therefore, these invariant conditions might be said to account for the cross-cultural regularities in human family systems. On the other hand, however, the variability that is found in these systems—variability, for example, in the principles of recruitment to the domestic group, the classification of kintypes, the norms which govern social relationships within the family, the rules which determine the distribution of inherited property, and so on—may be said to represent a limited range of institutionalized solutions to the problems, both sociological and psychological, created by those same invariant conditions. In sum, it might be argued that certain invariant biological conditions (bisexual reproduction and prolonged biological dependency) produce certain invariant sociological consequences (the biparental family and its caretaking functions) from which there flow certain invariant psychological consequences (ambivalence to parents and siblings), and that these consequences lead to variable cultural responses (norms and rules) which regulate the potentially disruptive effects of both dimensions—love and hate—of these ambivalent relationships.

I shall now argue that the invariant conditions that account for the cross-cultural regularities in family systems are no less important for the understanding of family behavior than are the culturally variable rules and norms that govern family relationships. I am not arguing, I hasten to add, that these rules and norms are merely epiphenomena—superstructure, as Marxists say. I am arguing, rather, that the emotional and motivational dispositions of family actors that require the elaboration of cultural rules and norms for their regulation continue to operate in these actors even after they require those rules and norms, and that their behavior, therefore, is a product (in the algebraic sense) of the simultaneous influence of both of these determinants.

Take, for example, filial behavior. Whatever the cultural values regarding parents might be, children's sentiments and attitudes regarding their parents are not formed exclusively by these culturally variable values. They are formed as well by their invariant, albeit socially acquired emotions of the type discussed earlier; and their filial sentiments and attitudes represent an interaction of these two sets of determinants. To be sure, to the degree that filial emotions conflict with filial values we would expect filial *behavior* to comply not so much with the actors' emotions as with their cultural values which, expressed in rules and norms, govern their duties and obligations to parents. Since, in such a case, filial emotions conflict with filial values, the former must be repressed. Inasmuch, however, as the parents remain their unconscious targets, these emotions are as powerful as they ever were, but they are expressed in various disguises—some more, some less disruptive in their social consequences.

In conclusion, if social relationships are governed by the attitudes and sentiments an actor has toward some Alter, and if these attitudes and sentiments are produced not only by culturally acquired values, but also by emotional and motivational dispositions acquired by the actor in his social experience with Alter, it is as foolish to ignore the emotional as it is to ignore the cultural determinants of their relationship. This is especially so in the case of family relationships, for many attitudes and sentiments which children hold toward parents and siblings are based on conceptions of them that are formed much before their acquisition of language—hence, before the acquisition of the cultural values which comprise the normatively expected conceptions of parents and siblings. That is, these attitudes and sentiments are formed on the basis of their personal experiences with their parents and siblings, experiences which, as was argued above, arouse conflicting emotions of love and hate, of attachment and resentment, and the like. Since, then, these emotions are usually reinforced by later experiences with parents and siblings, they inevitably play a significant role in the development of the attitudes and sentiments that inform their social relationships with them.

Religion and the Family

How, now, to turn to the second aspect of the theme of our conference, does the discussion of the family relate to religion? As students of religion we can never know the superhuman beings postulated by religious belief systems directly; we can only know them indirectly, i.e., by means of the conceptions that religious actors have of them. Indeed, with some few exceptions—for example, mystical experience and trance possession—the religious actors themselves do not claim to have direct knowledge of them. They, too, know them only indirectly—as they are represented in the collective representations of their culture, in their own mental representations of them, and in the rituals by which they attempt to relate to them.

If, then, we take these three sets of data as our evidence for the conceptions which religious actors have of superhuman beings, it seems safe to say (on the basis of a great deal of comparative research) that these conceptions are more or less isomorphic with the conceptions, unconscious as well as conscious, which, as family actors, they form of their family members, and more particularly the conceptions which as children they form of their caretakers, usually their parents, in their personal encounters with them. It also seems safe to say that the rituals by which they attempt to relate to these superhuman beings express, and sometimes gratify, the wishes that are instigated by the emotions which those caretakers arouse in them, most especially the emotions of dependency and love, of fear and hatred. Thus, if the child's dependency needs, for example, are gratified by a nurturant mother, it is not unlikely that as an adult he will worship a mother-like superhuman being(s) from whom he anticipates the gratification of his wish for continuing childlike dependency. Similarly, if certain of his childhood needs are frustrated, for example, by an authoritarian father, whom he consequently learns to fear or hate, it is not unlikely that as an adult he will propitiate a fatherlike superhuman being(s) so as to avoid his wrath which he fears, and/or to express his hostility to him, something he seldom does (not at least overtly) in his relationship with his father.

In short, I am suggesting that whatever the "objective" characteristics of his parents might be when seen through the lens of a camera, the child forms various mental representations of them which, given the fact that the child's lens is neither objective nor realistic, distort and exaggerate their characteristics. I am suggesting, further, that these parental representations, partly conscious, partly unconscious, constitute the *anlage* or conceptual schemata for the mental representations which he later forms of superhuman beings. I am suggesting, finally, that the psychological reality of superhuman beings, like that of the parents, is in no way affected by their physical reality. Thus, even if their parents have died and are no longer in the physical world, they continue to exist for their children in the latter's representational world—i.e., in their mental representations of them—and it is in the latter world that, even when they are alive, they have their important, i.e., their psychological reality. This condition also holds, *pari passu,* for gods, ghosts, and ancestors, to use Jordan's felicitous designation for the superhuman beings of East Asia (Jordan 1972).

With this conceptual orientation to the relationship between the family and religion, we may now examine the extent to which this schema applies to the East Asia materials. I should also note that if much of the focus of my discussion is on male actors, it is because the material herein has been typically presented from that perspective.

Family Tensions in East Asia

In order to confine my discussion to reasonable boundaries, I have decided to focus on lines of tension in the East Asian family. Since, however, filial piety and family solidarity have always received a great deal of attention in discussions of the East Asian family, such a focus may perhaps contribute some new dimensions to the subject.

One might expect the following lines of tension to be most salient in the families of East Asia. First, given the extraordinary relationship of nurturance and dependency characteristic of the mother and the son, most especially, so it seems, in Japan, I would expect considerable tension to develop between the father and the son: on the father's part because of the wife's obvious emotional preference for the son, on the son's part because his father is a most important competitor for his wish for the mother's exclusive attention. If nothing else, it is the father—not the son—who has a monopoly on the mother's sexuality. Moreover, since the father-husband is an especially important authority figure, both for the wife and the children, one whose jural, if not personal, authority requires obedience and respect, one would expect that this would constitute an equally important source of tension in the father-son relationship.

It must be noted here that although the mother-son relationship is described in many of these papers, none of them addresses the father-son, father-daughter, or mother-daughter relationships, nor, except in passing, the relationship among siblings. That this disregard of the latter relationships would not occur in a conference dealing, for example, with South Asia or the Middle East, only serves to underscore the pivotal emotional, though not jural, importance of the mother-son dyad in the East Asia family system. (It also means that my comments will be incomplete and somewhat distorted.)

Given the subordination of children to both parents, as well as the duties and obligations that the former owe the latter (which are summed up in the key concept of filial piety) and which continue even after their death, I would also expect considerable tension to develop not only between father and son, but also between mother and son. But there is an additional—and more important—reason that I would expect tension to develop in the latter relationship. Although the mother is extraordinarily nurturant to the son and attentive to his needs—which, of course, leads to the loving and dependent attachment to her that is stressed in all the papers—that very attentiveness can be expected to lead to three types of tension.

First, the mother's devotion, conceived as a "perfect act of unchanging selfless sacrifice" to quote Tanaka (1984), may produce a "deep feeling of guilt and indebtedness in the son," and such a feeling can only lead to profound (though probably unconscious) resentment. Second, the young son's intimate and persistent physical contact with the mother—he sleeps with her, is bathed by her, and so on—most probably arouses erotic feelings for her which, however, are necessarily frustrated, and, I assume, ultimately repressed. It is for that reason, I would assume, that the mother-son relationship is characterized, to quote Tanaka again, by "the continuous presence of unresolved libidinality." Third, the dependent attachment to the mother, which she herself encourages, is in conflict with the child's need for autonomy, including psychological separation and individuation (Mahler *et al.* 1975).

I would also expect considerable tension to develop in the husband-wife relationship: on the husband's part because of his subordinate place to the son in the wife's emotional life; and on the wife's part because, as Tanaka puts it, of the "unrecognition of sexuality in the marital relationship." Now if, as Tanaka also points out, the wife's relationship to her husband recapitulates that of the mother to her son. that is highly gratifying for the husband, especially since he can gratify his erotic needs outside of the marriage—hence, have his cake and eat it too—but it can only be frustrating to the wife whose erotic needs, however much she may sublimate them in her relationship with her son, are nevertheless frustrated in her marital relationship in which (to quote Tanaka again) "sexuality is very much downplayed." Indeed, I would argue that it is precisely because her sexual needs are frustrated in her role as wife that the woman invests such great affect in her role as mother, her nurturant relationship to her son being a sublimation of her frustrating erotic relationship with her husband.

I would argue, too, that the husband's relative disinterest in his wife as an erotic object is the last link in a feedback loop in which, having recoiled as a boy from the incestuous implications of his attachment to his highly affectionate mother, he marries a woman who in so many respects represents the mother. In Japan, for example, the husband not only calls his wife, "mother," following the birth of their first child, but since her relationship to him is, as Tanaka puts it, "not essentially different from her relationship to her young children"—implying that it is little different from his mother's relationship to him when he was a child—he comes to perceive her, so I would suggest, as a mother. In short, since the wife-husband relationship and the mother-son relationship are "dangerously similar" (to use Tanaka's words), it is hardly surprising that the wife becomes a nonerotic object for her husband.

The dynamics of that process are encapsulated in Freud's pithy comment concerning a class of males—the males of East Asia, of course, were far from his mind—concerning whom he writes, "Where they love they do not desire and where they desire they cannot love. They seek objects which they do not need to love, in order to keep their sensuality away from the objects they love" (Freud 1912:183). For such males, the wife is classified with the class of females who, like the mother, are viewed as asexual, and they are distinguished from the class of females (including prostitutes, concubines, and mistresses) who are viewed as sexual. The former class, being pure, are worthy of love; the latter, being impure, are worthy only of sex.

I would suggest, then, that the neo-Confucianist view of marriage, according to which, to quote Tu (1984), "mutual responsibility rather than romantic love" ought to characterize the conjugal relationship, is more a reflection of than a model for the actual relationship between the spouses. In either event, for the wife to be treated by her husband, as Ch'eng I reports his father to have treated his mother, with "full

respect" and "reverence," or for that same wife to live with her husband in "tranquility and correctness," and never to be the object of
"indecent liberties and improper intimacies,"—all these quotations
are taken from sources quoted by Tu—such a wife, I would suggest, is
not only sexually frustrated, but in the context of East Asian society she
is all the more resentful (perhaps unconsciously) because though *she* is
not the object of her husband's "indecent liberties and improper intimacies," she knows that other women—concubines, mistresses, or
whatever—are.

A fourth line of tension, as I see it, develops between siblings. It
seems reasonable to assume that the birth of a new child, especially a
son, means that the elder child is, to some degree, displaced by the
younger as the focal attention of the mother. In Korea this displacement is both symbolized and actualized in the sleeping arrangements
in which, as Lee (1984) describes it, the elder sibling is extruded from
his parents' bedroom following the birth of a younger sibling, and is
sent to sleep in the room of his paternal grandmother. But even in
Japan, where such extrusion does not occur, the rivalry between siblings for maternal love has its effects, so that it is little wonder that in
the *Kojiki* myths analyzed by Sofue (1984), 12 of the 15 myths which
deal with the relationship between brothers entail competition and
rivalry, and that in 8 of these 12 the rivalry culminates in fratricide.

Given such strong indications of sibling rivalry, it is little wonder,
too, that both in Japan and Korea the domestic unit comprises a stem,
rather than extended family. Moreover, although Lee contrasts the
Japanese and Korean stem family households with the extended family
household in China, in fact the situation in China (Hsu 1971; Yang
1969) is very little different from that in Japan and Korea, and for the
same reason: following the death of the father, friction between married siblings leads to the segmentation of the extended family and their
formation of independent households.

Family Tensions and Religion in East Asia

In the following sections I wish to examine some possible links between the putative tensions in the East Asian family discussed in the
previous section and certain aspects of East Asian religion. Before examining these links it is important to emphasize two points. First, I am
not suggesting that religious beliefs and rituals can be "reduced" to
sociological or psychological variables. I am suggesting, rather, that
social relationships, cognitive orientation, and motivational dispositions both inform and are reflected in belief and ritual systems,

whether sacred or secular. Second, in focusing on their relationship between family tensions and religion, I am not suggesting that the solidarious dimension of the family is not reflected in religion. Rather, that dimension is not the subject of my inquiry.

Ancestor Worship and the Father

Although ancestors are most often viewed as benign, it is also the case that sometimes they may be punitive. Fortes claimed that in East Asia, as well as West Africa, "the feature that stands out most conspicuously in all varieties of ancestor worship . . . is their punitive character" (Fortes 1977:145). Thus, in Korea, the dead (including ancestors and ghosts) are dangerous, so Kendall (1984) remarks, "simply because they are dead . . . and their touch brings illness or affliction." This is especially true in the case of ancestors who died with "unfulfilled desires." Restless ancestors, as well as ghosts and angry household gods, cause not only illness, but financial loss and domestic strife, as well. Similarly, Lee observes that if the ritual service for an ancestor is not performed, the ancestor spirit becomes a wandering ghost; and although, he further observes, ghosts have no power to punish their descendents directly, this implies, I would assume, that they do have power to punish them indirectly.

In his treatment of ancestor worship in China (Taiwan) Suenari (1984) does not deal with the punitive dimension of ancestors, but it is implicit in his emphasis on (what he calls) the "economic reciprocity" characteristic of family relationships, including that with ancestors. Like their relationship with the gods, the Chinese relationship with their ancestors is "contractual," which implies that the latter's punitive or nonpunitive action is contingent upon the offering or withholding of gifts by their descendents. This implication is explicit in the work of Emily Ahern on ancestor worship in Taiwan. According to Ahern's findings ancestors are not infrequently blamed for such serious misfortunes as insanity, serious infirmity and death (Ahern 1973: chap. 12).

The situation in Japan is no different. Thus, Morioka (1984) observes that for the lower class, at least, the function of ancestor worship is to "avert disaster" which would be caused by ancestors if their worship were neglected. Carmen Blacker makes the same point without restricting it, however, to the lower class. Thus, if "the ancestral dead are not correctly treated by their descendants, if the offerings or the obsequies necessary to their nourishment are neglected, then with frightening suddenness their nature will change. The kindly old grandfather, the sympathetic father, the loving mother will turn in an instant into a vicious and capricious tyrant, punishing the neglectful family with curses." (Blacker 1975:47–48).

In order to understand these findings, it is important to consider other data. First, approximately 50 percent of Japanese families, according to Morioka, continue to practice ancestor worship even when the *ie* system has collapsed. Second, in Korea, according to Lee, the ancestor tablet is kept in the ancestral shrine only until the fourth ascending generation, following which it is buried in the grave, which implies that the ancestor remains individuated only for a relatively short time, after which he is assimilated to the generic class of "ancestor."

Now although in ancestor worship, rites are performed for all one's ancestors, these findings suggest that the *cognitively salient* ancestors are not the genealogically remote ancestors, but rather the genealogically close and immediately dead ancestors—i.e., the parents and grandparents. The remote ancestors, of course, are important both jurally (to establish claims on property, to enhance the prestige of a clan line or to legitimize its rights) and politically (to inculcate respect for authority, beginning with the family and ending with the centralized state). But for the average individual, I would suggest, these corporate functions are second in importance to their "religious" functions. In the latter regard, an ancestor (like anyone else) is cognitively salient for a religious actor only to the degree that he has a clear and vivid mental representation of him, and the ancestors concerning whom he has the clearest and most vivid mental representations are his deceased parents and grandparents—those whom he himself has personally encountered. Hence, even though in ancestor worship the actor in principle attends to all of his ancestors, it is his immediate ancestors, especially his parents, who, so I would suggest, he has most in mind, or whose mental representation forms the template for his conception of the other ancestors. Fortes (1961:187) put it most succinctly in his remark that "ancestor worship is primarily the religious cult of deceased parents."

These claims are supported by Morioka's finding that (a) although traditionally a Japanese "ancestor" is the ancestor of the *ie*, with the collapse of the *ie* in urban families, "ancestor" has increasingly come to designate the "deceased bilateral kindred" (which most importantly means, I would suggest, the ascendance of the mother to the status of a cognitively salient ancestor), and that, (b) the "private" meanings of ancestor worship have superseded its "public" meanings. Consistent with my previous hypothesis, however, I would suggest that these private meanings were always foremost in the worshipper's mind (although the public meanings were, no doubt, the important formal meanings), and that the collapse of the *ie* merely permits their centrality to be acknowledged.

Even more important, however, is Morioka's finding that although many urban families do not own a *butsudan,* the rate of ownership dramatically increases with the death of a parent, and that even in extended family households (in which, presumably, the *ie* is still somewhat important) it increases significantly in households with widows. These two findings suggest once again that the cognitively and emotionally salient ancestors are the immediate dead. Moreover, taking Morioka's findings concerning widows into account, the ancestors need not even be lineal ancestors so long as they had been household members with whom the actor had sustained important social relationships.

If this is so, then inasmuch as ancestors are not only revered—an extension of filial piety—but also feared, I would suggest that both attitudes are a function of the mental representations that, as children, the actors had formed of their immediately deceased ancestors, most especially, but not exclusively, the father. The latter attitude, which is the one we are concerned with here, might be explained in the first instance by Fortes' hypothesis that it is the "authority component" of the father that is elevated to ancestorship. If, then, in addition to his positive feelings for him, the child also develops negative feelings toward the father, one would expect—given the over-arching value of filial piety—that he would probably repress these feelings, or at least not exhibit them in overt behavior. That upon his death the father—now an ancestor—is viewed as a potentially dangerous figure, capable of inflicting harm on his descendants, is then susceptible of two complementary interpretations.

First, the repressed hostility which was felt for the father when he was alive can now find an outlet in the culturally-constituted belief that ancestors are potentially dangerous. Specifically, that belief allows the child to project his erstwhile hostility toward the living father onto the dead ancestor, thereby transforming him from an ordinarily oppressive authority figure into a potentially dangerous one. The second interpretation is more complex. Clinical evidence indicates that hostility toward some person may generate death wishes (if only as an unconscious fantasy) toward him; should that person die, the actor, given that the "omnipotence of thoughts" is one of the characteristics of unconscious mentation, may unconsciously experience his death as resulting from his death wishes toward him. Given, then, that the principle of *lex talionis* informs not only many legal systems, but unconscious mentation as well, the belief that the deceased father is potentially dangerous might be explained by the unconscious conviction of the child that the former might harm him in retaliation for the 'harm' that he (the child) had inflicted on the father.

Goddesses, Religious Specialists and the Mother

Since the most notable feature of the mother-son relationship in East Asia is the mother's nurturance and the son's dependence, we would expect that dimension of the mother-son relationship to be reflected in East Asian religion. The extraordinary nurturant-dependent nature of the mother-son relationship in East Asia, at least in Japan, is stressed in the reports by Tanaka and Sofue. A "good mother," Tanaka observes, "is believed to care for and worry about her son eternally." Hence, the son's dependency (amae) on the mother persists not only over her lifetime, but even after her death when, as an ancestress, she is still "supposed to be watching over him." As a measure of what he characterizes as the son's "very strong dependency need" in regard to the mother, Sofue points to the fact that it is the favorite theme of Japanese popular culture. For him, therefore, this need comprises a "mother-complex." Whatever that expression may denote, it certainly connotes the formation by the son of a mental representation of the mother as extraordinarily loving and nurturant, one who can be expected to do anything in her power in the service of his welfare.

Such a maternal representation is too good to give up. Hence, it is little wonder that when the mother becomes an ancestor the son continues to expect that he can rely on her assistance. It is little wonder, too—though I would not have predicted it—that with the introduction of Buddhism to China, and thence to Japan, the infinitely compassionate Hindu god, Avalokitesvara, was transformed into the goddess, Kuanyin (China) or Kannon (Japan). That the amae relationship with the mother is transferred to Kannon—probably the most popular deity (actually Bodhisattva) in Japan—and that the benevolent dimension of the maternal representation is reflected in the collective representation of Kannon (just as the authority dimension of the paternal representation is reflected in the collective representation of the male ancestors) can be seen in the following statement of Teruko Furuya. (The translation is by Yohko Tsuji.)

Kannon's concern is not directed toward heaven or a utopia, but toward this world (in which many people still suffer). Kannon is benevolent and omnipotent. She never punishes us, nor gets angry with us. On the contrary, consistently and promptly she answers our selfish prayers, such as a desire to have an attractive child, a desire to pass an entrance examination for a prestigious school, a desire to get promoted at work, and so on. She is just like an *amai* mother who always listens to the desires of an indulged child.

Like the mother, Kannon is not only infinitely compassionate, but she has another quality that the mother does not have: she is also all-powerful, as the following quotation from Blacker (1975:94) indicates.

A man only has to think of the Bodhisattva Kannon to be saved from every conceivable calamity. A man hurled into a fiery pit has but to think of the Kannon for the fire to be quenched. A man floundering in an ocean of sea monsters has but to think of Kannon and he will neither sink nor drown. A man bombarded with thunderbolts has but to think of Kannon and not a hair of his head will be hurt. A man beset by goblins, demons, ghosts, giants, wild beasts or fearful fiery serpents has but to think of Kannon for these creatures to vanish.

Power of this magnitude, of course, is never found in any human being but it *is* found in the mental representations that a young child forms of his parents. In the child's eyes the parent, who literally has the power of life or death over him, is indeed omnipotent. Hence, when the omnipotence of the maternal representation of the Japnese child is conjoined with its benevolence, the result—I would suggest—is a maternal representation that is projected in the adult's collective representation of Kannon.

But the relationship between the religious devotee and Kannon is not the only manifestation of the child's *amae* relationship with the mother on the religious plane. It is also manifested, as Tsuji (1980) has suggested, both in the relationship between client and shaman (*miko*)—and here, I would include Korea as well as Japan—and in that between the members and founders (*kyoso*) of the new religions.

In Japan and Korea, though not in China, shamans are almost exclusively female, and the rare male shaman performs his role as a trasvestite. In Korea, according to Kendall, the shaman (*mansin*) is used to help the household overcome the afflictions—illness, financial loss, domestic strife—that are brought about by restless ancestors, ghosts, and angry household gods, as well as to help young women overcome infertility. According to Blacker, similar functions are served by the Japanese *miko* as well as by her modern counterpart, the *kyoso*, most of whom are also female. So far as the latter are concerned, Davis observes that the "great majority" of those who join a new religion hope "to receive some practical benefit—cure of disease, solution to some personal problem, support for some psychological difficulty, etc—from their affiliation" (Tsuji 1980:ms). In short, in both cases when faced with adversity, the adult reestablishes a dependency relationship with a *female* religious specialists that as a child he had experienced with his mother.

I might add that just as the devotees' relationship with these female religious specialists is best understood by reference to the family—as a recapitulation of their early experience with the mother—the recruitment of these women to their religious vocations is also best understood by reference to the family—to their experience as wives in a sexually frustrating marital relationship. This, in Korea, Kendall tells us, shamans are usually recruited to their calling in middle age, after suffering a "run of ill luck" as a result of possession by some god who claims them. In Japan, Sasaki (1984) writes, there are two ways of becoming a shaman: "One is by divine calling and the other by self-searching for shamanship." In the former case, the woman suffers from some mental and physical abnormality, including visual and auditory hallucinations, trance, decrease in appetite, severe palpitations of the heart, sleeplessness and loss of weight. If her condition is not improved by resort to modern medical specialists, she will visit a shaman to discover the cause of her affliction. Should it be diagnosed as resulting from spirit possession, the most important means for overcoming her afflictions is for her to become a shaman herself, and to serve the spirit or god who has possessed her. (In Okinawa, this often means agreeing to marry him.) After agreeing to become a shaman, her "abnormality" gradually disappears.

These women, according to Blacker, exhibit in their personal histories a "curiously uniform pattern,"

Nearly all of them in their early life betray symptoms of what could be called 'arctic hysteria.' They are sickly, neurotic, hysterical, odd, until a moment comes when exacerbated by suffering, these symptoms rise to a climactic interior experience of a mystical kind. A deity, by means of a dream or a possession, seizes them and claims them for his service. Thenceforward they are changed characters. Their former oddity and sickliness give way to a remarkable strength and magnetism of personality, which is conferred on them, together with various supernormal powers, by the deity who has possessed them (Blacker 1975:129)

The characteristics of these women—which are almost identical with the characteristics and mode of recruitment of Burmese shamans whom I investigated in the 1960's (Spiro 1978)—are the classical symptoms of conversion hysteria, a condition that is typically brought on by the repression of frustrated sexual needs. In this case, I would suggest, these frustrated needs are symbolically gratified by means of trance possession—i.e. by a hallucinatory experience—in which they are finally claimed by the most potent male of all, a god. If, then, the East Asian woman, like her counterpart in South and Southeast Asia, is often frustrated by her unfulfilled libidinal attachment to her father, as Roy (1975) observes in the case of India; if moreover, her unfulfilled desires continue to be frustrated in her sexually unsatisfactory relationship with her husband as occurs, so Tanaka and Koh suggest, both in Korea and Japan, and if, finally, the sublimation of her repressed libidinal desires in her relationship with her son is not entirely effective; if all this is true, then it is hardly surprising, as Blacker observes, that the women who become shamans or founders of new religions represent merely the tip of an iceberg. Nor is it surprising that some of these women—usually lower class and not highly educated—should find an outlet in these religious callings, especially since possession by a god serves not only to gratify their frustrated libidinal needs, but their status needs as well. From a position of subordination and relative powerlessness in the formal social structure, they suddenly become the medium for the gods themselves, so that their personality undergoes a transformation of corresponding magnitude (Blacker 1975).

Buddhist Monasticism and the Parents

As a final example of the relationship between tensions in the parent-child relationship and religion in East Asia, I wish to turn to Buddhist monasticism. The crucial feature of Buddhist monastic recruitment is found in the carrying out of the Buddha's injunction that in order to achieve the Supreme Goal of Buddhism it is necessary—in the words of the *Mahavagga Sutta*—that "family men go forth from home into homelessness."

Now what was peculiar to Indian civilization at the time of the Buddha, as Dutt (1962:43) observes in his magisterial history of Buddhist monks and monasteries in ancient India, is not that India produced saints and ascetics who renounced family and the world for a higher goal—religious manifestations of that type were also found in other civilizations as well—but that in India the "goers-forth" formed a community. Lancaster (1984) also stresses this point in regard to East Asia, but with an important twist that we shall note below. In ancient India, moreover, this community was "recognized as such not only by the people, but also by the State"—something which continues to be true of the Buddhist societies of Sri Lanka and Southeast Asia (Spiro 1982b)—whereas in East Asia the Sangha has most frequently met strong opposition from the people and the State alike.

The State aside, opposition to the Sangha is entirely understandable in the case of East Asia where "leaving home" is the ultimate act of filial impiety because as Lancaster observes, it means giving up the family name, removing oneself from the ancestral lineage by not having children, producing no descendants for the continuation of ancestor worship, and—on a more mundane note—causing trouble after death because monks leave no descendants to worship them.

It may also be remarked that, beginning with the Buddha himself, "leaving home" has meant abandoning not only parents, but also—since some "goers-forth" have been married when embarking upon their quest for Enlightenment—wives and children as well. The *locus classicus* is the *Vessantara Jataka,* the most famous Buddhist myth in Theravada Buddhist societies (*The Jataka* 1957:vol. 6). The Prince Vessantara, an earlier incarnation of the Buddha, abandoned his beloved wife and children in order to seek Enlightenment. To attain his quest he even gave his children as servants to a cruel Brahmin, and his wife to yet another. When his children, beaten and oppressed by the Brahmin, managed to escape and find their way back to Vessantara, he was filled with "dire grief"—his heart palpitated, his mouth panted, blood fell from his eyes—until he arrived at the insight that "All this pain comes from affection and no other cause; I must quiet this affection, and be calm." Having achieved that insight, he was able to abandon his children.

Such an attitude, as Ozaki reminds us, (1984), was already found in East Asia prior to the arrival of Buddhism, being present in Taoism as well. The following story of Lu Hsiu Ching, which I quote from Ozaki's chapter, indicates that very clearly.

Lu Hsiu Ching retired from the world to the mountains where he studied. He left the mountains for a while to look for some medicine. When he passed through his native place he stayed at his house for a few days. At that time his daughter began to run a fever all of a sudden and fell into a critical condition. The family pleaded with him to cure her. But Hsiu Ching left, saying: 'Having abandoned my family, I am in the midst of training. The house I stopped by is no different from an inn to me.'[1]

In both cases, Buddhist and Taoist alike, the attitude of the perfect "goer-forth" is best described in the famous injunction of the *Sutta Nipata.* "Having left son and wife, father and mother, wealth, and corn, and relatives, the different objects of desire, let one wander

1. That the pursuit of the religious life requires the rejection of family ties is, of course, not restricted to the salvation religions of Asia. Early Christianity (as the attitude of Jesus, both to his ties with his own family, as well as to family ties in general reveal) required an equally powerful rejection (cf. Mark 3:31ff, Luke 9:59ff, Luke 14:26).

alone like a rhinoceros" (*Sutta-Nipata,* verse 26 of the *Khaggavisana Sutta*). But, of course, for the typical Buddhist monk, "leaving home" does not entail wandering alone like a rhinoceros; instead, everywhere he enters a community of like-minded "goers-forth," a monastery.

Unless, as Lancaster perceptively observes, we recognize the "appeal of the monastery life, it is difficult to account for the fact [that despite the monks' violation of the sacred duty of filial piety] Buddhist monastic organizations thrived and became one of the most important features of the religious, economic and social life of China, Korea and Japan." In his discussion of monastic recruitment, Lancaster is entirely correct in stressing the appeal of the "pull" factors, as migration theorists call them, that attract young men to the monastery—special dress, ritual, mystical practices, and the like; but for the purposes of this paper, I should like to stress the "push" factors that motivate them to "leave home."

In attempting to understand these "push" factors it is important to stress that when the young man "goes forth," he does more than *leave* home—that is much too passive a term to characterize this process, especially in the societies of East Asia in which filial piety is an overriding value. Rather, he *abandons* home, i.e. he actively severs his ties with his parents and siblings, and he refrains from forming normally expectable ties with a wife and children. It is the *wish* to sever the former ties and to refrain from forming the latter which constitutes, I am suggesting, the "push" factor in his "leaving home." This suggestion is supported by the fact that (as has already been noted) "going forth" does not mean wandering alone like a rhinoceros, but rather substituting a voluntary community, based on religiomystical ties, for an involuntary one, based on biological-kinship ties. When it is considered, moreover, that the voluntary community, the monastery, has many of the characteristics of the family—indeed, in China, as Lancaster observes, the monastery became an actual family surrogate, even including fictive father-son relationships, fictive lineage formations, and fictive ancestral tablets—it becomes all the more obvious that it is not living in a family-like structure as such that the "goer-forth" rejects in "leaving home," but rather living in his own biological family.

And make no mistake about it. "Leaving home" *is* a rejection of the latter family, despite the monks' attempts to rationalize it, and thereby cope with the guilt induced by this act of filial impiety, by claiming that by transferring merit to deceased parents and thereby promoting their otherwordly welfare, the monastic vocation is in fact an expression of filial piety. This is tellingly demonstrated, for example, in Lancaster's data which show that 70 percent of the Korean monks he interviewed entered the monastery against the wishes of their parents, that they persist in their decision despite the fact that for as many as ten years their parents begged them to return home, that the resentment of their siblings for having to assume the entire burden for caring for their aged parents is well-known to them, and that their lingering guilt for having abandoned the parents is evidenced by their resistance to discuss this matter in their interviews.

The recognition that monastic recruitment violates the norm of filial piety—and the attendant psychological consequences of guilt, remorse, and rationalization attendant upon this violation—is clearly evident as well in the autobiographies of the five Korean nuns that Koh summarizes in her paper. To be sure, the "pull" factors in the nuns' motivation to enter the monastery—the traumata attendant upon such experiences as the death of a lover, marriage failure, frustrated childlessness, the remarriage of a father, the death of a mother, etc.—were even stronger, it is safe to say, than the "push" factors. Nevertheless, their recognition of their violation of the duty of filial piety, more especially since they had been importantly influenced by the Confucian ethic, is equally evident. Thus, one nun characterized her decision as "this unfilial act," but then immediately rationalized the decision by saying that as a Buddhist nun she could more effectively fulfill her filial duties. Another nun, though her father was a Christian minister, made the same claim. Their rejection of the family, their guilt, and their rationalizations are all evidenced in the fact that, as Koh observes, they all experienced "sorrow" about leaving home without their families' permission, and yet they nevertheless carried out their decision over the strong opposition of their families, and in the full realization that the latter would suffer "tremendous social stigma." Now, it may also be true, as Koh claims, that their decision, given their "sentimental and deep attachment" to their family members, is a measure of their self-reliance, but it is also a measure (I would argue) of their willingness, if not wish, to reject their families.

Since, however, the nuns' decisions to enter the monastery were traumatically motivated, I shall return to the monks in order to address the problem that is by now rather obvious: what "push" factors could possibly account for the fact that a young man, reared in a culture which places such strong emphasis on filial piety, is nevertheless motivated to violate his filial duties in such an extreme fashion?

The answer—or at least one of the answers—is to be found, I would suggest, in the wish to escape the tensions that, as discussed at the beginning of this chapter, are endemic in East Asia (but not only East

Asia) in the relationship between the boy and the other members of his family. These tensions include the fear and resentment engendered by the father, the incestuous and dependency anxiety aroused by the mother, and the rivalry induced by male siblings in his family of origin. They also include the Oedipally-induced fears concerning the formation of a sexual relationship with a woman other than the mother, as well as the anxiety about giving up his dependency orientation, both of which are aroused in anticipation of establishing a family of procreation. All of these tensions, I would submit, are experienced in some sense by most young men in East Asia. (For a Southeast Asia parallel example, cf. Spiro 1977.)

In most cases these tensions are of a magnitude that can be handled and overcome. In some few cases, however, they are too powerful to sustain in continuous and ongoing relationships with members of the family—especially since most of these tensions continue to be experienced interminably because of the stem and extended family households of East Asian societies. For such men the monastery is a marvelously contrived institution which, inasmuch as it is religiously sanctioned, permits them to avoid family relationships while at the same time providing cultural legitimacy for their violating the duty of filial piety by interpreting the seeming violation as motivated by a higher duty. Indeed, I would suggest that the resort to such an extreme solution, in spite of the sacred duty of filial piety, is convincing demonstration of how painfully those family tensions are experienced by them.

But we don't have to turn to those few who seek a solution in monasticism to assess their strength even for the majority that are able to cope with them. Thus, it is not accidental, I believe, that when they have the chance, even those who continue to recognize the duty of filial piety seize the opportunity to leave their homes, not for the monastery, but for the city. And once there, rather than forming stem or extended family households, most of them establish nuclear family households, as Tanaka and Lee have shown for Japan and Korea respectively. It is for that reason that I disagree with Lee's interpretation of the "modernization of the Korean family and religion as an extension of traditional familism." The traditional sentiment may still remain— after all we are still witnessing the first generation of this phenomenon—but the difference between the persistence of the sentiment of familism and its expression in the formation of a stem household is a difference that, as William James puts it, makes a difference.

I wish now to conclude this chapter with the mother-son relationship, the theme with which it began. I want to suggest that of all the tensions that motivate home-leaving, whether it be for a celibate life in the monastery or a married life in the city, the most important is the tension the son experiences in his relationship with the mother. Let us consider the choice of the monastery—because we can learn most from the more extreme case.

Since the monastery can be viewed, as we have already seen, as a kind of nonbiological family, it is not inaccurate to say about Buddhist monasticism everywhere—as Lancaster says about Buddhist monasticism in China—that the monk can "join the new group [the monastery] and break the binds of the family system and yet find within Buddhism a re-creation of the family." That is not, as I said, inaccurate, but it is not entirely accurate either, because although the monk can re-create in the monastery a relationship with a "father," "sons," and (male) "siblings," there is one relationship that he cannot re-create, that with a "mother"! And it is that pivotal relationship of the East Asian son, I would suggest, that the monk especially wishes to avoid by joining the monastery. For despite its highly pleasurable aspects, the young boy's relationship with the mother, as I have already stressed, has two potentially frightening dimensions, as well: a sexual dimension, on the one hand, and a symbiotic one (Mahler *et al.* 1975) on the other.

Thus, if the highly attentive mother is "seductive" in her relationship with the son, the intensity of the libidinal dimension in their relationship can become frightening for him because of its incestuous implications. Similarly, if, rather than being seductive, the mother is overprotective toward him, the exaggeration of his dependency on her can become frightening for the son because it signifies a regressive pull to the symbiotic state of early infancy in which the psychic differentiation between self and mother has not yet been achieved. If either alone can be frightening, the combination can be terrifying. In becoming a monk, then, the son not only escapes these frightening dimensions of his relationship with the mother, but he also—because of the monastic rule of celibacy—avoids their re-creation in a relationship with a wife. (For a more detailed analysis of these and other motives for monastic recruitment in Southeast Asia, see Spiro 1982b). I am suggesting, then, that the monastery is attractive to those few men for whom the relationships with mother and wife are too threatening to sustain because it allows them to escape the former and avoid the latter.

References

Ahern, Emily. 1973. *The cult of the dead in a Chinese village.* Stanford, Calif.: Stanford University Press.

Blacker, Carmen. 1975. *The Catalpa bow*. London: George Allen and Unwin.

Dutt, Sukumar. 1962. *Buddhist monks and monasteries of India*. London: George Allen and Unwin.

Fortes, Meyer. 1961. Pietas in ancestor worship. *Journal of the Royal Anthropological Institute* 91:166–91.

――――. 1977. Custom and conscience in anthropological perspective. *International Review of Psychoanalysis* 4:127–54.

Freud, Sigmund. 1968. On the universal tendency to debasement in the sphere of love. In *The standard edition of the complete psychological works of Sigmund Freud*, vol. 11 [1912]. London: The Hogarth Press.

Hsu, Francis L. K. 1971. *Under the ancestor's shadow*. Stanford, Calif.: Stanford University Press.

Jordan, David K. 1972. *Gods, ghosts and ancestors: Folk religion in a Taiwanese village*, Berkeley: University of California Press.

Kendall, Laurel. 1984. Korean shamanism: Women's rites and a Chinese comparison. In *Religion and the family in East Asia*, ed. George DeVos and Takao Sofue. Osaka: National Museum of Ethnology.

Koh, Hesung Chun. 1984. Religion and socialization of women in Korea. Ibid.

Lancaster, Lewis. 1984. Buddhism and family in East Asia. Ibid.

Lee, Kwang Kyu. 1984. Family and religion in traditional and contemporary Korea. Ibid.

Mahler, Margaret S., Fred Pine, and Anni Bergman. 1975. *The psychological birth of the human infant*. New York: Basic Books.

Morioka, Kiyomi. 1984. Ancestor worship in contemporary Japan: Continuity and change. In *Religion and the family*, ed. DeVos and Sofue.

Ozaki, Masaharu. 1984. The Taoist priesthood: From Tsai-chia to Ch'u-chia. Ibid.

Roy, Manisha. 1975. The Oedipus complex and the Bengali family in India (a study of father-daughter relations in Bengal). In *Psychological anthropology*, ed. Thomas E. Williams. The Hague: Mouton.

Sasaki, Kokan. Spirit possession as an indigenous religion in Japan and Okinawa. In *Religion and the family*, ed. DeVos and Sofue.

Sofue, Takao. 1984. Family and interpersonal relationships in early Japan. Ibid.

Spiro, Melford E. 1977. *Kinship and marriage in Burma*. Berkeley: University of California Press.

――――. 1978. *Burmese supernaturalism*. 2d exp. ed. Philadelphia: I.S.H.I.

――――. 1982a. *Oedipus in the Trobriands*. Chicago: University of Chicago Press.

――――. 1982b. *Buddhism and society: A great tradition and its Burmese vicissitudes*. 2d exp. ed. Berkeley: University of California Press.

Suenari, Michio. 1984. The "religious family" among the Chinese of central Taiwan. In *Religion and the family*, ed. DeVos and Sofue.

Tanaka, Masako. 1984. Maternal authority in the Japanese family. Ibid.

Tsuji, Yohko. 1980. *Females in Japanese religion*. Unpublished ms.

Tu, Wei-Ming. 1984. On neo-Confucianism and human relatedness. In *Religion and the family*, ed. DeVos and Sofue.

Yang, C. K. 1969. *Chinese communist society: The family and the village*. Cambridge: MIT Press.

Pali Texts (translations)

1957. *The Jataka*, ed. E. B. Cowell. London: Luzac and Co.

1881. *Sutta-Nipata*, transl. V. Fausboll. Oxford: Clarendon Press.

12   Symbolism and Functionalism in the Anthropological Study of Religion

Introduction

FOR THE HISTORIAN and sociologist of science, the history of social science provides many fascinating problems for inquiry, not the
least of which is the propensity of its practitioners to reject old approaches as false whenever a new approach acquires saliency. Even
Marxist and Hegelian social scientists for whom antitheses must necessarily eventuate in some kind of synthesis, nevertheless view the different approaches to sociocultural inquiry as constituting binary
opposites, one of which (their own) is believed (with all the fervor of a
Manichean) to represent the forces of light, the other the forces of
darkness. A relevant case is the rejection of functionalism by the practitioners of the new symbolist approach to religious anthropology, much
as the functionalists had rejected the evolutionary approach of the generation before them. The current symbolic approach, it might be
added, is part of the contemporary Zeitgeist; everywhere, in politics
and kinship, as well as in religion and myth, functionalism is out, symbolism is in, motivation is out, cognition is in, social processes are out,
mental processes are in.

Roughly speaking, we can distinguish at least three different anthropological approaches to the study of cultural symbols and symbol
systems; (a) phenomenological analysis of the philosophical meanings
of the symbols, (b) structural analysis of the logical relationships among
the symbols and (c) formal semantic analysis of their classificatory sche-

Reprinted from *Science of Religious Studies in Methodology*, edited by Lauri Honko.
Proceedings of the Study Conference of the International Association for the History of
Religion, Turku, Finland, Aug. 27–31, 1973. (The Hague: Mouton, 1979), pp. 322–39.

mata. Although these three approaches are obviously quite different from each other, they have in common an exclusive attention to symbols and symbol systems as such, and an avoidance of attention to the relationship between cultural symbols and social experience. The latter is viewed (at best) as theoretically uninteresting, and (at worst) as an intellectual sin against the Cartesian theory of the mind held by many of them.

The previous generation of functionalists were equally dogmatic in the opposite direction. For many of them, at least, the cognitive meaning of cultural symbol systems was more or less ignored in favor of their relationship either to the psychobiological needs of the social actors or to the functional requirements of their social system. With some few exceptions the cognitive meaning of the symbols, as such, was of little interest.

Despite the polemical opposition between symbolic and functionalist approaches, there is no intrinsic opposition between them. On the contrary, I would say (to paraphrase Kant) that functionalism without symbolism is blind, and symbolism without functionalism is lame. For, surely, the social functions of symbol systems largely depend on their cognitive meaning, and the meanings which symbol systems have for social actors derive from and are related to their social context. This, at least, is the thesis I wish to explore in this chapter, not, however, by a logical analysis of the postulates and theorems of these respective theoretical approaches, but by a concrete comparison of a subset of the set of symbol systems of traditional Judaism and Theravāda Buddhism, namely, their soteriological symbols. My choice of these two religions stems primarily from the fact that I happen to have conducted research in two communities—an Israeli kibbutz and a Burmese village—whose cultures are informed by these two religious traditions. Theravāda Buddhism comprises the most important idea system (religious or secular) in Burma; and although the kibbutz (a collective agricultural settlement) which I studied is atheist, its founders—those who created its institutions and established its ethos—were reared in, and internalized most of the basic concepts and values of, orthodox Judaism.

What I hope to do, then, is to compare some basic, or core, symbols of these religions with respect to their philosophical meaning—I shall forgo a structural and logical analysis of the symbols—and I shall then attempt to relate them to the cultural orientations and motivational dispositions found in Yeigyi, a village in Upper Burma, and Kiryat Yedidim, a kibbutz in central Israel.

The Soteriological Symbolism of Judaism and Buddhism

Introduction

Although, at first blush, no two religions appear to be as disparate as traditional Judaism[1] and Theravāda Buddhism,[2] when they are looked at more closely their basic concepts bear a remarkable resemblance to each other. Both religions are characterized by two sets of conceptual trinities—a trinity of faith and a trinity of soteriologically valued action—which, structurally viewed, are almost identical. If this proposition seems outrageous, consider, for example, the following data. In both religions there are three ultimately sacred symbols which are taken, in some important sense, to be the essential instruments of salvation, and which constitute the irreducible objects of devotion. This trinity—the trinity of faith, as I shall term it—consists of a sacred being (Jahweh—Buddha),[3] a sacred Law (Torah—Dhamma), revealed by the sacred being, and a sacred community (Israel—Saṅgha), which, prescriptively, lives in accordance with the Law. In the case of Buddhism, the Buddha, His Law, and His Order of Monks (Saṅgha) are the "Three Gems" in whom, daily, the Buddhist "take(s) Refuge." In Judaism, although there can be no god but God, "God, Torah, and Israel," as the tradition has it, "are one."

In any salvation religion, certain types of action are prescribed as necessary, if not sufficient, for the achievement of its soteriological goal. Again, Judaism and Buddhism seem to share a common trinity of soteriologically oriented action, viz., charity (ṣedakah—dāna), morality (miṣwah—sīla), and a form of intellectual activity—study or meditation (talmud torah—bhāvanā). For both, too, the latter type of action is the most important; for Buddhism, charity and morality are merely stages en route to bhāvanā; for Judaism, the study of Scripture is (as the Mishnah puts it) "equal to all the other commandments combined."

This structural similarity between these Judaic and Buddhist symbols seems to pose a serious challenge to that part of functionalist theory which maintains that there is some kind of "fit" between religious ideology, on the one hand, and society or personality, on the other.

1. By 'traditional Judaism' I refer to pre-World War I Eastern European orthodox Judaism, the faith in which the founders of Kiryat Yedidim were raised.
2. *Theravāda* Buddhism, the form of Buddhism found in South and Southeast Asia, is as different from *Mahāyāna* Buddhism found in Northern and Eastern Asia as, say Roman Catholicism differs from Calvinist Protestantism. In the rest of this paper I shall use 'Buddhism' to refer to its *Theravādist* form exclusively.
3. In this, and in all subsequent contrasted pairs of concepts, the first is Judaic, the second Buddhist.

Whether from a Weberian point of view, in which ideology influences behavior, or from Freudian, Manheimian, or Marxist points of view, in which ideology is a reflection, respectively, of unconscious conflict, social structure, or economic relations, it would not have been expected that these structurally similar symbols would be found in communities that are so markedly different in social structure, motivational disposition, and cultural ethos. Whereas the kibbutz is achievement-, work-, and group-oriented, village Burma is characterized, on each of these variables, by its polar opposite: work is not an intrinsic value, achievement (including change) is not an important goal, and individual concerns take precedence over group values.

Upon closer inspection, however, this challenge to the functionalist thesis becomes somewhat less formidable. When the Buddhist and Judaic symbols are compared in terms of their cultural and psychological meanings, their structural similarities are seen to be more apparent than real, for such a comparison reveals that whereas there is almost no point at which the Buddhist symbols articulate with the secular social order (either to give it value, on the one hand, or to provide a fulcrum by which it can be changed, on the other), the homologous Judaic symbols make contact with the social order at almost every point. For purposes of brevity I shall examine this thesis only with respect to those symbols which comprise the trinity of faith of these two religions.

Jahweh—Buddha

As traditionally depicted, Jahweh represents activity; He is a world-creating being. The Buddha, by contrast, represents passivity; He is a contemplative, world-negating being. Compare, for example, Michelangelo's wrathful Moses—for Judaism, Moses and Jahweh are, on many attributes, almost interchangeable—with the blissful calm of the traditional Buddha image.

Jahweh is not only a world creator, He is a world transformer. He is a Redeemer, who intercedes in the world to change it. The Buddha, on the other hand, teaches the Way to redemption, but He himself does not redeem. His Way, moreover, emphasizes the renunciation of the world, not its transformation.

Concretely, Jahweh redeemed Israel from Egypt, and, after a long struggle with a harsh desert environment and with their own "stubbornness," He brought them to the land of "milk and honey" which, however, was acquired only through conquest. The Exodus, Sinai, and the Conquest of the Land comprise, jointly, the symbols of the nuclear historical experience of Judaism. This set of symbols implies (a) that suffering can be overcome in this world, for (b) the world is potentially good, but that (c) to overcome suffering and to make the world good requires struggle.

The Buddha is almost the mirror image of Jahweh. As the Prince Gautama, he had tasted from birth the "milk and honey" of the royal court, only to reject it to become, in pursuit of Enlightenment, a wandering mendicant. It is the Buddha's renunciation of the world, and His ultimate attainment of Enlightenment which comprise the symbols of the nuclear historical experience of Buddhism. Milk and honey, this symbol set implies, (a) are an obstacle to be overcome, not a goal to be desired, for (b) though suffering can only be overcome by struggle, the struggle is not with impedimenta of the external world, but with one's own impulses (specifically, a "clinging" (*tanhā*) to the world), and (c) the aim of this struggle is not to change the world, for since (as we shall see) suffering is an irreducible attribute of all sentient existence, such an aim is but yet another snare on the way to liberation. The aim, rather, is to transcend the seductions of the world by achieving a state of detachment. It is no accident, surely, that monastic asceticism, which has never found a place in normative Judaism—the Essenes were viewed as heretics—is the key institution of Buddhism.

These differences between the Buddha and Jahweh, it should be noted, are dramatically symbolized in their respective festivals. The important holy days of Judaism commemorate those events which comprise Israel's nuclear historical experience—the redemption from slavery, the revelation of the Commandments, and deliverance into the Promised Land. The important Buddhist holy days commemorate the Buddha's nuclear experiences—His renunciation of the world and His deliverance from the realm of desire and attachment. If, then, sacred beings are not merely objects of devotion, but if they are also models for emulation, then, the Buddha is a model for the denigration of (and retreat from) the world, while Jahweh is a model for valuing the world and for attempting to change it.

Torah-Dhamma

The Buddhist Teaching, or Law (Dhamma), stresses two themes: suffering and release from suffering. Since, according to Buddhism, suffering (*dukkha*) is one of the three essential attributes of sentient existence—the other two are impermanence and nonself—any attempt to change the world which is based on the assumption that suffering can thereby be eliminated is irrational. Not only can such attempts not succeed, but they have the opposite effect; they not only increase suffering by increasing attachment (*tanhā*) to the world (the ultimate cause of suffering), but such attachment, in turn, precludes the attainment of nirvana, the only goal whose attainment signals the extinction of suffering.

Although the Judaic Law (Torah) is not blind to the existence of suffering, it views the latter not as an inevitable attribute of existence—after creating the world, God surveyed His handiwork, and pronounced it as "very good"—but as retribution for sin. By refraining from sin, i.e., by living in accordance with the Law, suffering can be avoided. Hence, according to the Prophets, if suffering is to be overcome, it is necessary to change the world in compliance with the Law. Since, then, life is basically (or, at least, potentially) good, to try to make of the world a place in which its goods can be experienced, is rational, not (as in Buddhism) irrational.

But this contrast between Torah and Dhamma can be drawn even more sharply. The laws of the Torah were given, as Jahweh told Israel, "so that ye may live by them." The Dhamma, on the contrary, was given so that (literally) one may die by them. Life, according to Buddhism, comprises an endless round of rebirths (all, from the lowest hell to the highest heaven, characterized by suffering), and the Law is the means by which the wheel of life can be brought to an end (through the achievement of nirvana).

In short, while the Dhamma stresses the rejection and transcendance of the world as a means to extinction of suffering, the Torah stresses the acceptance of the "yoke of the Law"—which, in effect, means the changing of the world—as the means to that end.

This difference between these two religions is exemplified in the difference between the Jewish and Buddhist male initiation ceremonies. (Neither has a female initiation.) In Burma, the initiation (*shimbuy*) is a reenactment and commemoration of the Buddha's transformation from world-embracing prince to world-rejecting mendicant. In Judaism, the initiation (*bar mitzva*) signals the acceptance of the yoke of the Law, an ontogenetic recapitulation of a phylogenetic experience.

Israel—Saṅgha

The true Buddhist is the monk. The monastic community (Saṅgha) is an elite, consisting of those few who possess the necessary spiritual qualifications (*pāramitā*) to practice the Dhamma in its entirety, including the 227 regulations that comprise the monastic Rule (Vinaya). Distinguished from this elite is the great mass of laymen who are spiritually qualified to follow only the Five Precepts (to refrain from lying, killing, stealing, drunkenness, and sexual immorality). The layman can only hope that the piety exhibited in his present birth will enable him to acquire sufficient merit so that, in a future birth, he too will have the qualifications for admission to the monastic order.

For Judaism, all of Israel is the elite, all are the Chosen People. Hence, all must observe the 613 commandments of the Torah. None can be exempt from their hereditary elitist status—and hence from this responsibility—for all equally received the Commandments on Sinai. "You only have I known of all the families of the earth," Jahweh warns, and, therefore, "I will visit upon you all your iniquities." Indeed, it is not far-fetched to argue that Israel is to the rest of mankind what the Saṅgha is to the Buddhist laity, for while all of Israel must observe the 613 commandments, the Gentiles need observe the seven Noachite laws only. (These include obedience to authority, reverence for the Divine Name, and abstinence from idolatry, incest, murder, robbery, and eating the flesh of a living animal.) This same theme is implicit in the prophetic notion of Israel as the Suffering Servant.

The comparison of the respective sacred communities of Buddhism and Judaism yields yet another important difference. In Buddhism neither laymen nor Saṅgha, whether separately or jointly, comprise a church, a corporate group. Even within the monastic order each monk (or, at any event, each monastery) is a law unto himself (or itself). This organizational feature of the Saṅgha parallels the ideological structure of Buddhism: each individual must seek his own salvation. As the Master stressed in a famous Sutta, monks must "wander alone like the rhinoceros," or, as He put it in yet another metaphor, they must "live as islands unto [themselves]."

For Judaism, on the other hand, the sense of corporate identity and corporate responsibility is keen. Because of a mythical kin tie—all Israel are "descendants of Abraham, Isaac, and Jacob"—and because of a corporate contract—they all entered into the covenant with God—"All Israel," according to the Mishnah, "is responsible one for the other." Hence, in the liturgical confession of sins, it is not "my" sins, but "our" sins that are confessed; and it is not for "my" sins, but for "our" sins that punishment is due. This sense of corporate responsibility, moreover, perdures through historical time, the sins of the ancestors being visited upon their descendants even unto three generations.

The Soteriological Goal

Although there is no reason to expect a univocal relationship between means and ends—many different roads, as they say, can lead to Rome—it is, nevertheless, not surprising that the dramatic differences between the belief systems of Buddhism and Judaism should be associated with radically different notions of redemption. Although both religions postulate similar conditions of proximate salvation—rebirth into some heaven-like existence—they postulate radically different conditions of ultimate salvation.

For Buddhism ultimate salvation consists in nirvana which, whatever else it might connote—and scholars and laymen alike differ concerning its meaning—signals the end of the wheel of rebirth. Since all forms of existence entail suffering, salvation means deliverance from all thirty-one realms of existence. In addition to the existential meaning of Buddhist salvation, attention must also be directed to its exclusively individualistic meaning. Nirvana is individualistic in two senses: the individual is both the object of salvation—the individual alone can be saved—and the instrument of salvation—the individual must save himself.

For Judaism, ultimate salvation consists in the attainment of the Kingdom of God, which is achieved, with the Messianic Coming, at the End of Days. Unlike the Buddhist case, however, salvation does not entail transcendence of the physical and social worlds as we know them, but, rather, in their transformation. In the words of the Prophet, the lion lies down with the lamb, the crooked is made straight, the people are comforted. It will be noted, moreover, that unlike the individualistic character of Buddhist salvation, that of Judaism is corporate. It is the group, Israel, that is saved, and it is the group, by its collective acceptance of the yoke of the Law, that is the instrument of salvation.

For Buddhism, then, salvation, (a) is individualistic, and (b) it consists in the transcendence of the world such that the normal and recognizable ethical, social, and political—not to mention physical and biological—categories are rendered nonexistent. For Judaism, salvation (a) is collective, and (b) it consists in the transformation, rather than the transcendence, of the sociopolitical world within the known spatiotemporal world (however much the latter might be modified).

Sacred Symbols and Social Behavior

Thus far, I have attempted to show that there are differences between Buddhist and Judaic soteriologies, that each of these soteriologies is associated with a set of three sacred symbols (a sacred being, a sacred law, and a sacred community) which, though structurally isomorphic, are semantically dissimilar. Although I have only touched the tip of the symbolic iceberg, I shall forgo the temptation to explore the other dimensions of these sacred symbols, and, instead, ask yet another question of them. Do these symbols essentially reflect the nature of the human mind? (Which, if such were the case, would suggest that the mind, unlike the claims of some linguistically oriented structuralists, operates not only according to binary oppositions, but also triadic complementaries.) And, if this question were to be answered in the affirmative, are such symbols created, as Lévi-Strauss once suggested about totemic symbols, because they are good to think, in splendid isolation from any social context? Although such hypotheses are very much in vogue today, no student, however, of either the Burmese or the Jews could entertain these hypotheses for long. Even ignoring the symbolic sets we have been examining—which, if space permitted, could be shown to be related to certain common dimensions of Jewish and Buddhist social life—the semantic differences in the individual symbols would alone infirm these hypotheses. These differences can be shown to be systematically related to differences in ethos and behavior found in village Burma and the Israeli kibbutz. To be sure, the explanations for these relationships are moot. Thus, some theorists would argue that the relationships are causal, although they would disagree about the direction of causality (one group contending that the ideas are prior, the other that the societal forms are prior). Since I wish to avoid such controversies—my own view, which is different from both, may be found in my two books on Burmese religion—I am content to observe that such relationships do in fact exist, and that these religious concepts serve to express (and perhaps to sustain) the basic components of the ethos of each culture.

Thus, the Buddhist symbol set, which denigrates the sociocultural world, which emphasizes the renunciation of the politicoeconomic world, and which aims at the transcendence of the spatiotemporal world is found in a society (Burma) which places little value on social and economic change, on achievement values, or on corporate responsibility; in a society whose cynosure is the world-renouncing monk, and whose ideal is the *arhant*, the individual who, oblivious to the suffering of others, seeks and attains salvation for himself.

The Judaic model which values the sociocultural world, and which emphasizes the transformation of the politicoeconomic world, is found in a society (the kibbutz) which places great value on social and economic revolution, on achievement, and on group responsibility; in a society whose cynosure and ideal alike is the *halutz*, whose personal goals are subordinate to, and who sacrifices his needs for, the transformation of society.

Needless to say, I am not concerned here with evaluating the relative merits of these different religious orientations and their social concommitants, nor, qua anthropologist, am I qualified to do so. I am even less concerned with evaluating the different character types that are associated with these different orientations, especially since both are the products of social and individual histories over which social actors have little if any responsibility. I would like instead to make two additional observations concerning the relationship between religious symbols and social behavior. The first is stimulated by a contrast between Buddhism and Judaism, the second by their similarity.

Religious Symbols and Social Behavior

I have already observed that the conceptions of ultimate salvation found in Judaism and Buddhism are found side by side with entirely different conceptions of proximate salvation. In both cases, moreover—and this is more important—the latter conceptions have usually been the more strongly cathected by the religious actors. If, as has often been the case, this latter fact is ignored, we are led not only to a distorted conception of the salient beliefs of the religious actors, but to a misleading interpretation of the relationship between religious symbols and social action.

For Buddhism, proximate salvation consists in rebirth in any of the many material paradises—the abodes of the *devas*—and, as all anthropological fieldwork in contemporary Buddhist societies has revealed, it is this form of salvation that the majority of their members most strongly desire. For although the aspiration for nirvana is reiterated by the average Buddhist in ritual formulae, the latter goal is for him more a cultural cliché than a personal motive; his *summum bonum* consists not in the extinction of desire, but in its satisfaction. And if rebirth in a heavenly abode is viewed as beyond his reach, he is happy to settle for rebirth as a wealthy and high status citizen of this planet, preferably of his present society. The Buddhist's preference for proximate salvation does not, however, require any changes in the semantics of the soteriological symbols discussed above. Moreover, the soteriological mechanism remains the same. Whether salvation is viewed in ultimate or proximate terms, it is achieved as the consequence of the impersonal law of karma, whose working is exclusively affected by individual action, and by the merit and demerit which such action produces.

For Judaism, too, it is a heavenly existence which constitutes proximate salvation, and although the End of Days occupies a central place in Jewish liturgy, the post-Exilic belief in an afterlife has been at least equally important in the soteriological concerns of post-Exilic and Diaspora Jewry. As in the case of Buddhism, this emphasis on proximate salvation requires little change in the semantics of the soteriological symbols of Judaism. It does, however, signal a change in the object of salvation from a corporate to an individualistic orientation. It is individual, not group, action which determines one's fate in the afterlife, and it is the individual, not the group, that is rewarded (or punished). The mechanism of salvation, however, is the same in both, salvation being achieved not by means of a karma-like mechanism, but by means of divine intercession. Whether from justice or mercy, God is influenced by human action to establish His Kingdom on earth (ultimate salvation), or to send the individual to His heavenly abode (proximate salvation).

In this connection, there are two psychologically interesting and historically significant aspects of the soteriology of the Eastern European founders of the kibbutz. The first aspect, already alluded to, is the restoration of corporate redemption to its pre-Exilic place of centrality. This reversal, it should be noted, occurred not only in the kibbutz movement, but it occurred much earlier in the nonsocialist Zionist movement of Eastern and Central Europe, as well as in the theology of Western European Reform Judaism. Whereas the kibbutz founders, however, placed equal stress on both the parochial (Jewish) and universal (international socialist) dimensions of the Messianic Days, General Zionism stressed its parochial dimension, and Reform Judaism its universal dimension. With respect to the theoretical concern of this paper, viz., the relationship between religious symbols and social action, this example illustrates the elementary principle that man manipulates his cultural symbols to serve his own needs. Man is as much the master, as the servant, of his cultural symbols.

Judaism and Buddhism, surely, are not the only religions in which alternative and even conflicting symbol systems exist side-by-side, and their differential appeal in different historical epochs, or to different social groups within the same historical epoch, remains a little-explored area of inquiry in religious research. Since these alternative symbol systems are equally normative, it seems not unlikely that their differential appeal might be explained by their differential cathexis by the social actors, in short, by their personality differences. But since in any society (especially if it constitutes a relatively endogamous breeding population), personality differences (either among its subgroups or its historical epochs) are a function of differences in social conditions and their attendant cognitive and affective consequences, these personality differences are, in turn, related to sociological differences. Since it would take us too far afield, however, to examine the possible sociological conditions that contributed to the renewed emphasis on corporate soteriology in nineteenth and early twentieth century Judaism, I shall only observe that it is another illustration of the thesis that religious symbols, no less than any others, do not spring Athena-like from the human mind; rather, they emerge from concrete social experiences which act upon the mind and influence its activity.

A second important aspect of the soteriology of the founders of the kibbutz is the elimination of divine intercession for the achievement of the soteriological goal. Kibbutz ideology, as I have already mentioned, is based on a thoroughly naturalistic metaphysics. As in the case of Buddhism, the soteriological aspirations of the kibbutz—if I may use a religious concept to characterize a secular belief system—are achieved by human action alone; its consequences, however, are not deemed to be governed by the law of karma, but by the laws of sociology and history. Although space, again, does not permit an examination of the conditions that might possibly produce such thoroughgoing naturalism, this aspect of kibbutz soteriology—the absence of divine intercession—leads to the final section of this paper.

Chercher la Femme

Buddhism and Judaism not only share a common trinity of formal soteriological symbols—a sacred person, a sacred law, and a sacred group—but these symbols share a common attribute—none of them is feminine. To be sure, it can be argued—and empirical support can be adduced for such an argument—that feminist elements have been bootlegged into both Buddhism and Judaism in the unconscious meanings of some of their other symbols. Nevertheless, at the level of their formal and conscious meanings, their symbols, including those that have been examined in this chapter, are primarily (Judaism) if not exclusively (Buddhism) masculine. I say "primarily" in the case of Judaism because Israel may be viewed as a combined male and female symbol since its empirical referent, the people of Israel, includes both males and females. Even this statement, however, must be qualified by the observation that the female component in the symbol, Israel, is only physically, but not ritually or jurally, relevant. God's covenant with Israel, which is the jural basis for its status as a sacred people, is renewed in, and symbolized by, the circumcision ritual, which is performed for males alone. That, nevertheless, physical membership in the group is determined by the mother—by Talmudic law, the child of a Jewish father and a non-Jewish mother is not a Jew—is one of those paradoxes which might be variously resolved by structuralist, psychoanalytic, and other theories which delight in paradox. Ritually, too, Israel is essentially a masculine symbol in that, traditionally, Jewish congregational worship requires a quorum of ten adult males. Although females, like minors, may participate in the worship, they may not be counted in the quorum.

Buddhism is even more exclusively masculine in its symbolism than Judaism. Not only is the historical Buddha, Gautama, a male, but all previous Buddhas have also been, and all future Buddhas will also be, males. Buddhahood can be attained only in a masculine form. The Saṅgha, too, is an exclusively male institution. In Judaism the physical Israel, at least, includes both sexes, even though jurally and ritually females are peripheral members. This is not the case even with respect to the physical Saṅgha. To be sure, in early Buddhism, females were permitted to become monks—over the objection, it should be noted, of the Buddha—but after a few short years they were, and they have continued to be, excluded from the order. A woman's aspiration to the monkhood must be deferred until her future rebirth as a male.

To summarize, then, Judaism and Buddhism alike are characterized by a pervasive and systematic exclusion of females and feminine symbols from soteriological, devotional, and liturgical significance. On this dimension Buddhism and Judaism may not only be classified together, but (among the great religions) they are members of a class which includes Islam, Confucianism and Protestantism, and which excludes Hinduism and Catholicism. Like Buddhism and Judaism, the latter two religions are also characterized by a soteriological trinity, but, unlike the former, they include an important feminine component. Now, of course, just as Lévi-Strauss and the structuralists can always find binary oppositions, so too I can be charged with always finding trinities. In each of these cases, however, the trinity was not discovered by fancy intellectual methods; rather trinities are enunciated by the social actors themselves, and the problem consists in deciding which, among alternative trinities, is most germane to the present discussion. Thus, for example, both Hinduism and Catholicism exhibit one type of trinity which is isomorphic with that of Judaism and Buddhism: a sacred being (Brahma and God), a sacred law (Dharma and the teachings of the Church), and a sacred group (Varna and the Church). Unanalyzed, these trinities are as exclusively masculine as their Judaic and Buddhist counterparts. But the Hindu "Brahma" and the Catholic "God," it will be recalled, are generic terms, best glossed as "divinity" or "godhead," each of which, depending on the interpretation, comprises three component deities or aspects of the godhead.

These divine trinities are, of course, well known. The Hindu trinity consists of Vishnu, Shiva, and one of the forms taken by the feminine principle—Sakte—variously conceived as Parvati, Kali, or Durga. The

Catholic trinity consists of God, Christ, and the Virgin Mary. In Catholic theology, to be sure, the Trinity refers to the triune God—Father, Son, and Holy Spirit. To the anthropologist, however, who follows the lead of the religious actor and his devotional concerns, the third member is not the Holy Spirit, but the Holy Virgin.

Now the difference between the presence or absence of a feminine symbol within the set of sacred symbols of a religion is not, I need emphasize, a trivial difference; and it certainly involves much more than a cognitive preference or lack of preference for binary oppositions (the opposition, in this case, of male and female). For, although I have thus far used the abstract concept, "feminine," in referring to the Virgin and Parvati, neither, as is well known, represents a generically conceived, abstract, female principle. Rather, both represent a specific type of female, and that type is not wife, or sister, or daughter, or aunt, but Mother. Both are expressly referred to as Mother. The difference, then, between the absence of a sacred female symbol in Judaism and Buddhism (as well as in Islam, Protestantism and Confucianism), on the one hand, and its presence in Catholicism and Hinduism, on the other, is the difference between the presence or absence of a Mother Goddess. And this difference, in turn, is related, on the one hand, to the general importance of familial symbols within the sacred symbol system, and to the role of women in the secular domain, on the other.

Of the four religions we are considering here, Buddhism has most systematically expunged all familial symbols from its sacred symbol system. It not only excludes all mother symbols, but it also excludes all father symbols. The Buddha is a male, but he is never designated as father. Judaism, too, excludes all mother symbols—though the prophets had to fight a long battle before the various Astartes were expunged from the religious life of the ancient Hebrews—but the Jewish God is an expressly conceived father symbol, as is the God of Islam and Protestantism. Hinduism, on the other hand, includes both father and mother symbols. With respect to the latter it might also be observed that the mother symbol is not restricted to the Goddess, for we can hardly ignore the symbolism of Mother India or of the sacred cow. It should also be added that in the form of baby Krishna, Hinduism, like Catholicism, includes the sacred child symbol—and why is the child a son rather than a daughter?—although father, mother, and son are not integrated to form one sacred family. Family symbolism, of course, is most pervasive in Catholicism. Not only does the earthly family find its isomorphic representation in the Divine Family of Father, Mother, and Son, but the priest is "father," the nun is "sister," and the Church (as well as the nun) is a "bride" (the Bride of Christ), and so on.

Now to pursue all the ramifications of the conceptual, not to mention the soteriological, differences in the sacred symbols of these religions would require a monograph. Here, I am interested only in the presence or absence of the Mother symbol. Since all human beings have mothers, why is this symbol such a salient feature in some religions, absent in others, and almost phobically avoided in still others? It is in their different answers to this type of question that contemporary symbolic approaches differ from functionalist approaches to the study of religion. The various symbolic approaches would attempt to answer this question by reference to the semantics, or syntax, or grammar of the symbol systems themselves, while the various functionalist approaches would look outside of the symbol systems for an explanation. A functionalist cannot ignore the obvious correlations, for example, between the following array of variables in India and China, respectively. The worship of mother goddesses in India is associated with an almost obsessive concern with the mother, the sacredness of the cow, the dietary importance of milk and milk products, the voluptuousness of sacred female iconography, and the heavy-breasted woman. The lesser importance of mother goddesses in China, on the other hand, is associated with the relative unimportance of the mother, the lack of concern with the cow, the rejection of milk and milk products, the absence of female iconography, and the flat-chested woman. Given what we know today about population genetics and the influence of cultural factors on biological selection, the possibility of a systematic relationship among these social, cultural and biological variables is not as farfetched as it might seem.

But these correlations do not provide an explanation for the difference between the presence or absence of mother symbols in different religions. Rather, they provide a broader context or frame in which such symbols are to be viewed, and their systematic covariation with a wide array of variables suggests to a functionalist that differences in symbols and symbol systems are best explained by differences in the social systems in which they are embedded and from which, *ex hypothesi*, they arise and derive their meaning. He would point, for example, to differences in cultural attitudes to sex, in the social status of women, in the roles of women as wives and mothers, and, if he is psychoanalytically oriented, to differences in the parent-child relationship and, especially, to the variable vicissitudes of the Oedipus complex.

On the basis of my own work in Buddhist Burma, I would suggest that the presence or absence of the mother goddess is systematically related to two feminine roles, those of mother and of wife, and to the differences in a single dimension of each of these roles, viz., the nur-

The Relationship Between the Presence or Absence
of Mother Goddesses and Certain Female Roles

	mother	wife
India	+	−
Catholicism (Italy)	+	−
Ceylon	+	−
Burma	+	+
Israel	+	+
Islam (Arab)	−	−
China	−	−
Calvinism (Reformation)	−	−

Key: mother: + = high nurturance
              − = low nurturance
     wife: + = high dominance
              − = low dominance

turance dimension of the mother role and the dominance dimension of
the wife role. Although preliminary research (to be published separately) supports this hypothesis, for our present purposes the specific
empirical findings are less important than the assumption underlying
its construction, viz., religious symbols—and cultural symbols in general—though created by the human mind, do not arise from a mental
tabula rasa. Although they are elaborated by philosophical thought,
and infused with theological and metaphysical meaning, these symbols
are ultimately the products of individual fantasies which are produced
by (and therefore vary with) different types of social experience. Like
private symbols they serve to express certain aspirations and needs
which arise from such experience, to resolve the conflicts that are induced by the experience, and to integrate them in a manner which
renders them existentially meaningful. For religious actors, religious
symbols are created not only to think by, but also—and much more
important—to live by.

Index

303